Beyond Consent

Nijhoff International Investment Law Series

Series Editors

Prof. Eric De Brabandere (*Leiden University*)
Prof. Tarcisio Gazzini (*University of East Anglia*)
Prof. Stephan W. Schill (*University of Amsterdam*)
Prof. Attila Tanzi (*University of Bologna*)

Editorial Board

Andrea K. Bjorklund (McGill University) – Juan Pablo Bohoslavsky (UNCTAD and Universidad Nacional de Rio Negro [Argentina]) – Chester Brown (University of Sydney) – Patrick Dumberry (University of Ottawa) – Michael Ewing-Chow (National University of Singapore) – Susan D. Franck (American University) – Ursula Kriebaum (University of Vienna) – Makane Mbengue (University of Geneva) – Catherine A. Rogers (Penn State Law) – Christian Tams (University of Glasgow) – Andreas Ziegler (University of Glasgow)

VOLUME 18

The titles published in this series are listed at *brill.com/iils*

Beyond Consent

Revisiting Jurisdiction in Investment Treaty Arbitration

By

Relja Radović

BRILL
NIJHOFF

LEIDEN | BOSTON

Cover illustration: Edvard Munch: Jurisprudence, 1887 © Munch Museum/Munch-Ellingsen Group/BONO 2020.

Library of Congress Cataloging-in-Publication Data

Names: Radović, Relja, author.
Title: Beyond consent : revisiting jurisdiction in investment treaty arbitration / by Relja Radović.
Description: Leiden, The Netherlands : Koninklijke Brill NV, [2021] | Series: Nijhoff international investment law series, 2351-9542 ; volume 18 | Includes bibliographical references and index. | Summary: "The process of jurisdictional regulation in investment treaty arbitration is governed by the principle of consensualism, which in theory confers the power to define the jurisdiction of arbitral tribunals on disputing parties exclusively. The practice of arbitral tribunals, however, has given the impression that tribunals are willing to establish jurisdiction on alternative and weaker bases than party consent. This book addresses the question to what extent party consent indeed defines the jurisdiction of arbitral tribunals"– Provided by publisher.
Identifiers: LCCN 2021014031 (print) | LCCN 2021014032 (ebook) | ISBN 9789004453685 (hardback) | ISBN 9789004453692 (ebook)
Subjects: LCSH: Arbitration agreements, Commercial. | Arbitration and award. | Consent (Law) | Investments, Foreign–Law and legislation. | International commercial arbitration. | Investments, Foreign (International law) | Commercial treaties.
Classification: LCC K2400 .R325 2021 (print) | LCC K2400 (ebook) | DDC 346/.092–dc23
LC record available at https://lccn.loc.gov/2021014031
LC ebook record available at https://lccn.loc.gov/2021014032

Typeface for the Latin, Greek, and Cyrillic scripts: "Brill". See and download: brill.com/brill-typeface.

ISSN 2351-9542
ISBN 978-90-04-45368-5 (hardback)
ISBN 978-90-04-45369-2 (e-book)

Copyright 2021 by Koninklijke Brill NV, Leiden, The Netherlands.
Koninklijke Brill NV incorporates the imprints Brill, Brill Nijhoff, Brill Hotei, Brill Sense, Brill Schöningh, Brill Fink, Brill mentis, Vandenhoeck & Ruprecht, Böhlau Verlag and V&R Unipress.
All rights reserved. No part of this publication may be reproduced, translated, stored in a retrieval system, or transmitted in any form or by any means, electronic, mechanical, photocopying, recording or otherwise, without prior written permission from the publisher. Requests for re-use and/or translations must be addressed to Koninklijke Brill NV via brill.com or copyright.com.

This book is printed on acid-free paper and produced in a sustainable manner.

To my grandfather

Contents

Acknowledgements XI
Summary XII
List of Graphs XIII
List of Abbreviations XIV

Introduction 1
1 Consensual and Arbitral Jurisdictional Regulation 1
2 Framing the Project 5
   2.1 *'Consent'* 5
   2.2 *'Jurisdiction'* 6
   2.3 *Scope of the Project* 7
3 Method 7
4 Outline 9
5 Relevance 10

1 The Process of Jurisdictional Regulation in Investment Treaty Arbitration 12
1 Introduction 12
2 The Significance of Consent 13
   2.1 *The Consensualism of International Adjudication* 14
   2.2 *The Function of Consent* 19
      2.2.1 The Origins of the Power to Adjudicate 20
      2.2.2 Dispute and Justiciability 22
      2.2.3 A Multistage Process 25
      2.2.4 The Contractual Nature of International Jurisdiction 30
   2.3 *A General Principle of International Law* 35
   2.4 *Some Contextual Considerations* 37
      2.4.1 Global Public Goods 37
      2.4.2 Protective Treaty Regimes 39
      2.4.3 A Hybrid Regime 42
3 Jurisdictional Regulation in Investment Treaty Arbitration 44
   3.1 *Legal Framework* 45
      3.1.1 The ICSID Convention 45
      3.1.2 'Arbitration Without Privity' 48
   3.2 *Agreement to Arbitrate* 52
      3.2.1 Offer and Acceptance 52

                3.2.2   Contract, Agreement, or Unilateral Act   55
                3.2.3   The Form of an Agreement to Arbitrate   57
        3.3   *The Substance of Jurisdictional Regulation*   59
                3.3.1   Arbitrable (Justiciable) Disputes   59
                3.3.2   Conditions of Access   62
    4   The Governing Legal Regime   63
        4.1   *The Law Governing Agreements to Arbitrate*   63
        4.2   *The Rules of Interpretation of Agreements to Arbitrate*   66
        4.3   *Three Stages of Jurisdictional Checks*   68
                4.3.1   Pre-Examination by Administrative Organs   69
                4.3.2   Examination by Arbitral Tribunals   70
                4.3.3   Post-Examination by Annulment Committees and Courts   73
        4.4   *The Power of Tribunals to Fill Gaps in Jurisdictional Regulation*   75
    5   Conclusion   78

2   **Arbitrator-Made Rules and the Procedural Aspects of Consensual Jurisdictional Regulation**   80
    1   Introduction   80
    2   Rules Weakening the Conditions of Access   81
        2.1   *The Jurisdiction/Admissibility Dichotomy*   81
        2.2   *Conditions Precedent as Issues of Admissibility*   84
        2.3   *Applicable Procedure as an Issue of Admissibility*   88
    3   Rules Bypassing the Conditions of Access   89
        3.1   *Bypassing Conditions Precedent*   89
                3.1.1   Futility   90
                3.1.2   The *Mavrommatis* Principle   92
                3.1.3   Identity of Disputes   92
        3.2   *Bypassing Fork-in-the-Road Clauses*   94
    4   Most-Favoured-Nation Clause as a Jurisdictional Panacea   98
        4.1   *Dispute Resolution as Substantive Protection*   98
        4.2   *Presumptions on the MFN-Dispute Resolution Conjunction*   100
                4.2.1   Conditions Precedent and Presumed Applicability   100
                4.2.2   Substantive Jurisdiction and Presumed Inapplicability   102
        4.3   *Presumptions in Practice*   105
    5   Conclusion   108

CONTENTS   IX

3   Arbitrator-Made Rules and the Substantive Aspects of Consensual
    Jurisdictional Regulation   110
    1   Introduction   110
    2   Rules with a Temporal Dimension   110
        2.1   *The Non-Retroactivity of Denial of Benefits*   110
        2.2   *The Extension of the Validity of Consent and the Continued Act
              Doctrine*   115
    3   Rules Expanding the Scope of Protection   119
        3.1   *The Broches Test*   120
        3.2   *Protecting Indirect Investments*   123
    4   Rules Expanding the Scope of Arbitrable Disputes:
        Example of Jurisdictional Bridging   127
    5   Conclusion   131

4   Arbitrator-Made Rules Imposing Additional Jurisdictional Limits   132
    1   Introduction   132
    2   Rules Restricting the Scope of Protection   132
        2.1   *The Objective Definition of 'Investment'*   133
              2.1.1   The ICSID Framework   133
              2.1.2   Non-ICSID Context   140
        2.2   *The Independent Legality Requirement*   143
        2.3   *The Objective Definition of 'Investor'*   148
    3   Rules Restricting the Scope of Arbitrable Disputes:
        Example of Umbrella Clauses   151
    4   Abuse of Process as a Jurisdictional Limit *in Statu Nascendi*   155
    5   Conclusion   159

5   Towards a New Jurisdictional Framework of Investment Treaty
    Arbitration   160
    1   Introduction   160
    2   The Impetus of Arbitral Jurisdictional Regulation   161
        2.1   *Traditional Concerns about Investment Arbitration*   161
              2.1.1   Commercial Law Approaches   162
              2.1.2   One-Sided System   165
              2.1.3   Biased Arbitrators and 'Adventurism' in
                     Jurisdictional Determinations   168
        2.2   *A Fresh Start: Changing Perspectives on Party Consent*   170
              2.2.1   Hard Perspective   171
              2.2.2   Soft Perspective   174

          2.2.3   The Specific Framework of Investor-State Dispute
                  Settlement   176
                  2.2.3.1   Substantive Opportunities for
                            Law-Making   177
                  2.2.3.2   Procedural Opportunities for
                            Law-Making   178
3   A Two-Layered Model of Jurisdictional Regulation in Investment
    Treaty Arbitration   180
    3.1   *Primary Rules*   181
    3.2   *Secondary Rules*   182
          3.2.1   Defining Secondary Rules   182
          3.2.2   Practice as a Source of Law   186
          3.2.3   Practical Application and the Doctrine of Evolutive
                  Jurisdictional Regulation   192
4   Some Challenges of the Proposed Model   198
    4.1   *The Development of Secondary Rules and the 'Impulse for
          Change'*   198
    4.2   *The Relationship between Primary and Secondary Rules
          Regarding Legal Change*   202
    4.3   *Control Mechanisms*   205
    4.4   *Transparency and the Availability of the Law-Making
          Material*   208
    4.5   *The Risk of Excessiveness and the Prospect of Stabilisation of
          Practice*   209
5   The Two-Layered Model of Jurisdictional Regulation and
    the International Legal Order   212
    5.1   *Investment Arbitration and Global Governance*   212
    5.2   *Trends towards Accepting Judicial Regulation in International
          Adjudication*   217
6   Conclusion   220

Final Conclusions   221

Bibliography   227
Table of Cases   249
Treaties   267
Miscellaneous Sources   269
Index   271

Acknowledgements

This book is a result of my doctoral research conducted at the University of Luxembourg between 2015 and 2019. I am grateful to the Luxembourg National Research Fund for funding my doctoral project as part of its AFR PhD scheme. I am very thankful to Professor Matthew Happold, my supervisor, and Professors Gilles Cuniberti and Herwig Hofmann, members of my supervisory committee, for their supervision and valuable guidance during my work. I am also thankful to the Faculty of Law of the National University of Singapore, the School of Regulation and Global Governance (RegNet) of the Australian National University, and the Max Planck Institute Luxembourg for Procedural Law, for allowing me to conduct parts of my research at their respective institutions. Finally, but most importantly, I am indebted to my doctoral comrades at the University of Luxembourg, Johannes Hendrik Fahner, Başak Bağlayan, Chrysa Alexandraki, and Simona Demková, for their friendship, support, and extraordinary ability to cope with me on an everyday basis.

Relja Radović
Belgrade, November 2020

Summary

The process of jurisdictional regulation in investment treaty arbitration is governed by the principle of consensualism, which in theory confers the power to define the jurisdiction of arbitral tribunals on disputing parties exclusively. The practice of arbitral tribunals, however, has given the impression that tribunals are willing to establish jurisdiction on alternative and weaker bases than party consent. This book addresses the question to what extent party consent indeed defines the jurisdiction of arbitral tribunals. It argues that the consensualism of investment treaty arbitration is eroded by the rise of arbitral law-making in the matters of jurisdiction. The book tracks the development of specific arbitrator-made jurisdictional rules, which direct the interpretation and application of party-provided jurisdictional rules but also impose additional jurisdictional limits. The development of such rules decreases the share of disputing parties in the process of jurisdictional regulation. The book addresses the need for the recognition of the regulatory function of arbitral tribunals and its integration into the jurisdictional framework of investment treaty arbitration. To that end, the book sketches a two-layered model of jurisdictional regulation in investment treaty arbitration, consisted of both party-defined and arbitrator-made rules. The recognition of arbitral law-making as a pertinent part of the jurisdictional structure of investment treaty arbitration would provide more legal certainty in the creation and application of arbitrator-made rules, and possibly rebuild consensualism, by allowing for a clear coordination between the two layers of jurisdictional regulation.

Graphs

1 Conferral of the authority to adjudicate as a multistage process   27
2 Consensual and non-consensual definition of jurisdiction   79
3 The relationship between primary and secondary jurisdictional rules   185

Abbreviations

AJIL	American Journal of International Law
BIT	Bilateral investment treaty
CUP	Cambridge University Press
ECHR	European Convention on Human Rights
ECmHR	European Commission on Human Rights
ECOWAS	Economic Community of West African States
ECT	Energy Charter Treaty
ECtHR	European Court of Human Rights
EJIL	European Journal of International Law
EU	European Union
EWCA	Court of Appeal of England and Wales
EWHC	High Court of England and Wales
HRC	Human Rights Committee
ICC	International Chamber of Commerce
ICJ	International Court of Justice
ICSID Convention	Convention on the Settlement of Investment Disputes Between States and Nationals of Other States
ICSID Rev-FILJ	ICSID Review – Foreign Investment Law Journal
ICSID	International Centre for Settlement of Investment Disputes
ILC	International Law Commission
ILM	International Legal Materials
JIDS	Journal of International Dispute Settlement
JIEL	Journal of International Economic Law
JWIT	Journal of World Investment & Trade
LCIA	London Court of International Arbitration
LPICT	Law & Practice of International Courts and Tribunals
MFN	Most-favoured nation
NAFTA	North American Free Trade Agreement
New York Convention	Convention on the Recognition and Enforcement of Foreign Arbitral Awards
OUP	Oxford University Press
PCA	Permanent Court of Arbitration
PCIJ	Permanent Court of International Justice
SADC	Southern African Development Community
SCC	Stockholm Chamber of Commerce
SGHC	High Court of Singapore
TDM	Transnational Dispute Management

ABBREVIATIONS

UN	United Nations
UNCITRAL	United Nations Commission on International Trade Law
UNCTAD	United Nations Conference on Trade and Development
UNTS	United Nations Treaty Series
USSC	Supreme Court of the United States
VCLT	Vienna Convention on the Law of Treaties
WTO	World Trade Organization

Introduction

1   Consensual and Arbitral Jurisdictional Regulation

The principle of consensualism is the fundamental principle of international law governing the settlement of disputes at the international level, and it is the foundational principle of investment treaty arbitration. It instructs that the jurisdiction of every investment arbitral tribunal is defined by party consent. The mention of 'arbitration' has led many authors to analogise with domestic laws and to observe the requirement of a contractual relationship between disputing parties. The discovery that this field of international dispute settlement has been developing as 'arbitration without privity' was announced as a radical departure from what was previously known about the consensualism of arbitration, although in a positive sense.[1] Others have been critical about such developments, announcing 'la marginalisation du consentement dans l'arbitrage international'[2] and contesting the idea of arbitrating investment disputes without prior contractual relationships.[3] These were reactions to arbitral practice, which, it is often noted, has been willing to establish jurisdiction on alternative and weaker bases. An overall impression was that something was changing about the consensualism of investment arbitration, either when it comes to the establishment of consensual bonds between disputing parties, or in terms of damaging the concept of state sovereignty.

The consensualism of investment treaty arbitration continues to raise controversies. There are several deficiencies in the existing literature concerning this topic. First, this topic has mostly been examined from the point of view of 'international arbitration' as a sufficiently defined category, which allegedly comprises both investment and commercial arbitration.[4] The usual narrative

---

1   Jan Paulsson, 'Arbitration Without Privity' (1995) 10 ICSID Rev-FILJ 232.
2   Brigitte Stern, 'Un coup d'arrêt à la marginalisation du consentement dans l'arbitrage international (A propos de l'arrêt de la Cour d'appel de Paris du 1er juin 1999)' (2000) 2000 Revue de l'Arbitrage 403. See also Brigitte Stern, 'ICSID Arbitration and the State's Increasingly Remote Consent: Apropos the Maffezini Case' in Steve Charnovitz, Debra P Steger, and Peter Van den Bossche (eds), *Law in the Service of Human Dignity: Essays in Honour of Florentino Feliciano* (CUP 2005) 259–60.
3   M Sornarajah, *Resistance and Change in the International Law on Foreign Investment* (CUP 2015) 139–47.
4   Monographs addressing the topic of consent to arbitration include Andrea Marco Steingruber, *Consent in International Arbitration* (OUP 2012); Ousmane Diallo, *Le consentement des parties à l'arbitrage international* (Presses Universitaires de France 2010).

goes that consent is required as in 'any form of arbitration'.[5] This type of analysis often fails to accommodate the principle of consensualism within a broader legal context, namely that of public international law. That accommodation is important because in the first step it explains the function of party consent. Second, the existing literature has focused on the establishment of consensual links between disputing parties, in contrast to the process of making of jurisdictional rules.[6] That focus fails to observe that the act of consenting does not imply a simple 'yes' or 'no' to arbitral jurisdiction, but it primarily means defining the scope of the authority to adjudicate in substance. Shifting the focus to the substantive aspects of the arbitral authority to adjudicate can reveal that the jurisdictional determinations that some commentators would qualify as unusual, adventuristic, expansionary, or simply wrong, involve complex issues in the process of jurisdictional regulation.[7]

Finally, an emerging view on the consensualism of investment arbitration rejects private law analogies and focuses on state consent. It considers that the authority of arbitral tribunals derives from state consent exclusively, observing it either as an act of state regulation over its subjects (as public law approaches to investment treaty arbitration do),[8] or as a unilateral obligation under international law.[9] The problem is that these approaches impose their view on how

---

5   Rudolf Dolzer and Christoph Schreuer, *Principles of International Investment Law* (2nd ed, OUP 2012) 254. See also Piero Bernardini, 'International Commercial Arbitration and Investment Treaty Arbitration: Analogies and Differences' in David D Caron and others (eds), *Practising Virtue: Inside International Arbitration* (OUP 2015) 52 (arguing that analogies between commercial and investment arbitration are based on their consensual foundations and the will of parties not to resort to other channels of dispute settlement such as local courts or diplomatic protection).

6   In addition to the literature at n 4, see Paulsson (n 1); Jacques Werner, 'The Trade Explosion and Some Likely Effects on International Arbitration' (1997) 14 J Int'l Arb 5. Specific jurisdictional questions are usually treated as topics for themselves, although occasionally included in the analyses of consent in general. See, for example, Guiguo Wang, 'Consent in Investor–State Arbitration: A Critical Analysis' (2014) 13 Chinese JIL 335.

7   By 'jurisdictional regulation' I mean the process of defining the jurisdiction of arbitral tribunals, or more precisely the process of defining the rules determining the limits of arbitral jurisdiction. This process is analysed in ch 1.

8   See, for example, Stephan W Schill, 'International Investment Law and Comparative Public Law—An Introduction' in Stephan W Schill (ed), *International Investment Law and Comparative Public Law* (OUP 2010) 10–7; Gus Van Harten, 'The Public-Private Distinction in the International Arbitration of Individual Claims against the State' (2007) 56 Int'l & Comp LQ 371.

9   See, for example, Michael D Nolan and Frédéric G Sourgens, 'Limits of Consent–Arbitration Without Privity and Beyond' in MÁ Fernández-Ballesteros and David Arias (eds), *Liber Amicorum Bernardo Cremades* (La Ley 2010) 873; David D Caron, 'The Interpretation of National Foreign Investment Laws as Unilateral Acts Under International Law' in

investment arbitration functions or is ought to function, without verifying the compliance of that view with the theoretical foundations of the international legal order, on the one hand, and the actual practice of arbitral tribunals, on the other.[10] Furthermore, these approaches also fail to observe the rationale of the principle of consensualism. They either do not go beyond sketching an investor-state jurisdictional bond,[11] or are quite state-centric and ignore the role of investors in the definition of the authority to adjudicate.[12]

This book attempts to fill these gaps in the existing scholarship. First, it examines the principle of consensualism in investment treaty arbitration from the perspective of public international law. I suggest that an analysis of this principle in international law generally can shed a different light on its function and practical implementation. Second, I observe the principle of consensualism in a broader context of the process of jurisdictional regulation. Simply put, consensualism governs the process of defining concrete jurisdictional rules. This perspective shifts the focus from the formalities of establishing consensual bonds, to the substance of party consent which sets or fails to set the limits of arbitral jurisdiction.

The central question of this book is to what extent party consent defines jurisdictional rules in the context of investment treaty arbitration. The traditional understanding of the principle of consensualism in public international law confers the exclusive power to define the authority to adjudicate on disputing parties.[13] My argument is that this principle is eroded in investment

---

Mahnoush H Arsanjani and others (eds), *Looking to the Future: Essays on International Law in Honor of W. Michael Reisman* (Martinus Nijhoff 2011) 649.

[10] For example, Van Harten maintains that consent of a home state can oblige its investors to arbitrate with their host states, although such proposition was rebutted very early in arbitral practice. cf Van Harten (n 8) 380; with *American Manufacturing & Trading Inc v Republic of Zaire*, ICSID Case No ARB/93/1, Award (21 February 1997) paras 5.17-18. Similarly, the theory qualifying state consent as a unilateral act under international law ignores the actual practice, which observes arbitration agreements established by virtue of state offer and investor acceptance.

[11] For example, the theory qualifying state consent as a unilateral act under international law fails to observe its implications relating to the substance of jurisdictional regulation. That theory would imply a rebuttal of the theory of reciprocity, according to which the jurisdiction of an international court or tribunal exists only within the limits of the overlap of the intentions of both disputing parties.

[12] For example, Van Harten criticises the reliance on investor consent and the constructions of arbitration agreements, because that associates investment treaty arbitration to commercial arbitration. See Van Harten (n 8) 380–1. However, as argued in this book, the significance of such consent and arbitration agreements derives from public international law.

[13] See ch 1, s 2.

treaty arbitration by the rise of arbitral law-making in the matters of jurisdiction. I label such arbitral law-making 'arbitral jurisdictional regulation', in contrast to 'consensual jurisdictional regulation' which is exercised by disputing parties. I hypothesize that the strength of the principle of consensualism is inversely proportional to the extent of arbitral jurisdictional regulation. I find that arbitral tribunals have generated rules that instruct the interpretation and application of party-defined jurisdictional rules, on the one hand, and impose independent jurisdictional limits, on the other. This proves my hypothesis true, because the development of arbitrator-made rules decreases the degree to which disputing parties define the authority to adjudicate of arbitral tribunals. In other words, while I do not find an erosion of the principle of consensualism in terms of how consensual bonds are established, I find such an erosion in the process of defining the authority to adjudicate.

In practice, to what extent arbitrator-made rules will be used to supplement the applicable set of jurisdictional rules depends from case to case, because every arbitration faces different jurisdictional questions and every tribunal derives jurisdiction from a different arbitration agreement, which is in turn derived from one of thousands of investment treaties. What is important is that when arbitrators engage in law-making, they create arbitration-transcending jurisdictional rules in general and prescriptive terms, observing general considerations not limited to the particular arbitration agreement. They find inspiration in various sources, such as analogies to other fields of law, policy considerations, personal beliefs and values, and so on.

The development of arbitrator-made jurisdictional rules challenges the validity of the principle of consensualism as the normative basis of investment treaty arbitration. For this reason, the jurisdictional regulatory activity of arbitral tribunals remains in an informal domain, and it has never been properly recognised, while its growth causes a perceived violation of the principle of consensualism. Because consensualism is the basic norm stemming from the foundations of the international legal order, and arbitral jurisdictional regulation is a fact of practice, it is hardly imaginable that the latter could substitute for or derogate the former in the normative sense. I therefore argue that arbitral jurisdictional regulation should be integrated in the normative framework of the principle of consensualism. This book advances a proposal of how that integration should be conducted, arguing that arbitral jurisdictional regulation should be recognised in principle, followed by a formalisation of the process of arbitral law-making. The recognition would provide for a clear coordination of primary (party-created) and secondary (arbitrator-created) jurisdictional rules by establishing the primacy of the former over the latter. At the same time, this would allow for more legal certainty in the event of silence of party-provided jurisdictional rules. The integration of the two sets of rules will ultimately restore the consensualism of investment treaty arbitration, by allowing disputing parties to implicitly agree or explicitly disagree with arbitrator-made jurisdictional rules.

2   Framing the Project

Before proceeding to the substance, it is necessary to first clarify the two basic notions used in this book, namely 'consent' (1) and 'jurisdiction' (2). I will also address the scope of the book (3).

2.1   'Consent'

The notion of consent can be approached from several perspectives. First, consent can be assigned formal and substantive meanings. *Formally*, consent is seen as an act. This perspective observes the instruments of expression of consent, such as arbitration agreements, declarations, treaty accessions, and so on. *Substantively*, consent means the intention of a party to submit to third-party dispute resolution, and to do so within defined limits. This perspective is adopted in this book and it targets the substance of party intentions which gives parameters defining the limits of arbitral jurisdiction. Consent is therefore not seen as a countable act, but as substance without clear beginning and end.

Second, consent can be assigned narrow and wide meanings. *Narrowly*, consent is required because of some framework regulation. For example, it can be argued that state consent is required for litigating before the International Court of Justice (ICJ) due to the requirements of its Statute.[14] In the same vein, it can be argued that party consent is necessary within the system of the International Centre for Settlement of Investment Disputes (ICSID) because that is what Article 25(1) of the Convention on the Settlement of Investment Disputes Between States and Nationals of Other States (ICSID Convention) stipulates.[15] The consequence of this view is that the perceived scope of the issues governed by party consent shrinks. In its *wide* meaning, consent is the necessary condition for conferring the authority to adjudicate on any

---

14   Statute of the International Court of Justice (signed 26 June 1945, entered into force 24 October 1945) 3 Bevans 1153, art 36.
15   Convention on the Settlement of Investment Disputes Between States and Nationals of Other States (signed 18 March 1965, entered into force 14 October 1966) 575 UNTS 159, art 25(1).

international court or tribunal because of the lack of a centralised legislative authority in the international legal order.[16] This view broadens the scope of the issues governed by party consent, so for example such issues include both the terms of an agreement to arbitrate and the ICSID Convention, as well as party conduct affecting the definition of arbitral jurisdiction.[17] This book observes the notion of consent in its wide meaning.

2.2 'Jurisdiction'

This book understands jurisdiction as the limits of the power to adjudicate. Jurisdiction therefore concerns the scope or the area of the conferred power to adjudicate, and as such is inextricably related to the notion of dispute.[18] In turn, the judicial resolution of a dispute always requires a jurisdictional title meaning a consensual foundation.[19] Besides the limits of the authority to adjudicate, disputing parties also define the conditions of its exercise, which makes them jurisdictional.[20]

The concept of jurisdiction should be distinguished from the concept of powers of international courts and tribunals, despite the fact that the two terms are often used interchangeably.[21] The latter concept refers to the actions undertaken by international courts and tribunals in exercising their judicial function, as is the case with the powers to rule on their jurisdiction, to manage the procedure, to grant provisional measures, to award remedies, and to interpret and revise decisions.[22] The relationship between powers and jurisdiction can be discussed, but because the focus of this book is jurisdiction, judicial powers will not be considered further.[23]

---

16   See ch 1, s 2.1.
17   See ch 1, s 2.2.
18   See ch 1, ss 2.2.1–2.2.2.
19   *Continental Shelf (Libyan Arab Jamahiriya/Malta)* (Application to Intervene) (1984) ICJ Rep 3, paras 35–7.
20   *Armed Activities on the Territory of the Congo (New Application: 2002) (Democratic Republic of the Congo v Rwanda)* (Jurisdiction and Admissibility) (2006) ICJ Rep 6, para 88.
21   See, for example, *Nuclear Tests (Australia v France)* (Judgment) (1974) ICJ Rep 253, para 23; *Nuclear Tests (New Zealand v France)* (Judgment) (1974) ICJ Rep 457, para 23; Luiz Eduardo Salles, 'Jurisdiction' in William A Schabas and Shannonbrooke Murphy (eds), *Research Handbook on International Courts and Tribunals* (Edward Elgar 2017) 253.
22   See Chester Brown, 'The Inherent Powers of International Courts and Tribunals' (2006) 76 British Yrbk Int'l L 195, 211–22.
23   For example, it is usually said that the conferral of jurisdiction implies the power to award remedies. The availability of that power can also be seen as a question of substantive jurisdiction, which disputing parties can control by limiting the scope of justiciable disputes to the issues of liability, appropriate remedies, or quantum. See Chester Brown, *A Common Law of International Adjudication* (OUP 2007) 187–9.

INTRODUCTION   7

This book starts by examining the principle of consensualism in international law generally, and therefore references are made to the notion of jurisdiction as common to international adjudication at large. However, international adjudication has grown enormously and it now addresses a great range of issues, from inter-state disputes to the matters of individual criminal responsibility. It can hence be objected that the nexus between party consent and the jurisdiction of international courts and tribunals is not obvious, especially bearing in mind the example of international criminal tribunals. The structure of the jurisdictional regulation that relates to international crimes, which is arguably entirely different from the one relating to internationally wrongful acts, is not the topic of this study. This book focuses on the jurisdiction of international courts and tribunals akin to the jurisdiction of domestic courts over civil matters, ie on the jurisdiction that orbits around the notion of dispute as a disagreement between two (or more) parties over their rights and obligations.

2.3   Scope of the Project

Investment arbitration is defined descriptively, insofar as it concerns disputes between foreign investors and their host states. It addresses disputes arising out of contracts, domestic laws, investment treaties, and occasionally customary international law. The jurisdiction of arbitral tribunals can be derived from a contract (directly) and from a domestic law or treaty (indirectly).[24] This study is limited to investment arbitrations whose jurisdiction is governed by public international law. In theory, the jurisdiction of arbitral tribunals governed by public international law can be derived from all these sources,[25] however in practice the most common source today are investment protection treaties. For this reason, the focus of this book is investment treaty arbitration, while references to contract- and statute-based arbitrations are made for the sake of completeness and/or comparison.

3   Method

This book focuses on arbitral decisions addressing the questions of jurisdiction. I seek to identify parts of arbitral reasoning that develop rules governing the jurisdiction of investment arbitral tribunals. What I am looking for

---

24   See ch 1, s 3.2.
25   See ch 1, s 4.1.

specifically are the instances in which arbitrators recognise, either explicitly or implicitly, regulatory deficiencies of party-provided jurisdictional rules and remedy them by developing additional, arbitrator-made rules. By arbitrator-made rules I consider premises formulated in general and prescriptive terms, which are not based on the terms of party-defined jurisdictional rules, but find inspiration elsewhere.[26] The sources of inspiration can be various, from analogies to other spheres of law to policy considerations, to personal beliefs and values. My focus is on the formulation of such premises and I am not interested in whether their substance is right or wrong.

I acknowledge that ICSID annulment committees and domestic courts reviewing arbitral decisions also participate in this law-making process, although to varying extents. I therefore also observe their decisions contributing to the production of rules. However, the leaders of this law-making activity are arbitral tribunals, and for that reason I refer to 'arbitral jurisdictional regulation', 'arbitral law-making', and 'arbitrator-made rules'. Unless addressed separately, my conclusions and recommendations for the improvement of the practice of arbitral tribunals apply *mutatis mutandis* to ICSID annulment committees and domestic courts.

This is not a quantitative but a qualitative study, and therefore it does not conduct an exhaustive empirical analysis of all the publicly available decisions within a specified period of time. The study focuses on the leading decisions creating streams of practice and bearing some precedential value. It also observes other, less prominent decisions that have challenged the existing practices or otherwise actively engaged in discourses on the content of arbitrator-made rules. Tracing the precedential effect of decisions in streams, their challenges, collisions, and possible reconciliations is particularly important in order to inquire to what extent arbitrator-made rules have gained some sort of normativity. This study takes into account decisions rendered and reported until 31 December 2019.

---

26   In contrast, the standard approach to the analysis of arbitral work observes the interpretation of treaty provisions. See, for example, Matthew Weiniger, 'Jurisdiction Challenges in BIT Arbitrations – Do You Read a BIT by Reading a BIT or by Reading into a BIT?' in Loukas A Mistelis and Julian DM Lew (eds), *Pervasive Problems in International Arbitration* (Kluwer Law International 2006) 254 (arguing that through interpretation 'the provisions of BITs are capable of being melded in any direction the tribunal wishes'); Gabrielle Kaufmann-Kohler, 'Interpretation of Treaties: How Do Arbitral Tribunals Interpret Dispute Settlement Provisions Embodied in Investment Treaties?' in Loukas A Mistelis and Julian DM Lew (eds), *Pervasive Problems in International Arbitration* (Kluwer Law International 2006) 257 (discussing the consistency of arbitral decisions pertaining to what is called here arbitral law-making through the prism of treaty interpretation).

Investment law scholarship at large has been criticised for the dominance of external and deductive perspectives focusing on arbitral decisions.[27] This criticism suggests that the proper perspective is internal and inductive, shifting the focus to arbitrations as a process of interaction between parties and arbitrators.[28] While this criticism certainly has merit in the analysis of the process of arbitral decision-making, it is not sustainable when it comes to the discovery of the meaning of principles, concepts, and rules across international law. Deduction is inevitable in the analysis of the jurisdictional framework of investment treaty arbitration, the process of jurisdictional regulation, and consensualism as their governing principle. For this reason, this book does not attempt to reverse methodological directions, and it rather follows the classical canons of the examination of judicial practice.

4   Outline

This book is divided into five chapters. Chapter 1 examines the process of jurisdictional regulation in investment treaty arbitration. It argues that the principle of consensualism continues to govern this process, conferring on disputing parties the exclusive power to define jurisdictional rules. The chapter argues that consensualism is a persistent feature of international adjudication and investment treaty arbitration due to the absence of a central legislative authority, and that it has not been affected by contextual developments in these fields. The following three chapters examine the formation of arbitrator-made jurisdictional rules. They are structured according to the effects of arbitrator-made rules, thus demonstrating their significance from the practical perspective. Chapter 2 analyses the rules that facilitate the access to international arbitration by relaxing the procedural aspects of consensual jurisdictional regulation, ie the conditions of access defined by disputing parties. Chapter 3 analyses the rules that facilitate the access to international arbitration by relaxing the substantive aspects of consensual jurisdictional regulation. Chapter 4 focuses on the rules that hinder the access to international arbitration by introducing sharper limits of arbitral jurisdiction. These three chapters do not present an exhaustive catalogue of arbitrator-made jurisdictional rules but discuss their most prominent examples. Other examples can develop. Finally, Chapter 5 argues that arbitral jurisdictional regulation should be integrated

---

27   Frédéric Gilles Sourgens, *A Nascent Common Law: The Process of Decisionmaking in International Legal Disputes between States and Foreign Investors* (Brill Nijhoff 2015) 25.
28   ibid 25–9.

in the jurisdictional framework of investment treaty arbitration. It first finds the driving force behind arbitral jurisdictional regulation, and then sets forth a two-layered model of jurisdictional regulation consisting of primary (party-created) and secondary (arbitrator-created) jurisdictional rules. The chapter also discusses some challenges of the proposed model and situates it in a broader context of the international legal order.

5 Relevance

This book engages in the ongoing debate about the future of investor-state dispute settlement. Among the concerns identified by the United Nations Commission on International Trade Law (UNCITRAL) Working Group III in the discussion about the reform of investor-state dispute settlement, the issues of consistency and correctness of arbitral decisions are dealt with by the proposed model (in regard to jurisdiction).[29] The issue of consistency is particularly important regarding the jurisdictional sphere, because it concerns secondary/structural and precise rules (as opposed to primary and flexible standards) which do not tolerate inconsistency.[30] Correctness of arbitral decisions is a persistent consideration which requires internal support and guidance, as opposed to external/institutional amendments.[31] Furthermore, despite some arguments in favour of abandoning investor-state dispute settlement at the international level, the discussion at the UNCITRAL Working Group III shows that the system is probably here to stay with more or less amendments.[32] The possible establishment of an appellate mechanism or a multilateral investment court, as well as the already commenced process of

---

29 UNCITRAL Working Group III, 'Possible Reform of Investor-State Dispute Settlement (ISDS)' (5 September 2018) UN Doc A/CN.9/WG.III/WP.149, paras 9–10; UNCITRAL, 'Report of Working Group III (Investor-State Dispute Settlement Reform) on the Work of Its Thirty-Sixth Session (Vienna, 29 October–2 November 2018)' (6 November 2018) UN Doc A/CN.9/964, paras 25–63.

30 Julian Arato, Chester Brown and Federico Ortino, 'Parsing and Managing Inconsistency in Investor-State Dispute Settlement' (2020) 21 JWIT 336.

31 Anna De Luca and others, 'Responding to Incorrect Decision-Making in Investor-State Dispute Settlement: Policy Options' (2020) 21 JWIT 374.

32 UNCITRAL, 'Report of Working Group III (Investor-State Dispute Settlement Reform) on the Work of Its Thirty-Eighth Session (Vienna, 14–18 October 2019)' (23 October 2019) UN Doc A/CN.9/1004, para 25 (indicating reform options, namely an appellate mechanism, a multilateral investment court, and the issues of selection and appointment of arbitrators and adjudicators).

establishing separate investment courts led by the European Union (EU),[33] present another opportunity for good implementation of the proposed model. From the normative perspective, these amendments would provide better conditions for the proposed model, such as an increased availability of decisions and a stronger power of jurisdictional review. From the institutional perspective, they would bring new incentives for formulating uniform approaches in arbitral decision- and law-making.

This book also engages in a broader scholarly discourse about the functioning of international adjudication. Because the international judiciary remains dispersed, lacking any means of comprehensive regulation, and governed by the principle of consensualism, it is imaginable that other fields could face the same phenomenon of developing judicial and/or arbitral jurisdictional regulation. Therefore, this study should not be taken as an exclusive examination of investment treaty arbitration, but rather as an experiment in one field that can reveal indicators about the functioning of international adjudication in general. Investment treaty arbitration presents an excellent sample for such an experiment, because its jurisdictional structure can be called rudimentary compared to other international courts and tribunals: each arbitral tribunal derives jurisdiction from an arbitration agreement, which is in turn usually based on a single article of an investment treaty. Despite the recent tendencies towards an expansion of jurisdictional and procedural regulation in investment treaties, they will not eliminate the need for the arbitral regulatory activity, simply because of the dynamics of arbitration and the continuous emergence of new jurisdictional questions. In the meantime, the jurisdiction of investment tribunals remains regulated in minimalist terms, which increases the visibility of the arbitral regulatory activity on the trajectory from a preliminary objection to a jurisdictional determination. The findings of this study can serve as the basis for further investigations of similar phenomena in other fields of international adjudication.

33 See Comprehensive Economic and Trade Agreement Between Canada and the European Union (signed 30 October 2016, not in force) c 8, s F; EU-Vietnam Investment Protection Agreement (signed 30 June 2019, not in force) c 3; EU-Singapore Investment Protection Agreement (signed 19 October 2018, not in force) c 3.

CHAPTER 1

The Process of Jurisdictional Regulation in Investment Treaty Arbitration

1   Introduction

International adjudication is a good example of change in the international legal order. It is a commonplace that international law used to focus on interstate relations without any (permanent) adjudicatory mechanisms. The opening of first international courts and tribunals marked the beginning of a new era.[1] When non-state actors, such as individuals, groups, and corporations acquired direct rights in international legal instruments, it became obvious that international law had begun to govern actual everyday life.[2] And such direct rights ceased to be utopian once non-state actors acquired the right to pursue claims against states in international forums.[3] Certainly, the proliferation of international courts and tribunals, which has put into practice the judicial protection of such diverse interests, has prompted an enormous development of the relevant procedural law.

---

1   While the settlement of international disputes by a third party was not a new phenomenon, the idea of empowering a permanent body with that task characterises the end of the 19th and the beginning of the 20th century. See Vanda Lamm, *Compulsory Jurisdiction in International Law* (Edward Elgar 2014) 9; and Ole Spiermann, *International Legal Argument in the Permanent Court of International Justice: The Rise of the International Judiciary* (CUP 2005) 14–5.

2   Although conferring direct rights on individuals or groups was not alien to international law in earlier times, the period after the Second World War is considered the peak time of such developments, aimed to establish control of state behaviour towards its subjects, which have primarily taken place in the spheres of human rights and investment protection.

3   For the argument that what makes a right is the possibility of enforcement, see Hillel Steiner, 'Working Rights' in Matthew H Kramer, NE Simmonds, and Hillel Steiner, *A Debate Over Rights: Philosophical Enquiries* (OUP 1998) 235–47. See also *Ashby v White* (1703) 92 ER 126 (Holt CJ Dissent) ('If the plaintiff has a right, he must of necessity have a means to vindicate and maintain it, and a remedy if he is injured in the exercise or enjoyment of it, and, indeed it is a vain thing to imagine a right without a remedy; for want of right and want of remedy are reciprocal [...]'). But for the argument that procedural enforcement rights in international law do not stem from substantive rights, particularly in the context of investment treaty arbitration, see Eric De Brabandere, *Investment Treaty Arbitration as Public International Law: Procedural Aspects and Implications* (CUP 2014) 55–70.

Despite these developments, some aspects of international law are not prone to change. While new rules governing international adjudication and the judicial process are being developed on an everyday basis, it is reasonable to take at least some principles for granted.[4] These fundamentals of the international legal order in general, and of international adjudication in particular, require new rules to adjust to their requirements. The consensualism of international adjudication belongs to this group.

This chapter examines the process of jurisdictional regulation in investment treaty arbitration. It starts from general international law and the consensualism of international adjudication, and proceeds to the specific context of investment treaty arbitration. The argument of this chapter is that consensualism, as a general principle of international law, continues to govern the process of jurisdictional regulation in investment treaty arbitration, and confers the power to define jurisdictional rules on disputing parties exclusively. The principle of consensualism has persisted because of the function it exercises in the absence of a central legislative authority, and it has not been affected by contextual developments in the theory and practice of international law and international investment law. Section 2 firstly discusses party consent as the basis of jurisdictional regulation in international law. Section 3 then turns to the framework of investment treaty arbitration, navigating through the process of jurisdictional regulation. Section 4 analyses the legal regime governing jurisdictional rules defined by disputing parties. Section 5 concludes.

2 The Significance of Consent

Almost every defence in international adjudication starts by challenging jurisdiction on the grounds of a lack of consent.[5] At the same time, scholarly

---

[4] Besides the fundamentals of the international legal order and international adjudication, which are discussed in this chapter, it has also been argued that international courts and tribunals share some common procedural aspects. See generally Chester Brown, *A Common Law of International Adjudication* (OUP 2007). But, for the claim that every tribunal in international law is a 'self-contained system', see *Prosecutor v Duško Tadić* (Decision on the Defence Motion for Interlocutory Appeal on Jurisdiction) ICTY-94-1 (2 October 1995) para 11.

[5] The phenomenon that one state is at the same time both the issuer of consent and the party contesting its existence or scope is regarded as 'the paradox of consent': CL Lim and OA Elias, *The Paradox of Consensualism in International Law* (Brill 1998) 202. An older research has found jurisdictional issues being raised in 87 out of 102 awards in 82 investment cases: Susan D Franck, 'Empirically Evaluating Claims About Investment Treaty Arbitration' (2007) 86 North Carolina L Rev 1, 24, 52.

challenges of consensualism in international law generally have become increasingly visible.[6] They vary, from the arguments that international law is reforming,[7] to those favouring law-making around state consent within the existing system.[8] The requirement of consent in international law is often regarded as unfair and outdated. These objections have appeared together with an increased regulation of state conduct at the international level, followed by demands for further acceleration of that trend, often motivated by humanitarian or moral concerns.[9] A valid question is why do we still talk about consent. To answer this question, this section firstly addresses the theory behind the consensualism of international adjudication (1). It then proceeds to the function of this principle (2), and to its status as a general principle of international law (3). Finally, some contextual considerations significant for the field of investment treaty arbitration are addressed (4).

2.1   *The Consensualism of International Adjudication*

The system of international adjudication is built around one cardinal deficiency: the lack of a higher authority above sovereigns.[10] Sovereignty is an inexhaustible topic in (international) law.[11] Only one of its many aspects is important in the present context: states are the basic subjects of international

---

[6]   See, for example, Andrew T Guzman, 'Against Consent' (2012) 52 Virginia J Int'l L 747; and Laurence R Helfer, 'Nonconsensual International Lawmaking' (2008) 2008 Univ Illinois L Rev 71. But see also, on the inevitability of consent, despite its paradoxes, Lim and Elias (n 5).

[7]   Such suggestions derive from various perspectives on international law, such as realpolitik, international hegemonic law, and the impact of globalisation. For an overview see Duncan B Hollis, 'Why State Consent Still Matters—Non-State Actors, Treaties, and the Changing Sources of International Law' (2005) 23 Berkeley J Int'l L 137, 137–9.

[8]   For example Guzman (n 6).

[9]   The literature cited above analyses the means of non-consensual law-making almost exclusively in the context of national security, human rights, and environmental issues. For the argument that states cannot benefit from state immunity, and that their consent is not necessary for establishing the jurisdiction of foreign courts in the matters of grave violations of international human rights law, see *Jurisdictional Immunities of the State (Germany v Italy: Greece intervening)* (Dissenting Opinion of Judge Cançado Trindade) (2012) ICJ Rep 179.

[10] For a critical view on the role of state sovereignty in international law, see Sir Hersch Lauterpacht, *The Function of Law in the International Community* (reprint, OUP 2011) 3ff.

[11] For classical works on this topic, see GWF Hegel, *Elements of the Philosophy of Right* (CUP 1991) 275ff; Carl Schmitt, *Political Theology: Four Chapters on the Concept of Sovereignty* (University of Chicago Press 2005); Hans Kelsen, *General Theory of Law and State* (Harvard University Press 1945) 383–6; HLA Hart, *The Concept of Law* (3rd ed, OUP 2012) 215–8; and, for a summary of the Schmitt v Kelsen debate in the context of international law, Martti Koskenniemi, *From Apology to Utopia: The Structure of International Legal Argument* (CUP 2005) 226–40.

law and there is no authority above them.[12] No centralised regulatory authority exists, which would be capable of imposing rights and obligations on states, or for that matter on other possible subjects of international law such as individuals and companies.

That states are the principal law-makers of international law is a truism.[13] A statement of the Permanent Court of International Justice (PCIJ) in the *Lotus* case from the 1920s, has become the best-known authority on the issue:

> International law governs relations between independent States. The rules of law binding upon States therefore *emanate from their own free will* as expressed in conventions or by usages generally accepted as expressing principles of law and established in order to regulate the relations between these co-existing independent communities or with a view to the achievement of common aims. Restrictions upon the independence of States cannot therefore be presumed.[14]

The same reasoning has been followed by the ICJ, which does not omit to mention sovereignty next to any obligation of the state.[15] The nexus between the two notions is twofold: from one perspective, any obligation of the state limits its sovereignty;[16] from another, sovereignty gives the capacity to the state to undertake obligations and to act as a law-maker in the international scene.[17]

---

12 *Reparation for Injuries Suffered in the Service of the United Nations* (Advisory Opinion) (1949) ICJ Rep 174, 177–80.

13 Rosalyn Higgins, 'International Law and the Reasonable Need of Governments to Govern. Inaugural Lecture, London School of Economics and Political Science 22nd November, 1982' in Rosalyn Higgins, *Themes and Theories: Selected Essays, Speeches, and Writings in International Law*, vol 2 (OUP 2009) 784 ('states are still the most important of the actors in the international legal system, and their sovereignty is at the heart of this system').

14 *The Case of the SS 'Lotus' (France v Turkey)* (Judgment) (1927) PCIJ Ser A—No 10, 4, 18 (emphasis added). For a commentary see Spiermann (n 1) 247–63. Koskenniemi argues that this excerpt reflects the absolutist pure fact approach to sovereignty: Koskenniemi, *Apology* (n 11) 255–6.

15 See, for example, *Military and Paramilitary Activities in and against Nicaragua (Nicaragua v United States of America)* (Merits) (1986) ICJ Rep 14, para 269.

16 This view follows the argument that sovereignty is a question of fact, and that any restrictions upon it result from an agreement among states, relying on the theory of 'absolute sovereignty'. Koskenniemi, *Apology* (n 11) 231–3. See also *Case of the SS 'Wimbledon' (UK, France, Italy, Japan, and Poland intervening v Germany)* (Judgment) (1923) PCIJ Ser A—No 1, 15, 25; *Customs Régime Between Germany and Austria (Protocol of March 19th, 1931)* (Advisory Opinion) (1931) PCIJ Ser A/B—No 41, 37, 52.

17 This view follows the argument that sovereignty is a legal quality granted to states by international law. See *Wimbledon* (n 16) 25 ('the right of entering into international engagements is an attribute of State sovereignty'); Koskenniemi, *Apology* (n 11) 229–30; James

Whichever direction is taken in this loop, the creation of international obligations is impossible without the involvement of the concept of state sovereignty, either as an object or a subject of law-making.[18] The insistence that consent is the basis of each and every obligation of the state has been noted alongside the rise of positivism, when the concept of state sovereignty emerged in the centre of legal thought.[19]

States create their own procedural obligations, as distinct from substantive law, such as to submit disputes to judicial or arbitral resolution.[20] However, I suggest that the fact that states' submissions to adjudication 'emanate from their own free will' should not be regarded as strictly connected to the notion of sovereignty as such, but rather to the other side of the same coin: the lack of a higher authority in international law capable of regulating the resolution of disputes arising within that system. As I will argue in Chapter 5, when analysing the practice of investment tribunals, the idea of sovereignty has been lost behind the principle of consensualism in the context of public-private adjudication.[21] The principle of consensualism is inclusive of both public and

---

Crawford, 'Sovereignty as a Legal Value' in James Crawford and Martti Koskenniemi (eds), *The Cambridge Companion to International Law* (CUP 2012) 122–3.

18   *Customs Régime Between Germany and Austria (Protocol of March 19th, 1931)* (Dissenting Opinion of M Adatci, Mr Kellogg, Baron Rolin-Jaequemyns, Sir Cecil Hurst, M Schücking, Jonkheer van Eysinga, and M Wang) (1931) PCIJ Ser A/B—No 41, 74, 76–8. Further on the two approaches of 'the State as an entity of an absolute legal and moral value', on the one hand, and '[t]he positivist doctrine, grounded as it is on the conception of international law based on the sovereign will of the State', on the other, see Sir Hersch Lauterpacht, *Private Law Sources and Analogies of International Law (with Special Reference to International Arbitration)* (Longmans 1927, reprint Lawbook Exchange 2013) 43–51.

19   Mónica García-Salmones Rovira, *The Project of Positivism in International Law* (OUP 2013) 56; Horia Ciurtin, 'Paradoxes of (Sovereign) Consent: On the Uses and Abuses of a Notion in International Investment Law' in Crina Baltag (ed), *ICSID Convention after 50 Years: Unsettled Issues* (Kluwer Law International 2017) 38–41.

20   *Status of Eastern Carelia* (Advisory Opinion) (1923) PCIJ Ser B—No 5, 7, 27 ('It is well established in international law that no State can, without its consent, be compelled to submit its disputes with other States either to mediation or to arbitration, or to any other kind of pacific settlement.'); *Legality of Use of Force (Yugoslavia v Belgium)* (Provisional Measures) (1999) ICJ Rep 124, para 20 ('Whereas the Court, under its Statute, does not automatically have jurisdiction over legal disputes between States parties to that Statute or between other States to whom access to the Court has been granted; whereas the Court has repeatedly stated "that one of the fundamental principles of its Statute is that it cannot decide a dispute between States without the consent of those States to its jurisdiction" […]; and whereas the Court can therefore exercise jurisdiction only between States parties to a dispute who not only have access to the Court but also have accepted the jurisdiction of the Court, either in general form or for the individual dispute concerned;').

21   See ch 5, s 2.2.2.

private actors and it persists because, due to the lack of a higher authority, it represents the only possible means of the conferral of the power to adjudicate. Sovereignty can be seen as assigning states the status of an *initiator* of international jurisdictional relationships, but it does not grant them the exclusivity of regulation over international dispute settlement.

A jurisdictional relationship is initiated by expression of at least one 'free will' to commit to international jurisdiction, ie consent, which can be done both *ex ante* and *ex post* to the dispute itself. And while consenting in advance, either in treaties constituting special courts,[22] in separate declarations,[23] or jurisdictional treaty provisions,[24] is common today, these are not examples of 'compulsory jurisdiction' as they are customarily referred to.[25] At most, these are examples of the appearance of compulsory jurisdiction: if a state consents in advance to adjudication in respect of a class of disputes, from the point of view of the other party (another state or, more often, a private person) to a concrete dispute within that class, it appears as if its opponent is subject to a compulsory jurisdiction.[26] But from the point of view of the law, the compulsory component is lacking, because the state had decided by virtue of its own free will to accept the jurisdiction of an adjudicatory body. Furthermore, a conferral of the authority to adjudicate is not complete without the participation of both disputing parties in a sort of a contractual relationship, which I discuss

---

[22] For example, Convention for the Protection of Human Rights and Fundamental Freedoms, as amended by Protocols Nos 11 and 14 (opened for signature 4 November 1950, entered into force 3 September 1953; Protocol No 11 entered into force 1 November 1998; Protocol No 14 entered into force 1 June 2010) 213 UNTS 222 (ECHR) arts 19, 34.

[23] Statute of the International Court of Justice (signed 26 June 1945, entered into force 24 October 1945) 3 Bevans 1153 (ICJ Statute) art 36(2); *Anglo-Iranian Oil Co (UK v Iran)* (Individual Opinion of President McNair) (1952) ICJ Rep 93, 116 ('the machinery provided by that paragraph is that of "contracting-in", not of "contracting-out" ').

[24] This can be done in regard to specifically defined disputes, as in Convention on the Prevention and Punishment of the Crime of Genocide (adopted 9 December 1948, entered into force 12 January 1951) 78 UNTS 277, art IX; or (legal) disputes in general, as in European Convention for the Peaceful Settlement of Disputes (signed 29 April 1957, entered into force 30 April 1958) 320 UNTS 243, art 1.

[25] See, for example, Cesare PR Romano, Karen J Alter, and Yuval Shany, 'Mapping International Adjudicative Bodies, the Issues, and Players' in Cesare PR Romano, Karen J Alter, and Yuval Shany (eds), *The Oxford Handbook of International Adjudication* (OUP 2014) 6; Bernard H Oxman, 'Complementary Agreements and Compulsory Jurisdiction' (2001) 95 AJIL 277 (in general); Lamm (n 1) (as for the ICJ in particular); Gary Born, 'A New Generation of International Adjudication' (2012) 61 Duke LJ 775 (as for specialised forums).

[26] See in this respect Stanimir A Alexandrov, 'The Compulsory Jurisdiction of the International Court of Justice: How Compulsory Is It?' (2006) 5 Chinese JIL 29.

in more detail further in this chapter.[27] Given that the other disputing party usually takes action only after a dispute has arisen, 'compulsory jurisdiction' presents only another instance of *ex ante* consent, which only initiates a conferral of the adjudicative power.

In contrast to express consent (expressed either before or after a dispute has arisen, the latter by special agreement or *compromis*), a jurisdictional relationship can also be established implicitly. According to the *forum prorogatum* doctrine, if one party files a claim for adjudication without any expression of consent of the other party, the other party can consent to adjudication by simply not objecting to jurisdiction for the lack of consent.[28] This doctrine is not often seen in practice,[29] which is understandable given that jurisdictional challenges are a powerful and efficient tool in the hands of respondents.

Because the cardinal notion here is the will or intention, or more precisely its manifestation, the concept of consent should not be understood formalistically.[30] Examining whether consent to adjudication has been given or not is not a simple reading exercise. It rather requires an inquiry into the will of the concerned party.[31] The questions are whether an obligation to submit a dispute for adjudication can be identified,[32] and whether the party had the intention of undertaking that obligation.[33] Furthermore, because the power to adjudicate can be limited in different ways, the usual question appearing before adjudicators is not whether consent has been given at all, but rather

---

27   See s 2.2.4.
28   See ICJ, Rules of Court (adopted 14 April 1978, entered into force 1 July 1978) (ICJ Rules) art 38(5); *Haya de la Torre* (*Colombia v Peru*) (Judgment) (1951) ICJ Rep 71, 78.
29   Until 2011, in only two clear instances (but arguably up to seven) the ICJ had jurisdiction based on the *forum prorogatum* doctrine. See Table 3, Item 6 in Mariko Kawano, 'The Role of Judicial Procedures in the Process of the Pacific Settlement of International Disputes' (2009) 346 Recueil des Cours 9, 472. The *Haya de la Torre* case should be added to this list.
30   The term 'consent' refers to the substance which can be expressed in different forms: Vienna Convention on the Law of Treaties (signed 23 May 1969, entered into force 27 January 1980) 1155 UNTS 331 (VCLT) art 11.
31   *Factory at Chorzów* (*Germany v Poland*) (Claim for Indemnity) (Jurisdiction) (1927) PCIJ Ser A—No 9, 4, 32 ('When considering whether it has jurisdiction or not, the Court's aim is always to ascertain whether an intention on the part of the Parties exists to confer jurisdiction upon it.').
32   *Maritime Delimitation and Territorial Questions* (*Qatar v Bahrain*) (Jurisdiction and Admissibility) (1994) ICJ Rep 112, paras 21–30.
33   *Aegean Sea Continental Shelf* (*Greece v Turkey*) (Judgment) (1978) ICJ Rep 3, paras 100–7; *Application of the Convention on the Prevention and Punishment of the Crime of Genocide* (*Bosnia and Herzegovina v Yugoslavia*) (Preliminary Objections) (1996) ICJ Rep 595, paras 17, 37.

whether a particular issue is covered by consent.[34] Accordingly, 'a search for consent' usually prompts an inquiry into the will of disputing parties, as manifested in any useful documents, or as the case may be—in their silence.

The requirement of consent to adjudication shows that international adjudication is still more of an exception than a rule. It is a preserved rule that disputing parties must provide their consent defining the authority to adjudicate, despite the possibility to do so both before and after a dispute has arisen. This is a crucial difference from municipal judicial systems, which usually provide a general access to courts.[35] And while in municipal systems such access is provided by the state as a central regulatory authority, no such authority exists in international law that could provide the same.

2.2 *The Function of Consent*

Jurisdiction can be defined in many ways.[36] One crucial notion stands at the centre of every definition: the power (or authority) to adjudicate.[37] The theories about the empowerment of international courts and tribunals often address the delegation of interpretative powers by states as law-makers, and view international adjudicators as agents[38] or trustees of states.[39] This perspective can be supported by the additional argument that states delegate parts of their domestic jurisdiction to investment tribunals.[40] It is suggested here that international adjudicators can also be viewed as agents or trustees in a somewhat different empowering trajectory, which is advocated in this study. It is maintained here that every international jurisdiction is constituted by the delegation of the *power to adjudicate* by disputing parties to international adjudicators.[41] This view is supported by the fact that dispute resolution at the

---

34 *Ambatielos (Greece v United Kingdom)* (Merits: Obligation to Arbitrate) (1953) ICJ Rep 10, 19 ('the question is whether the consent given by the Parties in signing the Declaration of 1926 to arbitrate a certain category of disputes, does or does not extend to the Ambatielos claim').

35 Chittharanjan F Amerasinghe, *Jurisdiction of International Tribunals* (Kluwer Law International 2003) 56–8; Romano, Alter, and Shany (n 25) 5–6.

36 See Amerasinghe, *Jurisdiction* (n 35) ch 2; and Chittharanjan F Amerasinghe, *Jurisdiction of Specific International Tribunals* (Martinus Nijhoff 2009) 5–8 ('jurisdiction' is not a term of art).

37 Yuval Shany, *Questions of Jurisdiction and Admissibility before International Courts* (CUP 2016) 22.

38 Karen J Alter, 'Agents or Trustees? International Courts in Their Political Context' (2008) 14 European J Int'l Relations 33, 34.

39 ibid 38–44.

40 See, for one such argument, Shany, *Questions* (n 37) 32–3.

41 Shany argues that states do not delegate the judicial, but the decision-making power to international courts and tribunals, because states themselves do not possess the power to

international level forms a separate international legal relationship from the one governing substantive relations between disputing parties.[42]

The mere mention of 'jurisdiction' implies some area of competence with defined borders. Consent to adjudication grants the power to adjudicate and at the same time defines the limits of that power. I describe the process of this definition in four steps. First, I identify the delegators of the power to adjudicate (1). Second, I analyse the concepts of dispute and justiciability (2). I then discuss the formation of jurisdictional borders as a multistage process (3), and the contractual nature of international jurisdiction (4).

2.2.1   The Origins of the Power to Adjudicate

The first question is who delegates the power to adjudicate. Do states parties to a treaty, as law-makers, authorise a tribunal to interpret and give meaning to treaty provisions, or do parties to a dispute authorise a tribunal to settle their differences? It has been argued that the former presents a traditional paradigm of public international law, while the latter characterises other legal systems.[43] The core of my argument is that under public international law the authority to adjudicate is delegated by disputing parties exclusively. In the words of the ICJ, 'when States sign an arbitration agreement, they [...] entrust an arbitration tribunal with the task of settling a dispute in accordance with the terms agreed by the parties, who define in the agreement the jurisdiction of the tribunal

---

adjudicate over each other: ibid 27–8. While technically true, this distinction loses importance if one takes into account, as Shany himself does, that states make delegation with the condition of employing judicial methodologies, thus defining the adjudicative power as a sub-category of decision-making. Furthermore, because the power to adjudicate is delegated by disputing parties to a concrete dispute, no question of authority to adjudicate of one state over another is involved. See s 2.2.1 below.

42   Note the separate conferral of substantive rights and procedural remedies in international law; see De Brabandere (n 3) 55–70.

43   Anthea Roberts, 'Clash of Paradigms: Actors and Analogies Shaping the Investment Treaty System' (2013) 107 AJIL 45, 60–1. See also Julia Hueckel, 'Rebalancing Legitimacy and Sovereignty in International Investment Agreements' (2012) 61 Emory LJ 601, 618–21 (relying on the principal-agent theory); Anne van Aaken, 'Control Mechanisms in International Investment Law' in Zachary Douglas, Joost Pauwelyn, and Jorge E Viñuales (eds), *The Foundations of International Investment Law: Bringing Theory into Practice* (OUP 2014) 410–5 (using economic contract and principal-agent theories); but see Alec Stone Sweet and Florian Grisel, *The Evolution of International Arbitration: Judicialization, Governance, Legitimacy* (OUP 2017) 22–33 (discussing the principal-agent theory in international arbitration, both commercial and investment, in three models: contractual, judicial, and pluralist-constitutional).

and determine its limits'.[44] The crux of this statement is not the statehood of delegating entities, but their status as disputing parties. That is why the inclusion of non-state actors in international adjudication has faced no difficulty in regard to this basic premise of the principle of consensualism.

This proposition can be tested very briefly. Judicial interpretations of international law are incidental (the applicable law is determined and interpreted *for* the dispute), non-exclusive (the same set of rules can be interpreted by various courts and tribunals), and non-binding (for either the same or other courts and tribunals). In contrast, judicial settlement of a dispute is central (the jurisdiction of a court or tribunal is established for a particular dispute), ideally exclusive (jurisdictional overlaps are seen as problematic), and always binding (both on disputing parties and other courts and tribunals as *res judicata*). Consider one example: the only decision finding genocide in an inter-state dispute, and for that purpose interpreting the Genocide Convention extensively, was delivered in a case between two states which did not exist at the time of that Convention's drafting.[45] The case was brought to the ICJ not because of the trust the drafting states conferred on it as the 'guardian of the Convention', but because of the applicability of the jurisdictional clause between the two disputing states.[46] The Court's interpretation of the Convention is not binding on other tribunals, or for that matter on the ICJ itself,[47] unlike its finding of genocide and the determination of legal consequences.[48]

This is not to say that the judicial task to interpret the law should be undermined, but that task should rather be seen in light of the judicial function to settle disputes. In short, dispute resolution is the primary task of international judicial bodies, whereas interpretation of the applicable law is their secondary

---

44 *Arbitral Award of 31 July 1989 (Guinea-Bissau v Senegal)* (Judgment) (1991) ICJ Rep 53, para 49.

45 *Application of the Convention on the Prevention and Punishment of the Crime of Genocide (Bosnia and Herzegovina v Serbia and Montenegro)* (Judgment) (2007) ICJ Rep 43.

46 See *Bosnia and Herzegovina v Yugoslavia* (Preliminary Objections) (n 33); cf *Armed Activities on the Territory of the Congo (New Application: 2002) (Democratic Republic of the Congo v Rwanda)* (Jurisdiction and Admissibility) (2006) ICJ Rep 6, paras 64–70 (lacking jurisdiction due to a reservation to the jurisdictional clause in the Genocide Convention).

47 *Application of the Convention on the Prevention and Punishment of the Crime of Genocide (Croatia v Serbia)* (Judgment) (2015) ICJ Rep 3, para 125 (repeating that it is only the Court's choice not to deviate from previous practice without 'very particular reasons to do so').

48 ICJ Statute (n 23) art 59 ('The decision of the Court has no binding force except between the parties and in respect of that particular case.').

task.[49] Any discussion about jurisdiction, therefore, must begin from the notion of dispute.

2.2.2   Dispute and Justiciability

The best-known definition of 'dispute' is the one offered by the PCIJ in the *Mavrommatis* case, holding that a dispute 'is a disagreement on a point of law or fact, a conflict of legal views or of interests between two persons'.[50] The central element of that definition is the 'positive opposition' of the parties' claims and/or views on the compliance with certain obligations or the existence of certain rights.[51] The ICJ has opined that an inquiry into the existence of a dispute is an 'objective determination': the Court will inquire whether there is a dispute in substance by examining facts, and mere assertion or denial of its existence is not conclusive.[52] The positions or attitudes of the parties pertaining to the existence of a dispute do not need to be stated expressly, and they can be inferred.[53] The Court will analyse actions taken by the parties,[54] but also various other factors that are instructive on the awareness of the mutual opposition of views.[55] The existence of a dispute is a matter of substance, not form, and procedural conditions precedent to the institution of proceedings do not play a role in the formation of a dispute.[56]

---

49   See Iain GM Scobbie, 'The Theorist as Judge: Hersch Lauterpacht's Concept of the International Judicial Function' (1997) 8 EJIL 264, 277–8 (discussing Lauterpacht's recognition of the creativity of the international judicial function in connection to the development of law as a secondary task, and compared to the primary role to settle disputes).

50   *Mavrommatis Palestine Concessions (Greece v UK)* (Judgment) (1924) PCIJ Ser A—No 2, 6, 11.

51   *Interpretation of Peace Treaties with Bulgaria, Hungary and Romania (First Phase)* (Advisory Opinion) (1950) ICJ Rep 65, 74; *South West Africa Cases (Ethiopia v South Africa; Liberia v South Africa)* (Preliminary Objections) (1962) ICJ Rep 319, 328.

52   *Interpretation of Peace Treaties* (n 51) 74; *South West Africa* (n 51) 328; see also *Obligations concerning Negotiations relating to Cessation of the Nuclear Arms Race and to Nuclear Disarmament (Marshall Islands v United Kingdom)* (Judgment) (2016) ICJ Rep, paras 38–41.

53   *Land and Maritime Boundary between Cameroon and Nigeria (Cameroon v Nigeria: Equatorial Guinea intervening)* (Preliminary Objections) (1998) ICJ Rep 275, para 89.

54   For example, public statements; see *Alleged Violations of Sovereign Rights and Maritime Spaces in the Caribbean Sea (Nicaragua v Colombia)* (Preliminary Objections) (2016) ICJ Rep, para 73.

55   For the variety of documents and statements, as well as their historical context, see *Application of the International Convention on the Elimination of All Forms of Racial Discrimination (Georgia v Russian Federation)* (Preliminary Objections) (2011) ICJ Rep 70, paras 35–9.

56   But they may assist in finding the existence of a dispute and its subject-matter: ibid para 30. Equally, the existence of a dispute cannot satisfy procedural conditions to the

The term 'dispute' has a general meaning, which applies unless there are indicators that a special meaning should prevail in a specific case.[57] Adjudicators assess objectively the existence of a dispute, although their view on what amounts to a dispute might evolve.[58] However, in every case the term 'dispute' in its general meaning must be read in conjunction with the applicable jurisdictional clause because the latter defines the subject-matter of the justiciable disputes.[59] Claimants can, of course, present their claims in a way that is necessary to trigger the aimed jurisdictional clause, which is why the determination of the subject-matter of the dispute is also left to an objective assessment of the adjudicator.[60] Moreover, one factual situation can give rise to multiple disputes, relating to multiple bodies of law, which can also be subject to different adjudicative mechanisms.[61] This scenario shows the necessity of an objective approach to the existence of a dispute and its subject-matter.

An old controversy in international law is whether some disputes are inherently non-justiciable. Arguments have been advanced that 'legal' should be separated from 'non-legal' or 'political' disputes, only the former being suitable for judicial resolution.[62] While the legal/political divide has some parallels in

---

institution of proceedings: *Armed Activities on the Territory of the Congo* (n 46) para 91. cf *Marshall Islands v UK* (n 52) para 41 ('a dispute exists when it is demonstrated, on the basis of the evidence, that the respondent was aware, or could not have been unaware, that its views were "positively opposed" by the applicant'). The latter approach has been seen as a formalisation of pre-litigation procedures; see Michael A Becker, 'The Dispute That Wasn't There: Judgments in the Nuclear Disarmament Cases at the International Court of Justice' (2017) 6 Cambridge Int'l LJ 4, 10–20.

57 *Georgia v Russia* (n 55) para 29.
58 See, on the changing standard of the existence of a dispute, Lorenzo Palestini, 'Forget About Mavrommatis and Judicial Economy: The Alleged Absence of a Dispute in the Cases Concerning the Obligations to Negotiate the Cessation of the Nuclear Arms Race and Nuclear Disarmament' (2017) 8 JIDS 557; Vincent-Joël Proulx, 'The World Court's Jurisdictional Formalism and Its Lost Market Share: The Marshall Islands Decisions and the Quest for a Suitable Dispute Settlement Forum for Multilateral Disputes' (2017) 30 Leiden JIL 925.
59 *Georgia v Russia* (n 55) para 30.
60 Luiz Eduardo Salles, 'Jurisdiction' in William A Schabas and Shannonbrooke Murphy (eds), *Research Handbook on International Courts and Tribunals* (Edward Elgar 2017) 248–9.
61 *United States Diplomatic and Consular Staff in Tehran* (*United States of America v Iran*) (Judgment) (1980) ICJ Rep 3, paras 36–7; *Georgia v Russia* (n 55) para 32.
62 Known as the 'doctrine of the limitation of the judicial process' or the 'doctrine of non-justiciable disputes': Lauterpacht, *Function* (n 10) 4–5. See also Hermann Mosler, 'Political and Justiciable Legal Disputes: Revival of an Old Controversy?' in Bin Cheng and ED Brown (eds), *Contemporary Problems of International Law: Essays in Honour of Georg Schwarzenberger on His Eightieth Birthday* (Stevens & Sons 1988) 219–23.

domestic constitutional theories,[63] it seems more fruitful to seek its roots in an earlier state practice of conditioning the jurisdiction of arbitral tribunals in inter-state cases with the absence of states' 'vital interests' (which was determined unilaterally).[64] This can be understandable for an early age of international adjudication, when its new role in the international community was waiting to be grasped. But the argument has persisted. After upholding jurisdiction in the *Nicaragua* case, the ICJ was faced with the withdrawal of the US from the proceedings, maintaining that the dispute, as a political one, was not appropriate for judicial settlement.[65] Some 30 years later, a similar approach was taken by China in the *South China Sea* arbitration.[66]

Non-justiciability based on the legal/political distinction has been criticised heavily by Hersch Lauterpacht. His seminal book *The Function of Law in the International Community* is dedicated entirely to the concept of justiciability. Lauterpacht begins by pointing out that the term 'justiciability' has different meanings, and that only one of them pertains to the legal/political divide.[67] A popular opinion was that not all international relations were regulated legally, and that international law was characterised by considerable gaps and inherent incompleteness.[68] Lauterpacht opposed distinguishing 'legal' from 'political' disputes.[69] All international disputes are legal, just as all are political.[70] The history of international dispute settlement does not show the dependence of the justiciability of disputes on their (a)political nature; rather, justiciability depends on the will of states to submit to international adjudication.[71]

---

63 Edward McWhinney, 'Judicial Settlement of Disputes: Jurisdiction and Justiciability' (1990) 221 Recueil des Cours 9, 68.

64 ibid 73. See also, for a discussion on the origins of the doctrine, Lauterpacht, *Function* (n 10) 7–16.

65 US Department of State File No P85 0009-2151 reported in Marian Nash Leich, 'Contemporary Practice of the United States Relating to International Law' (1985) 79 AJIL 431, 439. See also Iran's argument in *Tehran* (n 61) para 35.

66 *The South China Sea Arbitration (The Republic of the Philippines v The People's Republic of China)*, PCA Case No 2013-19, Award on Jurisdiction and Admissibility (29 October 2015) paras 133–7 (maintaining that the dispute essentially concerned state sovereignty).

67 Lauterpacht, *Function* (n 10) 19–22 (distinguishing justiciability as a question of the suitability of a dispute for judicial settlement, from justiciability as a question of the existence of jurisdiction).

68 ibid 59–64. See also Ian Brownlie, 'The Justiciability of Disputes and Issues in International Relations' (1967) 42 British Yrbk Int'l L 123, 124–36 (identifying various other bases of non-justiciability).

69 Lauterpacht, *Function* (n 10) 174–90. See also Mosler (n 62) 223–4.

70 Lauterpacht, *Function* (n 10) 161–8.

71 ibid 153–61.

THE PROCESS OF JURISDICTIONAL REGULATION 25

This stream of thought has prevailed in practice. The fact that a dispute forms part of a wider political controversy, or itself has a political aspect, cannot annul the established authority to adjudicate.[72] Edward McWhinney argues that the criteria of justiciability have become more pragmatic, inquiring if judicial involvement could solve a problem.[73] For him, justiciability is a question of judicial restraint and activism, pertaining to the issues of timing, the availability and appropriateness of other solutions, and the capacities of judges.[74] While such considerations are useful from the point of view of dispute management, from the point of view of the authority to adjudicate the justiciability of a dispute depends solely on party consent.[75]

2.2.3 A Multistage Process

A dispute submitted to a judicial body must objectively exist[76] and be sufficiently determined.[77] The adjudicators will verify that the dispute falls within the scope of their jurisdiction, because a tribunal 'must conform to the terms by which the Parties have defined [its] task'.[78] Such terms, however, often cannot be found at one place and result from a complex process of their definition.

Scholars have distinguished between jurisdiction *in abstracto*, ie the potential of a judicial body to adjudicate certain classes of disputes (sometimes called 'foundational' or simply 'jurisdiction'), and jurisdiction *in concreto*, ie jurisdiction over a concrete dispute, which is established by its referral for resolution (also known as 'specific' or 'competence').[79] But this distinction is

---

72   *Tehran* (n 61) para 37. See also *Legal Consequences of the Construction of a Wall in the Occupied Palestinian Territory* (Advisory Opinion) (2004) ICJ Rep 136, para 41.
73   McWhinney (n 63) 74, 174–6.
74   ibid 175. See also Brownlie (n 68) 142 ('justiciability is a matter of policy').
75   Lauterpacht, *Function* (n 10) 24, 171–3.
76   *Nuclear Tests (Australia v France)* (Judgment) (1974) ICJ Rep 253, paras 55–9.
77   Sir Robert Jennings, 'Reflections on the Term "Dispute"' in Ronald St John Macdonald (ed), *Essays in Honour of Wang Tieya* (Martinus Nijhoff 1994) 404 (concluding that the competence of the ICJ exists in respect of disputes that 'have been reduced to a series of quite specific issues of the kind a court can deal with in an essentially adversarial process').
78   *Delimitation of the Maritime Boundary in the Gulf of Maine Area (Canada/United States of America)* (Judgment) (1984) ICJ Rep 246, para 23.
79   Shany, *Questions* (n 37) 22–6, 63–83. In the same direction, see Sir Gerald Fitzmaurice, 'The Law and Procedure of the International Court of Justice, 1951-4: Questions of Jurisdiction, Competence and Procedure' (1958) 34 British Yrbk Int'l L 1, 8–9; Georges Abi-Saab, *Les exceptions préliminaires dans la procédure de la Cour internationale* (Pedone 1967) 61–3. See also *Corfu Channel (UK v Albania)* (Preliminary Objection) (Dissenting Opinion by Judge ad hoc Daxner) (1948) ICJ Rep 15, 33, 39–40 (differentiating between two uses of the term 'jurisdiction' in the context of the ICJ, namely 'to recognize the Court as an organ

not flawless. First, it places international courts and tribunals in a multilateral context only, and it undermines the role played by party consent in the definition of jurisdiction. A bilateral relationship between two disputing parties can establish both foundational and specific jurisdiction. Second, the distinction observes party consent as a required act, which is separate from and comes after the multilateral framework.[80] However, party consent can also constitute consent to a multilateral instrument itself,[81] and a separate act incorporating the latter's terms by reference.[82] Third, the distinction fails to identify the proper source of normativity of a conferral of the power to adjudicate.[83]

When jurisdictional regulation takes place in multiple stages, it is more fruitful to regard such stages as pertinent parts of the intentions of disputing parties to confer the power to adjudicate.[84] The truth is that every definition of the authority to adjudicate is made in multiple stages. On a spectrum between no authority and the full authority to adjudicate in a concrete case, disputing parties take many steps towards its definition: they accept framework or constitutive treaties, they conclude compromissory clauses or special jurisdictional

---

instituted for the purpose *jus dicere* and in order to acquire the ability to appear before it' and 'to determine the competence of the Court, i.e., to invest the Court with the right to solve concrete cases').

80 To resolve the problem caused by attaching the notion of consent to specific jurisdiction and concrete disputes, Shany argues that consent expressed in compromissory clauses or acceptances of the ICJ optional clause could be seen as *promises* of future consent, or as *waivers* of the requirement of consent. See Shany, *Questions* (n 37) 25–6.

81 For example, the establishment of human rights courts, where states in constitutive treaties consent to the settlement of disputes with private parties. Withdrawals of consent also take place at the multilateral level, by cancelling the adjudicative body or amending its jurisdiction, as illustrated by the case of the Tribunal of the Southern African Development Community.

82 Christoph H Schreuer and others, *The ICSID Convention: A Commentary* (2nd ed, CUP 2009) 938 ('In the case of ICSID arbitration, the agreement to arbitrate incorporates the Convention by reference.').

83 According to this division, the actual normative conferral of the power to adjudicate can take place both at the level of foundational and at the level of specific jurisdiction. Yuval Shany, 'Jurisdiction and Admissibility' in Cesare PR Romano, Karen J Alter, and Yuval Shany (eds), *The Oxford Handbook of International Adjudication* (OUP 2014) 790–3. This suggestion only refers the definition of jurisdiction back to the examination of consent and its content, and to inquiries into the party intention to put into motion a (until then dysfunctional) foundational instrument.

84 See Amerasinghe, *Jurisdiction* (n 35) 77–82; and Amerasinghe, *Specific Jurisdiction* (n 36) 14–7 (criticising the distinction between two stages of conferring jurisdiction on the ICJ, firstly by virtue of its Statute and secondly by virtue of a jurisdictional clause or an agreement; both steps are necessary for the definition of jurisdiction, and one is meaningless without the other).

agreements, but they also define detailed jurisdictional rules, such as case-specific extensions or limitations of jurisdiction. Referrals of cases to tribunals should not be excluded from this spectrum, because they often exercise an important function in the definition of the authority to adjudicate. That is the case in investment arbitration where they perfect agreements to arbitrate,[85] but also at the heart of the *forum prorogatum* doctrine. Viewed from this perspective, the ICSID Convention is not the governor, but the substance of consent, together with, for example, an investor's request for arbitration perfecting an agreement to arbitrate. These steps are often unilateral from the point of view of individual parties, but their overlapping intentions will eventually amount to the formation of a jurisdictional link between them. This means that at some point on this spectrum normativity will be apparent, insofar as there will be sufficient evidence of the parties' shared intention to confer the power to adjudicate. But what is more important is that none of these steps works alone, and only together can they provide a full picture of the jurisdictional framework applicable to a dispute. Graph 1 presents the conferral of the authority to adjudicate as a multistage process.

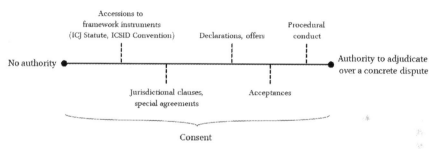

GRAPH 1   Conferral of the authority to adjudicate as a multistage process

Multiple layers of jurisdictional regulation can often demonstrate a regulatory conflict. For example, one layer of jurisdictional regulation might contain a 'self-judging' clause, which excludes jurisdiction in matters that states themselves consider their domestic affairs.[86] Lauterpacht, acting as a judge of the ICJ, argued that such clauses were contrary to the power of the Court to rule

---

85   See s 3.2.1 below.
86   Also known as 'automatic reservations': James Crawford, 'The Legal Effect of Automatic Reservations to the Jurisdiction of the International Court' (1980) 50 British Yrbk Int'l L 63; Stephan Schill and Robyn Briese, ' "If the State Considers": Self-Judging Clauses in International Dispute Settlement' in Armin von Bogdandy and Rüdiger Wolfrum (eds), *Max Planck Yearbook of United Nations Law*, vol 13 (Martinus Nijhoff 2009) 87–91.

on its own competence (*compétence de la compétence*), which was regulated in the ICJ Statute as another layer of jurisdictional regulation.[87] The European Court of Human Rights (ECtHR) was willing to find territorial reservations to its jurisdiction invalid because of the conflict with the object and purpose of the European Convention on Human Rights (ECHR).[88] The ECHR itself defines the scope of its application using the term 'jurisdiction', which bears a territorial connotation.[89] For the sake of securing the respect for human rights to everyone under states' control or power, the ECtHR had to reinterpret that term.[90] Just as a general limitation of the ECHR's application to the contracting states' territories was inconsistent with that objective, the same inconsistency would be caused by a similar individual territorial limitation of the ECtHR's jurisdiction.[91] Concrete acceptances of jurisdiction, therefore, cannot be isolated from the regulatory context to which the parties have equally agreed.[92]

Solutions to these examples of conflict can both affirm and deny jurisdiction,[93] although in any case the question of severability of the invalid clause appears decisive.[94] This issue can be analysed from the point of view of Shany's argument that the importance of the legitimising role of consent differs among

---

87   *Certain Norwegian Loans (France v Norway)* (Separate Opinion of Sir Hersch Lauterpacht) (1957) ICJ Rep 9, 34, 43–8; *Interhandel (Switzerland v United States of America)* (Preliminary Objections) (Dissenting Opinion of Sir Hersch Lauterpacht) (1959) ICJ Rep 6, 95, 103–6. Judge Lauterpacht relied on Article 36(6) of the ICJ Statue, however the same power can be considered inherent to the judicial function: Chester Brown, 'The Inherent Powers of International Courts and Tribunals' (2006) 76 British Yrbk Int'l L 195, 212. See also *Right of Passage over Indian Territory (Portugal v India)* (Preliminary Objections) (1957) ICJ Rep 125, 141–4 (where India argued that a reservation in the Portuguese acceptance of the ICJ's jurisdiction contradicted the object and purpose of Article 36(2) ICJ Statue, which was not accepted by the Court, holding that the clause only reserved the possibility of a partial denunciation of that acceptance).

88   *Loizidou v Turkey* App No 15318/89 (ECtHR, 23 March 1995) paras 65–89.

89   ECHR (n 22) art 1.

90   *Soering v The United Kingdom* App No 14038/88 (ECtHR, 7 July 1989) para 86; *Loizidou* (n 88) para 62.

91   *Loizidou* (n 88) paras 72, 75. See also Alexander Orakhelashvili, 'The Concept of International Judicial Jurisdiction: A Reappraisal' (2003) 3 LPICT 501, 528–9.

92   *Interhandel* (Lauterpacht) (n 87) 104 ('Sovereign States are free to append to their Acceptance any kind of reservation or limitation—subject only to the qualification that reservations and limitations which are contrary to the Statute cannot be acted upon by the Court.').

93   Judge Lauterpacht held that the invalidity of the reservation invalidated the entire declaration accepting the jurisdiction of the ICJ. The ECtHR in *Loizidou,* on the other hand, separated the invalid reservation from the declaration and upheld its jurisdiction.

94   *Certain Norwegian Loans* (Lauterpacht) (n 87) 55–9; *Interhandel* (Lauterpacht) (n 87) 116–7; *Loizidou* (n 88) para 97.

courts, as does the priority given to the enforcement of substantive law.[95] The *Loizidou* case offers another important explanation for possible different outcomes: the regulatory context. In that case, the ECtHR made an explicit distinction between itself and the ICJ, referring to the ICJ's general jurisdiction and capacity to settle any dispute referred to it by two states, on the one hand, and the ECtHR's supervisory role over the ECHR, on the other.[96] Further, the ECtHR found that the Turkish invalid reservation was severable from its declaration, on the basis of, *inter alia,* the general practice of unconditional acceptance of the ECtHR's jurisdiction.[97]

The regulatory context is crucial here. On the one hand, jurisdictional agreements and clauses need to define the authority to adjudicate of the ICJ almost from scratch, because the framework regulation does not define the borders of the Court's competence in detail.[98] On the other hand, consent to the jurisdiction of the ECtHR appears as an adhesional acceptance of a comprehensively defined judicial framework.[99] It is always instructive to inquire whether the broader regulatory framework contains a norm that can resolve the conflict. Thus, Judge Lauterpacht might have been wrong for not remedying self-judging clauses by relying on the ICJ Statute, although that seems reasonably impossible in light of his other argument that the defect in question invalidated the essence of advance consent.[100]

The jurisdictional criteria that must be observed by arbitrators in investment treaty arbitration can be traced across multiple levels. Take the example of the jurisdiction *ratione personae.* In the ICSID context, personal jurisdiction is defined at no less than three levels. First, at the level of the ICSID Convention, jurisdiction is limited to disputes 'between a Contracting State (or any constituent subdivision or agency of a Contracting State designated to the Centre by that State) and a national of another Contracting State', accompanied by

---

[95] Shany, *Questions* (n 37) 43.
[96] *Loizidou* (n 88) para 84.
[97] ibid paras 90–8.
[98] The ICJ Statute regulates the access to the Court only, which defines its personal jurisdiction, limiting it to states: ICJ Statute (n 23) art 35. See *Fisheries Jurisdiction (Spain v Canada)* (Jurisdiction) (1998) ICJ Rep 432, para 44 (noting that conditions and reservations to declarations accepting the Court's jurisdiction under the optional clause 'do not by their terms derogate from a wider acceptance already given', but 'operate to define the parameters of the State's acceptance of the compulsory jurisdiction of the Court').
[99] Defining both personal and substantive jurisdictions; see ECHR (n 22) arts 32-4.
[100] *Certain Norwegian Loans* (Lauterpacht) (n 87) 48–55; *Interhandel* (Lauterpacht) (n 87) 106–7.

a definition of 'National of another Contracting State'.[101] When a state consents in advance, it usually defines a class of entities that can, by virtue of their own consent, perfect a jurisdictional relationship. In other words, the state defines the addressees of the expressed willingness to litigate/arbitrate, which is a technique not peculiar to investment law.[102] This level of regulation is also important because definitions of 'investor' are linked to the rules defining the jurisdiction *ratione materiae*.[103] Finally, the acceptance of the offer by an investor perfects the jurisdictional bond and definitively defines the limits of the personal jurisdiction of a tribunal.[104]

2.2.4 The Contractual Nature of International Jurisdiction

As seen so far, the jurisdiction of international courts and tribunals is defined by party consent, or more precisely, by the parties' common intention to confer the power to adjudicate on an international forum. The function of common intentions implies the contractual nature of the conferral of the power to adjudicate, which is obvious when such intentions are expressed in a direct agreement. The contractual nature of international jurisdiction is reinforced by the fact that international courts and tribunals cannot exercise jurisdiction over a non-party to a jurisdictional agreement,[105] and over disputes that a non-party might have with the litigating parties.[106] This suggestion can be challenged on the grounds that the evolution of the international judiciary, which now often allows private parties to access courts and tribunals by simply instituting proceedings, has moved away from the contractual nature of international

---

[101] Convention on the Settlement of Investment Disputes Between States and Nationals of Other States (signed 18 March 1965, entered into force 14 October 1966) 575 UNTS 159 (ICSID Convention) art 25(1)-(2).

[102] See ECHR (n 22) art 34 ('The Court may receive applications from any person, nongovernmental organisation or group of individuals claiming to be the victim of a violation by one of the High Contracting Parties of the rights set forth in the Convention or the Protocols thereto.'); Energy Charter Treaty (signed 17 December 1994, entered into force 16 April 1998) 2080 UNTS 95 (ECT) art 26(1) ('Disputes between a Contracting Party and an Investor of another Contracting Party').

[103] To qualify as an investor, a person or a company must own or control an 'investment', which also determines the substantive jurisdiction of a tribunal.

[104] See s 3.2.1 below.

[105] *Monetary Gold Removed from Rome in 1943* (*Italy v France, UK, and USA*) (Preliminary Question) (1954) ICJ Rep 19, 32; *East Timor* (*Portugal v Australia*) (Judgment) (1995) ICJ Rep 90, para 26; *Larsen v Hawaiian Kingdom*, PCA Case No 1999-01, Award (5 February 2001) para 11.17.

[106] *Continental Shelf* (*Libyan Arab Jamahiriya/Malta*) (Application to Intervene) (1984) ICJ Rep 3, paras 28–37.

jurisdiction, towards a generalised jurisdictional regulation by virtue of multilateral treaties.[107]

However, contractual bonds continue to form the skeleton of international jurisdiction, regardless of the external appearance. Even 'opt-in' acceptances of international jurisdiction observe the contractual nature. For example, the ICJ has qualified the link established between two disputing states, which have accepted the optional clause under Article 36(2) of the ICJ Statute, as a 'contractual relation'.[108] That contractual relation is established by virtue of an offer (by the first accepting state) and acceptance (by the later accepting state).[109] The shared intentions of the parties give the content to their agreement.[110] Basically, there is always an underlying agreement between disputing parties regardless of the form as long as its content can be identified.[111] The mechanism of offers and acceptances is notable because, as it will be seen further in this chapter, it is also used in the establishment of jurisdictional relationships in investment treaty arbitration.

---

107 Shany, 'Jurisdiction and Admissibility' (n 83) 784; Shany, *Questions* (n 37) 64. See particularly Cesare PR Romano, 'The Shift From the Consensual to the Compulsory Paradigm in International Adjudication: Elements for a Theory of Consent' (2007) 39 Int'l L & Politics 791. Romano analyses the development of a 'compulsory paradigm' in which 'consent is largely formulaic either because it is implicit in the ratification of treaties creating certain international organizations endowed with adjudicative bodies or because it is jurisprudentially bypassed and litigation is often undertaken unilaterally': ibid 794–5. Romano's analysis, however, does not challenge the requirement of consent as such, but rather how it is implemented within judicial institutional frameworks. Also, Romano takes a state-centric perspective, in contrast to the dispute-centric perspective advocated in this study.

108 *Right of Passage over Indian Territory* (n 87) 146. See also *The Electricity Company of Sofia and Bulgaria (Belgium v Bulgaria)* (Preliminary Objection) (Separate Opinion by M Anzilotti) (1939) PCIJ Ser A/B—No 77, 86, 87 ('an agreement'); *Spain v Canada* (n 98) para 46 ('consensual bond'); *Military and Paramilitary Activities in and against Nicaragua (Nicaragua v United States of America)* (Jurisdiction and Admissibility) (1984) 1984 ICJ Rep 392, para 60 ('the declarations, even though they are unilateral acts, establish a series of bilateral engagements with other States accepting the same obligation of compulsory jurisdiction'). See also Orakhelashvili (n 91) 520–7.

109 *Land and Maritime Boundary between Cameroon and Nigeria* (n 53) para 25.

110 This is best evidenced in the theory of reciprocity, according to which each party can rely on the conditions and reservations contained in the declaration of the other party. See *Certain Norwegian Loans (France v Norway)* (Judgment) (1957) ICJ Rep 9, 24.

111 See *Monetary Gold Removed from Rome in 1943* (n 105) 31 (where an offer to submit the dispute to the ICJ was contained in a statement, which was then accepted by a declaration deposited with the Court; the Court referred to Article 36(1) of the Statute, thus implying the existence of a special agreement). See also, regarding separate acceptances of the Court's jurisdiction, *Corfu Channel (United Kingdom of Great Britain and Northern Ireland v Albania)* (Preliminary Objection) (Judgment) (1948) ICJ Rep 15, 28.

Because parties are masters of their contracts, the contractual nature of international jurisdiction requires the observance of the parties' intentions throughout the proceedings. In *Certain Norwegian Loans,* the ICJ gave effect to a self-judging clause contained in one acceptance of the optional clause, because its validity was not challenged by the parties and the Court held that the clause constituted 'an expression of their common will relating to the competence of the Court'.[112] Procedural conduct appears here as another layer in the multistage process of jurisdictional regulation.

Multilateral and institutional contexts do not affect the contractual nature of international jurisdiction. Human rights bodies have been willing to declare invalid reservations to their jurisdiction on account of the main intention of the state to accede to a wider legislative context of which such forums form part.[113] The intention to accede to an adjudicative mechanism whose jurisdiction is pre-defined in a multilateral treaty, is not any less consensual than the intention to define international jurisdiction from scratch. The only difference is that the acceptance of a modelled framework means accepting its pre-defined jurisdictional borders, which can be said to form what Shany calls the 'foundational jurisdiction' of international courts.[114] But without the intention to accede, definitions of international jurisdictions in multilateral or framework instruments remain only dead letters. What gives normativity to pre-defined jurisdictional borders are the subsequent steps taken by disputing parties, forming jurisdictional agreements. The impossibility to redefine their terms does not rebut the contractual nature. There is nothing wrong with 'take it or leave it' contractual models: what remains crucial is the mere possibility of choice.[115]

---

112   *Certain Norwegian Loans* (Judgment) (n 110) 27. In fact, Norway relied on a self-judging clause contained in the French acceptance of the Court's jurisdiction. See also *Rights of Nationals of the United States of America in Morocco (France v United States of America)* (Judgment) (1952) ICJ Rep 176 (where the same self-judging clause did not bar the Court's jurisdiction because it was not invoked, nor was the jurisdiction of the Court challenged in general).

113   *Loizidou* (n 88) paras 65–89; *Rawle Kennedy v Trinidad and Tobago* Comm No 845 (HRC, 31 December 1999) paras 6.1-8.

114   Shany distinguishes foundational from specific jurisdiction, whereby the former regulates outer limits of the jurisdiction of a particular court, ie its jurisdiction *in abstracto,* while the latter provides jurisdiction of the court over a specific dispute. Shany, *Questions* (n 37) 22–6.

115   An analogy can be drawn to the sphere of private law disputes and arbitration rules of arbitration institutions. The fact that such rules become part of the disputing parties' contract does not mean that the parties are free to amend them as they wish. For example, should a state and a foreign investor provide in their contract that the disputes arising from that contract will be settled under the ICSID's auspices, the ICSID Convention and

The inability of private persons as disputing parties to substantively influence the terms of jurisdictional borders has equally no effect on the contractual nature of international jurisdiction. From their perspective, international courts and tribunals indeed can appear as exercising a de facto compulsory jurisdiction over states.[116] The contractual nature, however, does not stem from the appearance, but from the necessity of party consent in the establishment of the normative legitimacy of an international forum.[117] When it comes to ad hoc mechanisms, such as arbitral tribunals, this necessity appears obvious in the fact that without an underlying agreement of the disputing parties there cannot be a tribunal in the first place. When it comes to institutionalised adjudicatory bodies, such as treaty-based courts, the empowering role of the private parties' consent is often ignored due to their one-sided character.[118] What is crucial in observing the contractual nature in such scenarios is that states do not impose jurisdiction on private persons as their sovereigns, but offer them, as to subjects of international law, the possibility to enter a jurisdictional relationship as litigating equals.[119] It follows that the contractual analogy has not disappeared from international adjudication, but it has shifted from bilaterally negotiated, to adhesion contractual models.

Qualifying the jurisdiction of international courts and tribunals as contractual in nature is not directed at diminishing the prospects of private parties' access to such forums. While the term 'compulsory jurisdiction' can be used in a descriptive sense, insisting on a changing nature of international jurisdiction is both unnecessary and erroneous. The principle of *pacta sunt servanda* alone

---

arbitration rules will be considered part of their contract, however without the possibility of altering the basic ICSID jurisdictional rules, except to the extent allowed by them. See Emmanuel Gaillard, 'Some Notes on the Drafting of ICSID Arbitration Clauses' (1988) 3 ICSID Rev-FILJ 136, 139–42.

116 See, regarding investment arbitration, Born (n 25) 838. Born also invokes the fact that many states are pressured to conclude investment treaties providing for arbitration.

117 Allen Buchanan and Robert O Keohane, 'The Legitimacy of Global Governance Institutions' in Rüdiger Wolfrum and Volker Röben (eds), *Legitimacy in International Law* (Springer 2008) 25–6 (consent as the expression of normative legitimacy).

118 Because such bodies are normally established to allow private persons to address their claims against states, and not *vice versa*. That does not mean that the expression of consent of private parties does not matter. See s 3.1.2 below.

119 International law recognises that rights can be conferred on private persons by virtue of international agreements: *LaGrand (Germany v US)* (Judgment) (2001) ICJ Rep 466, para 77. The conferral of the right to litigate at the international level on an equal footing with states can be contrasted with the regulation of the jurisdiction of international criminal courts, where states (or international organisations through their powers) use sovereign prerogatives to subject their nationals and other individuals under their jurisdiction to another level of criminal jurisdiction.

suffices to recognise the compulsory after the consensual. The main point behind the contractual nature is that the definition of the power to adjudicate of international courts and tribunals, and particularly the source of its normativity, rests on party consent.

Because the jurisdiction of international courts and tribunals is contractual in nature, increased caution is necessary not to exceed its limits.[120] An arbitrator breaching the limits of his adjudicative power defined by party consent commits an excess of powers.[121] The power of international courts and tribunals to decide on the issues of their own jurisdiction, also known as the *compétence de la compétence,* is the first tool at the disposal of international adjudicators aimed at satisfying that necessity.[122] Admittedly, *compétence de la compétence* had taken a long time to become a rule in international law.[123] That observation does not diminish its importance in the international legal order, and the slow establishment of the rule in international law could be explained by the slow and insecure steps in the early years of international adjudication.[124] The *compétence de la compétence* power can be seen as a simple necessity in the international legal order, given the lack of a hierarchy of courts capable of determining each other's jurisdiction, and bearing in mind that deferral of jurisdictional questions to states would be a problem in itself, possibly preventing adjudication.[125] The second tool at the disposal of international adjudicators is the option of raising jurisdictional questions on their

---

120 See Attila M Tanzi, 'On Judicial Autonomy and the Autonomy of the Parties in International Adjudication, with Special Regard to Investment Arbitration and ICSID Annulment Proceedings' (2020) 33 Leiden JIL 57 (discussing the tension between party autonomy and judicial autonomy); and ibid 66–8 (noting that in jurisdictional matters judicial autonomy operates to the full extent to the detriment of party autonomy).

121 Following the Roman law maxim *arbiter nihil extra compromissum facere potest.* Bin Cheng, *General Principles of Law as Applied by International Courts and Tribunals* (Stevens & Sons 1953) 259–66; W Michael Reisman, 'The Breakdown of the Control Mechanism in ICSID Arbitration' (1989) 1989 Duke LJ 739, 745–7.

122 Brown, 'Inherent Powers' (n 87) 212.

123 Lauterpacht, *Private Law* (n 18) 207–8; Ibrahim FI Shihata, *The Power of the International Court to Determine Its Own Jurisdiction: Compétence de la Compétence* (Springer 1965) 11ff.

124 Arguably, the acceptance was slow because first arbitrations were initiated by virtue of special treaties, and it might have been assumed that states have retained the principal power of their interpretation. See Lauterpacht, *Private Law* (n 18) 247–8 (regarding the *Pious Fund of California* case, where the Tribunal affirmed its *compétence de la compétence,* however on unclear grounds); and Shihata, *Power* (n 123) 16–7 (regarding the *Colombian Bond* cases, where a restrictive approach to jurisdiction was upheld, reserving the issues of the conferral of jurisdiction to states).

125 Fitzmaurice, 'Jurisdiction, Competence and Procedure' (n 79) 28. See also Shihata, *Power* (n 123) 24–7.

own initiative: *proprio motu* or *ex officio,* depending on whether they are considered *able*[126] or *required* to do so.[127] The use of these tools is delicate, because it should not be conducted so as to impose an improper burden of proof on the party attempting to access the forum.[128] Jurisdiction is not to be proven, but established,[129] and therefore a matter for adjudicators.[130] However, admittedly this is a more complex issue because the establishment of jurisdiction means an inquiry into the intentions of disputing parties,[131] including the possibility of finding such intentions by implication.[132] This means that the facts pertaining to the parties' intentions must be examined in jurisdictional determinations.

2.3   A General Principle of International Law

It is clear what consent does. A more complicated question is where the requirement of consent to international adjudication can be found. Its origins can be traced to the theoretical foundations of the international legal order

---

126   Fitzmaurice, 'Jurisdiction, Competence and Procedure' (n 79) 28–9.
127   *Tehran* (n 61) para 33. As regards the terminology, see *Legality of Use of Force (Serbia and Montenegro v Belgium)* (Preliminary Objections) (Separate Opinion of Judge ad hoc Kreća) (2004) ICJ Rep 371, para 43 ('In the practice of the Court the expressions ex officio and *proprio motu* are used as interchangeable, although there exist differences in the meaning of these two expressions. The expression *"proprio motu"* implies the discretionary authority of the Court to take action on its own initiative. The action taken by the Court "ex officio" is an expression of the duty of the Court by virtue of its judicial function.').
128   *Spain v Canada* (n 98) para 38 ('there is no burden of proof to be discharged in the matter of jurisdiction').
129   *Border and Transborder Armed Actions (Nicaragua v Honduras)* (Jurisdiction and Admissibility) (1988) ICJ Rep 69, para 16 ('The existence of jurisdiction of the Court in a given case is however not a question of fact, but a question of law to be resolved in the light of the relevant facts.'); *Fisheries Jurisdiction (Germany v Iceland)* (Merits) (1974) ICJ Rep 175, para 18 ('It being the duty of the Court itself to ascertain and apply the relevant law in the given circumstances of the case, the burden of establishing or proving rules of international law cannot be imposed upon any of the Parties, for the law lies within the judicial knowledge of the Court.').
130   *Spain v Canada* (n 98) para 37 ('The Court points out that the establishment or otherwise of jurisdiction is not a matter for the parties but for the Court itself. Although a party seeking to assert a fact must bear the burden of proving it [...], this has no relevance for the establishment of the Court's jurisdiction [...]' [references omitted]).
131   *Factory at Chorzów* (n 31) 32.
132   *Monetary Gold Removed from Rome in 1943* (n 105) 32; *Haya de la Torre* (n 28) 78. This is particularly so given the lack of formality of the expression of consent; see *Rights of Minorities in Upper Silesia (Minority Schools) (Germany v Poland)* (Judgment) (1928) PCIJ Ser A—No 15, 4, 23.

and the lack of an ultimate regulatory authority. It follows that the requirement of consent does not need to be clearly identified as a rule of international law. Even the Vienna Convention on the Law of Treaties (VCLT) regulates only the means of expression of consent, whereas the requirement of consent in the formation of international obligations remains implied.[133]

Nevertheless, considering the important implications of the requirement of consent throughout the international legal order, it is fruitful to position it within the wide and complex network of international legal norms. First, the requirement of consent is a norm of general significance. It is not a feature of a particular field of international law or a self-contained regime, but it permeates all corners of international law in general. It can be therefore considered part of the corpus of norms dubbed 'general international law'.[134] It can even be said that it presents the basic norm of international adjudication in general.[135] But its status as a *rule* of law is less clear. A proper formulation of the requirement of consent can hardly be imagined, and that requirement rather appears as a product of logic.[136] Consent is, therefore, closer to the category of principles, and it is most often thus labelled.[137] More importantly, it is consulted as such in practice. Courts and tribunals often resort to the notion of consent seeking instruction in the interpretation of concrete jurisdictional rules.[138] The principle of consensualism, therefore, belongs to the corpus of norms dubbed 'general principles of *international* law', as opposed to the general principles of law derived from national legal systems, because

---

133 VCLT (n 30) art 11.
134 See Christian Tomuschat, 'What Is "General International Law"?' in *Guerra y Paz: 1945-2009. Obra homenaje al Dr. Santiago Torres Bernárdez* (Universidad Del País Vasco 2010) 342–4 (discussing the basic rules and principles stemming from the 'axiomatic premises of the international legal order', and particularly from the sovereign equality of states).
135 Kelsen finds the basic norm of international law in the proposition that 'states ought to behave as they have customarily behaved', forming the basis for the *pacta sunt servanda* principle as a customary norm of general international law, and whose functioning is, in my opinion, impossible without the involvement of the notion of consent. See Hans Kelsen, *Principles of International Law* (Rinehart & Company 1952) 418. Following Kelsen's definition of basic norm as the highest norm whose validity cannot be further questioned, it can be argued that the requirement of consent, resulting from the sole absence of a customary norm providing for compulsory adjudication, is the basic norm of the system of international adjudication taken separately.
136 cf Tomuschat (n 134) 342 (regarding the basic rules and principles of the VCLT).
137 *Monetary Gold Removed from Rome in 1943* (n 105) 32; *Larsen v Hawaiian Kingdom* (n 105) para 11.20; Fitzmaurice, 'Jurisdiction, Competence and Procedure' (n 79) 66.
138 For example, the ICJ has resorted to the principle of consensualism to qualify the conditions of seisin as jurisdictional (as opposed to the conditions of admissibility). See *Armed Activities on the Territory of the Congo* (n 46) para 88.

THE PROCESS OF JURISDICTIONAL REGULATION 37

it is inherent to the international legal order and retains general application as its main feature.[139]

2.4 *Some Contextual Considerations*

While the function of consent in investment treaty arbitration has been inherited from general public international law, it is valid to ask whether several specific views on investment treaty arbitration add something to this issue. Three characterisations are important here: international investment law and arbitration as a global public good (1), as a protective regime of international law (2), and as a hybrid regime (3).

2.4.1 Global Public Goods

Contemporary thinking on the life of the international community recognises that international regulation is needed for the provision of certain goods.[140] For example, human rights have been recognised as public goods on the global scale, which are to be provided through international regulation by international human rights law.[141] 'Global public goods' follow the usual definitions of public goods: these are goods that provide benefits to a community (in this case the international community), and which are characterised by non-rivalry and non-excludability.[142] The question is whether the need for the provision of global public goods has affected the foundations of the international legal order, or managed to circumvent the formalism of consent. Although scholars have indeed found that some alternative routes in international regulation have been paved, there is no evidence that the consensualism of the (formal) international legal order decays as the principal regulatory tool.[143]

---

139 See, for the concept, M Cherif Bassiouni, 'A Functional Approach to General Principles of International Law' (1990) 11 Michigan J Int'l L 768, 772; Patrick Dumberry, 'The Emergence of the Concept of "General Principle of International Law" in Investment Arbitration Case Law' (2020) 11 JIDS 194, 200–2.

140 Daniel Bodansky, 'What's in a Concept? Global Public Goods, International Law, and Legitimacy' (2012) 23 EJIL 651, 655 ('Just as the state is needed to provide public goods at optimal levels nationally, international governance is needed to provide the optimal level of global public goods.' [references omitted]).

141 Inge Kaul and Ronald U Mendoza, 'Advancing the Concept of Public Goods' in Inge Kaul and others (eds), *Providing Global Public Goods: Managing Globalization* (OUP 2003) 95–9; Birgit Lindsnaes, 'The Global and the Regional Outlook: How Can Global Public Goods Be Advanced from a Human Rights Perspective?' in Erik André Andersen and Birgit Lindsnaes (eds), *Towards New Global Strategies: Public Goods and Human Rights* (Martinus Nijhoff 2007) 74.

142 See Kaul and Mendoza (n 141) 95; Bodansky (n 140) 652–4.

143 Nico Krisch, 'The Decay of Consent: International Law in an Age of Global Public Goods' (2014) 108 AJIL 1, 34. See also, for an explanation of alternative routes in law-making,

International economic law has not been immune to the global public goods discourse.[144] *International investment law* is said to qualify as such, being both non-rivalrous (because its use by one party does not impair the use by others), and non-excludable (because it facilitates capital flow and advances economic growth regarding both members and non-members of the investment law system).[145] Although the actual achievements of such benefits are debatable,[146] the effects of this discourse in investment law can be anticipated: just as human rights are sometimes perceived as requiring to be secured by international regulation, an expansion of international investment regulation might be justified by the necessity of securing investor protection.

Another approach examines whether *international adjudication* could be or provide a global public good.[147] In the absence of tangible benefits of international adjudication (which are still in the theorising sphere), such an argument is harder to maintain. One such benefit is arguably the practice of investment tribunals, which clarifies the content of the law.[148] If the international community's recognition of the benefits of judicial dispute settlement would grow at one point to the extent of formulating a requirement for its securing, this might have repercussions on the consensualism of international adjudication. In my opinion, that would involve restructuring the foundations of the international legal order.

There is no sign, however, that the consensualism of investment treaty arbitration has suffered due to the global public goods discourse. The idea of global public goods can only bring new considerations in the interpretation of investment treaties and in the work of investment tribunals.

Armin Steinbach, 'The Trend towards Non-Consensualism in Public International Law: A (Behavioural) Law and Economics Perspective' (2016) 27 EJIL 643.

144 Barnali Choudhury, 'International Investment Law as a Global Public Good' (2013) 17 Lewis & Clark L Rev 481; Stephan W Schill, 'The Jurisprudence of Investment Treaty Tribunals: Between Public Good and Common Concern' in Tullio Treves, Francesco Seatzu, and Seline Trevisanut (eds), *Foreign Investment, International Law and Common Concerns* (Routledge 2014) 9; Stephan W Schill, 'Crafting the International Economic Order: The Public Function of Investment Treaty Arbitration and Its Significance for the Role of the Arbitrator' (2010) 23 Leiden JIL 401, 416; Petros C Mavroidis, 'Free Lunches? WTO as Public Good, and the WTO's View of Public Goods' (2012) 23 EJIL 731.

145 Choudhury (n 144) 502–4.

146 ibid 505–13 (referring to the failures to bring such benefits because of the well-known legitimacy issues in investment law).

147 See generally Joshua Paine, 'International Adjudication as a Global Public Good?' (2018) 29 EJIL 1223.

148 Schill, 'Jurisprudence' (n 144) 9; Schill, 'International Economic Order' (n 144) 416.

2.4.2 Protective Treaty Regimes

There is another, perhaps less ambitious, analogy to human rights: the emergence of protective regimes of international law. The 20th century was revolutionary in the departure from the concept of treaty-contracts.[149] A new type of treaties emerged, by virtue of which states did not establish reciprocal rights and obligations protecting their individual interests, but aimed to give effect to certain values in the international community.[150] This type of treaties is most notable in the sphere of human rights.[151] The central idea here is that the obligations undertaken by states in human rights treaties are not subjective but objective, which determines how such obligations are interpreted and applied in practice.[152]

The system of international investment law is a network of thousands of different treaties. Bilateral investment treaties (BITs), the core of that system, are often titled as agreements 'for reciprocal promotion and protection of investments'. Despite such labelling, there is little reciprocal in them. They grant foreign investors direct rights,[153] who can rely on them regardless of the home state's behaviour.[154] What can be qualified as reciprocal in BITs is the mutual liberalisation of the conditions for investing, prospectively leading to an increased investment exchange,[155] although even in that respect BITs have traditionally been seen as reflecting economic inequalities among states.[156] As

---

149 Treaties as contracts between states dominated international legal thinking throughout history. Lord McNair, *The Law of Treaties* (Clarendon Press 1961) 6 ('the treaty as a concept of international law has been mainly indebted in the course of its development to the agreement or contract of private law').

150 See generally Lea Brilmayer, 'From "Contract" to "Pledge": The Structure of International Human Rights Agreements' (2007) 77 British Yrbk Int'l L 163; see particularly ibid 170 ('Reciprocity is not the glue that holds a rights regime together; the glue that holds a rights regime together is shared commitment to moral principle.').

151 ibid 168–72.

152 *Austria v Italy* App No 788/60 (ECmHR, 11 January 1961) 19.

153 Zachary Douglas, *The International Law of Investment Claims* (CUP 2009) 32–8.

154 ibid 17–9. But see, for a proposal of restructuring investment treaties to enable more influence of home states on investment claims, Anthea Roberts, 'Triangular Treaties: The Extent and Limits of Investment Treaty Rights' (2015) 56 Harvard Int'l LJ 353.

155 Which is often stated in BIT preambles. See, for example, UK Model BIT (2008) pmbl <https://investmentpolicy.unctad.org/international-investment-agreements/treaty-files/2847/download> accessed 20 August 2020 ('Recognising that the encouragement and reciprocal protection under international agreement of such investments will be conducive to the stimulation of individual business initiative and will increase prosperity in both States;').

156 It is often recalled that BITs were invented by developed countries in order to protect their investments in developing countries. See Kenneth J Vandevelde, 'A Brief History of International Investment Agreements' (2005) 12 UC Davis J Int'l L & Policy 157, 168–75.

far as investors are concerned, binding their rights to the rights of states would contradict the whole purpose of depoliticizing and internationalising investment protection and investor-state disputes.[157]

Accordingly, investment law is often compared to human rights law.[158] Despite the lack of 'humanity' as a core ideal, the parallel is well founded. Both regimes are founded on inter-state agreements granting direct rights to private parties. The granted rights are to some extent similar: the protection from expropriation and the standard of fair and equitable treatment can be compared to the rights to property, fair trial, and non-discrimination.[159] Both regimes empower international adjudicators to review state conduct possibly violating such rights.[160] And both provide specific secondary rules of state responsibility.[161] Some procedural differences that can be found among the two regimes, such as the exhaustion of local remedies and the publicity of judgments/awards, are not decisive for this analogy, because they can be implemented differently in both regimes.[162] After all, human rights and the

---

157 However, Roberts argues that the depoliticization of investment disputes does not necessarily imply granting investors *absolute* rights to the exclusion of all powers of states parties to investment treaties over such disputes. Roberts, 'Triangular Treaties' (n 154) 388–95.

158 José Enrique Alvarez, 'The Public International Law Regime Governing International Investment' (2009) 344 Recueil des Cours 193, 234–46; Thomas W Wälde, 'The Specific Nature of Investment Arbitration' in Philippe Kahn and Thomas W Wälde (eds), *New Aspects of International Investment Law* (Martinus Nijhoff 2007) 60.

159 See Protocol No 1 to the European Convention for the Protection of Human Rights and Fundamental Freedoms (signed 20 March 1952, entered into force 18 May 1954) 213 UNTS 262, art 1; cf ECHR (n 22) arts 6, 14; with *The Loewen Group Inc and Raymond L Loewen v United States of America*, ICSID Case No ARB(AF)/98/3, Award (26 June 2003) para 123. See also *Mondev International Ltd v United States of America*, ICSID Case No ARB(AF)/99/2, Award (11 October 2002) paras 141–4 (discussing the practice of the ECtHR).

160 De Brabandere (n 3) 27–9.

161 Commentary to art 33, para 4 in ILC, 'Responsibility of States for Internationally Wrongful Acts', *Yearbook of the International Law Commission 2001*, vol II (Part Two) (UN 2007) 95.

162 The exhaustion of domestic remedies can be required in investment arbitration, while some human rights courts do not contain that requirement. cf ICSID Convention (n 101) art 26; with *Essien v The Gambia* ECW/CCJ/APP/05/05 (ECOWAS Court of Justice, 14 March 2007) paras 20–8. Although party consent is required for publishing investment awards, most of them are public today, followed by further efforts to improve the transparency of investor-state arbitrations. See ICSID Convention (n 101) art 48(5); United Nations Convention on Transparency in Treaty-Based Investor-State Arbitration (signed 10 December 2014, entered into force 18 October 2017). In comparison, human rights courts can restrict the publicity of their cases: ECtHR, Rules of Court (in force 14 November 2016) art 33(2).

protection of foreign investors share common roots in the old standards of the protection of aliens.[163]

Dispute settlement mechanisms are the crucial elements of protective regimes. They secure the enforceability of the granted rights, which some would argue makes them meaningful.[164] The context of protective regimes and their objectiveness (in terms of the pursued aims) possibly affect the work of judges and arbitrators. First, the perception of a regime as protective can make room for the judicial development of doctrines that significantly affect the interpretation and application of the written law. For example, the ECtHR has the 'living instrument' doctrine, which instructs that the ECHR should be interpreted in accordance with the contemporary circumstances.[165] Second, because such protective regimes are 'one-sided', insofar as they grant rights to beneficiaries who can bring claims against states for violation of those rights, but not *vice versa,* suspicions exist that adjudicators can favour the beneficiaries in legal interpretations.[166] Investment arbitration in particular is criticised for systemic one-sidedness,[167] but it is important to note that this problem is not peculiar to that field.[168] In addition, some authors argue that investment arbitration is troubled by professional bias of arbitrators, which increases their siding potential.[169]

I will turn to possible practical effects of these concerns in Chapter 5. From the normative point of view, the principle of consensualism cannot be affected

---

163   Alvarez, 'Regime' (n 158) 238–40.
164   Kelsen, *Principles* (n 135) 140, 143–44; Wälde, 'Specific Nature' (n 158) 56; Sergio Puig, 'No Right Without a Remedy: Foundations of Investor-State Arbitration' (2014) 35 Univ Penn J Int'l L 829.
165   *Tyrer v The United Kingdom* App No 5856/72 (ECtHR, 25 April 1978) para 31; *Loizidou* (n 88) para 72.
166   This is a consequence of the dispute resolution setting, where the interests of treaty parties are not apparent or directly involved in concrete disputes. Anthea Roberts, 'Power and Persuasion in Investment Treaty Interpretation: The Dual Role of States' (2010) 104 AJIL 179, 184; Alex Mills, 'Antinomies of Public and Private at the Foundations of International Investment Law and Arbitration' (2011) 14 JIEL 469, 490.
167   Martti Koskenniemi, 'It's Not the Cases, It's the System' (2017) 18 JWIT 343. cf Wälde, 'Specific Nature' (n 158) 54–7 (rebutting one-sidedness, because '[g]overnments can at any time apply national law to the investor's operation located in their country', which is compensated by the international protection).
168   The 'expansionist problem', which in asymmetrical systems usually resembles favouring claimants, can be linked to the disappearance of states' 'gatekeeping functions' in transnational dispute resolution. See Robert O Keohane, Andrew Moravcsik, and Anne-Marie Slaughter, 'Legalized Dispute Resolution: Interstate and Transnational' (2000) 54 Int'l Org 457, 459.
169   Gus Van Harten, *Investment Treaty Arbitration and Public Law* (OUP 2007) 172–3.

by these considerations concerning protective regimes. But it cannot be isolated from them in arbitral work either. For example, insofar as it is believed that investment treaties should be interpreted so as to serve better the protection of investors, jurisdictional rules can be interpreted among the same lines.

2.4.3 A Hybrid Regime

Apart from the ICSID, whose private law character I will challenge shortly, investment arbitration often employs commercial law dispute settlement mechanisms, such as those provided by the International Chamber of Commerce (ICC), the Stockholm Chamber of Commerce (SCC), and the UNCITRAL arbitration rules. In addition, it is often commented that the investment arbitration community is dominated by commercial lawyers, and that commercial law approaches dominate arbitral practice.[170] The link to commercial mechanisms and approaches prompts the question whether the nature of investment arbitration is indeed clear, and whether there are any related factors that can affect the principle of consensualism.

Investment law in its entirety is often called a hybrid. The hybridity of investment arbitration is usually alleged due to the mixture of public and private interests and procedural elements.[171] But it seems settled now that public features dominate, at least when it comes to the crux of investment treaty disputes and the applicable law, that is public international law.[172] New qualifications have emerged: investment law and arbitration can be seen as part

---

[170] Wälde, 'Specific Nature' (n 158) 54; Stephan W Schill, 'W(h)Ither Fragmentation? On the Literature and Sociology of International Investment Law' (2011) 22 EJIL 875, 880, 888.

[171] Zachary Douglas, 'The Hybrid Foundations of Investment Treaty Arbitration' (2003) 74 British Yrbk Int'l L 151; Douglas, *Claims* (n 153) 6–10; Mills, 'Antinomies' (n 166) 488–98; Alex Mills, 'The Public–Private Dualities of International Investment Law and Arbitration' in Chester Brown and Kate Miles (eds), *Evolution in Investment Treaty Law and Arbitration* (CUP 2011) 108–111; José E Alvarez, 'Is Investor-State Arbitration "Public"?' (2016) 7 JIDS 534; Guillermo J Garcia Sanchez, 'The Blurring of the Public/Private Distinction or the Collapse of a Category? The Story of Investment Arbitration' (2018) 18 Nevada LJ 489.

[172] Andrea K Bjorklund, 'The Public Interest in International Investment Law' in August Reinisch, Mary E Footer, and Christina Binder (eds), *International Law and... Select Proceedings of the European Society of International Law* (Hart 2016) 152; Stephan W Schill, 'International Investment Law and Comparative Public Law—An Introduction' in Stephan W Schill (ed), *International Investment Law and Comparative Public Law* (OUP 2010) 10–7; Gus Van Harten, 'The Public-Private Distinction in the International Arbitration of Individual Claims against the State' (2007) 56 Int'l & Comp LQ 371. Both Schill and van Harten correctly characterise investment arbitration as public adjudication due to the public law nature of disputes, however they maintain that this dispute settlement system is not based on traditional agreements to arbitrate. The latter argument is not endorsed in this study.

of a developing *global administrative law*.[173] Investment arbitration represents an additional layer of judicial control of governmental conduct, using international standards of protection.[174] This seems a logical conclusion from the historical perspective. Other means of investor protection have existed, such as internationalised contracts,[175] and the introduction of investment protection treaties was meant to depart from that practice.[176] If the intention behind what is today the corpus of investment treaties was indeed to abandon private instruments and to establish regulatory regimes, there is no room for adding a private facet to investment arbitration, despite the involvement of private interests. Otherwise, any field of international law granting direct rights to private persons could be called a hybrid.

The hybridity that I would like to maintain concerns the application of commercial law approaches, coupled with the employment of commercial dispute settlement mechanisms, in investment arbitration practice. This is certainly a contextual but systemic problem of investment arbitration. Indeed, the diversity of involved actors bears the potential of creating a schizophrenic environment of approaches to the interpretation and application of investment treaties,[177] which can be found in some practical examples.[178] For this reason, calls for more consistent public (international) law approaches are common.[179] It

---

[173] See generally Gus Van Harten and Martin Loughlin, 'Investment Treaty Arbitration as a Species of Global Administrative Law' (2006) 17 EJIL 121; Benedict Kingsbury and Stephan Schill, 'Investor-State Arbitration as Governance: Fair and Equitable Treatment, Proportionality and the Emerging Global Administrative Law' (2009) New York University Public Law and Legal Theory Working Papers, Paper 146; Daniel Kalderimis, 'Investment Treaty Arbitration as Global Administrative Law: What This Might Mean in Practice' in Chester Brown and Kate Miles (eds), *Evolution in Investment Treaty Law and Arbitration* (CUP 2011) 145.

[174] Van Harten and Loughlin (n 173) 145–8; Van Harten, *Public Law* (n 169) 45.

[175] M Sornarajah, *Resistance and Change in the International Law on Foreign Investment* (CUP 2015) 78ff.

[176] James Crawford, 'International Protection of Foreign Direct Investments: Between Clinical Isolation and Systematic Integration' in Rainer Hofmann and Christian J Tams (eds), *International Investment Law and General International Law: From Clinical Isolation to Systemic Integration?* (Nomos 2011) 19 ('The BIT phenomenon involves [...] a rejection of the internationalization of contracts.').

[177] See Roberts, 'Clash of Paradigms' (n 43) 53–7.

[178] See Thomas W Wälde, 'Interpreting Investment Treaties: Experiences and Examples' in Christina Binder and others (eds), *International Investment Law for the 21st Century: Essays in Honour of Christoph Schreuer* (OUP 2009) 725 (on confusing styles of treaty interpretation).

[179] Schill, 'Introduction' (n 172) 23–35; and, more hostilely, Wälde, 'Specific Nature' (n 158) 61 ('We should therefore be ready to emancipate ourselves from the tyranny of the

seems that the whole purpose of qualifying international investment law as 'global administrative' is breaking the ties to commercial arbitration.[180] One can note a process of further 'publicization' of investment law and arbitration, in both substance[181] and form,[182] which can erase the perceived limits of that system to monetary losses. Despite these developments, the fact remains that the investment law community includes commercial lawyers and arbitrators,[183] and this branch of law remains perceived by many as 'commercial'.[184]

This hybridity is another contextual issue whose possible practical effects are analysed in Chapter 5. These considerations cannot affect the consensualism of investment treaty arbitration in the normative sense, but they are important in the practical application of that principle and should be recognised as a systemic fragility. Despite the public foundations of the system, actors coming from the commercial law sphere might approach jurisdictional issues differently from what is usually expected under public international law.

3 Jurisdictional Regulation in Investment Treaty Arbitration

The jurisdiction of investment arbitral tribunals has been analysed extensively in the existing scholarship.[185] My focus are not detailed jurisdictional limits,

---

commercial arbitration paradigm when the specific nature and purpose of investment arbitration clearly requires so.').

180 Van Harten and Loughlin (n 173) 148 ('Rather than being viewed as an offshoot of commercial arbitration, investment arbitration should be treated as a unique, internationally-organized strand of the administrative law systems of states.').

181 For example, efforts are made to link investment protection to other spheres of public international law, such as human rights and environmental law.

182 Efforts are also made to improve the procedural aspects of investment arbitration, such as the transparency of the process and the independence and permanency of adjudicators (for example through the establishment of an investment court system).

183 Sergio Puig, 'Social Capital in the Arbitration Market' (2014) 25 EJIL 387, 401–2; Joost Pauwelyn, 'The Rule of Law without the Rule of Lawyers? Why Investment Arbitrators Are from Mars, Trade Adjudicators from Venus' (2015) 109 AJIL 761, 773.

184 See also Charles N Brower and Shashank P Kumar, 'Investomercial Arbitration: Whence Cometh It? What Is It? Whither Goeth It?' (2015) 30 ICSID Rev-FILJ 35, 36 ('the real distinction today is between investomercial arbitration on the one hand, and strictly private-party arbitration on the other').

185 See generally, among many others, Filippo Fontanelli, *Jurisdiction and Admissibility in Investment Arbitration: The Practice and the Theory* (Brill 2018); Yas Banifatemi (ed), *Jurisdiction in Investment Treaty Arbitration* (Juris 2018); Andrea Marco Steingruber, *Consent in International Arbitration* (OUP 2012) pt III; Amerasinghe, *Specific Jurisdiction* (n 36) ch 7; Michael Waibel, 'Investment Arbitration: Jurisdiction and Admissibility' in Marc Bungenberg and others (eds), *International Investment Law: A Handbook* (CH Beck/

but the process of jurisdictional regulation. I will show that the process is not perfect, allowing for deficiencies among party-defined jurisdictional rules and requiring further regulatory activity on a trajectory towards jurisdictional determinations in concrete cases. How tribunals have dealt with such deficiencies and made jurisdictional rules is analysed in Chapters 2 to 4. In this section, I address the legal framework of the process of jurisdictional regulation (1), the formation of agreements to arbitrate (2), as well as the substance of jurisdictional rules provided in such agreements (3).

3.1   *Legal Framework*

The legal framework of the process of jurisdictional regulation involves two particularly significant elements, namely the ICSID Convention (1) and the phenomenon that scholarship calls 'arbitration without privity' (2).

3.1.1   The ICSID Convention

To truly depoliticize investment disputes, a forum for their resolution was required. This is where the ICSID comes in.[186] Established by virtue of the ICSID Convention,[187] it gradually took the role of the major, albeit not the only, mechanism for the settlement of investment disputes.[188] It is often said that the ICSID was initially meant to serve the settlement of contractual disputes between states and foreign investors, its jurisdiction being extended in the subsequent practice to treaty-based disputes.[189] However, this assumption should not be taken for granted.[190]

      Hart/Nomos 2015) 1212; Christoph Schreuer, 'Consent to Arbitration' in Peter Muchlinski, Federico Ortino, and Christoph Schreuer (eds), *The Oxford Handbook of International Investment Law* (OUP 2008) 830; David AR Williams QC, 'Jurisdiction and Admissibility' in Peter Muchlinski, Federico Ortino, and Christoph Schreuer (eds), *The Oxford Handbook of International Investment Law* (OUP 2008) 868. See also the special issue 'Jurisdiction and Admissibility in Investment Arbitration' (2017) 16(1) LPICT.

186   See generally Ibrahim FI Shihata, 'Towards a Greater Depoliticization of Investment Disputes: The Roles of ICSID and MIGA' (1986) 1 ICSID Rev-FILJ 1.

187   ICSID Convention (n 101). See Crina Baltag, 'The ICSID Convention: A Successful Story – The Origins and History of the ICSID' in Crina Baltag (ed), *ICSID Convention after 50 Years: Unsettled Issues* (Kluwer Law International 2017) 4–20.

188   At the time of writing, the ICSID administered four times more cases than the second largest arbitration administrator in this filed, the PCA (more than 600 and 150, respectively). See UNCTAD, Investment Policy Hub, Investment Dispute Settlement Navigator <https://investmentpolicy.unctad.org/investment-dispute-settlement> accessed 20 August 2020.

189   Sornarajah, *Resistance* (n 175) 122; M Sornarajah, *The International Law on Foreign Investment* (3rd ed, CUP 2010) 300.

190   See s 3.1.2.

Party consent is central to the ICSID system.[191] This is obvious given that the ICSID is nothing more than an institutionalised arbitration mechanism, which only administers individual arbitrations. A point of differentiation from traditional arbitral institutions is, however, notable: besides regulating the structure and operation of the ICSID, the ICSID Convention also defines the basic substantive limits of the jurisdiction of the tribunals established under its auspices,[192] and provides a limited review mechanism.[193] Still, the Convention is explicit that its acceptance does not imply consent to arbitrate concrete cases.[194] Individual agreement to arbitrate remains the central means of conferring the power to adjudicate on individual tribunals.[195] The ICSID mechanism does not appear any different from any other arbitration framework in this respect, be it public or private. Both the Permanent Court of Arbitration (PCA)[196] and commercial arbitration regimes[197] follow the same pattern. The ICSID and other arbitration mechanisms therefore accommodate the contractual nature of international adjudication.

The ICSID Convention went one step further in fortifying the consensualism of international adjudication. Unlike commercial arbitration mechanisms, the ICSID system was produced by diplomatic efforts resulting in a treaty.[198] The demands for the protection of the requirement of consent were so strong in the drafting process, that they led to the establishment of a pre-arbitral, administrative procedure (so-called 'screening process') for a preliminary verification of the satisfaction of that requirement.[199] The drafters even

---

191 'Report of the Executive Directors on the Convention on the Settlement of Investment Disputes Between States and Nationals of Other States, 1965' (1993) 1 ICSID Reports 23, para 23 ('Consent of the parties is the cornerstone of the jurisdiction of the Centre.').
192 ICSID Convention (n 101) art 25.
193 ibid art 52.
194 ibid pmbl ('Declaring that no Contracting State shall by the mere fact of its ratification, acceptance or approval of this Convention and without its consent be deemed to be under any obligation to submit any particular dispute to conciliation or arbitration').
195 ibid art 25(1) ('The jurisdiction of the Centre shall extend to any legal dispute […] which the parties to the dispute consent in writing to submit to the Centre.').
196 Arbitration Rules of the Permanent Court of Arbitration (in force 17 December 2012) (PCA Rules) art 1(1). See also UNCITRAL Arbitration Rules (with new article 1, paragraph 4, as adopted in 2013) (in force 1 April 2014) (UNCITRAL Rules) art 1(1).
197 Rules of Arbitration of the International Chamber of Commerce (in force 1 March 2017) (ICC Rules) art 6; Arbitration Rules of the Arbitration Institute of the Stockholm Chamber of Commerce (in force 1 January 2017) (SCC Rules) pmbl.
198 *History of the ICSID Convention*, vol I (ICSID 1970) 2–10.
199 *History of the ICSID Convention*, vol II–2 (ICSID 1968) 769 (Broches). See further, for the drafting history of the 'screening process', ibid 769–75. The 'screening' is provided for in ICSID Convention (n 101) art 36(3). This process allows the ICSID Secretary-General to

THE PROCESS OF JURISDICTIONAL REGULATION   47

went so far to exclude the possibility of consenting by *forum prorogatum*.[200] While full determination of a tribunal's jurisdiction is for that tribunal itself to make,[201] the screening process was intended to allow for a preliminary check of whether any discussion on the existence of consent is possible in the first place. Other arbitration institutions conduct similar checks, although to a lower degree.[202]

The ICSID system is also distinct because, being a denationalized mechanism, its awards are not reviewable by domestic courts and it provides a specific annulment mechanism.[203] The ICSID annulment proceedings provide a safeguard of the consensualism of investment arbitration,[204] although a limited one, because to annul an award the excess of powers by the tribunal must be 'manifest'.[205] Even if annulment would be regarded as neglecting party consent, due to a limited review of jurisdictional determinations, that cannot be credited to an erosion of the consensualism as such, but rather to the finality of arbitral awards[206] and the transfer of the power to make jurisdictional determinations to arbitral tribunals.[207] The mere possibility of review of arbitral jurisdictional determinations is already extraordinary, and party consent is therefore safeguarded throughout the ICSID process.

---

deny registration of a request for arbitration if 'the dispute is manifestly outside the jurisdiction of the Centre'.

200 A Broches, 'The Convention on the Settlement of Investment Disputes: Some Observations on Jurisdiction' (1966) 5 Columbia J Transnat'l L 263, 273.

201 ICSID Convention (n 101) art 41(1) ('The Tribunal shall be the judge of its own competence.'). See also PCA Rules (n 196) art 23(1); UNCITRAL Rules (n 196) art 23(1); ICC Rules (n 197) arts 6(3), 6(5). The SCC Rules imply that power of tribunals.

202 Brooks Daly, Evgeniya Goriatcheva, and Hugh Meighen, *A Guide to the PCA Arbitration Rules* (OUP 2014) 23, 84; ICC Rules (n 197) art 6(3)-(4); SCC Rules (n 197) art 12.

203 ICSID Convention (n 101) arts 52, 53, 54.

204 *History of ICSID II-2* (n 199) 850 (Broches); Schreuer and others (n 82) 938; Reisman (n 121) 745–7, 750–5.

205 ICSID Convention (n 101) art 52(1)(b). But see Schreuer and others (n 82) 933–4 (on the absence of clear boundaries between different grounds for annulment).

206 *History of the ICSID Convention*, vol II–1 (ICSID 1968) 423 (Bertram); Mark B Feldman, 'The Annulment Proceedings and the Finality of ICSID Arbitral Awards' (1987) 2 ICSID Rev-FILJ 85, 90.

207 This suggestion raises theoretical questions. If tribunals indeed act as agents or trustees of disputing parties, as discussed above, their decision on the scope of their jurisdiction would be made on behalf of disputing parties. Paradoxically, any challenge of an arbitral jurisdictional determination would thus contradict the delegating act (party consent) itself.

3.1.2 'Arbitration Without Privity'

Modern investment law has introduced expressions of state consent in a new type of treaties: investment protection treaties, primarily bilateral but also multilateral. Modern investment treaties have proliferated since the late 1950s, and their development has been analysed extensively.[208] It is often observed that first investment treaties did not include provisions on investor-state arbitration and that such provisions appeared only with the 'second generation' BITs.[209] Another source of investment protection possibly allowing for international arbitration is domestic legislation. A number of states have special laws providing for arbitrating disputes between them and investors concerning foreign investment protections (which can be both contractual and statutory).[210] Although this route of access to international investment arbitration is arguably the oldest one,[211] its importance has diminished due to the dominance of investment treaties. Expressions of state consent to international arbitration can therefore be found in a variety of sources not involving direct investor-state contracts.

BITs, as the most important source of the contemporary investment law, usually provide for both state-to-state and investor-state arbitration. State-to-state arbitration portrays the classical paradigm of inter-state dispute settlement, whereby two states parties to a treaty are at the same time two prospective

---

[208]   See, among many others, Kenneth J Vandevelde, *Bilateral Investment Treaties: History, Policy, and Interpretation* (OUP 2010); Vandevelde, 'Brief History' (n 156); Andrew T Guzman, 'Why LDCs Sign Treaties That Hurt Them: Explaining the Popularity of Bilateral Investment Treaties' (1997) 38 Virginia J Int'l L 639; Zachary Elkins, Andrew T Guzman, and Beth A Simmons, 'Competing for Capital: The Diffusion of Bilateral Investment Treaties, 1960 – 2000' (2006) 60 Int'l Org 811.

[209]   Joost Pauwelyn, 'Rational Design or Accidental Evolution? The Emergence of International Investment Law' in Zachary Douglas, Joost Pauwelyn, and Jorge E Viñuales (eds), *The Foundations of International Investment Law: Bringing Theory into Practice* (OUP 2014) 29–31; Vandevelde, 'Brief History' (n 156) 174–5.

[210]   UNCTAD maps more than 50 countries with investment laws providing for access to international arbitration. Data available at UNCTAD, Investment Policy Hub, Investment Laws Navigator <https://investmentpolicy.unctad.org/investment-laws> accessed 20 August 2020.

[211]   Domestic laws as a source of consent were mentioned already in the drafting of the ICSID Convention. See Commentary to art II, para 8 in Preliminary Draft of a Convention on the Settlement of Investment Disputes Between States and Nationals of Other States of 15 October 1963 in *History of ICSID II-1* (n 206) 205; and, for the first case relying on the offer-acceptance theory and a domestic law, *Southern Pacific Properties (Middle East) Limited v Arab Republic of Egypt*, ICSID Case No ARB/84/3, Decision on Preliminary Objections to Jurisdiction (14 April 1988).

THE PROCESS OF JURISDICTIONAL REGULATION   49

disputing parties.[212] Investor-state arbitration raises problems, because investors are not parties to investment treaties, and therefore the formation of consensual links between investors and states was unclear. The answer was found in the offer-acceptance theory: by including a dispute settlement clause in an investment treaty, states *offer* to investors to arbitrate their prospective disputes, while investors can *accept* that offer, and thus perfect an arbitration agreement, by instituting arbitration.[213] Given the lack of a prior contractual relationship between the investor and the state, this development was famously described by Jan Paulsson as 'arbitration without privity'.[214] The first arbitration construing an offer to arbitrate in a BIT did not face objections from the respondent state,[215] however Paulsson was very sharp in his conclusions: 'this is not a sub-genre of an existing discipline. It is dramatically different from anything previously known in the international sphere.'[216]

Technically speaking, however, Paulsson's 'arbitration without privity' is not an accurate description of the jurisdictional relationship between an investor and a state.[217] More to the point is Thomas Wälde's opinion that privity has not disappeared from investor-state relations, but moved to the sphere of legal fictions, because arbitration is impossible without an underlying arbitration agreement.[218] While it is true that there is no privity in the sense of negotiated two-sided contracts,[219] there is nothing unusual in the shift towards the one-sided, adhesion contract analogy.[220] Because adhesion contracts in fact

---

212   Aron Broches, 'Bilateral Investment Protection Treaties and Arbitration of Investment Disputes' in Aron Broches, *Selected Essays: World Bank, ICSID, and Other Subjects of Public and Private International Law* (Martinus Nijhoff 1995) 447.
213   Rudolf Dolzer and Christoph Schreuer, *Principles of International Investment Law* (2nd ed, OUP 2012) 254–60; Steingruber, *Consent* (n 185) 196–212; Schreuer, 'Consent to Arbitration' (n 185) 830.
214   Jan Paulsson, 'Arbitration Without Privity' (1995) 10 ICSID Rev-FILJ 232.
215   *Asian Agricultural Products Ltd v Republic of Sri Lanka,* ICSID Case No ARB/87/3, Final Award (27 June 1990).
216   Paulsson, 'Privity' (n 214) 256. See also Jacques Werner, 'The Trade Explosion and Some Likely Effects on International Arbitration' (1997) 14 J Int'l Arb 5, 6 ('It is nothing short of a revolution of the classic arbitration theory, which postulates that arbitration is the product of a contract [...]').
217   And later acknowledged: Jan Paulsson, 'The Tipping Point' in Meg Kinnear and others (eds), *Building International Investment Law: The First 50 Years of ICSID* (Kluwer 2016) 86.
218   Wälde, 'Specific Nature' (n 158) 59–60. See also Paulsson, 'Privity' (n 214) 247, 250 (in the context of the NAFTA and the ECT, arguing that privity is created at the time of initiation of arbitration).
219   Andrea K Bjorklund, 'Contract without Privity: Sovereign Offer and Investor Acceptance' (2001) 2 Chicago JIL 183 ('Yet despite a lack of privity in negotiating the agreement, the parties to an arbitration still have an "arbitral contract." ').
220   See s 2.2.4 above.

exist, I would not call privity 'fictional'. Surely, factually equal opportunities to influence the content of arbitration agreements are lacking. While in regular contractual relations the lack of such opportunities is usually attributed to the economic supremacy of one party, here that is a consequence of the treaty-making capacity of states.[221]

Paulsson's conclusions were also inaccurate in another respect: the offer-acceptance theory was not new in international law. When the idea of what will become the ICSID Convention emerged in 1961, it was stated that the prospective mechanism would imitate the mechanism of the ICJ: consent could be expressed either by a unilateral undertaking or by an agreement regarding a concrete dispute.[222] Both the commentary to a preliminary draft[223] and the Report of 1965[224] indicated the possibility of state consent being expressed by an offer, perfected into an arbitration agreement by investor's acceptance, which was assumed with the rise of BITs.[225] If the ICSID system was meant to follow the already known mechanisms of expressing consent, primarily those from the ICJ Statute, unilateral undertakings amounting to offers were one such known mechanism.[226] The innovative aspect of modern investment law was the introduction of a new genre of treaties, and not the technique for the establishment of consensual links.

Paulsson's 'Arbitration Without Privity' is undoubtedly one of the most influential works in investment law. One can find it, for example, as one of the motivations for Zachary Douglas' characterisation of the field as *sui generis* (or a hybrid), somewhere between public and private.[227] However, such views

---

[221] The requirement of consent is sometimes said to protect states exclusively, which leads to a complete disregard of agreements that are formed in combination with investors' consent. The argument is that investors always seek consent of states, being interested in instituting arbitrations, and not *vice versa*. See Ciurtin (n 19) 50. That view is, however, over-simplistic: the prime example of the investors' reliance on consensualism and their own consent is the problem of counterclaims.

[222] Note by A Broches, General Counsel transmitted to the Executive Directors of 28 August 1961, para 4 in *History of ICSID II-1* (n 206) 2. See also Note by the President to the Executive Directors of 28 December 1961, para 5 in ibid 5.

[223] See Preliminary Draft of a Convention on the Settlement of Investment Disputes Between States and Nationals of Other States of 15 October 1963 in *History of ICSID II-1* (n 206) 205.

[224] Report of the Executive Directors (n 191) para 24 ('Thus, a host State might in its investment promotion legislation offer to submit disputes arising out of certain classes of investments to the jurisdiction of the Centre, and the investor might give his consent by accepting the offer in writing.').

[225] Broches, 'Bilateral Investment Protection' (n 212) 452–3.

[226] See s 2.2.4 above. See also, for the same analogy between the ICJ optional clause and offers to arbitrate in investment treaties, Alexandrov (n 26).

[227] Douglas, 'Foundations' (n 171); Douglas, *Claims* (n 153) 6–10.

might be complicating what is in fact much simpler. There is no doubt that the emergence of investment protection treaties has introduced new elements in international law and raised questions of the theoretical accommodation and qualification of investors' rights. But reaching to completely different (or 'opposite') fields of law, such as private law, for help seems impulsive.

The view on consent through the lens of private law or commercial arbitration is questionable. 'Arbitration without privity' might be seen as innovative through this lens, but hardly from the public international law point of view. One public international law perspective suggests that jurisdictional clauses in investment treaties constitute unilateral obligations of states, rejecting the offer-acceptance theory altogether.[228] An important objection to this theory is that it fails to explain the required reciprocity of consents for establishing jurisdiction. As demonstrated above, international adjudication requires contractual foundation, which does not mean that the offer-acceptance construction is unknown to it.[229] It only appears that the traditional common law concept of privity is not a feature of international jurisdictional relationships,[230] which logically follows the separation between procedural devices and substantive rights and obligations in international law.[231]

Furthermore, the insistence on the private law perspective is odd, given the fact that the basic premise of the requirement of consent in commercial arbitration is irrelevant in the public international law environment.[232] The

---

228 See generally Michael D Nolan and Frédéric G Sourgens, 'Limits of Consent – Arbitration Without Privity and Beyond' in MÁ Fernández-Ballesteros and David Arias (eds), *Liber Amicorum Bernardo Cremades* (La Ley 2010) 873; Yulia Andreeva, 'Interpreting Consent to Arbitration as a Unilateral Act of State: A Case Against Conventions' (2011) 27 Arb Int'l 129. See also, regarding investment laws, David D Caron, 'The Interpretation of National Foreign Investment Laws as Unilateral Acts Under International Law' in Mahnoush H Arsanjani and others (eds), *Looking to the Future: Essays on International Law in Honor of W. Michael Reisman* (Martinus Nijhoff 2011) 649.

229 See s 2.2.4 above.

230 In the English law, 'privity' has stood for a contractual relation between two parties which prevents the enforcement of its provisions by a third party (an alien to the contract). In the present context, agreements are formed for the purpose of settling disputes that arise under public international law and can concern various sources of substantive obligations. Therefore, transposition of the traditional understanding of privity is both unnecessary and impossible. See Vernon Valentine Palmer, *The Paths to Privity: A History of Third Party Beneficiary Contracts at English Law* (Austin & Winfield 1992) 1–5.

231 De Brabandere (n 3) 55–70.

232 As discussed above, the consensualism of international adjudication stems from the foundations of the international legal order. In contrast, in private law the requirement of consent stems from a policy choice and legislative decision to establish the jurisdiction of courts as a default rule, with a limited possibility to 'opt-out' from the default rule by agreeing on arbitration. Domestic legislators can make different policy choices

drafting of the ICSID Convention even reveals a rejection of the immixture with private law arbitration.[233] There is no need to draw conclusions from the private law sphere, either when defending,[234] or criticising[235] the consensualism of investment treaty arbitration 'without privity', or even when seeking its explanation in a rebuttal of the offer-acceptance construction in its entirety.[236] That is not to say that I categorically reject the assistance of private law analogies. Such analogies can be helpful, as they have often been throughout the history of international law, but only when international law itself does not offer satisfactory explanations. In this case, investment arbitration follows the standard international law model of the conferral of the power to adjudicate.

3.2 Agreement to Arbitrate

The establishment of the authority to adjudicate in investment arbitration is, as in any other type of international adjudication, a multistage process.[237] It involves the formation of jurisdictional agreements by matching party intentions (1). Further questions are what is the nature of investor-state jurisdictional agreements (2) and whether they require a specific form (3). Of course, jurisdictional bonds can also be created by virtue of direct contracts between investors and states, however as this scenario is typical for contractual disputes, it is not in the focus of this study.

3.2.1 Offer and Acceptance

The offer-acceptance theory in the establishment of the jurisdiction of investment tribunals has been recognised from the field's beginning. Arbitral tribunals have reaffirmed this theory in practice. The first tribunal to base its jurisdiction on an offer to arbitrate made by a state to investors in a BIT did not say much about the theory because it did not present a controversy.[238] Other

---

and swap the default rule and the exception. See generally Gilles Cuniberti, *Rethinking International Commercial Arbitration: Towards Default Arbitration* (Edward Elgar 2017).

233   For example, in the context of drafting the grounds for annulment, see *History of ICSID II-1* (n 206) (Broches) ('He suggested that the parallel with commercial arbitration should not be drawn too closely because the Convention sought to establish a new jurisdiction. The parallel if any lay with the International Court of Justice rather than with commercial arbitration.').
234   See Paulsson, 'Privity' (n 214) 255; Wälde, 'Specific Nature' (n 158) 57–61.
235   See Sornarajah, *Resistance* (n 175) 144–6.
236   See Nolan and Sourgens (n 228).
237   See s 2.2.3 above.
238   See *Asian Agricultural Products Ltd v Sri Lanka* (n 215).

THE PROCESS OF JURISDICTIONAL REGULATION   53

tribunals, however, elaborated on the issue. For example, the Tribunal in the *Millicom v Senegal* case stated:

> The Arbitral Tribunal does not see why it would be necessary, as the Respondent asserts [...], to adopt a two-step procedure pursuant to which, before submitting a request, the party intending to act would have to request authorization from the Contracting State which it would have no right to refuse, unless otherwise specifically stated. It is more reasonable to view this [the jurisdictional clause in the relevant BIT] as a unilateral offer and a commitment by Senegal to submit itself to ICSID jurisdiction;[239]

The wording of purported jurisdictional clauses can be controversial. Following the understanding that consent pertains to the intention of a party to submit to international adjudication, such an intention must be evident in the relevant clause.[240] One can distinguish between the clauses expressing consent to arbitration, on the one hand, and those making only a promise of future consent, on the other.[241] Furthermore, some clauses merely mention the option of concluding special agreements between investors and their host states to submit their disputes to arbitration.[242] Therefore, textual analysis and other means of interpretation are central in the inquiry whether a clause expresses the intention to accept arbitration.[243] Even if the intention is evident, offers

---

239   *Millicom International Operations BV and Sentel GSM SA v The Republic of Senegal*, ICSID Case No ARB/08/20, Decision on Jurisdiction of the Arbitral Tribunal (16 July 2010) para 63. See also, among many others, *American Manufacturing & Trading Inc v Republic of Zaire*, ICSID Case No ARB/93/1, Award (21 February 1997) paras 5.19-20; *Lanco International Inc v The Argentine Republic*, ICSID Case No ARB/97/6, Preliminary Decision on the Jurisdiction of the Arbitral Tribunal (8 December 1998) para 44; *LG&E Energy Corp, LG&E Capital Corp, and LG&E International Inc v Argentine Republic*, ICSID Case No ARB/02/1, Decision of the Arbitral Tribunal on Objections to Jurisdiction (30 April 2004) para 73; *Pan American Energy LLC and BP Argentina Exploration Company v The Argentine Republic and BP America Production Company and others v The Argentine Republic*, ICSID Cases Nos ARB/03/13 and ARB/04/8, Decision on Preliminary Objections (27 July 2006) para 33.
240   See s 2.1 above.
241   Broches, 'Bilateral Investment Protection' (n 212) 449–51; Schreuer and others (n 82) 206–9; Dolzer and Schreuer (n 213) 258; Steingruber, *Consent* (n 185) 202–5 (all regarding BIT clauses).
242   Broches, 'Bilateral Investment Protection' (n 212) 449 (regarding BIT clauses); Schreuer and others (n 82) 200–2 (regarding host state legislation) and 209 (regarding BIT clauses); Dolzer and Schreuer (n 213) 256 (regarding host state legislation); Steingruber, *Consent* (n 185) 205 (regarding BIT clauses).
243   Cf *Churchill Mining Plc v Republic of Indonesia*, ICSID Case No ARB/12/14, Decision on Jurisdiction (24 February 2014) paras 154–239 (finding that a treaty clause providing that

only initiate the establishment of jurisdictional relationships, and they do not constitute jurisdictional bonds. Therefore, offers do not amount to a proper jurisdictional regulation.

Investors can accept offers to arbitrate made by states by initiating arbitration.[244] In doing so, an investor expresses his own consent and perfects an arbitration agreement with the offering state. As the Tribunal in *Generation Ukraine v Ukraine* put it:

> [...] it is firmly established that an investor can accept a State's offer of ICSID arbitration contained in a bilateral investment treaty by instituting ICSID proceedings. There is nothing in the BIT to suggest that the investor must communicate its consent in a different form directly to the State;[245]

By perfecting an arbitration agreement, an investor establishes a jurisdictional relationship with the state and fixes the scope of arbitrable disputes. Investors are not obliged to do so only after a dispute has arisen and they can accept offers to arbitrate in advance,[246] which commentators advise to avoid the risk of withdrawal of an offer.[247] The risk for investors is obvious: a host state can repeal an investment law or terminate a treaty that contains an offer to arbitrate, and thus eliminate the access to international arbitration. A jurisdictional

---

the state 'shall assent' to arbitration did establish advance consent); with *Planet Mining Pty Ltd v Republic of Indonesia*, ICSID Case No ARB/12/40, Decision on Jurisdiction (24 February 2014) paras 152–98 (finding that a clause providing that the state 'shall consent in writing [to arbitration ...] within forty-five days of receiving such a request from the investor', did not establish advance consent).

244   Schreuer and others (n 82) 202–5, 211–4; Schreuer, 'Consent to Arbitration' (n 185) 834, 836–7; Dolzer and Schreuer (n 213) 256–60; Steingruber, *Consent* (n 185) 200–1, 206–7.

245   *Generation Ukraine Inc v Ukraine*, ICSID Case No ARB/00/9, Award (16 September 2003) para 12.2.

246   *ADC Affiliate Limited and ADC & ADMC Management Limited v The Republic of Hungary*, ICSID Case No ARB/03/16, Award of the Tribunal (2 October 2006) para 363 (where the claimants consented to arbitration by a separate letter sent before initiating arbitration); Luke Eric Peterson, 'Venezuela Sees a New BIT Claim – By Another Oil Services Provider That Suffered Expropriation in 2009' (*Investment Arbitration Reporter*, 20 December 2016) <www.iareporter.com/articles/venezuela-sees-a-new-bit-claim/> accessed 15 October 2018 (reporting an arbitration initiated in 2016, where the claimant 'appear[ed] to have accepted the ICSID arbitration offer contained in the Barbados-Venezuela BIT several years ago, in advance of the taking effect of Venezuela's denunciation of the ICSID Convention').

247   Broches, 'Bilateral Investment Protection' (n 212) 453; Schreuer and others (n 82) 213; Schreuer, 'Consent to Arbitration' (n 185) 834, 837.

clause in an investment treaty lacks full normativity and becomes binding towards disputing parties only after the acceptance of the offer. While the issue of withdrawal is problematic from the perspective of investor protection,[248] it does not raise controversies as regards the functioning of jurisdictional regulation: in any event jurisdictional regulation comes into being only upon the establishment of an agreement between the state and the investor. The investor's acceptance determines the definite scope of arbitrable disputes, which by simple logic can be only up to the extent defined in the offer.[249] Otherwise, the investor would make a counteroffer, which would require acceptance from the respondent state.[250]

A jurisdictional link comes into being once both disputing parties have expressed their consent to a sufficient degree to evidence its existence. This is known as the 'time of consent',[251] and at this moment consensual jurisdictional regulation is supposedly complete.

3.2.2 Contract, Agreement, or Unilateral Act

The Court of Appeal of England and Wales (EWCA) once held that 'the agreement to arbitrate which results by following the Treaty route is not itself a treaty' but 'an agreement between a private investor on the one side and the relevant State on the other'.[252] The Court noted that an arbitration agreement could be governed by international law, simply because 'it is closely connected with the international Treaty which contemplated its making, and which

---

248 See Steingruber, *Consent* (n 185) 222–3 (discussing three normative proposals in favour of the irrevocability of offers to arbitrate: investors' reliance on the irrevocability of consent, investors' consent by implication, and arbitration agreements as unilateral contracts).

249 Schreuer and others (n 82) 203.

250 While acceptances can be only narrower than offers to arbitrate, states can accept an extended jurisdiction in a particular arbitration when such extension is requested by an investor. See s 3.2.3 below. The notion of counteroffer is often inspired by private law sources, which despite good illustration, cannot have heavier value than analogies. See, for example, Hege Elisabeth Kjos, *Applicable Law in Investor–State Arbitration: The Interplay Between National and International Law* (OUP 2013) 136.

251 Schreuer and others (n 82) 217–9; Schreuer, 'Consent to Arbitration' (n 185) 855–6. See also *Tradex Hellas SA (Greece) v Republic of Albania*, ICSID Case No ARB/94/2, Decision on Jurisdiction (24 December 1996) 29 (request for arbitration unable to accept offer to arbitrate because it was filed before the entry into force of the BIT); and *Generation Ukraine Inc v Ukraine* (n 245) para 12.6 ('Ukraine's consent to ICSID arbitration in Article VI(3) of the BIT was naturally conditional upon a future event, *viz.* Ukraine's ratification of the ICSID Convention.').

252 *Occidental Exploration & Production Company v The Republic of Ecuador* [2005] EWCA Civ 1116 [33].

contains the provisions defining the scope of the arbitrators' jurisdiction'.[253] Several scholars have qualified investor-state arbitration agreements as contracts.[254] Besides the question of the governing law, to which I will come back shortly, these terminological differences do not raise major issues because they essentially refer to the very same phenomenon, namely the overlapping consent and shared intentions of disputing parties.

In contrast, some scholars see state consent to arbitration as a unilateral obligation under international law. They argue that state consent is a standing obligation which does not require any action on the part of investors to become truly binding.[255] I argued above that international adjudication in general, investment treaty arbitration included, has essentially contractual foundations, meaning that the authority to adjudicate is always vested on a tribunal by virtue of disputing parties' mutual consent.[256] Arguments about state consent as a unilateral obligation can be made with clear policy objectives,[257] but they contradict the prevailing understanding in arbitral practice.[258] They also fail to explain the basic features of the conferral of the power to adjudicate in international law. The unilateral act theory ignores the fact that international jurisdiction cannot be established unilaterally, involving action on the part of only one actor, but at least bilaterally. Only after the match of two intentions to accept the jurisdiction of an international tribunal, can offers to arbitrate become binding because only after that moment they cannot be withdrawn.[259] Needless to say that thus established jurisdiction becomes binding on both the state and the investor. Furthermore, the unilateral act theory cannot explain the concept of reciprocity in the establishment of jurisdiction,

---

253   ibid.
254   James Crawford, 'Treaty and Contract in Investment Arbitration' (2008) 24 Arb Int'l 351, 361; Steingruber, *Consent* (n 185) 81–2; Andrea Marco Steingruber, 'Some Remarks on Veijo Heiskanen's Note *"Ménage à Trois?* Jurisdiction, Admissibility and Competence in Investment Treaty Arbitration"' (2014) 29 ICSID Rev-FILJ 675, 689; Brower and Kumar (n 184) 44.
255   Nolan and Sourgens (n 228) 873; Andreeva (n 228); Caron (n 228) 653–5; Veijo Heiskanen, 'Comment on Andrea Marco Steingruber's Remarks on Veijo Heiskanen's Note *"Ménage à Trois?* Jurisdiction, Admissibility and Competence in Investment Treaty Arbitration"' (2014) 29 ICSID Rev-FILJ 669, 671–2.
256   See s 2.2.4 above.
257   For example, Andreeva relies on state consent as unilateral act in order to argue in favour of restrictive approaches to its interpretation: Andreeva (n 228) 137–46.
258   See nn 239 and 245 above and the accompanying text.
259   Schreuer and others (n 82) 254–6. See also *Rumeli Telekom AS and Telsim Mobil Telekomunikasyon Hizmetleri AS v Republic of Kazakhstan*, ICSID Case No ARB/05/16, Award (29 July 2008) paras 333–5.

which observes consent of two parties only to the extent of their overlap and therefore only the parties' shared intentions. This is the antonym of a unilateral commitment.

The EWCA's view was correct. An arbitration agreement between a state and an investor is not a treaty, because it does not qualify as treaties are defined in international law today.[260] But treaties are not the one and only kind of agreements in international law.[261] What is crucial in characterising something as an agreement are the shared intentions of two parties and their mutual consent. That is the essence of every agreement.[262] Although without much normative value, in order to avoid confusion, investor-state jurisdictional bonds established by an offer and an acceptance are probably best defined as agreements under public international law (as opposed to treaties, which are concluded between states and international organisations, and contracts, which are governed by domestic laws).[263]

3.2.3   The Form of an Agreement to Arbitrate

Early scholarly writings have considered special agreements necessary for bringing disputes between states and investors to international arbitration.[264] This suggestion has been rebutted by a quick recognition of the offer-acceptance theory, which complies with the general understanding that conferrals of international jurisdiction do not need to be made in a single document or another specific form.[265] However, offers and acceptances must be expressed in writing. The ICSID Convention requires this explicitly,[266] while

---

[260] VCLT (n 30) art 2(1)(a); Vienna Convention on the Law of Treaties Between States and International Organizations or Between International Organizations (signed 21 March 1986, not in force) 25 ILM 543, art 2(1)(a) (these conventions define treaties as instruments between states and/or international organisations).

[261] See Kirsten Schmalenbach, 'Article 1' in Oliver Dörr and Kirsten Schmalenbach (eds), *Vienna Convention on the Law of Treaties: A Commentary* (Springer 2012) 19–25 (on the exclusion of agreements with non-state entities and persons [like individuals and private organisations, churches, and sub-state units] from the scope of the VCLT).

[262] See generally Kelvin Widdows, 'What Is an Agreement in International Law?' (1980) 50 British Yrbk Int'l L 117 (discussing party intentions as the crucial element in the establishment of binding commitments).

[263] Schreuer and others (n 82) 249. See further s 4.1 below.

[264] For example, M Sornarajah, *The International Law on Foreign Investment* (CUP 1994) 267.

[265] *Aegean Sea Continental Shelf* (n 33) para 96; *Qatar v Bahrain* (n 32) para 23.

[266] ICSID Convention (n 101) art 25(1) ('The jurisdiction of the Centre shall extend to any legal dispute [...] which the parties to the dispute consent in writing to submit to the Centre.').

oral establishment of jurisdiction from scratch is hardly imaginable in respect of any international court or tribunal.[267]

The possibility of establishing jurisdiction by conduct or acquiescence is questionable. Filing a request for arbitration accepting an offer to arbitrate is in itself an expression of consent by conduct,[268] although technically it satisfies the requirement of consent in writing.[269] The functioning of *forum prorogatum* is more difficult. Some scholars argue that *forum prorogatum* is not applicable in international arbitrations generally,[270] while the ICSID system does not allow investors to initiate arbitrations without any prior expression of state consent due to the 'screening' of requests.[271] Other arbitration mechanisms might be more open to this option.[272] Regardless of the institutional framework, *forum prorogatum* can be relevant when it comes to extensions or modifications of existing jurisdictional relationships, for example in the case of counterclaims.[273]

There is another scenario. Jurisdictional agreements may provide ambiguous rules, fertile for the arguments that the scope of the tribunal's substantive jurisdiction is limited. By not raising jurisdictional objections, the respondent can factually extend jurisdiction, considering that an objection could lead to its restriction.[274] This scenario is more delicate, as it clashes with the tribunal's

---

[267]   While some steps in the multistage process of creation of the authority to adjudicate could perhaps be taken orally, the most important such steps are usually taken in written instruments, such as treaties, declarations, written submissions etc. A major difficulty concerns the evidence of oral consent.

[268]   *Limited Liability Company Amto v Ukraine*, SCC Case No 080/2005, Final Award (26 March 2008) para 46 ('A request for arbitration is by its very nature a consent to arbitrate because a legal proceeding cannot be requested by a party without their own participation in the proceeding. To request legal process is to submit to this process.').

[269]   Schreuer and others (n 82) 211–2.

[270]   Chittharanjan F Amerasinghe, *International Arbitral Jurisdiction* (Brill 2011) 51–3.

[271]   Broches, 'Convention' (n 200) 273.

[272]   Other arbitration frameworks allow the conclusion of arbitration agreements by not raising jurisdictional objections. W Laurence Craig, William W Park, and Jan Paulsson, *International Chamber of Commerce Arbitration* (3rd ed, Oceana 2000) 21 (regarding the ICC framework); Kaj Hobér, *International Commercial Arbitration in Sweden* (OUP 2011) 96 (regarding the Swedish law, which is applicable to arbitrations under the SCC's auspices).

[273]   See, for example, *Perenco Ecuador Limited v The Republic of Ecuador*, ICSID Case No ARB/08/6, Decision on Perenco's Application for Dismissal of Ecuador's Counterclaims (18 August 2017) paras 35, 43–4.

[274]   Schreuer and others (n 82) 221–5. This issue relates to other two questions. The first one is the timing when the respondent is supposed to raise jurisdictional objections. See ICSID Rules of Procedure for Arbitration Proceedings (in force 10 April 2006) (ICSID Arbitration Rules) art 41(1) ('Any objection that the dispute or any ancillary claim is not within the jurisdiction of the Centre or, for other reasons, is not within the competence of the

power and/or duty to raise jurisdictional questions on its own initiative, which I will examine shortly.[275] Considering that parties and arbitrators can value jurisdictional issues differently, at least occasionally arbitrators will defer to the parties' decision not to raise objections.[276] Furthermore, scholars have argued that non-compliances with 'procedural' limits of consent can be cured by procedural conduct, whereas those with 'jurisdictional' limits cannot.[277] Since a clear limit between the two categories is uncertain,[278] and because extensions of jurisdiction by acquiescence can concern substantive jurisdiction, the distinction based on curability does not seem satisfactory.

3.3 The Substance of Jurisdictional Regulation

The content of arbitration agreements is well-known to the investment law readership, and it does not offer a great spectrum of varieties. I will only briefly address the parameters used to define justiciable disputes (1) and the conditions of bringing disputes to adjudication (2), paying attention to the issues that they usually fail to regulate.

3.3.1 Arbitrable (Justiciable) Disputes

Agreements to arbitrate regulate the substantive jurisdiction of tribunals by defining justiciable disputes. The ICSID Convention requires that a dispute must be 'legal' and that it must arise 'directly out of an investment'.[279] BITs

---

Tribunal shall be made as early as possible.'). The other question concerns the clarity of the respondent's intention not to raise jurisdictional objections. This is a factual question, which probably requires explicit consent or direct pleading on the merits, because a delay in raising jurisdictional objections cannot imply consent: Schreuer and others (n 82) 222, 225, 527–8.

275 See s 4.3.2 below. Wass suggests resolving this conflict by inquiring whether the jurisdictional requirement at stake relates to party interests only, or to non-party interests. He notes that in the ICSID arbitration context this criterion would normally give priority to the possibility of acquiescence: Jack Wass, 'Jurisdiction by Estoppel and Acquiescence in International Courts and Tribunals' (2015) 86 British Yrbk Int'l L 155, 191–4.

276 For some examples in case law, see Schreuer and others (n 82) 528–30. Schreuer distinguishes between the jurisdictional issues that can be disposed by not raising objections, and the objective requirements of the ICSID Convention, which, according to him, cannot. However, as evidenced by some examples discussed by Schreuer himself, that distinction is debatable.

277 Douglas, *Claims* (n 153) 141, 152 (differentiating between jurisdiction, on the one hand, and admissibility and seisin, on the other); Steingruber, 'Remarks' (n 254) 681–2, 684, 687 (arguing that objections to admissibility and conditions of consent should not be examined by tribunals on their own initiative, unlike the terms defining the scope of jurisdiction).

278 See ch 2, s 2.

279 ICSID Convention (n 101) art 25(1).

often refer only to an 'investment dispute' or simply to a 'dispute' between an investor of one contracting state and the other contracting state, but some BITS go into more detail and define an 'investment dispute'.[280] Justiciable disputes can be limited to specific substantive issues, such as the protection from expropriation and the amount of compensation for expropriation.[281] Agreements to arbitrate often fail to regulate some questions. For example, do openly worded clauses allow arbitrating any investor-state dispute (like contractual disputes and state counterclaims arising from domestic legislation) or only the disputes arising from the relevant treaty?

Various treaty clauses are relevant, such as those defining 'investment', umbrella clauses, and (arguably) most-favoured nation (MFN) clauses. What is often left open are questions like whether the notion of investment has an objective meaning that must be taken into account in addition to the treaty's definition, and whether certain criteria should be considered inherent to any definition of 'investment', even if not mentioned explicitly. Umbrella clauses often leave unanswered the question whether they cover direct contractual relationships between states and investors only, or whether they also cover contracts concluded by state-controlled entities and affiliates of investors. Most MFN clauses do not regulate the question of their general application to dispute settlement clauses, but also nuanced issues such as whether they can affect substantive, personal, and temporal jurisdiction.

When it comes to personal jurisdiction, investment treaties provide definitions of 'investor'. The ICSID Convention has its own requirements, such as that of different investor nationality from the host state.[282] Here as well many questions remain open, such as whether the notion of investor has an objective meaning, and whether state-owned companies can be considered 'private' foreign investors.

---

280   For example, Agreement on Free Trade and Economic Partnership Between Japan and the Swiss Confederation (signed 19 February 2009, entered into force 1 September 2009) art 94(1) (' "investment dispute" means a dispute between a Party and an investor of the other Party that has incurred loss or damage by reason of, or arising out of, an alleged breach by the former Party of any obligation under this Chapter with respect to the investor or its investment').

281   For example, Accord entre les Gouvernements du Royaume de Belgique et du Grand-Duché de Luxembourg et le Gouvernement de l'Union des républiques socialistes soviétiques, concernant l'encouragement et la protection réciproques des investissements (signed 9 February 1989, entered into force 18 August 1991) art 10(1) ('[t]out differend [...] relatif au montant ou au mode de paiement des indemnites dues en vertu de l'article 5').

282   ICSID Convention (n 101) art 25(1)-(2).

Temporal jurisdiction can be defined specifically, usually relying on the time when a dispute arises,[283] but also on the time of the relevant facts or acts.[284] When such a definition is not provided, the temporal jurisdiction of tribunals is defined indirectly through the rules governing the temporal validity of investment treaties and the substantive investor protection guarantees that give rise to disputes.[285] While these rules are usually sufficient for jurisdictional determinations, other questions with a temporal dimension can arise. For example, whether an expired offer to arbitrate can be used in some circumstances by investors to perfect an arbitration agreement and bring their dispute to arbitration. Investment treaties may allow states to deny benefits to investors, including the offer to arbitrate, however usually omitting to regulate whether that can be done retroactively, after the perfection of an arbitration agreement.

As these questions have appeared in practice, new questions can be expected to continue arising. In parallel with the distinction between 'rules' and 'standards', whereby the latter in theory allow for flexibility in their application,[286] it can be argued that disputing parties draw only the main lines of arbitral jurisdiction, while more detailed questions are left to tribunals. However, the matters of jurisdiction require precise definitions of the authority to adjudicate and cannot be formulated in terms of 'standards'.[287] Furthermore, the principle of consensualism relates primarily to the question *who* defines the authority to adjudicate. I will show in Chapters 2 to 4 that

---

283 For example, Agreement Between the Belgium-Luxembourg Economic Union and the Government of the Republic of Mozambique on the Reciprocal Promotion and Protection of Investments (signed 18 July 2006, entered into force 1 September 2009) art 12(1) ('This Agreement [...] shall not apply to any dispute concerning an investment which arose, or any claim concerning an investment which was settled, before its entry into force.').

284 See discussion in *Industria Nacional de Alimentos SA and Indalsa Perú SA v The Republic of Peru,* ICSID Case No ARB/03/4, Decision on Annulment (5 September 2007) paras 41, 94–5.

285 VCLT (n 30) art 28 (non-retroactivity of treaties). See also Agreement Between the Belgo-Luxembourg Economic Union, on the one hand, and the Serbia and Montenegro, on the other hand, on the Reciprocal Promotion and Protection of Investments (signed 4 March 2004, entered into force 12 August 2007) art 13 ('This Agreement shall also apply to investments made before its entry into force [...] and shall be applicable from the date of its entry into force.').

286 See Pierre Schlag, 'Rules and Standards' (1985) 33 UCLA L Rev 379, 400–18 (on the vices and virtues of rules and standards, although criticising the reliance on such features to draw a clear and sharp boundary between the two categories).

287 ibid 382–3 ('The paradigm example of a rule has a hard empirical trigger and a hard determinate response. [...] A standard, by contrast, has a soft evaluative trigger and a soft modulated response.').

arbitral tribunals have addressed the above unregulated questions, and I will argue in Chapter 5 that that activity amounts to law-making. If the principle of consensualism confers the power to regulate jurisdiction on disputing parties exclusively,[288] factual jurisdictional regulation by any other party erodes the principle.

3.3.2 Conditions of Access

Conditions of access can be various, and equally can leave a number of questions open. For example, investors can be required to negotiate with host states, to litigate investment disputes in domestic courts for some time,[289] or to exhaust local remedies, before accessing arbitration. Treaties usually do not regulate whether in certain circumstances such requirements can be disregarded. When investors are required to first resort to domestic courts, arbitrators must assess the identity of the two claims and proceedings (domestic and international) to see whether the requirement has been complied with, without any pre-defined criteria. Investors can also be precluded from accessing international arbitration if they have resorted to domestic courts, by virtue of fork-in-the-road clauses. These clauses usually do not define the criteria for their triggering, pertaining to a comparison of the two sets of claims and proceedings (domestic and international). Investors often attempt to bypass certain conditions relying on MFN clauses and third-party BITs which offer easier conditions of access. In this scenario, the lack of rules on the applicability of MFN clauses to dispute resolution clauses becomes apparent again. Other uncertainties about conditions of access exist, such as whether they limit the jurisdiction of tribunals or qualify somewhat differently, which can have implications on their rigidity. Finally, it is questionable whether certain conditions of access limit the jurisdiction of arbitral tribunals independently of the text of arbitration agreements, such as those preventing investors from artificially bringing themselves under the protection of an investment treaty and benefiting from an offer to arbitrate.

---

288 See s 2.2.
289 Periods vary, usually from few months to two years: Christoph Schreuer, 'Calvo's Grandchildren: The Return of Local Remedies in Investment Arbitration' (2005) 4 LPICT 1, 3; Facundo Pérez Aznar, 'Local Litigation Requirements in International Investment Agreements: Their Characteristics and Potential in Times of Reform in Latin America' (2016) 17 JWIT 536, 540–1. But see Indian proposal of a five-year local litigation requirement: India Model BIT (2015) art 15(2) <https://investmentpolicy.unctad.org/international-investment-agreements/treaty-files/3560/download> accessed 20 August 2020.

4 The Governing Legal Regime

Arbitration agreements are governed by international law (1), which provides relatively clear rules of interpretation (2). Arbitration agreements are examined on multiple occasions, which gives opportunities for identifying possible regulatory deficiencies and for attempts at their remedying (3). Nevertheless, the current system does not confer on arbitral tribunals a formal power to fill gaps in jurisdictional regulation (4).

4.1 *The Law Governing Agreements to Arbitrate*

Agreements to arbitrate between states and investors are governed by public international law. This point was not obvious, though. In 1985, the EWCA in *Dallal v Bank Mellat* held that international law could not govern an arbitration agreement establishing the jurisdiction of the US-Iran Claims Tribunal.[290] Key to that conclusion was that the arbitration agreement was not concluded between states but private persons, and '[i]f private law rights are to exist, they must exist as part of some municipal legal system, and public international law is not such a system'.[291] But the EWCA fell into a trap: it confused the substantive rights and obligations for the arbitration agreement. It is now generally accepted, in investment law particularly but following general international law, that jurisdiction and merits are not governed by the same law.[292] Even if the link were correct, in international investment law the substantive rights are not 'private' but pretty much public: these are international legal guarantees of treatment of foreign investors. This rebuts another presumption adopted by the EWCA, namely that international law governs inter-state relations only.

International law is not exclusive, and it is flexible enough to accommodate various actors and relationships.[293] States and private persons have at times

---

[290] *Dallal v Bank Mellat* [1985] QB 441 (EWCA) 456.

[291] ibid. See also *Serbian Loans (France v The Kingdom of the Serbs, Croats, and Slovenes)* (Judgment) (1929) PCIJ Ser A—No 20, 5, 41 ('Any contract which is not a contract between States in their capacity as subjects of international law is based on the municipal law of some country.').

[292] Schreuer and others (n 82) 248–9; Dolzer and Schreuer (n 213) 263; Christoph Schreuer, 'Jurisdiction and Applicable Law in Investment Treaty Arbitration' (2014) 1 McGill J Disp Resol 1, 3.

[293] This is also supported by a reverse argument: the conduct of states that can engage international law obligations is not limited to 'sovereign' acts and can equally be private or 'commercial': Commentary to art 4, para 6, and commentary to art 12, para 10, in ILC (n 161) 41, 56. Furthermore, states also conclude treaties under public international law

preferred to subject their contracts to international law, and that legal system provided avenues for their accommodation.[294] Still, the assumption that international law governs inter-state relations exclusively, and that any legal relationship with private persons must be based in domestic law, is occasionally maintained. Veijo Heiskanen has argued that state consent and investor consent to arbitration are governed by two different legal systems: international and domestic, respectively.[295] He finds some support in the *Dallal* decision, where the EWCA drew a parallel between the US-Iran Claim Tribunal and the so-called statutory arbitration.[296] What must be more appreciated is that even the EWCA turned its analysis back to examining the validity of arbitral jurisdiction under international law and its voluntary and direct acceptance by private parties (ie consent) besides that of sovereigns.[297]

The later opinion of the EWCA in the *Occidental* case, that an arbitration agreement can be governed by international law, should be supported.[298] The Court even expressed reservations regarding the *Dellal* reasoning.[299] The EWCA in *Occidental* was right in relying on the nexus between the arbitration agreement and the relevant BIT.[300] Translated into the language of the contractual nature of international adjudication advocated above, when a jurisdictional relationship is initiated with reference to the international legal space (by a state making an offer), it can only be perfected with regard to the same legal space (by an investor accepting the offer). And because consent concerns the intention of its issuer, the crucial question is to what legal system consent refers to in substance, explicitly or implicitly. For this reason, offers to arbitrate made in domestic laws produce effects

---

executing commercial transactions among them: FA Mann, 'The Proper Law of Contracts Concluded by International Persons' (1959) 35 British Yrbk Int'l L 34, 34–41.

294 Mann (n 293) 43–56. Mann challenges the statement made by the PCIJ, quoted at n 291 above, arguing that the PCIJ could not have prevented the development of international law since the 1920s: ibid 47–8.

295 Veijo Heiskanen, 'Forbidding *Dépeçage*: Law Governing Investment Treaty Arbitration' (2009) 32 Suffolk Transnat'l L Rev 367; Heiskanen, 'Comment' (n 255) 672–3.

296 Heiskanen, '*Dépeçage*' (n 295) 384–5.

297 *Dallal v Bank Mellat* (n 290) 460–1.

298 *Occidental Exploration & Production Company v Ecuador* (n 252) [33].

299 ibid [34] ('If English law recognises the binding force of a "quasi-statutory" adjudication at the international level, it is, in our view, hard to see why it should not be possible for a State and an investor to enter into an agreement to arbitrate of the type contemplated by the present Bilateral Investment Treaty subject to international law.').

300 ibid [33]. See also Crawford, 'Treaty and Contract' (n 254) 361; Campbell McLachlan, Laurence Shore, and Matthew Weiniger, *International Investment Arbitration: Substantive Principles* (2nd ed, OUP 2017) 74–5.

in international law,[301] as do contracts regulating the jurisdiction of investment tribunals.[302]

The fact that domestic courts can review the validity and scope of arbitration agreements and set aside awards in the non-ICSID context does not affect the authority of public international law. Zachary Douglas has argued that the decisive factor for the governance of international law over procedural questions, including the validity and scope of arbitration agreements, is the applicability of state immunity before domestic courts, which he found inapplicable to investment arbitrations due to their characterisation as 'commercial'.[303] However, domestic law does not displace international law. First, domestic courts apply international law to arbitration agreements, which must be taken as a different question from the scope and standard of review applied by domestic courts.[304] It is hardly imaginable that a court would apply domestic law to an arbitration agreement by default, ignoring international law as the parties' choice.[305] Second, as Douglas himself has noticed, the competence of domestic courts is a consequence of state choices, either explicit, such as qualifying matters as 'commercial' in treaties, or implicit, such as referring to the New York Convention and selecting the seat of arbitration and the procedural rules.[306] State choices must be considered pertinent part of their consent in the definition of the authority to adjudicate. The principle of consensualism allows disputing parties to denationalize their arbitrations, and their intent to make awards reviewable before domestic courts amounts to nothing else

---

301　*PNG Sustainable Development Program Ltd v Independent State of Papua New Guinea*, ICSID Case No ARB/13/33, Award (5 May 2015) para 264.
302　*Ceskoslovenska Obchodni Banka AS v The Slovak Republic*, ICSID Case No ARB/97/4, Decision of the Tribunal on Objections to Jurisdiction (24 May 1999) paras 35, 49-59; *Lighthouse Corporation Pty Ltd and Lighthouse Corporation Ltd IBC v Democratic Republic of Timor-Leste*, ICSID Case No ARB/15/2, Award (22 December 2017) para 142.
303　Douglas, 'Foundations' (n 171) 219-24.
304　See in this respect Relja Radović, 'Arbitral Jurisdictional Regulation in Investment Treaty Arbitration and Domestic Courts' (2021) JIDS (forthcoming).
305　See UNCITRAL Model Law on International Commercial Arbitration of 1985, with amendments as adopted in 2006 (UNCITRAL Model Law) art 34(2)(a)(i) <https://uncitral.un.org/sites/uncitral.un.org/files/media-documents/uncitral/en/19-09955_e_ebook.pdf> accessed 4 April 2021 ('[...] the said agreement is not valid *under the law to which the parties have subjected it* or, failing any indication thereon, under the law of this State;' [emphasis added]).
306　Douglas, 'Foundations' (n 171) 220-4. See particularly United Nations Convention on Jurisdictional Immunities of States and Their Property (signed 2 December 2004, not in force) annex ('With respect to article 17: The expression "commercial transaction" includes investment matters.').

but the application of this principle.[307] Public international law remains the ultimate governing legal system.

4.2 *The Rules of Interpretation of Agreements to Arbitrate*

Some tribunals have argued that consent must be clear and unambiguous,[308] while others have maintained that such a requirement is not founded in international law.[309] Indeed, imposing that requirement would favour states in cases of uncertainty, which would contradict a well-established understanding in international law that jurisdictional clauses should not be interpreted differently from other rules, and that there is neither a restrictive nor a liberal approach to jurisdictional interpretation.[310] This opinion has been widely accepted by investment tribunals.[311]

The standard rules on treaty interpretation are therefore relevant, and they have been in the focus of scholarship.[312] However, their relevance is not

---

307 In the ICSID context, the denationalization is effected by the stipulation in the ICSID Convention that awards will not be subject to any additional review, including that of domestic courts, and which forms part of state consent. See ICSID Convention (n 101) art 53.

308 *Plama Consortium Limited v Republic of Bulgaria*, ICSID Case No ARB/03/24, Decision on Jurisdiction (8 February 2005) para 198; *Wintershall Aktiengesellschaft v Argentine Republic*, ICSID Case No ARB/04/14, Award (8 December 2008) paras 167, 172. See also *Vladimir Berschader & Moïse Berschader v The Russian Federation*, SCC Case No 80/2004, Award (21 April 2006) paras 177, 181, 206, 208 (firstly criticising the 'clear and unambiguous' standard as a general principle in interpreting jurisdictional clauses, but then applying the same standard to the issue of MFN-dispute settlement conjunction).

309 *Suez, Sociedad General de Aguas de Barcelona SA, and InterAguas Servicios Integrales del Agua SA v The Argentine Republic*, ICSID Case No ARB/03/17, Decision on Jurisdiction (16 May 2006) para 64; *Suez, Sociedad General de Aguas de Barcelona SA, and Vivendi Universal SA v The Argentine Republic*, ICSID Case No ARB/03/19, and *AWG Group Ltd v The Argentine Republic*, UNCITRAL arbitration, Decision on Jurisdiction (3 August 2006) para 66.

310 *Oil Platforms (Islamic Republic of Iran v United States of America)* (Preliminary Objection) (Separate Opinion of Judge Higgins) (1996) ICJ Rep 847, para 35.

311 See, for example, *Amco Asia Corp and others v The Republic of Indonesia*, ICSID Case No ARB/81/1, Award on Jurisdiction (25 September 1983) para 14(i); *Ceskoslovenska Obchodni Banka AS v Slovakia* (n 302) para 34; *El Paso Energy International Company v The Argentine Republic*, ICSID Case No ARB/03/15, Decision on Jurisdiction (27 April 2006) paras 68–70; *Mondev International Ltd v USA* (n 159) para 43; *Austrian Airlines v The Slovak Republic*, UNCITRAL ad hoc arbitration, Final Award (9 October 2009) para 121; *Spyridon Roussalis v Romania*, ICSID Case No ARB/06/1, Award (7 December 2011) para 867.

312 See J Romesh Weeramantry, *Treaty Interpretation in Investment Arbitration* (OUP 2012) 13–4; Daniel Rosentreter, *Article 31(3)(c) of the Vienna Convention on the Law of Treaties and the Principle of Systemic Integration in International Investment Law and Arbitration* (Nomos 2015) 247–56; Tarcisio Gazzini, *Interpretation of International Investment Treaties* (Hart 2016) 56–60; Michael Waibel, 'International Investment Law

straightforward, because it is unclear whether tribunals interpret arbitration agreements or offers to arbitrate made in investment treaties/legislation. Because jurisdictional objections normally allege that the respondent state has not consented to arbitration, tribunals usually interpret treaties and domestic laws purportedly containing offers to arbitrate. This causes unclarity regarding the specific rules of interpretation of treaties, on the one hand, and domestic laws, on the other.

When it comes to treaties, international law is clear: the rules on interpretation contained in the VCLT are applicable either directly as treaty rules or indirectly as customary international law.[313] However, arbitral tribunals are often criticised for using the Vienna tools wrongly and/or inconsistently,[314] or for employing other means of treaty interpretation that cannot be found in the VCLT.[315]

Offers to arbitrate made in domestic laws are more complex, given that they are often characterised as unilateral acts of states. First, unilateral acts of states are interpreted differently from treaties.[316] Second, domestic law should instruct the interpretation of offers made in domestic laws.[317] This approach is problematic. First, the tribunals that characterise domestic laws as unilateral acts at the same time qualify them as offers.[318] This is a contradiction: unilateral acts are binding and effective without any counteraction,[319] whereas offers

---

and Treaty Interpretation' in Rainer Hofmann and Christian J Tams (eds), *International Investment Law and General International Law: From Clinical Isolation to Systemic Integration?* (Nomos 2011) 29.

[313] See, for example, *Tokios Tokelės v Ukraine,* ICSID Case No ARB/02/18, Decision on Jurisdiction (29 April 2004) para 27; Gazzini (n 312) 56–7.

[314] Trinh Hai Yen, *The Interpretation of Investment Treaties* (Brill 2014) ch 2.

[315] Weeramantry (n 312) 157–64; Wälde, 'Interpreting' (n 178) 725.

[316] See, for the rules on interpretation of unilateral acts, Caron (n 228) 655–73; and Michele Potestà, 'The Interpretation of Consent to ICSID Arbitration Contained in Domestic Investment Laws' (2011) 27 Arb Int'l 149, 160–8.

[317] *PNG Sustainable Development Program Ltd v Papua New Guinea* (n 301) para 265; *Zhinvali v Georgia* referred to in *Mobil Corporation, Venezuela Holdings BV, and others v Bolivarian Republic of Venezuela,* ICSID Case No ARB/07/27, Decision on Jurisdiction (10 June 2010) para 81. See also *SPP v Egypt,* mentioning 'general principles of statutory interpretation', referred to in ibid para 79.

[318] *PNG Sustainable Development Program Ltd v Papua New Guinea* (n 301) para 264; *Mobil Corporation, Venezuela Holdings BV, and others v Venezuela* (n 317) para 85; *CEMEX Caracas Investments BV and CEMEX Caracas II Investments BV v Bolivarian Republic of Venezuela,* ICSID Case No ARB/08/15, Decision on Jurisdiction (30 December 2010) para 79.

[319] *Nuclear Tests (Australia v France)* (Judgment) (1974) ICJ Rep 253, para 43; *Nuclear Tests (New Zealand v France)* (Judgment) (1974) ICJ Rep 457, para 46. cf Jarrod Hepburn, 'Domestic Investment Statutes in International Law' (2018) 112 AJIL 658, 667–93, and

require acceptance.³²⁰ Second, because the definition of the authority to adjudicate takes place at the international level, tribunals cannot ignore the international law rules of interpretation, which are considered more important than domestic rules.³²¹ This latter point reflects the international law governance of arbitration agreements, and evidences the unsustainability of a high dependence on diverse domestic rules on interpretation.³²² That does not mean that domestic laws should be disregarded completely. Legislation can be relevant, for example, for determining the substance of consent.³²³ Nevertheless, what results from this very complex picture is much simpler: faced with unclarity regarding the rules of interpretation of unilateral acts, investment tribunals resort to the VCLT and other rules of treaty interpretation by analogy.³²⁴

4.3 Three Stages of Jurisdictional Checks

Jurisdictional examinations carry the prospect of identifying deficiencies in party-provided jurisdictional rules. This section discusses this possibility and observes the opportunity for remedying deficiencies in jurisdictional

---

particularly 673 (extending the unilateral act analysis to the substantive investor protections, which indeed imply unilateral obliging and do not require acceptances).

320   See s 3.2.1 above. It should be borne in mind that by accepting an offer to arbitrate, an investor does not merely trigger a state commitment to arbitrate, but also undertakes the same commitment on his part.

321   *PNG Sustainable Development Program Ltd v Papua New Guinea* (n 301) para 265 ('Where the principles of interpretation under the State's domestic law conflict with international law principles, international law principles will ordinarily prevail [...]'); *Mobil Corporation, Venezuela Holdings BV, and others v Venezuela* (n 317) para 85 ('Those unilateral acts must accordingly be interpreted according to the ICSID Convention itself and to the rules of international law governing unilateral declarations of States.'); *CEMEX Caracas Investments BV and CEMEX Caracas II Investments BV v Venezuela* (n 318) para 79 ('they must be interpreted according to the ICSID Convention and to the principles of international law governing unilateral declarations of States'); *Zhinvali v Georgia* referred to in *Mobil Corporation, Venezuela Holdings BV, and others v Venezuela* (n 317) para 81 ('the Tribunal must follow that national law guidance, but always subject to ultimate governance by international law').

322   See also S Mullen and E Whitsitt, 'ICSID and Legislative Consent to Arbitrate: Questions of Applicable Law' (2017) 32 ICSID Rev-FILJ 92, 114–5 (concluding that taking into account domestic principles of interpretation did not make much effective difference in practice).

323   *Mobil Corporation, Venezuela Holdings BV, and others v Venezuela* (n 317) para 96(i); *CEMEX Caracas Investments BV and CEMEX Caracas II Investments BV v Venezuela* (n 318) para 89(a).

324   *PNG Sustainable Development Program Ltd v Papua New Guinea* (n 301) paras 265 (VCLT), 269 (the principle of effectiveness); *Mobil Corporation, Venezuela Holdings BV, and others v Venezuela* (n 317) para 96(ii) (VCLT); *CEMEX Caracas Investments BV and CEMEX Caracas II Investments BV v Venezuela* (n 318) para 89(b) (VCLT).

regulation. I analyse the jurisdictional examinations conducted by administrative organs of arbitration institutions (1), arbitral tribunals (2), and ICSID annulment committees and local courts (3).

4.3.1 Pre-Examination by Administrative Organs

All the major arbitration institutions used for the resolution of investor-state disputes provide some form of preliminary review of arbitration agreements conducted by administrative organs such as secretariats. The ICSID system has the 'screening' procedure conducted by the Secretary-General, who can refuse to register a request for arbitration if 'the dispute is manifestly outside the jurisdiction of the Centre';[325] the ICC and SCC systems confer a similar power on collective bodies,[326] while the Secretary-General of the PCA conducts a similar review without any formal empowerment in writing.[327] These processes have been a subject of extensive scholarly analyses (particularly in the ICSID context).[328] None of these processes is meant to make full and final jurisdictional determinations: tribunals remain the judges of their competence, and in cases of doubt administrative bodies must defer jurisdictional questions to tribunals. Administrative organs can decide not to proceed with arbitrations only if it is manifest or obvious that the submitted dispute would be outside the tribunal's jurisdiction.

One aspect of these processes is relevant, though. Consider the example of an investor who brings a dispute to international arbitration relying on a BIT clause which requires him to firstly resort to domestic courts. Wishing to bypass this requirement, the investor invokes the MFN clause contained in the same BIT and a third-party BIT which does not require domestic litigation. Depending on the rigidity of its approach, an administrative organ can hold that the dispute is manifestly outside the jurisdiction because the investor's jurisdictional construction is wrong, on the one hand, or defer to the tribunal

---

325 ICSID Convention (n 101) art 36(3).
326 ICC Rules (n 197) art 6(3)-(4) ('The arbitration shall proceed if and to the extent that the Court is prima facie satisfied that an arbitration agreement under the Rules may exist.'); SCC Rules (n 197) art 12 ('The Board shall dismiss a case, in whole or in part, if: (i) the SCC manifestly lacks jurisdiction over the dispute;').
327 Daly, Goriatcheva, and Meighen (n 202) 23, 84.
328 See, for example, Eloïse Obadia and Frauke Nitschke, 'Institutional Arbitration and the Role of the Secretariat' in Chiara Giorgetti (ed), *Litigating International Investment Disputes: A Practitioner's Guide* (Brill 2014) 80; Sergio Puig and Chester Brown, 'The Secretary-General's Power to Refuse to Register a Request for Arbitration under the ICSID Convention' (2012) 27 ICSID Rev-FILJ 172; Martina Polasek, 'The Threshold for Registration of a Request for Arbitration under the ICSID Convention' (2011) 5 Disp Resol Int'l 177.

the question of the applicability of the MFN clause to the dispute resolution clause, on the other. Therefore, administrative organs have an opportunity to filter jurisdictional constructions advanced by claimants that will be considered by arbitral tribunals.[329] Administrative organs can thus set the agenda of tribunals regarding the regulatory deficiencies that will be considered and prospectively remedied. This effect is unwelcome, given that the function of administrative organs is not to make jurisdictional determinations. Administrative organs should take a more technical approach in preliminary reviews, with the aim of mitigating possible censoring effect on the jurisdictional questions referred to tribunals.[330]

4.3.2   Examination by Arbitral Tribunals

Arbitral tribunals are judges of their own competence,[331] and therefore the principal jurisdictional determinations in arbitral processes are made by them. Jurisdictional questions can come before tribunals in two ways. The first one is the power of tribunals to raise jurisdictional issues on their own initiative, *proprio motu* or *ex officio*.[332] Investment tribunals largely follow general international law in this respect.[333] More commonly, jurisdictional questions arrive before tribunals through objections by disputing parties, which are the usual first line of defence of respondents. It is not unimaginable that a tribunal itself raises a jurisdictional question relating to deficiencies in party-provided jurisdictional rules,[334] but most of them are discovered through objections. Regulatory deficiencies in jurisdictional rules can also be implicit in claimants' requests for arbitration, and complex jurisdictional constructions may imply supplementing the given set of jurisdictional rules by their mere affirmation.

---

329   See generally Relja Radović, 'Screening Powers in Investment Arbitration: Questions of Legal Change and Legitimacy' in Freya Baetens (ed), *Legitimacy of Unseen Actors in International Adjudication* (CUP 2019) 452.

330   ibid.

331   ICSID Convention (n 101) art 41(1); PCA Rules (n 196) art 23(1); UNCITRAL Rules (n 196) art 23(1); ICC Rules (n 197) art 6(3), (5). See also Brown (n 87) 212 (*compétence de la compétence* as an inherent power of international courts and tribunals).

332   As noted earlier, these two terms reflect the difference between the *possibility* and the *duty* of tribunals to raise jurisdictional issues. See s 2.2.4, n 127 above.

333   cf *Anglo-Iranian Oil Co* (McNair) (n 23) 116–7; with ICSID Arbitration Rules (n 274) r 41(2); and *Mihaly International Corporation v Democratic Socialist Republic of Sri Lanka*, ICSID Case No ARB/00/2, Award (15 March 2002) para 56.

334   See, for example, *Phoenix Action Ltd v The Czech Republic*, ICSID Case No ARB/06/5, Award (15 April 2009) para 82 (where the Tribunal rejected the arguments of both the Claimant and the Respondent regarding the applicability of the *Salini* criteria to the definition of 'investment', arguing that a more appropriate set of criteria needs to be developed).

Arbitral tribunals, therefore, have most of the opportunities for addressing the deficiencies of party-provided jurisdictional rules. At this point, two preliminary remarks concerning arbitral activism are necessary.[335] First, the power (or even more so, the duty) of arbitral tribunals to raise jurisdictional issues on their own initiative conflicts with the principle of consensualism which gives disputing parties the possibility to define jurisdiction by procedural conduct, or with what is frequently referred to as 'party autonomy'.[336] The former implies an objectively defined jurisdictional framework, while the latter confers the full definition of jurisdiction on disputing parties. This is paradoxical, because the arbitral power to raise jurisdictional issues is meant to ensure that the arbitral tribunal is not acting outside its mandate, thus safeguarding the principle of consensualism.[337] Hence tribunals have taken different approaches to this power in practice: they have been willing to both examine jurisdiction on their own initiative and to defer to the parties' procedural conduct on the very same questions.[338] Activism appears decisive. Second, despite the pressure on disputing parties to raise jurisdictional objections as soon as possible,[339] some tribunals have tolerated belated objections.[340] This is another paradox: both phenomena rely on the parties' definition of

---

335 In this context, the term 'activism' refers to the willingness of arbitrators to make more or less use of their discretionary powers. This view should be distinguished from the one that observes arbitral activism as an excess of authority. See, for the latter view, Andrea K Bjorklund, 'Are Arbitrators (Judicial) Activists?' (2018) 17 LPICT 49.

336 See above, on consent by conduct and acquiescence, s 3.2.3; De Brabandere (n 3) 99–101 (arguing that party autonomy plays a limited role in investment arbitration because of the public law concepts like *jura novit curia*); Tanzi (n 120) 66–8 (arguing that in jurisdictional matters judicial autonomy prevails over party autonomy).

337 Schreuer and others (n 82) 528. This is particularly obvious if a party fails to participate in proceedings, in which case it must be assured that it has consented to adjudication, and therefore courts and tribunals *must* examine their own jurisdiction *ex officio*. See ICJ Statute (n 23) art 53(2); ICSID Arbitration Rules (n 274) r 42(4).

338 cf *MTD Equity Sdn Bhd and MTD Chile SA v Republic of Chile*, ICSID Case No ARB/01/7, Award (25 May 2004) paras 93–4; and *Ioannis Kardassopoulos v Georgia*, ICSID Case No ARB/05/18, Decision on Jurisdiction (6 July 2007) paras 108–12 (qualifying the Claimants as investors under the ICSID Convention and the relevant investment treaties on the Tribunals' own initiative); with *Saipem SpA v People's Republic of Bangladesh*, ICSID Case No ARB/05/7, Decision on Jurisdiction and Recommendation on Provisional Measures (21 March 2007) para 73 (noting that the Respondent has abandoned its objection that the Claimant was not a private investor and considering the corresponding requirement of the ICSID Convention met).

339 ICSID Arbitration Rules (n 274) r 41(1).

340 Schreuer and others (n 82) 527–8; Christoph Schreuer, 'Belated Jurisdictional Objections in ICSID Arbitration' (2010) 7(1) TDM <www.transnational-dispute-management.com/article.asp?key-1533> accessed 20 August 2020.

jurisdiction, either implicit or explicit. Moreover, tribunals have held that they can open seemingly closed jurisdictional questions throughout the process.[341] Here again, arbitral activism and restraint appear decisive.

When examining jurisdictional issues, arbitral tribunals find themselves in the sphere of law, as generally understood in international law.[342] Jurisdiction is not to be proved, and therefore no burden of proof is imposed on disputing parties.[343] This is a consequence of qualifying as law, in accordance with the principle of *jura novit curia*.[344] Even if there were a burden, it would be shared by tribunals, following the said principle and their power to raise jurisdictional issues.[345] Investment tribunals, as other courts, analyse arguments in favour and against jurisdiction, and follow those arguments whose force is 'preponderant'.[346] This means that deficiencies in party-provided jurisdictional rules will be discussed in terms of law, not facts, and the answers to the issues raised by such deficiencies will be equally framed in terms of law. Arbitral tribunals are hence given an opportunity to discuss possible remedies to jurisdictional regulatory deficiencies in general and prescriptive terms.

---

341 See *Waguih Elie George Siag and Clorinda Vecchi v The Arab Republic of Egypt*, ICSID Case No ARB/05/15, Award (1 June 2009) para 311–4 (holding that a belated jurisdictional objection has been waived, but nevertheless deciding to examine the merits of the objection). This might not be possible when a tribunal has already decided on a jurisdictional objection; see *Siemens AG v The Argentine Republic*, ICSID Case No ARB/02/8, Award (6 February 2007) para 68 (however, the Tribunal did not reach its conclusions on formalistic grounds, and it noted that it had 'no doubt about its findings'). But some tribunals and annulment committees have held that the power of tribunals to examine jurisdiction on their own initiative grants them the power to reconsider earlier jurisdictional rulings; see *Standard Chartered Bank (Hong Kong) Limited v Tanzania Electric Supply Company Limited*, ICSID Case No ARB/10/20, Decision on the Application for Annulment (22 August 2018) paras 150–73.

342 *Nicaragua v Honduras* (n 129) para 16..

343 *Spain v Canada* (n 98) para 38.

344 *Fisheries Jurisdiction (United Kingdom v Iceland)* (Merits) (1974) ICJ Rep 3, para 17; *Fisheries Jurisdiction (Germany v Iceland)* (Merits) (1974) ICJ Rep 175, para 18 ('the burden of establishing or proving rules of international law cannot be imposed upon any of the Parties, for the law lies within the judicial knowledge of the Court').

345 See also Frédéric G Sourgens, 'By Equal Contest of Arms: Jurisdictional Proof in Investor-State Arbitrations' (2013) 38 North Carolina J Int'l L & Com Reg 875, 923–6.

346 *Factory at Chorzów* (n 31) 32; *Nicaragua v Honduras* (n 129) para 16; *Spain v Canada* (n 98) 38. This approach was accepted very early in investment arbitration; see in that respect *SPP v Egypt*, as reported by Solveiga Palevičienė, 'Consent to Arbitration and the Legacy of the *SPP v. Egypt* Case' (2014) 7 Baltic J Law & Politics 149, 155. This approach is related to the rejection of liberal or restrictive interpretation of jurisdictional instruments; see nn 310–311 above.

4.3.3 Post-Examination by Annulment Committees and Courts

Within the ICSID system, arbitral awards can be annulled if, among other grounds, 'the Tribunal has manifestly exceeded its powers' or 'the award has failed to state the reasons on which it is based'.[347] Non-ICSID awards are reviewable by domestic courts, either in the set aside proceedings at the seat of arbitration,[348] or in the recognition and/or enforcement proceedings before other domestic courts.[349] Can these control mechanisms identify deficiencies in party-defined jurisdictional rules and engage in their remedying?

Acting outside jurisdiction undoubtedly qualifies as excess of powers under the ICSID Convention.[350] The problem is that the excess of powers must be 'manifest' to justify annulment, which can have a limiting effect on the review conducted by committees. What that formulation means is debatable,[351] but ICSID committees have formed a jurisprudence on the matter.[352] As one committee put it: '[i]f an excess of powers is to be the cause of an annulment, the *ad hoc* Committee must so find with certainty and immediacy, without it being necessary to engage in elaborate analyses of the award'.[353] This principled pronouncement did not stop the Committee from examining detailed jurisdictional issues, namely the objective definition of 'investment',[354] which falls within the category that I will further argue to form arbitral law-making.

An alternative approach holds that 'manifest' refers to the gravity of excess. The *Vivendi v Argentina* annulment decision is often considered an example of

---

347 ICSID Convention (n 101) art 52(1)(b), (e).
348 UNCITRAL Model Law (n 305) art 34.
349 Convention on the Recognition and Enforcement of Foreign Arbitral Awards (signed 10 June 1958, entered into force 7 June 1959) 330 UNTS 38, art v.
350 Schreuer and others (n 82) 943–4.
351 Christoph Schreuer, 'From ICSID Annulment to Appeal Half Way Down the Slippery Slope' (2011) 10 LPICT 211, 216–21; Laurens JE Timmer, 'Manifest Excess of Powers as a Ground for the Annulment of ICSID Awards' (2013) 14 JWIT 775, 789–90, 791–802.
352 See, among many others, *Mr Patrick Mitchell v The Democratic Republic of the Congo*, ICSID Case No ARB/99/7, Decision on the Application for Annulment of the Award (1 November 2006) para 20; *MTD Equity Sdn Bhd and MTD Chile SA v Republic of Chile*, ICSID Case No ARB/01/7, Decision on Annulment (21 March 2007) paras 44–8; *Industria Nacional de Alimentos SA and Indalsa Perú SA v The Republic of Peru*, ICSID Case No ARB/03/4, Decision on Annulment (5 September 2007) paras 99–102; *Impregilo SpA v Argentine Republic*, ICSID Case No ARB/07/17, Decision of the ad hoc Committee on the Application for Annulment (24 January 2014) paras 125–32.
353 *Mr Patrick Mitchell v Congo* (n 352) para 20. See also Schreuer and others (n 82) 938 (holding that 'manifest' does not indicate gravity but ease with which an excess of powers is perceived).
354 *Mr Patrick Mitchell v Congo* (n 352) paras 27–33.

this alternative.[355] Here again the understanding of the term 'manifest' did not prevent the Committee from addressing nuanced jurisdictional issues, and the Committee was able to elaborate on the distinction between treaty claims and contract claims using the 'fundamental basis of the claim' criterion.[356]

It can be debated whether a non-manifest excess of jurisdiction is possible at all,[357] but that discussion loses much of its importance in light of the above examples. They demonstrate that in any event committees are able to address detailed jurisdictional issues. In contrast, some committees have not been willing to analyse jurisdictional issues that could help remedy certain deficiencies in party-made jurisdictional rules.[358] This finally implies that the intensity of review, and consequently the engagement in the attempts to remedy deficiencies in the given jurisdictional framework, depends mostly on the activism and restraint of annulment committees of the same kind as that of arbitral tribunals.[359]

---

355 *Compañiá de Aguas del Aconquija SA and Vivendi Universal v Argentine Republic*, ICSID Case No ARB/97/3, Decision on Annulment (3 July 2002) para 115 ('Given the clear and serious implications of that decision for Claimants in terms of Article 8(2) of the BIT, and the surrounding circumstances, the Committee can only conclude that that excess of powers was manifest.'). It should be noted, however, that the Committee faced the question of non-exercise of jurisdiction, as opposed to its overstepping, which could have influenced the holding that 'manifest' referred to the seriousness of excess of powers. See ibid para 86.

356 ibid paras 98–103.

357 cf Philippe Pinsolle, 'Jurisdictional Review of ICSID Awards' (2004) 5 JWIT 613, 618–20 (arguing that jurisdiction must be fully reviewed, because jurisdictional determinations cannot be right or wrong to a certain degree; a tribunal either has or does not have jurisdiction); with *Hussein Nuaman Soufraki v The United Arab Emirates*, ICSID Case No ARB/02/7, Decision of the ad hoc Committee on the Application for Annulment of Mr Soufraki (5 June 2007) paras 117–9.

358 *Impregilo SpA v Argentina* (n 352) paras 140–1 (refusing to examine the applicability of the MFN clause to the dispute resolution clause, and arguing that the Committee had no authority to determine whether the Tribunal's interpretation of these clauses was correct); *Suez, Sociedad General de Aguas de Barcelona SA, and Interagua Servicios Integrales de Agua SA v Argentine Republic*, ICSID Case No ARB/03/17, Decision on Argentina's Application for Annulment (14 December 2018) paras 173–80 (taking a similar approach in respect of the same issue). See also *Hussein Nuaman Soufraki v UAE* (n 357) para 116 ('the *ad hoc* Committee reiterates that it is not empowered to correct alleged "errors" committed by the Tribunal, and a series of errors is no more necessarily a ground for annulment than a single error').

359 As for the activism and restraint of annulment committees affecting the intensity of their review, see Schreuer, 'Annulment' (n 351) 215–21 (on extensions of the grounds for annulment) and 222–4 (referring to 'hyperactive' annulment committees); Timmer (n 351) 803 (identifying committees' restraint to annul awards for manifest excess of powers).

Another ground for annulment within the ICSID framework relates to the duty to state the reasons.[360] Annulment committees review the completeness and coherence of the given reasons, which is a good opportunity for verifying the methodologies employed by arbitral tribunals when dealing with jurisdictional problems.[361] However, here again the activism of committee members can introduce more substantial review by the back door. In *Patrick Mitchell v Congo*, the Committee identified an objective element in the definition of 'investment' and held that because the award did not discuss that element, it was not sufficiently reasoned.[362] This ground for annulment therefore gives committees a bigger manoeuvring space should they be willing to engage in a dialogue with arbitral tribunals on the correct solutions to regulatory jurisdictional questions.

When it comes to domestic courts reviewing non-ICSID awards, their approaches differ from country to country. However, most domestic courts, at least in major jurisdictions, exercise *de novo* review of jurisdictional questions.[363] Domestic courts therefore can exercise a more prudential review of jurisdictional questions than ICSID annulment committees. This gives domestic courts the same opportunities as that of arbitral tribunals to identify deficiencies in the given set of jurisdictional rules and to suggest solutions to the difficulties that they cause.

4.4 The Power of Tribunals to Fill Gaps in Jurisdictional Regulation

The next question is whether jurisdictional examiners are empowered to remedy deficiencies in party-provided jurisdictional frameworks by supplementing

---

360 ICSID Convention (n 101) art 52(1)(e).
361 Schreuer and others (n 82) 1003ff (regarding insufficient and inadequate reasons). As for the standard applied by committees, see *Impregilo SpA v Argentina* (n 352) para 180 (a committee 'shou[l]d not be concerned with the correctness of the Tribunal's reasoning but is confined to ascertaining whether the reasoning would allow an informed reader to understand how the Tribunal reached its conclusions').
362 *Mr Patrick Mitchell v Congo* (n 352) paras 39–41. cf *Malaysian Historical Salvors Sdn Bhd v The Government of Malaysia*, ICSID Case No ARB/05/10, Decision on the Application for Annulment (16 April 2009) para 80 (finding that the same objective element—contribution to the economic development of the host state—was not part of the definition of 'investment', and annulling the award for the manifest excess of power).
363 See Radović, 'Domestic Courts' (n 304); and, for example, *The Republic of Ecuador v Occidental Exploration & Production Co* [2006] EWHC 345 (Comm) [7] ('It is now well – established that a challenge to the jurisdiction of an arbitration panel under section 67 [of the Arbitration Act 1996] proceeds by way of a re – hearing of the matters before the arbitrators. The test for the court is: was the Tribunal correct in its decision on jurisdiction? The test is not: was the Tribunal entitled to reach the decision that it did.' [emphasis omitted]).

them with independent input. This is first and foremost a question of authority. The principle of consensualism grants disputing parties the exclusive authority to define the terms of their submission to adjudication,[364] while the *compétence de la compétence* power grants courts and tribunals the authority to verify the existence and extent of their jurisdiction.[365] This is, therefore, a distinction between regulators and examiners, or as often held in legal scholarship, between law-makers and law-appliers.

Is this distinction a strict one? *Compétence de la compétence* is often said to relate to the judicial function,[366] and considered an inherent power of international courts and tribunals.[367] Despite this fact, it is hard to talk about a unified concept of *compétence de la compétence*.[368] Furthermore, little discussion can be found on the issue of what kind of answers international courts and tribunals are entitled to give to jurisdictional questions. It is implied that courts and tribunals can only *interpret* the given jurisdictional framework and cannot supplement it with new jurisdictional rules. This proposition is debatable when jurisdictional determinations involve general principles of international law whose meaning is quite dependant on judicial activity.[369] But when

---

364 See s 2 above.
365 *Nottebohm Case (Liechtenstein v Guatemala)* (Preliminary Objection) (1953) ICJ Rep 111, 119–20. But see Shihata, *Power* (n 123) 27–30. Shihata takes into account so-called self-judging clauses and argues that the exercise of *compétence de la compétence* takes place in two stages: in the first step the disputing parties determine whether the dispute falls within the reserved domain, while in the second step the tribunal determines whether it has jurisdiction. Bearing in mind the problems arising in regard to such clauses, this distinction between two stages is disputable; see s 2.2.3 above.
366 *Interpretation of the Greco-Turkish Agreement of 1 December 1926 (Final Protocol, Article IV)* (Advisory Opinion) (1928) PCIJ Ser B—No 16, 4, 20 ('as a general rule, any body possessing jurisdictional powers has the right in the first place itself to determine the extent of its jurisdiction'); *Nottebohm* (n 365) 120 ('The judicial character of the Court and the rule of general international law referred to above are sufficient to establish that the Court is competent to adjudicate on its own jurisdiction in the present case.').
367 Brown (n 87) 212.
368 Laurence Boisson de Chazournes, 'The Principle of *Compétence de la Compétence* in International Adjudication and Its Role in an Era of Multiplication of Courts and Tribunals' in Mahnoush H Arsanjani and others (eds), *Looking to the Future: Essays on International Law in Honor of W. Michael Reisman* (Martinus Nijhoff 2011) 1043–4. See also ibid 1043–58 (distinguishing between extensive, restrictive, and *sui generis* effects of this power). According to Boisson de Chazournes, the ICSID system demonstrates the restrictive effect of *compétence de la compétence*, due to the explicit limitations of the ICSID jurisdiction in Article 25 ICSID Convention.
369 For example, the doctrines of *res judicata* and *lis pendens* in international law. See Kaj Hobér, '*Res Judicata* and *Lis Pendens* in International Arbitration' (2014) 366 Recueil des Cours 99, 287–402.

it comes to substantive jurisdiction, which is central in the present analysis, it seems generally accepted that courts and tribunals are not entitled to do anything else but to interpret the will of disputing parties,[370] and apply legal conclusions to the relevant facts.[371] It can be counter-argued that interpretation in itself is more than law-application,[372] but what matters in this discussion about authority is that tribunals must assert that their jurisdictional decisions are based on the will of disputing parties. Indeed, the absence of such an assertion would invalidate their entire work.

There are possibilities, however, for blurring the distinction between the definition and the application of jurisdictional rules. One way is to maintain that certain issues are not jurisdictional but 'procedural', even if only for the sake of terminology. The *Abaclat and others v Argentina* case is the most famous example of an extensive reliance on the power of a tribunal to 'fill gaps' in the rules of procedure, with the effect of affirming its competence.[373] In fact, the ICSID system empowers tribunals only to define procedural rules for the conduct of arbitration in the absence of a relevant written rule,[374] which can be seen as another inherent power of international courts and tribunals.[375] By qualifying certain rules as 'procedural' instead of 'jurisdictional', as is often done regarding the conditions of access,[376] different types of rules can be

---

370　*Nottebohm* (n 365) 119 ('an international tribunal has the right to decide as to its own jurisdiction and has the power to *interpret* for this purpose the instruments which govern that jurisdiction' [emphasis added]). Shihata identifies several techniques in the practice of the ICJ for determining jurisdiction, most importantly through the methods of interpretation of jurisdictional instruments. See Shihata, *Power* (n 123) 188–206. See also ibid 205 ('In this respect, not only the International Court, but, in fact, all courts can only try to "read the mind of the parties" by applying the techniques of interpretation and evidence most suited to their function and to the legal system in which they work.').

371　For the question how tribunals should approach facts at the jurisdictional level, see *Phoenix Action Ltd v Czechia* (n 334) paras 61–4 (holding that the facts that are relevant for the establishment of jurisdiction must be proved).

372　See generally Ingo Venzke, *How Interpretation Makes International Law: On Semantic Change and Normative Twists* (OUP 2012).

373　*Abaclat and others v The Argentine Republic*, ICSID Case No ARB/07/5, Decision on Jurisdiction and Admissibility (4 August 2011) paras 521–8.

374　ICSID Convention (n 101) art 44 ('If any question of procedure arises which is not covered by this Section or the Arbitration Rules or any rules agreed by the parties, the Tribunal shall decide the question.'); ICSID Arbitration Rules (n 274) r 19 ('The Tribunal shall make the orders required for the conduct of the proceeding.').

375　Brown (n 87) 215.

376　See ch 2, s 2.2.

confused, including the confusion of their addressees for creators. In addition, the introduction of the category of 'procedural' rules itself amounts to law-making, bearing in mind the absence of that classification in the written law and its practical impact.[377]

5   Conclusion

Consensualism is a persistent feature of international adjudication, and that is so in the first place because of the logic behind the international legal order. The consensualism of international adjudication persists because it represents the only means of defining the authority to adjudicate. There are no prospects that this will change. Even the theory that state consent to arbitration (more precisely, an offer to arbitrate) might in future reach the status of a customary rule,[378] which faces some practical obstacles,[379] does not exceed the classical understanding of consent (or at least the known controversies regarding customary international law and consent). Specific views on investment arbitration are not capable of affecting consensualism, from a strict point of view. Their contribution is contextual insofar as the views on investment law and arbitration as a global public good, a protective regime, or from the commercial arbitration point of view, can introduce new considerations relating to party consent and jurisdictional regulation. International adjudication, including investment treaty arbitration, is in its essence founded on a contractual relationship between disputing parties. Once disputing parties enter a jurisdictional relationship, they define the authority to adjudicate of an arbitral tribunal, but usually leaving a number of jurisdictional questions open. Answering these questions appears necessary on a trajectory towards jurisdictional determinations. Arbitral tribunals, as any other international court or tribunal, have the power to rule on their own competence, but not to fill regulatory gaps. In the following chapters, I will demonstrate that arbitral tribunals have answered opened jurisdictional questions in general and prescriptive terms and generated

---

377   See ch 2, s 2.1.
378   Mathias Audit and Mathias Forteau, 'Investment Arbitration without BIT: Toward a Foreign Investment Customary Based Arbitration?' (2012) 29 J Int'l Arb 581.
379   Specifically, the requirement of an agreement in writing: ICSID Convention (n 101) art 25(1).

jurisdictional rules. Graph 2 presents the arbitral regulatory activity as a non-consensual part of the process of jurisdictional regulation, which contests the premise that the definition of the authority to adjudicate is within the disputing parties' exclusive domain.

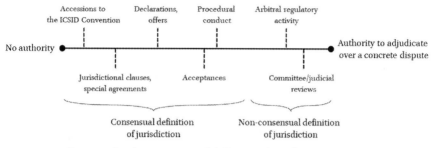

GRAPH 2   Consensual and non-consensual definition of jurisdiction

CHAPTER 2

Arbitrator-Made Rules and the Procedural Aspects of Consensual Jurisdictional Regulation

1   Introduction

The following three chapters analyse the creation of jurisdictional rules by arbitral tribunals in practice. In order to clearly demonstrate the importance of arbitrator-made rules, they are classified according to their effects. This chapter discusses the arbitrator-made rules that relax the procedural jurisdictional limits defined by disputing parties, while Chapter 3 discusses the arbitrator-made rules that relax the substantive jurisdictional limits defined by disputing parties. Chapter 4 then addresses the arbitrator-made jurisdictional rules that introduce sharper limits of arbitral jurisdiction, both procedural and substantive, and therefore hinder the access to international arbitration. The term 'procedural' in this sense is strictly descriptive, referring to the conditions of access to arbitration, and it should not be confused with the normative qualification of some conditions of access as 'procedural' (as opposed to jurisdictional in a narrower sense), which has been developed in practice.[1] The premise of this book is that the principle of consensualism grants disputing parties the power to define the authority to adjudicate (ie jurisdiction) of arbitral tribunals and therefore all terms of such definitions are jurisdictional. The method of my inquiry is announced in the Introduction.

Arbitrator-made rules affect the procedural aspects of consensual jurisdictional regulation in several respects. Section 2 analyses the rules weakening party-defined conditions of access, specifically regarding the development of a dichotomy between 'procedural' and 'jurisdictional' conditions of access and the detachment of some of them from party consent. Section 3 examines the rules providing avenues for bypassing party-defined conditions of access. Finally, Section 4 analyses the possible role of MFN clauses in overcoming jurisdictional barriers and specifically the formation of presumptions in favour and against their applicability to dispute settlement clauses.

---

1 See s 2 below.

2   Rules Weakening the Conditions of Access

The ICSID Convention and most investment treaties do not define the concept of admissibility. That concept has been developed in practice. I discuss first its formulation (1), and then the qualification of various conditions precedent (2), as well as of the applicable procedure as pertaining to the admissibility of claims (3).

2.1   *The Jurisdiction/Admissibility Dichotomy*

Legal scholarship shows a great interest in the concept of admissibility of claims. Its existence and separation from the notion of jurisdiction is generally accepted,[2] although arguments exist that the concept of admissibility is unjustified in the context of investment arbitration.[3] Furthermore, even if the concept is firmly established, the boundary between admissibility and jurisdiction, as well as its practical relevance, remains unclear.[4]

Academic interest was prompted by the developments in arbitral practice. The *SGS v Philippines* decision on jurisdiction was an early example of differentiation between the two concepts. The Tribunal held that jurisdiction is

---

[2] See, among many others, Jan Paulsson, 'Jurisdiction and Admissibility' in Gerald Aksen (ed), *Global Reflections on International Law, Commerce and Dispute Resolution: Liber Amicorum in Honour of Robert Briner* (ICC 2005) 601; Gerold Zeiler, 'Jurisdiction, Competence, and Admissibility of Claims in ICSID Arbitration Proceedings' in Christina Binder and others (eds), *International Investment Law for the 21st Century: Essays in Honour of Christoph Schreuer* (OUP 2009) 76; Veijo Heiskanen, 'Ménage à Trois? Jurisdiction, Admissibility and Competence in Investment Treaty Arbitration' (2014) 29 ICSID Rev-FILJ 231; Michael Waibel, 'Investment Arbitration: Jurisdiction and Admissibility' in Marc Bungenberg and others (eds), *International Investment Law: A Handbook* (CH Beck/Hart/Nomos 2015) 1212; Filippo Fontanelli and Attila Tanzi, 'Jurisdiction and Admissibility in Investment Arbitration: A View from the Bridge at the Practice' (2017) 16 LPICT 3; August Reinisch, 'Jurisdiction and Admissibility in International Investment Law' (2017) 16 LPICT 21; Filippo Fontanelli, *Jurisdiction and Admissibility in Investment Arbitration: The Practice and the Theory* (Brill 2018); David L Earnest, 'The Duty of Arbitrators to Delimitate between Jurisdiction and Admissibility in Investor-State Arbitration: A Developed Consensus or an Enduring Lacuna?' (2018) 17 LPICT 135.

[3] See generally Christer Söderlund and Elena Burova, 'Is There Such a Thing as Admissibility in Investment Arbitration?' (2018) 33 ICSID Rev-FILJ 525.

[4] One major difference between the two concepts might concern the possibility of review: Paulsson (n 2) 601. However, such a general claim is possibly too bold, and issues of admissibility can also be reviewed by ICSID annulment committees: Fontanelli and Tanzi (n 2) 12–4. Further on the difficulties in distinguishing between the two concepts, see Fontanelli (n 2) 129ff.

determined by the applicable BIT and the ICSID Convention, while admissibility concerns some impediment for the exercise of jurisdiction over a claim.[5] Later tribunals have gone further in the attempts to define the two concepts clearly. The *Hochtief* Tribunal held that '[j]urisdiction is an attribute of a tribunal and not of a claim, whereas admissibility is an attribute of a claim but not of a tribunal'.[6] Another tribunal considered that 'an objection to jurisdiction goes to the ability of a tribunal to hear a case while an objection to admissibility aims at the claim itself and presupposes that the tribunal has jurisdiction'.[7] The rationale behind the distinction is therefore in the question whether the defect at stake concerns the authority of the tribunal to adjudicate, or the claim itself and its suitability for adjudication. It follows that conditions of admissibility are not related to party consent but to various other questions.[8] The inspiration for the differentiation between the two concepts can be traced to the practice of the ICJ.[9]

In opposition, some tribunals have disputed the jurisdiction/admissibility dichotomy. They have considered the concept of admissibility inappropriate in the ICSID context because it is not mentioned in that Convention,[10] but some tribunals have also observed the lack of its definition in the applicable BIT[11]

---

5   *SGS Société Générale de Surveillance SA v Republic of the Philippines*, ICSID Case No ARB/02/6, Decision of the Tribunal on Objections to Jurisdiction (29 January 2004) para 154.

6   *Hochtief AG v The Argentine Republic*, ICSID Case No ARB/07/31, Decision on Jurisdiction (24 October 2011) para 90.

7   *Ioan Micula and others v Romania*, ICSID Case No ARB/05/20, Decision on Jurisdiction and Admissibility (24 September 2008) para 63. See also *Waste Management Inc v United Mexican States*, ICSID Case No ARB(AF)/98/2, Dissenting Opinion of Keith Highet (8 May 2000) para 58; and *Supervision y Control SA v The Republic of Costa Rica*, ICSID Case No ARB/12/4, Award (18 January 2017) paras 268–76.

8   See Chittharanjan F Amerasinghe, *International Arbitral Jurisdiction* (Brill 2011) 97–100 (giving examples of the criteria of (in)admissibility of claims from the law of diplomatic protection, and noting that some criteria can become conditions of jurisdiction if qualified as such in the parties' agreement).

9   See *Hochtief AG v Argentina* (n 6) para 95; Reinisch (n 2) 23–4; Söderlund and Burova (n 3) 527–8.

10 *CMS Gas Transmission Company v The Republic of Argentina*, ICSID Case No ARB/01/8, Decision of the Tribunal on Objections to Jurisdiction (17 July 2003) para 41; *Enron Corporation and Ponderosa Assets LP v The Argentine Republic*, ICSID Case No ARB/01/3, Decision on Jurisdiction (14 January 2004) para 33; *Pan American Energy LLC and BP Argentina Exploration Company v The Argentine Republic* and *BP America Production Company and others v The Argentine Republic*, ICSID Cases Nos ARB/03/13 and ARB/04/8, Decision on Preliminary Objections (27 July 2006) para 54.

11 *Ambiente Ufficio SpA and others v The Argentine Republic*, ICSID Case No ARB/08/9, Decision on Jurisdiction and Admissibility (8 February 2013) para 572.

and the rules of procedure.¹² Yet, these tribunals, with one exception,¹³ appear to take a more pragmatic approach, rather than focusing on abstract concepts, admitting that a negative finding leads to the same outcome (dismissing the case), regardless of the classification of the issue as going to jurisdiction or admissibility.¹⁴

If the distinction is accepted, which conditions of access pertain to jurisdiction and which pertain to admissibility? According to one stream, if a condition appears together with the manifestation of consent to arbitration, it limits that consent and therefore pertains to jurisdiction.¹⁵ This approach follows the ICJ practice.¹⁶ Other tribunals have considered the delimitation less sharp and inquired into the function of each condition. They have observed that some conditions of access do not establish consent to arbitrate but regulate how already established consent or a 'right to arbitrate' should be exercised.¹⁷ These requirements are 'procedural' as opposed to 'jurisdictional', because they define the procedure for setting arbitration in motion.¹⁸ What follows the recognition of different function of different conditions, is the perceived need for more flexibility in their application.¹⁹ In other words, requirements that do

---

12 *Methanex Corporation v The United States of America*, UNCITRAL ad hoc arbitration, Partial Award (7 August 2002) para 123.
13 See *Urbaser SA and CABB v The Argentine Republic*, ICSID Case No ARB/07/26, Decision on Jurisdiction (19 December 2012) paras 112–27 (challenging the concept of admissibility in relation to conditions precedent on many grounds, both practical an theoretical).
14 *Burlington Resources Inc v Republic of Ecuador*, ICSID Case No ARB/08/5, Decision on Jurisdiction (2 June 2010) para 340.
15 *SGS Société Générale de Surveillance SA v The Philippines* (n 5) para 154; *Ioan Micula and others v Romania* (n 7) para 64; *Impregilo SpA v Argentine Republic*, ICSID Case No ARB/07/17, Concurring and Dissenting Opinion of Professor Brigitte Stern (21 June 2011) para 83; *Abaclat and others v The Argentine Republic*, ICSID Case No ARB/07/5, Dissenting Opinion of Georges Abi-Saab (4 August 2011) para 23.
16 *Armed Activities on the Territory of the Congo (New Application: 2002) (Democratic Republic of the Congo v Rwanda)* (Jurisdiction and Admissibility) (2006) ICJ Rep 6, para 88.
17 *Hochtief AG v Argentina* (n 6) para 90; *Abaclat and others v The Argentine Republic*, ICSID Case No ARB/07/5, Decision on Jurisdiction and Admissibility (4 August 2011) paras 494–5; *İçkale İnşaat Limited Şirketi v Turkmenistan*, ICSID Case No ARB/10/24, Award (8 March 2016) para 242; *Casinos Austria International GmbH and Casinos Austria Aktiengesellschaft v Argentine Republic*, ICSID Case No ARB/14/32, Decision on Jurisdiction (29 June 2018) para 279.
18 *İçkale İnşaat Limited Şirketi v Turkmenistan* (n 17) para 242; *Casinos Austria International GmbH and Casinos Austria Aktiengesellschaft v Argentina* (n 17) para 279.
19 See, regarding the conditions of admissibility generally, *SGS Société Générale de Surveillance SA v The Philippines* (n 5) para 170 ('This is a matter of admissibility rather than jurisdiction, and there is a degree of flexibility in the way it is applied.' [reference omitted]); *Supervisión y Control SA v Costa Rica* (n 7) para 270(a) ('There is greater procedural

not condition the authority to adjudicate are less strict. This gives tribunals discretion in determining whether a non-compliance with such requirements prevents proceeding to the merits. Therefore, drawing an analogy to other fields of international adjudication, investment tribunals have adopted a principled distinction between jurisdiction and admissibility, although allowing their own criteria to classify individual questions to these categories.

2.2 Conditions Precedent as Issues of Admissibility

I now turn to the conditions precedent that are defined in the domain of consensual jurisdictional regulation, but which have been requalified by arbitral tribunals as pertaining to the admissibility of claims. A deficiency of explicit regulation regarding the character of conditions precedent makes regulatory space for tribunals.[20] Claimants are normally interested in facilitating the access to arbitration and, given the flexibility that accompanies the concept of admissibility, they argue that conditions precedent do not limit the jurisdiction of arbitral tribunals. However, tribunals can also requalify jurisdictional conditions as those of admissibility on their own initiative.[21]

Investors are often required to notify the host state of the dispute, to wait for some time before instituting arbitration (cooling-off or waiting periods), and to attempt to settle the dispute through negotiations. Tribunals have formed two streams of practice: one maintains that such conditions pertain to jurisdiction,[22] and the other maintains that they pertain to the admissibility of

---

flexibility if the tribunal has jurisdiction.'). See also *Casinos Austria International GmbH and Casinos Austria Aktiengesellschaft v Argentina* (n 17) para 275 ('Such less formalistic approach is more in line with the object and purpose of investment treaties to promote and protect foreign investment for the development of economic cooperation between States.').

20 cf US Model BIT (2012) art 26 <https://investmentpolicy.unctad.org/international-investment-agreements/treaty-files/2870/download> accessed 20 August 2020 ('Conditions and Limitations on Consent of Each Party').

21 *İçkale İnşaat Limited Şirketi v Turkmenistan* (n 17) para 239 ('The Tribunal considers that these two provisions [Article 41 ICSID Convention and Rule 41(2) ICSID Arbitration Rules] provide it with the authority to decide independently, within its *Kompetenz-Kompetenz*, and without being bound by the Parties' legal positions, as to whether the objection raised by the Respondent under Article VII(2) of the BIT constitutes an objection to jurisdiction or an objection to admissibility. Indeed, if this were not the case, and if the Tribunal were to be considered bound by the legal argument of the Parties, the Tribunal might have to reach a decision that it does not consider to be legally correct.').

22 *Enron Corporation and Ponderosa Assets LP v Argentina* (n 10) para 88; *Murphy Exploration and Production Company International v Republic of Ecuador*, ICSID Case No ARB/08/4, Award on Jurisdiction (15 December 2010) paras 140–56; *Tulip Real Estate Investment and Development Netherlands BV v Republic of Turkey*, ICSID Case No ARB/11/28, Decision

claims.[23] The first stream follows the classical understanding that every condition appearing with consent to arbitration is jurisdictional.[24] Accordingly, such conditions are always mandatory.[25] The second stream looks at these conditions as part of the procedure to be followed by investors when setting the dispute settlement mechanism in motion.[26] It recognises the need for flexibility in the application of such conditions, that they should not be regarded as strictly mandatory, and that tribunals have discretion in their application.[27] An early example was the *Lauder* decision, where the Tribunal held that a waiting period was 'not a jurisdictional provision, i.e. a limit set to the authority of the Arbitral Tribunal to decide on the merits of the dispute, but a procedural rule that must be satisfied by the Claimant'.[28] This led the Tribunal to reject an 'overly formalistic approach' in its application.[29] Another tribunal maintained that a 'six-month [waiting] period is procedural and directory in nature, rather than jurisdictional and mandatory' and '[n]on-compliance with the six month period, therefore, does not preclude this Arbitral Tribunal from proceeding'.[30]

on Bifurcated Jurisdictional Issue (5 March 2013) para 72; *Almasryia for Operating & Maintaining Touristic Construction Co LLC v State of Kuwait,* ICSID Case No ARB/18/2, Award on the Respondent's Application under Rule 41(5) of the ICSID Arbitration Rules (1 November 2019) paras 39, 48.

23   *Abaclat and others v Argentina* (Decision) (n 17) para 496; *RREEF Infrastructure (GP) Limited and RREEF Pan-European Infrastructure Two Lux Sàrl v Kingdom of Spain,* ICSID Case No ARB/13/30, Decision on Jurisdiction (6 June 2016) para 225; *Supervisión y Control SA v Costa Rica* (n 7) para 340. See also Arrêt du 29 janvier 2019, Cour d'Appel de Paris, Pôle 1 - Chambre 1 (France) 16/20822, 4.

24   *Tulip Real Estate Investment and Development Netherlands BV v Turkey* (n 22) paras 61, 63 (referring to the practice of the ICJ).

25   *Murphy Exploration and Production Company International v Ecuador* (n 22) paras 140–56. See also *Generation Ukraine Inc v Ukraine,* ICSID Case No ARB/00/9, Award (16 September 2003) para 14.3 ('This Tribunal would be hesitant to interpret a clear provision of the BIT in such a way so as to render it superfluous, as would be the case if a "procedural" characterisation of the [negotiation] requirement effectively empowered the investor to ignore it at its discretion.').

26   *Ronald S Lauder v The Czech Republic,* UNCITRAL ad hoc arbitration, Final Award (3 September 2001) para 187.

27   *SGS Société Générale de Surveillance SA v Islamic Republic of Pakistan,* ICSID Case No ARB/01/13, Decision of the Tribunal on Objections to Jurisdiction (6 August 2003) para 184; *Bayindir Insaat Turizm Ticaret Ve Sanayi AS v Islamic Republic of Pakistan,* ICSID Case No ARB/03/29, Decision on Jurisdiction (14 November 2005) paras 99–100, 102; *Alps Finance and Trade AG v The Slovak Republic,* UNCITRAL ad hoc arbitration, Award (5 March 2011) paras 201–2.

28   *Ronald S Lauder v Czechia* (n 26) para 187.

29   ibid para 190.

30   *Biwater Gauff (Tanzania) Ltd v United Republic of Tanzania,* ICSID Case No ARB/05/22, Award (24 July 2008) para 343.

Qualifying conditions precedent as procedural and pertaining to the admissibility of claims allows tribunals to observe other factors, such as procedural economy, when deciding whether to allow the arbitration to proceed.[31] Notably, tribunals make these qualifications in general terms, observing the general function of notification and waiting/negotiation requirements.[32] This leads to concrete results: requalifying conditions precedent from jurisdiction to admissibility relaxes the conditions of access to arbitration.

Another known condition precedent requires investors to litigate before domestic courts for a defined period of time before initiating arbitration.[33] Practice is again divided: some tribunals qualify local litigation requirements as conditions of jurisdiction,[34] while others regard them as pertaining to the admissibility of claims.[35] The latter group of tribunals assert discretion in the application of these requirements. The Tribunal in *Abaclat and others v Argentina* considered that a local litigation requirement did not pertain to state consent but to the 'implementation of consent' and therefore to the admissibility of claims.[36] The Tribunal held that it had to assess whether a disregard

---

31 SGS *Société Générale de Surveillance SA v Pakistan* (n 27) para 184 ('it does not appear consistent with the need for orderly and cost-effective procedure to halt this arbitration at this juncture and require the Claimant first to consult with the Respondent before re-submitting the Claimant's BIT claims to this Tribunal'). See also *Western NIS Enterprise Fund v Ukraine*, ICSID Case No ARB/04/2, Order (16 March 2006) para 7.

32 See, for example, *Biwater Gauff (Tanzania) Ltd v Tanzania* (n 30) para 343 ('Its [the waiting requirement's] underlying purpose is to facilitate opportunities for amicable settlement. Its purpose is not to impede or obstruct arbitration proceedings, where such settlement is not possible.').

33 See generally Christoph Schreuer, 'Calvo's Grandchildren: The Return of Local Remedies in Investment Arbitration' (2005) 4 LPICT 1, 3–5; Facundo Pérez Aznar, 'Local Litigation Requirements in International Investment Agreements: Their Characteristics and Potential in Times of Reform in Latin America' (2016) 17 JWIT 536.

34 *Wintershall Aktiengesellschaft v Argentine Republic*, ICSID Case No ARB/04/14, Award (8 December 2008) paras 133–53; *Impregilo SpA v Argentine Republic*, ICSID Case No ARB/07/17, Award (21 June 2011) para 94; *ICS Inspection and Control Services Limited (United Kingdom) v The Argentine Republic*, PCA Case No 2010-9, Award on Jurisdiction (10 February 2012) paras 258–62; *Daimler Financial Services AG v Argentine Republic*, ICSID Case No ARB/05/1, Award (22 August 2012) paras 193–4; *Kiliç İnşaat İthalat İhracat Sanayi Ve Ticaret Anonim Şirketi v Turkmenistan*, ICSID Case No ARB/10/1, Award (2 July 2013) paras 6.3.1-15.

35 *Hochtief AG v Argentina* (n 6) para 96; *İçkale İnşaat Limited Şirketi v Turkmenistan* (n 17) paras 241–2; *Casinos Austria International GmbH and Casinos Austria Aktiengesellschaft v Argentina* (n 17) paras 279–80; *Telefónica SA v The Argentine Republic*, ICSID Case No ARB/03/20, Decision of the Tribunal on Objections to Jurisdiction (25 May 2006) para 93.

36 *Abaclat and others v Argentina* (Decision) (n 17) para 496.

of the local litigation requirement precluded proceeding with the case.[37] In exercising that discretion, tribunals have observed various factors like fairness, efficiency,[38] and appropriateness.[39] Here again, tribunals have qualified local litigation requirements as conditions of jurisdiction or admissibility in general terms. They have based the qualifications on generalised and theoretical views on conditions precedent[40] and the functioning of consent to arbitration,[41] producing practical effects on the rigidity of the access to arbitration.

The Supreme Court of the United States (USSC) has supported the distinction between jurisdictional and procedural conditions in the investment arbitration context, but inspired by the US domestic law. In *BG Group plc v Argentina,* the USSC held that a local litigation requirement was not a condition of consent of the respondent state, but a procedural requirement in initiating arbitration.[42] The USSC drew an analogy to contractual relationships,[43] and then held that the fact that the instrument in question was a treaty did not make any difference, applying the US domestic law to treaties.[44] The USSC was manifestly wrong: assessing whether conditions precedent relate to jurisdiction or admissibility, courts should observe the governing law of arbitration agreements, which is public international law.[45] In light of what has been said

---

37 ibid paras 579–80.
38 ibid para 579.
39 *İçkale İnşaat Limited Şirketi v Turkmenistan* (n 17) paras 262–3. See also *Casinos Austria International GmbH and Casinos Austria Aktiengesellschaft v Argentina* (n 17) para 319 (considering the fair administration of international justice and the principle of good faith).
40 *Abaclat and others v Argentina* (Decision) (n 17) paras 579, 581 (stating that the dispute resolution clause including a local litigation requirement 'is a system aimed at providing the disputing parties with a fair and efficient dispute settlement mechanism', and then holding that the purpose of the local litigation requirement is to give a fair opportunity to the host state to resolve the dispute within its own domestic system).
41 cf *Kiliç İnşaat İthalat İhracat Sanayi Ve Ticaret Anonim Şirketi v Turkmenistan* (n 34) para 6.2.1 ('It is a fundamental principle that an agreement is formed by offer and acceptance.'); with *İçkale İnşaat Limited Şirketi v Turkmenistan* (n 17) paras 243–4 (rebutting the offer-acceptance theory and advancing the theory of unilateral state consent).
42 *BG Group plc v Republic of Argentina* (2014) 572 US ___, 8 ('It determines *when* the contractual duty to arbitrate arises, not *whether* there is a contractual duty to arbitrate at all.').
43 ibid 6 ('In answering the question, we shall initially treat the document before us as if it were an ordinary contract between private parties.').
44 ibid 10 (stating that '[a]s a general matter, a treaty is a contract, though between nations', that '[i]ts interpretation normally is, like a contract's interpretation, a matter of determining the parties' intent', and referring to several precedents in that respect; the USSC did not pay any attention to the international law rules of treaty interpretation).
45 Fabio G Santacroce, 'Navigating the Troubled Waters between Jurisdiction and Admissibility: An Analysis of Which Law Should Govern Characterization of Preliminary

above, had it applied public international law and the practice of investment tribunals, the USSC could have reached the same outcome.[46]

2.3   Applicable Procedure as an Issue of Admissibility

The principal problem in *Abaclat and others v Argentina* was the introduction of mass claims in investment arbitration. Out of its many questions,[47] only one is relevant for the present discussion. The Tribunal allowed mass claim proceedings, as a hybrid which starts as an aggregate but continues as a representative process due to the large number of the claimants.[48] The key to that conclusion was divorcing, although arguably wrongly, the applicable procedure from party consent and analysing it through the lens of admissibility.[49] According to the Tribunal, the mass aspect of the process did not concern party consent but the 'modalities and implementation of the ICSID proceedings', and therefore related to the admissibility of the claims and not jurisdiction.[50] This meant that the Tribunal did not need to look for special consent to a mass claim process.[51] Acknowledging that the ICSID framework did not have appropriate rules for processing mass claims, the Tribunal asserted the power to fill gaps in the applicable procedure, which made the mass claim process admissible.[52] The Tribunal was explicit that it did not have the power to

---

Issues in International Arbitration' (2017) 33 Arb Int'l 539, 565–6; Friedrich Rosenfeld, 'Arbitral Praeliminaria – Reflections on the Distinction between Admissibility and Jurisdiction after *BG v. Argentina*' (2016) 29 Leiden JIL 137, 152.

46   cf *BG Group plc v Republic of Argentina* (Roberts CJ dissenting) (2014) 572 US __, 6–7 (referring to the arbitral decisions that considered local litigation requirements as conditions of jurisdiction) and 14 ('None of them—not a single one [case cited by the majority]—involves an agreement between sovereigns or an agreement to which the person seeking to compel arbitration is not even a party.').

47   See, among many others, Hans van Houtte and Bridie McAsey, '*Abaclat and Others v Argentine Republic:* ICSID, the BIT and Mass Claims' (2012) 27 ICSID Rev-FILJ 231; Andrea Marco Steingruber, '*Abaclat and Others v Argentine Republic:* Consent in Large-Scale Arbitration Proceedings' (2012) 27 ICSID Rev-FILJ 237; SI Strong, 'Mass Procedures in *Abaclat v. Argentine Republic* – Are They Consistent with the International Investment Regime?' in Marianne Roth and Michael Geistlinger (eds), *Yearbook on International Arbitration*, vol 3 (NWV Verlag 2013) 261; Berk Demirkol, 'Does an Investment Treaty Tribunal Need Special Consent for Mass Claims?' (2013) 2 Cambridge Int'l LJ 612; Ridhi Kabra, 'Has *Abaclat v Argentina* Left the ICSID with a 'Mass'Ive Problem?' (2015) 31 Arb Int'l 425.

48   *Abaclat and others v Argentina* (Decision) (n 17) para 488.

49   Relja Radović, 'Problematizing *Abaclat's* Mass Claims Investment Arbitration Using Domestic Class Actions' (2017) 4 McGill J Disp Resol 1, 12–5.

50   *Abaclat and others v Argentina* (Decision) (n 17) para 492.

51   ibid paras 489–92.

52   ibid paras 521–47.

modify the existing rules of procedure or adopt full sets of rules,[53] but it factually reached that end,[54] which is visible in the changes it has implemented throughout the process.[55] The Tribunal was led by the same theoretical distinction between conditions of consent and conditions of 'implementation of consent' as in the context of the local litigation requirement,[56] disregarding the fact that the applicable procedure was defined together with its power to adjudicate in the BIT and the ICSID Convention. Another tribunal dealing with a related case criticised *Abaclat's* disregard of party consent in a multi-party scenario.[57] Although it did not consider to involve a 'mass aspect' (meaning a large number of claimants causing serious repercussions on the process), the latter tribunal also discussed the issues of procedure and the manageability of the case in the context of admissibility.[58]

3   Rules Bypassing the Conditions of Access

Regardless of the qualification of conditions of access as relating to jurisdiction or admissibility, tribunals have developed specific rules allowing for their circumvention or easier satisfaction. These rules have been developed in the context of conditions precedent (1) and fork-in-the-road clauses (2).

3.1   *Bypassing Conditions Precedent*

While the qualification of conditions precedent as relating to admissibility in itself provides flexibility in their application, the rules discussed here allow bypassing conditions precedent regardless of their character. Arbitral tribunals have developed three rules in particular affecting the application of conditions

---

53   ibid para 524.
54   ibid para 525 ('the filling of the gap does not consist of an amendment of the written rule itself, but rather of an adaptation of its application in a specific case'). See also Radović (n 49) 16–7.
55   See, for the introduction of a representative relief, Radović (n 49) 18–20.
56   See s 2.2 above.
57   *Giovanni Alemanni and others v The Argentine Republic*, ICSID Case No ARB/07/8, Decision on Jurisdiction and Admissibility (17 November 2014) para 289.
58   ibid paras 321–5. The Tribunal distinguished 'between those objections that raise the issue whether the Parties have duly consented to the dispute being brought to ICSID arbitration (which fall more on the "jurisdictional" side of the line) and those objections that raise the question whether, even if the Parties have duly consented, there nevertheless exist reasons why the Tribunal should decline to hear the dispute in the form in which the dispute is brought before it, even though it possesses the formal competence to do so (which thus fall more on the "admissibility" side of the line)': ibid para 260.

precedent: the futility exception (1), the *Mavrommatis* principle (2), and the identity of disputes test (3).

3.1.1 Futility

Conditions precedent such as attempts at amicable settlement or local litigation can be avoided if they are futile.[59] The exception is usually not regulated explicitly,[60] which gives regulatory space to tribunals, and scholars have recognised the exception's development in practice.[61] The sources of inspiration for the futility exception are clearly external to party-provided jurisdictional rules: from analogies to the law of diplomatic protection and the exhaustion of domestic remedies,[62] to previous investment decisions as established practice,[63] to constructions of logic,[64] to no clearly indicated sources.[65] Bearing this in mind, some tribunals have opined that if a futility exception does not

---

[59] See, in the context of the exhaustion of domestic remedies, James R Crawford and Thomas D Grant, 'Local Remedies, Exhaustion Of' in Rüdiger Wolfrum (ed), *The Max Planck Encyclopedia of Public International Law,* vol 6 (OUP 2012) 900 ('A remedy which is practically or legally unavailable to the claimant is not a real remedy in this sense.').

[60] cf India Model BIT (2015) art 15(1) <https://investmentpolicy.unctad.org/international-investment-agreements/treaty-files/3560/download> accessed 20 August 2020 (requiring that 'there are no available domestic legal remedies capable of reasonably providing any relief'); Agreement Between the United States of America, the United Mexican States, and Canada (signed 30 November 2018 and 10 December 2019, entered into force 1 July 2020) art 14.D.5(1)(b), fn 25 (requiring that 'recourse to domestic remedies was obviously futile').

[61] Christoph Schreuer, 'Travelling the BIT Route: Of Waiting Periods, Umbrella Clauses and Forks in the Road' (2004) 5 JWIT 231, 238.

[62] *Ambiente Ufficio SpA and others v Argentina* (n 11) para 599 and paras 600–7 (the Tribunal argued that the futility exception from the law of diplomatic protection was relevant via Article 31(3)(c) of the VCLT); *Giovanni Alemanni and others v Argentina* (n 57) paras 315–6. See also *Ethyl Corporation v The Government of Canada,* UNCITRAL ad hoc arbitration, Award on Jurisdiction (24 June 1998) para 84.

[63] *Occidental Petroleum Corporation and Occidental Exploration and Production Company v The Republic of Ecuador,* ICSID Case No ARB/06/11, Decision on Jurisdiction (9 September 2008) para 94; *Teinver SA, Transportes de Cercanías SA, and Autobuses Urbanos del Sur SA v The Argentine Republic,* ICSID Case No ARB/09/1, Decision on Jurisdiction (21 December 2012) paras 126–9.

[64] *BG Group Plc v The Republic of Argentina,* UNCITRAL ad hoc arbitration, Final Award (24 December 2007) para 147 (declining to apply the futility exception from the law of diplomatic protection, but holding that interpreting a local litigation requirement as absolute could lead to absurd results allowing states to avoid arbitration by preventing local litigation).

[65] *Consorzio Groupement LESI-DIPENTA v People's Democratic Republic of Algeria,* ICSID Case No ARB/03/08, Award (10 January 2005) para 32(iv).

appear in the relevant BIT it would be impossible to accept its existence.[66] Others have accepted the futility exception in principle, but have expressed reservations towards reading it freely into treaty texts.[67] Nevertheless, the futility exception now seems generally accepted and it has been recognised even by some tribunals which have not been able or forced to apply it.[68]

A bigger controversy is the threshold that should be applied under this exception. Some tribunals have not addressed this issue at all and proceeded immediately to the facts.[69] Others have addressed it, mostly in the context of local litigation requirements. One approach requires an 'obvious futility' of local litigation.[70] Another approach argues that 'obvious futility' is a too strict standard, and adopts the standard formulated by the International Law Commission (ILC) regarding the exhaustion of domestic remedies, namely that '[t]here are no reasonably available local remedies to provide effective redress, or the local remedies provide no reasonable possibility of such redress'.[71] Some tribunals have gone beyond the futility exception as such, and attempted to formulate a specific test stemming from the purpose of local litigation requirements. According to the Tribunal in *Urbaser v Argentina*, this requirement imposes a tougher burden on states, who should not only avoid futility but ensure that investors have proper opportunities to address their claims.[72] The value of this decision is that it recalls that regardless of the declared threshold of futility, the terms of the requirement at stake must be observed.[73] The practice on the

---

66   *İçkale İnşaat Limited Şirketi v Turkmenistan* (n 17) para 260.
67   *ICS Inspection and Control Services Limited (United Kingdom) v Argentina* (n 34) paras 265–7.
68   *Abaclat and others v Argentina* (Decision) (n 17) para 584; *Daimler Financial Services AG v Argentina* (n 34) paras 190–1; *Kiliç İnşaat İthalat İhracat Sanayi Ve Ticaret Anonim Şirketi v Turkmenistan* (n 34) paras 8.1.1-21; *Ömer Dede and Serdar Elhüseyni v Romania*, ICSID Case No ARB/10/22, Award (5 September 2013) paras 256, 259–60.
69   *Occidental Petroleum Corporation and Occidental Exploration and Production Company v Ecuador* (n 63) para 94; *Teinver SA, Transportes de Cercanías SA, and Autobuses Urbanos del Sur SA v Argentina* (Jurisdiction) (n 63) paras 126–9.
70   *ICS Inspection and Control Services Limited (United Kingdom) v Argentina* (n 34) para 269 ('This is not a case of obvious futility, where the relief sought is patently unavailable within the Argentine legal system.').
71   *Ambiente Ufficio SpA and others v Argentina* (n 11) paras 608–11. For this exception regarding the exhaustion of local remedies in diplomatic protection, see art 15(a) in ILC, 'Diplomatic Protection', *Yearbook of the International Law Commission 2006*, vol II (Part Two) (UN 2013) 26.
72   *Urbaser SA and CABB v Argentina* (n 13) para 131.
73   See also *Murphy Exploration and Production Company International v Ecuador* (n 22) para 135 ('[…] the obligation to negotiate is an obligation of means, not of results. There is no obligation to reach, but rather to try to reach, an agreement. To determine whether negotiations would succeed or not, the parties must first initiate them.').

threshold of futility is therefore less settled, but what appears well-established is that the futility exception exists independently of treaty texts.

3.1.2 The *Mavrommatis* Principle

The PCIJ has established in its practice the so-called *Mavrommatis* principle, according to which the Court will not decline jurisdiction if some conditions were not met at the time of its seizure but have become satisfied subsequently before the ruling on jurisdiction, so that the requesting party could simply reinstitute the proceedings.[74] The ICJ continues to apply this principle.[75] The same principle has been applied by investment tribunals. Some tribunals have been openly inspired by the ICJ practice.[76] Others have not been clear on this point, simply holding that 'it would be highly formalistic' to decline jurisdiction when the claimant could immediately start new arbitration.[77] The application of this principle has direct effects on conditions precedent, because it results in declining to send the parties to other (prior) dispute settlement means such as negotiation and local litigation. The usual motive is that the time has already passed and the parties have not been able to settle their dispute outside arbitration.[78]

3.1.3 Identity of Disputes

The requirement to litigate before domestic courts for some time before resorting to arbitration raises another question: when should the requirement be considered satisfied? Answering this question assumes developing criteria

---

74 *Mavrommatis Palestine Concessions (Greece v UK)* (Judgment) (1924) PCIJ Ser A—No 2, 6, 34.
75 *Application of the Convention on the Prevention and Punishment of the Crime of Genocide (Croatia v Serbia)* (Preliminary Objections) (2008) ICJ Rep 412, paras 81–91.
76 *Philip Morris Brands Sàrl, Philip Morris Products SA, and Abal Hermanos SA v Oriental Republic of Uruguay*, ICSID Case No ARB/10/7, Decision on Jurisdiction (2 July 2013) paras 144–8; *Teinver SA, Transportes de Cercanías SA, and Autobuses Urbanos del Sur SA v Argentina* (Jurisdiction) (n 63) para 135; *Casinos Austria International GmbH and Casinos Austria Aktiengesellschaft v Argentina* (n 17) paras 320–7. See also *Salini Impregilo SpA v Argentine Republic*, ICSID Case No ARB/15/39, Decision on Jurisdiction and Admissibility (23 February 2018) para 139 (following *Philip Morris v Uruguay*).
77 *TSA Spectrum de Argentina SA v Argentine Republic*, ICSID Case No ARB/05/5, Award (19 December 2008) para 112; *Ethyl Corporation v Canada* (n 62) para 85.
78 *Philip Morris Brands Sàrl, Philip Morris Products SA, and Abal Hermanos SA v Uruguay* (n 76) para 146; *Teinver SA, Transportes de Cercanías SA, and Autobuses Urbanos del Sur SA v Argentina* (Jurisdiction) (n 63) para 135; *TSA Spectrum de Argentina SA v Argentina* (n 77) para 111; *Ethyl Corporation v Canada* (n 62) para 85; *Casinos Austria International GmbH and Casinos Austria Aktiengesellschaft v Argentina* (n 17) paras 319, 328.

indicating compliance with the requirement. Developing uniform criteria seems unrealistic, because of different formulations of the requirement, on the one hand, and differently organised local judiciaries, on the other. Nevertheless, tribunals have tried to do so and have achieved a certain degree of consistency.

One option is to apply the 'triple identity' test, which targets the identity of the parties, the object of the dispute, and the cause of action.[79] However, tribunals have considered this test too strict, and focused on the subject matter of disputes instead. The Tribunal in *Philip Morris v Uruguay* started from the notion of 'dispute' in the BIT, arguing that it was a broad one and not limited to breaches of the BIT.[80] This led the Tribunal to conclude that local litigation did not necessarily need to concern the same cause of action as arbitration;[81] it also held that the litigating parties did not need to be the same as in arbitration.[82] According to this Tribunal, the litigated and arbitrated disputes do not need to be the same.[83] The only requirement is that the subject matter of disputes and the facts must be 'substantially similar' in domestic litigation and arbitration.[84] The Tribunal therefore justified its approach on the grounds of treaty interpretation, although it remains unclear how it came up with the criterion of substantial similarity. The Tribunal in *Teinver v Argentina* held that the same subject matter must be considered by local courts and arbitration.[85] This Tribunal drew an analogy to the exhaustion of domestic remedies in the ICJ practice, rejecting the proposition that the parties and the cause of action must be identical.[86] Another tribunal explicitly rejected the 'triple identity'

---

79 See, for these criteria in the *res judicata* doctrine, *Marco Gavazzi and Stefano Gavazzi v Romania*, ICSID Case No ARB/12/25, Decision on Jurisdiction, Admissibility, and Liability (21 April 2015) para 166.

80 *Philip Morris Brands Sàrl, Philip Morris Products SA, and Abal Hermanos SA v Uruguay* (n 76) paras 105–11.

81 ibid para 113.

82 ibid para 114. The Tribunal found that one of the Claimants satisfied the local litigation requirement in the interest of the other Claimants.

83 ibid para 105.

84 ibid paras 110, 113. See also *Casinos Austria International GmbH and Casinos Austria Aktiengesellschaft v Argentina* (n 17) paras 297, 303–5.

85 *Teinver SA, Transportes de Cercanías SA, and Autobuses Urbanos del Sur SA v Argentina* (Jurisdiction) (n 63) para 134.

86 ibid paras 132–3. See also *Salini Impregilo SpA v Argentina* (n 76) paras 128–33. Interestingly, the Tribunal in *Salini Impregilo v Argentina* isolated the notion of 'dispute' in the local litigation requirement from the rest of the dispute settlement provision. While Article 8(1) of the Argentina-Italy BIT referred to a 'dispute regarding an investment between an investor of one of the Contracting Parties and the other Party, regarding the issues regulated by this Agreement', Article 8(2) simply referred to 'the dispute'. This was not analysed by the Tribunal regarding the issue of cause of action, and the differences between the

test on the ground that treaty breaches could not be litigated domestically.[87] It further held that 'the most reasonable test [...] requires that disputes brought before local courts be of a nature that permits resolution to substantially the same extent as if brought before an international arbitral tribunal pursuant to an investment treaty'.[88]

It can also be asked what type of actions investors should undertake to comply with the requirement of local litigation. The principal contribution from this angle of analysis is the confirmation that local litigation does not necessarily need to concern the same cause of action[89] or the same relief[90] as that pursued in arbitration. It is important that the claimant has brought an entire dispute to local courts, although it remains questionable whether the cause of action and the remedy pursued domestically could lead to the settlement of the entire dispute, ie to the same extent as in arbitration.[91]

Despite the attempts to incorporate their conclusions into interpretative narratives, tribunals have created objective criteria orbiting around the notion of subject matter of dispute, which are determinative in the application of local litigation requirements. These loose criteria, setting out the standard for the implementation of local litigation requirements, relax in consequence the conditions of access to arbitration.

3.2   Bypassing Fork-in-the-Road Clauses

When investors can choose between multiple dispute settlement means, fork-in-the-road clauses make their choice of forum final. If an investor attempts to initiate proceedings before more than one forum, what criteria guide the triggering of a fork-in-the-road clause? This is not an interpretive question, as are questions about the existence of a fork-in-the-road clause[92] and its coverage of different forums.[93] Treaty texts usually lack any indicators, meaning

---

two paragraphs were analysed only regarding the identity of the parties. See ibid paras 115(1)-(2).
87   *Ömer Dede and Serdar Elhüseyni v Romania* (n 68) para 249.
88   ibid para 253.
89   *Urbaser SA and CABB v Argentina* (n 13) para 181.
90   *Wintershall Aktiengesellschaft v Argentina* (n 34) paras 118, 196.
91   *Urbaser SA and CABB v Argentina* (n 13) paras 179–82. See also *Philip Morris Brands Sàrl, Philip Morris Products SA, and Abal Hermanos SA v Uruguay* (n 76) para 112.
92   See, for example, *Beijing Urban Construction Group Co Ltd v Republic of Yemen*, ICSID Case No ARB/14/30, Decision on Jurisdiction (31 May 2017) para 71 (interpreting the word 'or' in the jurisdictional clause as a fork-in-the-road).
93   For example, whether a fork-in-the-road clause applies between local litigation and international arbitration only, or between different arbitral forums as well. See Damien

that tribunals are required to create criteria identifying two disputes as sufficiently identical to trigger a fork-in-the-road clause. Investment tribunals have not created a uniform practice, and have established two streams with smaller variations, although with dominance of one of them.

One stream of practice advocates for the 'triple identity' test, comprising the identity of the parties, the object of the dispute, and the cause of action.[94] Some tribunals have relied on some of these criteria in isolation, such as the cause of action,[95] the object,[96] the parties,[97] or on a combination of two of

---

Charlotin and Luke Eric Peterson, 'The Merck v. Ecuador Award (Part One): Arbitrators Wave Away Jurisdictional Objections – Including on Exhaustion – and Warn That Non-Compliance With Interim Orders Could Aggravate Treaty Breach' (*Investment Arbitration Reporter*, 27 March 2018) <www.iareporter.com/articles/the-merck-v-ecuador-award-part-one-arbitrators-wave-away-ecuadors-jurisdictional-objections-including-on-exhaustion-and-warn-that-ecuadors-non-compliance-with-interim-orders/> accessed 3 January 2019.

94 *Azurix Corp v The Argentine Republic,* ICSID Case No ARB/01/12, Decision on Jurisdiction (8 December 2003) paras 88–90; *Toto Costruzioni Generali SpA v The Republic of Lebanon,* ICSID Case No ARB/07/12, Decision on Jurisdiction (11 September 2009) para 211; *Hulley Enterprises Limited (Cyprus) v The Russian Federation,* PCA Case No AA 226, Interim Award on Jurisdiction and Admissibility (30 November 2009) para 597; *Mobil Exploration and Development Argentina Inc Suc Argentina and Mobil Argentina Sociedad Anónima v The Argentine Republic,* ICSID Case No ARB/04/16, Decision on Jurisdiction and Liability (10 April 2013) para 139; *Hulley Enterprises Limited (Cyprus) v The Russian Federation,* PCA Case No AA 226, Final Award (18 July 2014) paras 1256–72.

95 *Middle East Cement Shipping and Handling Co SA v Arab Republic of Egypt,* ICSID Case No ARB/99/6, Award (12 April 2002) para 71; *Desert Line Projects LLC v The Republic of Yemen,* ICSID Case No ARB/05/17, Award (6 February 2008) para 136. See also *Occidental Exploration and Production Company v The Republic of Ecuador,* LCIA Case No UN3467, Final Award (1 July 2004) paras 52, 57–8.

96 *Olguín v Republic of Paraguay,* ICSID Case No ARB/98/5, Decision on Jurisdiction (8 August 2000) para 30.

97 *Chevron Corporation and Texaco Petroleum Company v The Republic of Ecuador,* PCA Case No 2009-23, Third Interim Award on Jurisdiction and Admissibility (27 February 2012) paras 4.78-9 (starting from the 'triple identity' test, and after expressing some doubts about its sharpness, concluding that the wording of the fork-in-the-road clause implied that there needs to be the identity of the parties); *Charanne BV and Construction Investments SARL v The Kingdom of Spain,* SCC Case No V 062/2012, Final Award (21 January 2016) paras 398–410 (dismissing the objection based on the fork-in-the-road clause solely on the ground of the identity of the parties, which made the examination of the other two criteria unnecessary; but admitting that sometimes the identity of the parties should be analysed flexibly, to prevent avoidance of a fork-in-the-road); *Champion Trading Company and others v Arab Republic of Egypt,* ICSID Case No ARB/02/9, Decision on Jurisdiction (21 October 2003) para 3.4.3 (holding that the fork-in-the-road clause required the identity of the parties).

them.[98] The inspiration for the 'triple identity' test can be found in general legal doctrines such as *res judicata* and *lis pendens*.[99] The analogy seems well founded, because both these doctrines and fork-in-the-road clauses prevent parallel and sequential resolution of the same dispute by multiple forums. An important consideration in the application of these clauses is the coordination between contract and treaty claims, but also between treaty claims and domestic administrative challenges, which has led scholars to support the reliance on the above-mentioned criteria.[100] The 'triple identity' test serves the interests of investors, because it rarely leads to the triggering of fork-in-the-road clauses.

A different stream of practice observes the 'foundational basis of a claim'. In *Pantechniki v Albania*, the Sole Arbitrator applied this test, which was not disputed by the parties.[101] The test was inspired by the discourses in the context of distinguishing contractual and treaty disputes.[102] What was disputed, however, was what amounted to the fundamental basis of a claim, and the Sole Arbitrator held that the relevant question was 'whether claimed entitlements have the same normative source'.[103] He held that 'there comes a time when it is no longer sufficient merely to assert that a claim is founded on the Treaty' and that it must be determined whether the treaty claim was autonomous from the contract,[104] which the Sole Arbitrator found not to be the case because the Claimant was seeking the same relief on the same fundamental basis in both contractual and treaty disputes.[105] This test, therefore, looks beyond causes

---

98   Usually combining cause of action and parties: *Alex Genin, Eastern Credit Limited Inc, and AS Baltoil v The Republic of Estonia*, ICSID Case No ARB/99/2, Award (25 June 2001) paras 331–4; *Ronald S Lauder v Czechia* (n 26) paras 161–6; *Enron Corporation and Ponderosa Assets LP v Argentina* (n 10) paras 97–8; *CMS Gas Transmission Company v Argentina* (n 10) para 80.

99   *Enron Corporation and Ponderosa Assets LP v Argentina* (n 10) para 97; *Azurix Corp v Argentina* (n 94) para 88; *Chevron Corporation and Texaco Petroleum Company v Ecuador* (n 97) para 4.77.

100 Schreuer, 'Travelling the BIT Route' (n 61) 239–49.

101 *Pantechniki SA Contractors & Engineers (Greece) v The Republic of Albania*, ICSID Case No ARB/07/21, Award (30 July 2009) para 61.

102 ibid (referring to the 2002 annulment decision in *Vivendi v Argentina*). See *Compañiá de Aguas del Aconquija SA and Vivendi Universal v Argentine Republic*, ICSID Case No ARB/97/3, Decision on Annulment (3 July 2002) paras 98–101.

103 *Pantechniki SA Contractors & Engineers (Greece) v Albania* (n 101) paras 61–2.

104 ibid para 64.

105 ibid para 67. See also *Supervision y Control SA v Costa Rica* (n 7) paras 308–21 (applying the same test in the context of a waiver/withdrawal of claims requirement).

of action into the factual basis of claims, and it has been adopted elsewhere for that particular reason.[106] A major downside of this test is the lack of clear criteria and the consequent uncertainty. Furthermore, the *Vivendi* annulment decision, which revived the 'foundational basis of a claim' test in the context of the treaty/contract claims distinction, arguably considered the cause of action decisive in the test,[107] although on a separate note it viewed the fork-in-the-road clause not limited to treaty claims given the broadness of the term 'dispute'.[108]

An argument exists that the presence of the notion of 'dispute' in BITs should lead to the harmonisation of the rules applied to local litigation requirements and forks-in-the-road.[109] Some tribunals have indeed started from that notion and derived the criteria of the identity of causes of action and parties from specific definitions of 'investment dispute'.[110] But the same reliance on treaty terms and the notion of 'dispute' can be made in the opposite direction, to rebut the formalities such as those of the 'triple identity' test.[111] Tribunals appear to conflict regarding the purpose and functioning of fork-in-the-road clauses on a general level, and the reliance on treaty terms has rather a justificatory role in legal reasoning. Treaty-transcending criteria therefore take precedence over the actual terms of treaties, creating objective standards for the application of fork-in-the-road clauses. Because the 'triple identity' test dominates in practice compared to the 'fundamental basis of a claim' test, the widespread acceptance of the former in effect relaxes the conditions of access to arbitration.

---

106 *H&H Enterprises Investments Inc v The Arab Republic of Egypt,* ICSID Case No ARB/09/15, Award (6 May 2014) paras 366–85.
107 *Compañiá de Aguas del Aconquija SA and Vivendi Universal v Argentina* (n 102) paras 93–115; see also, for such a reading of this decision, *Occidental Exploration and Production Company v Ecuador* (n 95) paras 52–3.
108 *Compañiá de Aguas del Aconquija SA and Vivendi Universal v Argentina* (n 102) para 55.
109 Pérez Aznar (n 33) 554–5. See also Michal Swarabowicz, 'Identity of Claims in Investment Arbitration: A Plea for Unity of the Legal System' (2017) 8 JIDS 280 (supporting standardisation from a broader perspective).
110 *Ronald S Lauder v Czechia* (n 26) paras 158–61; *Alex Genin, Eastern Credit Limited Inc, and AS Baltoil v Estonia* (n 98) para 325; *Middle East Cement Shipping and Handling Co SA v Egypt* (n 95) para 71. See also *Nissan Motor Co Ltd (Japan) v The Republic of India,* PCA Case No 2017-37, Decision on Jurisdiction (29 April 2019) paras 210–3.
111 *H&H Enterprises Investments Inc v Egypt* (n 106) para 367; *Compañiá de Aguas del Aconquija SA and Vivendi Universal v Argentina* (n 102) para 55.

98   CHAPTER 2

4   Most-Favoured-Nation Clause as a Jurisdictional Panacea

The applicability of MFN clauses to dispute resolution clauses is possibly the most-examined topic in international investment law and arbitration.[112] I examine here only one aspect of that debate: the creation of presumptions governing the issue. I first set the scene by discussing the increased blending of dispute settlement clauses with the substantive investor protections (1). I then address the two presumptions (in favour and against the applicability of MFN clauses to dispute resolution clauses) that have appeared in practice (2), and finally I discuss the operation of these presumptions in practice (3).

4.1   *Dispute Resolution as Substantive Protection*
MFN clauses indisputably apply to the substantive investor protections.[113] The issue is their applicability to dispute settlement clauses, ie procedural norms which do not regulate the lawfulness of state conduct, but establish the jurisdiction of arbitral tribunals. The theoretical conceptions about the distinction between 'substantive' and 'procedural' rules and their function provide

---

112   See, among many others, Rudolf Dolzer and Terry Myers, 'After *Tecmed:* Most-Favored-Nation Clauses in Investment Protection Agreements' (2004) 19 ICSID Rev-FILJ 49; Dana H Freyer and David Herlihy, 'Most-Favored-Nation Treatment and Dispute Settlement in Investment Arbitration: Just How "Favored" Is "Most-Favored"?' (2005) 20 ICSID Rev-FILJ 58; Yannick Radi, 'The Application of the Most-Favoured-Nation Clause to the Dispute Settlement Provisions of Bilateral Investment Treaties: Domesticating the "Trojan Horse"' (2007) 18 EJIL 757; Scott Vesel, 'Clearing a Path Through a Tangled Jurisprudence: Most-Favored-Nation Clauses and Dispute Settlement Provisions in Bilateral Investment Treaties' (2007) 32 Yale J Int'l L 125; Jarrod Wong, 'The Application of Most-Favored-Nation Clauses to Dispute Resolution Provisions in Bilateral Investment Treaties' (2008) 3 AJWH 171; Nartnirun Junngam, 'An MFN Clause and BIT Dispute Settlement: A Host State's Implied Consent to Arbitration by Reference' (2010) 15 UCLA J Int'l L & For Aff 399; Zachary Douglas, 'The MFN Clause in Investment Arbitration: Treaty Interpretation Off the Rails' (2011) 2 JIDS 97; Martins Paparinskis, 'MFN Clauses and International Dispute Settlement: Moving beyond *Maffezini* and *Plama*?' (2011) 26 ICSID Rev-FILJ 14; Sam Wordsworth and Chester Brown, 'A Re-Run of *Siemens, Wintershall* and *Hochtief* on Most-Favoured-Nation Clauses: *Daimler Financial Services AG v Argentine Republic*' (2015) 30 ICSID Rev-FILJ 365.
113   However, it is disputable whether MFN clauses can import new substantive rights, not provided for in the basic BIT. cf *EDF International SA, SAUR International SA, and León Participaciones Argentinas SA v Argentine Republic,* ICSID Case No ARB/03/23, Award (11 June 2012) para 929 (importing an umbrella clause); with *Teinver SA, Transportes de Cercanías SA, and Autobuses Urbanos del Sur SA v The Argentine Republic,* ICSID Case No ARB/09/1, Award (21 July 2017) paras 884–92 (rejecting the importation of an umbrella clause).

a fertile soil for the arguments both in favour and against the applicability of MFN clauses to dispute resolution clauses in principle.

The very first decision that allowed the application of an MFN clause to a dispute settlement clause, *Maffezini v Spain*, held that 'today dispute settlement arrangements are inextricably related to the protection of foreign investors',[114] and stressed the importance of dispute settlement arrangements for the protection of foreign investors.[115] Other tribunals have gone beyond establishing a link between dispute settlement and substantive protection. The Tribunal in *Gas Natural v Argentina* held that the 'provision for international investor-state arbitration in [BITs] is a significant substantive incentive and protection for foreign investors',[116] 'that assurance of independent international arbitration is an important – perhaps the most important – element in investor protection',[117] and that it therefore formed part of 'the bundle of protections granted to foreign investors'.[118] Another tribunal maintained that the access to international arbitration 'is a protective right that sits alongside the guarantees against arbitrary and discriminatory measures, expropriation, and so on'.[119] The mingling of dispute settlement clauses with the rules of substantive protection is therefore motivated by their protective function towards investors, inclining tribunals not to draw any line between substantive and procedural rules.[120]

A different stream of practice has observed a very strong separation between substantive and procedural rules and built arguments against the applicability of MFN clauses to dispute resolution clauses.[121] According to these tribunals,

---

114   *Emilio Agustín Maffezini v The Kingdom of Spain*, ICSID Case No ARB/97/7, Decision of the Tribunal on Objections to Jurisdiction (25 January 2000) para 54.
115   ibid para 55.
116   *Gas Natural SDG SA v The Argentine Republic*, ICSID Case No ARB/03/10, Decision of the Tribunal on Preliminary Questions on Jurisdiction (17 June 2005) para 31.
117   ibid para 49.
118   ibid para 29.
119   *Hochtief AG v Argentina* (n 6) para 68.
120   *Suez, Sociedad General de Aguas de Barcelona SA, and InterAguas Servicios Integrales del Agua SA v The Argentine Republic*, ICSID Case No ARB/03/17, Decision on Jurisdiction (16 May 2006) para 57; *Suez, Sociedad General de Aguas de Barcelona SA, and Vivendi Universal SA v The Argentine Republic*, ICSID Case No ARB/03/19, and *AWG Group Ltd v The Argentine Republic*, UNCITRAL arbitration, Decision on Jurisdiction (3 August 2006) para 59.
121   *Vladimir Berschader & Moïse Berschader v The Russian Federation*, SCC Case No 80/2004, Award (21 April 2006) paras 185–208; *Telenor Mobile Communications AS v The Republic of Hungary*, ICSID Case No ARB/04/15, Award (13 September 2006) para 92; *Wintershall Aktiengesellschaft v Argentina* (n 34) para 168; *European American Investment Bank AG (Austria) v The Slovak Republic*, PCA Case No 2010-17, Award on Jurisdiction (22

the different nature of procedural clauses from those granting the substantive investor protections precludes their mingling and militates against the applicability of MFN clauses to dispute settlement clauses.

The value of the opinions that dispute settlement clauses form part of investment protection, however, should not be overemphasised. They can neither change the character of dispute settlement clauses, nor break the traditional separation between substantive and procedural rules in international law, and they have a justificatory role in allowing the application of MFN clauses to dispute settlement clauses.[122] However, this is an important contribution for the present discussion: by stressing the protective nature of dispute settlement arrangements, or rejecting their shared character with substantive protections, tribunals set the scene for the creation of principled presumptions in favour or against the applicability of MFN clauses to dispute settlement clauses.

4.2 *Presumptions on the MFN-Dispute Resolution Conjunction*

The issue of the applicability of MFN clauses to dispute settlement provisions appeared with the attempts to bypass conditions precedent and thus facilitate the access to international arbitration (1). The solutions created in that context proved problematic with the attempts to establish substantive jurisdiction via the same route (2).

4.2.1 Conditions Precedent and Presumed Applicability

In 2000, the *Maffezini v Spain* Tribunal allowed a local litigation requirement to be bypassed via an MFN clause and a third-party BIT which did not contain such a requirement.[123] The Tribunal created a presumption in favour of the applicability of MFN clauses to dispute resolution clauses, which is visible in its general formulation, on the one hand,[124] and the system of exceptions from

---

October 2012) paras 445–52; *Kiliç İnşaat İthalat İhracat Sanayi Ve Ticaret Anonim Şirketi v Turkmenistan* (n 34) para 7.3.9. See also *Tecnicas Medioambientales Tecmed SA v The United Mexican States*, ICSID Case No ARB(AF)/00/2, Award (29 May 2003) para 69.

122 Relja Radović, 'Between Rights and Remedies: The Access to Investment Treaty Arbitration as a Substantive Right of Foreign Investors' (2019) 10 JIDS 42.

123 *Emilio Agustín Maffezini v Spain* (n 114) para 64.

124 ibid para 56 ('From the above considerations it can be concluded that if a third party treaty contains provisions for the settlement of disputes that are more favorable to the protection of the investor's rights and interests than those in the basic treaty, such provisions may be extended to the beneficiary of the most favored nation clause as they are fully compatible with the *ejusdem generis* principle.').

that presumption, on the other.[125] This precedent has been followed by many other tribunals which have faced the same issue of bypassing local litigation requirements using MFN clauses.[126] Confirming the principle, the Tribunal in *Gas Natural v Argentina* considered that '[u]nless it appears clearly that the state parties to a BIT or the parties to a particular investment agreement settled on a different method for resolution of disputes that may arise, most-favored-nation provisions in BITs should be understood to be applicable to dispute settlement'.[127] Another formulation of the presumption targets specific wording of MFN clauses. The Tribunal in *Impregilo v Argentina* held that 'in cases where the MFN clause has referred to "all matters" or "any matter" regulated in the BIT, there has been near-unanimity in finding that the clause covered the dispute settlement rules', on which basis it concluded that the MFN clause was applicable to dispute settlement.[128]

The rule supported by these tribunals presumes the applicability of MFN clauses to dispute settlement clauses and instructs tribunals to inquire whether treaty drafters have intended to exclude the possibility of that conjunction. Tribunals have anticipated different possible indicators of exclusion, such as special dispute settlement arrangements (*Gas Natural*) and narrow wording of an MFN clause (*Impregilo*). The absence of such indicators militates in favour of concluding that an MFN clause is applicable to a dispute settlement clause.[129] Therefore, the central value of the presumption is the definition of the

---

125   ibid paras 62–3 ('As a matter of principle, the beneficiary of the clause should not be able to override public policy considerations that the contracting parties might have envisaged as fundamental conditions for their acceptance of the agreement in question, particularly if the beneficiary is a private investor, as will often be the case.' The Tribunal named the exhaustion of domestic remedies, fork-in-the-road clauses, selection of a specific arbitration forum, arbitral institutionalised system and rules of procedure, as examples of such public policy considerations.).

126   *Siemens AG v The Argentine Republic*, ICSID Case No ARB/02/8, Decision on Jurisdiction (3 August 2004) paras 102–3; *Telefónica SA v Argentina* (n 35) paras 105–6; *Suez, Sociedad General de Aguas de Barcelona SA, and InterAguas Servicios Integrales del Agua SA v Argentina* (n 120) para 60; *Suez, Sociedad General de Aguas de Barcelona SA, and Vivendi Universal SA/AWG v Argentina* (n 120) para 62; *National Grid plc v The Argentine Republic*, UNCITRAL ad hoc arbitration, Decision on Jurisdiction (20 June 2006) para 92. A rebuttable presumption in favour of the applicability of MFN clauses to dispute settlement provisions has also been supported by scholars: Radi (n 112) 764–71; Stephan W Schill, *The Multilateralization of International Investment Law* (CUP 2009) 173–93.

127   *Gas Natural SDG SA v Argentina* (n 116) para 49.

128   *Impregilo SpA v Argentina* (Award) (n 34) para 108.

129   See conclusion in ibid.

interpretative question and the direction of the interpretative process towards seeking the indicators of exclusion.[130] This effect has been explicitly recognised in practice.[131]

Some tribunals have shown awareness that general premises can lead to dangerous effects, shifting the focus to concrete conditions precedent as minor jurisdictional issues. In *Hochtief v Argentina*, the Tribunal firstly concluded that an MFN clause was applicable to the dispute settlement clause 'in principle', invoking the latter's protective purpose and establishing it on an equal footing with the rules of substantive protection.[132] But then, the Tribunal held that the local litigation requirement did not constitute new rights of investors but a procedural rule in the implementation of the right to arbitrate, that it concerned the admissibility of claims and not jurisdiction, which enabled its bypassing via the MFN clause.[133] It has become apparent that not all jurisdictional limits can be tackled using an MFN clause, or as one tribunal put it, some claimants have tried to apply MFN clauses 'beyond appropriate limits'.[134] However, these tribunals have not faced major jurisdictional extensions themselves, and therefore despite such reservations they have rather affirmed the general applicability of MFN clauses to dispute settlement provisions. Furthermore, this has not been a universal trend, and some tribunals have insisted on qualifying local litigation requirements as jurisdictional while bypassing them via an MFN clause.[135]

4.2.2 Substantive Jurisdiction and Presumed Inapplicability

When *Maffezini* and other tribunals were formulating the presumption, they did not distinguish between the questions of jurisdiction and admissibility. Indeed, the *Maffezini* Tribunal itself qualified the local litigation requirement as jurisdictional.[136] Although these tribunals have faced relatively minor issues (bypassing conditions precedent), the generality of their presumption opened the door for using the same route towards more serious

---

130 See, for examples of setting interpretive questions, *Telefónica SA v Argentina* (n 35) para 100; *Suez, Sociedad General de Aguas de Barcelona SA, and InterAguas Servicios Integrales del Agua SA v Argentina* (n 120) paras 56–7; *Suez, Sociedad General de Aguas de Barcelona SA, and Vivendi Universal SA/AWG v Argentina* (n 120) paras 58–9.
131 *Wintershall Aktiengesellschaft v Argentina* (n 34) para 184; *Teinver SA, Transportes de Cercanías SA, and Autobuses Urbanos del Sur SA v Argentina* (Jurisdiction) (n 63) para 173.
132 *Hochtief AG v Argentina* (n 6) paras 59–72.
133 ibid paras 77–99. See also *Teinver SA, Transportes de Cercanías SA, and Autobuses Urbanos del Sur SA v Argentina* (Jurisdiction) (n 63) para 182.
134 *National Grid plc v Argentina* (n 126) para 92.
135 *Impregilo SpA v Argentina* (Award) (n 34) paras 94, 108.
136 *Emilio Agustín Maffezini v Spain* (n 114) para 36.

jurisdictional questions (like extending the scope of justiciable disputes). On some occasions, substantive jurisdiction was indeed extended with the help of an MFN clause: in *RosInvest v Russia*, the Tribunal allowed the Claimant to rely on an MFN clause to extend its jurisdiction over the issue of occurrence of expropriation;[137] the Tribunal in *Le Chèque Déjeuner* thus established jurisdiction over the alleged breaches of the fair and equitable treatment, which were not arbitrable under the basic BIT.[138] While the *RosInvest* Tribunal showed restraint towards general considerations on the issue,[139] the Tribunal in *Le Chèque Déjeuner* showed more openness for such endeavours,[140] and applied the same presumption as in the cases discussed above.[141]

The tribunals that have expressed conceptual struggles with the MFN-dispute resolution conjunction have been more willing to engage in the discourse on that issue. In *Plama v Bulgaria*, the Tribunal was asked to incorporate consent to ICSID arbitration with a broader scope through an MFN clause. Reacting to *Maffezini*, the Tribunal held

> that the principle with multiple exceptions as stated by the tribunal in the *Maffezini* case should instead be a different principle with one, single exception: an MFN provision in a basic treaty does not incorporate by reference dispute settlement provisions in whole or in part set forth in another treaty, unless the MFN provision in the basic treaty leaves no doubt that the Contracting Parties intended to incorporate them.[142]

---

137 *RosInvestCo UK Ltd v The Russian Federation*, SCC Case No V 079/2005, Award on Jurisdiction (October 2007) paras 124–39.
138 *Le Chèque Déjeuner and CD Holding Internationale v Hungary*, ICSID Case No ARB/13/35, Decision on Preliminary Issues of Jurisdiction (3 March 2016) paras 135–222.
139 *RosInvestCo UK Ltd v Russia* (n 137) para 137.
140 The Tribunal addressed the general applicability of MFN clauses to dispute settlement clauses and often referred to the work of the ILC on the matter, although the only other arbitral decision commented by the Tribunal was the jurisdictional decision in *RosInvest v Russia*. See *Le Chèque Déjeuner and CD Holding Internationale v Hungary* (n 138) paras 165–6, 203–5, 207–15.
141 ibid para 159 ('Had the parties intended the MFN clause to be so limited, it would have been straightforward to set out a restriction to this effect in express terms either in the MFN clause itself or elsewhere in the Treaty. [...] To be capable of overturning the fundamental, non-discriminatory object and purpose of an MFN clause, the language of any limitation must have clearly and unambiguously in contemplation a restriction on the operation of the MFN clause itself.') and para 177 ('unrestricted language in an MFN clause should, as a matter of treaty interpretation, give rise to a presumption against limitation').
142 *Plama Consortium Limited v Republic of Bulgaria*, ICSID Case No ARB/03/24, Decision on Jurisdiction (8 February 2005) para 223.

The Tribunal thus created a reversed presumption, which has been endorsed by other tribunals facing the attempts to broaden the scope of substantive jurisdiction to non-justiciable issues under the basic BIT.[143] Its main value is that it sets the opposite direction of the interpretative process, so that it must be demonstrated that treaty parties have intended to include dispute settlement provisions within the reach of an MFN clause.[144] In other words, the reversed presumption described in *Plama* seeks the indicators of inclusion of dispute settlement provisions within the reach of an MFN clause. Some tribunals have integrated this approach in broader narratives on the consensualism of international adjudication, as the Tribunal in *Daimler v Argentina* did when it required 'affirmative evidence' for the establishment of consent and therefore jurisdiction.[145]

A functional reading of the case law on the topic in its totality argues that MFN clauses are applicable to dispute settlement clauses in respect of conditions precedent (as conditions of admissibility) but not in respect of substantive jurisdiction.[146] Yet, it is striking that such a distinction is usually absent in the formation of the premises on the applicability of MFN clauses to dispute settlement provisions. Precisely the absence of that distinction in *Maffezini* paved the way to the arguments in favour of establishing substantive jurisdiction via an MFN clause, to the equally generalised rebuttal in *Plama,* and eventually to the continuation of the generalised discourse about the applicability of MFN clauses to dispute settlement clauses in principle.[147] Tribunals rejecting

---

143 *Telenor Mobile Communications AS v Hungary* (n 121) para 90; *Vladimir Berschader & Moïse Berschader v Russia* (n 121) paras 178–81; *ST-AD GmbH (Germany) v The Republic of Bulgaria,* PCA Case No 2011-06, Award on Jurisdiction (18 July 2013) para 391. See also, in the context of the conditions of access, *H&H Enterprises Investments Inc v Egypt* (n 106) para 358; *ICS Inspection and Control Services Limited (United Kingdom) v Argentina* (n 34) para 282.

144 See *Plama Consortium Limited v Bulgaria* (n 142) paras 203–7; *Salini Costruttori SpA and Italstrade SpA v The Hashemite Kingdom of Jordan,* ICSID Case No ARB/02/13, Decision on Jurisdiction (15 November 2004) para 118.

145 *Daimler Financial Services AG v Argentina* (n 34) paras 175–6. See also *ICS Inspection and Control Services Limited (United Kingdom) v Argentina* (n 34) para 280.

146 UNCTAD, 'Most-Favoured-Nation Treatment', *UNCTAD Series on Issues in International Investment Agreements II* (UN 2010) 66–84; and *Teinver SA, Transportes de Cercanías SA, and Autobuses Urbanos del Sur SA v Argentina* (Jurisdiction) (n 63) para 169 (relying on the UNCTAD's admissibility/scope of jurisdiction dichotomy). But see ILC, 'Final Report of the Study Group on the Most-Favoured-Nation Clause' (29 May 2015) UN Doc A/CN.4/L.852, para 113 ('But there is no explanation in the UNCTAD report as to why it treats cases relating to the 18-month litigation requirement as concerning admissibility rather than as concerning jurisdiction.').

147 See particularly *Vladimir Berschader & Moïse Berschader v Russia* (n 121) para 181 ('The tribunal in the *Gas Natural* case suggested that as a matter of principle MFN provisions

the MFN-dispute settlement conjunction usually express conceptual struggles with the idea, rather than focusing on specific jurisdictional issues. One conceptual problem is the strong separation between 'substantive' and 'procedural' rules of international law.[148] This separation has practical aspects: one tribunal concluded that if MFN clauses could establish an obligation to consent, narrower consent in the basic BIT than in a third-party BIT would cause a breach of the MFN clause, but this could not establish jurisdiction.[149] Tribunals have also pointed out that jurisdictional clauses are severable from the rest of BITs and function as an 'agreement on their own'.[150] Another conceptual problem concerns the qualification of conditions precedent as related to admissibility: as I analysed above, many tribunals have insisted that such conditions qualify as jurisdictional,[151] and moreover some have done so precisely in rejection of the applicability of MFN clauses to dispute settlement provisions.[152] This latter group of tribunals has not allowed bypassing conditions precedent, such as local litigation requirements, via MFN clauses, in regard to which the entire *Maffezini* stream emerged in the first place. Finally, even the tribunals that have acknowledged the jurisdiction/admissibility distinction have applied the discussed presumptions as their starting point of examination.[153] The relevance of the presumptions in favour or against the applicability of MFN clauses to dispute settlement clauses therefore seems unavoidable.

4.3 *Presumptions in Practice*

The traditional narrative is that the applicability of MFN clauses to dispute settlement clauses concerns treaty interpretation and the wording of the concrete

---

in BITs should be understood to be applicable to dispute settlement provisions unless it appears clearly that the parties intended otherwise. [...] Instead, the present Tribunal will apply the principle that an MFN provision in a BIT will only incorporate by reference an arbitration clause from another BIT where the terms of the original BIT clearly and unambiguously so provide or where it can otherwise be clearly inferred that this was the intention of the contracting parties.' [reference omitted]).

148 See above n 121.
149 *Menzies Middle East and Africa SA et Aviation Handling Services International Ltd v République du Sénégal*, ICSID Case No ARB/15/21, Award (5 August 2016) para 141.
150 *Plama Consortium Limited v Bulgaria* (n 142) para 212; *H&H Enterprises Investments Inc v Egypt* (n 106) para 358. See also *European American Investment Bank AG (Austria) v Slovakia* (n 121) paras 445–6.
151 See above nn 22, 34.
152 *Wintershall Aktiengesellschaft v Argentina* (n 34) paras 160–97; *ICS Inspection and Control Services Limited (United Kingdom) v Argentina* (n 34) paras 274–317; *Daimler Financial Services AG v Argentina* (n 34) paras 179–281; *Kılıç İnşaat İthalat İhracat Sanayi Ve Ticaret Anonim Şirketi v Turkmenistan* (n 34) paras 7.1.1-9.1.
153 For example, *Hochtief AG v Argentina* (n 6) paras 59–72.

MFN clause, concealing the influence of any other factors.[154] However, survey of the case law reveals that tribunals have approached the question from a conceptual point of view and established general rules related to the essence of MFN clauses.[155] These presumptions set the burden of argumentation in the interpretative process.[156] In short, the presumption in favour of the MFN-dispute settlement conjunction seeks the indicators of its exclusion so that the party arguing against it bears the burden of argumentation, while the presumption against such conjunction functions in the same manner but in the opposite direction. The formation of presumptions objectivises the interpretative process, but that does not mean that tribunals are deprived of all discretionary space. The assessment of what amounts to an indicator of contrary intention, in particular, remains at tribunals' discretion. Tribunals have thus attributed different weight to narrow or open formulations of MFN clauses,[157]

---

154 For an example of an interpretive twist discovering the application of a presumption, see *AnY Ltd v Czech Republic*, ICSID Case No UNCT/15/1, Decision on Jurisdiction (9 February 2017) paras 93–107 (the Tribunal declared that an MFN clause could be applicable to dispute settlement clauses, but then gave preference to specific wording of the dispute settlement clause which specified arbitrable causes of action; however, the Tribunal factually applied the presumption against the applicability of MFN clauses to the matters of consent, because it relied on the fact that this was one of the UK BITs without the additional paragraph explicitly allowing the application of the MFN clause to the dispute settlement clause). Furthermore, tribunals generally tend to deny the relevance of any presumptions, despite their factual applications; see *Kiliç İnşaat İthalat İhracat Sanayi Ve Ticaret Anonim Şirketi v Turkmenistan* (n 34) paras 7.6.4–5, 7.8.10 (stating that it will not engage in discussions on general presumptions about the reach of MFN clauses and denying their applicability, but then verifying the interpretative outcome against the presumption against the MFN-dispute settlement conjunction suggested in legal scholarship); *Professor Christian Doutremepuich and Antoine Doutremepuich v The Republic of Mauritius*, PCA Case No 2018-37, Award on Jurisdiction (23 August 2019) para 197 ('The Tribunal is of the view that there is no principled argument for or against the application of an MFN clause to dispute resolution provisions, i.e. there is no general rule that MFN clauses *always* or *never* apply to dispute resolution. Rather, according to the Tribunal, MFN clauses *may* apply to dispute resolution provisions, provided that this is what the contracting States intended.' [emphasis in the original]).

155 Tribunals often emphasise their understanding of the function and purpose of MFN clauses. See, for example, *Le Chèque Déjeuner and CD Holding Internationale v Hungary* (n 138) paras 161–3 (on the purpose of MFN clauses to eliminate discrimination among foreign investors). See further Michael Waibel, 'Putting the MFN Genie Back in the Bottle' (2018) 112 AJIL 60, 61–2 (on the importance of the general understandings regarding the typical meaning of MFN clauses both in their drafting and application).

156 See n 131 above.

157 Regarding openly formulated clauses, cf *Impregilo SpA v Argentina* (Award) (n 34) para 108; with *Vladimir Berschader & Moïse Berschader v Russia* (n 121) paras 184–94. Regarding narrowly formulated clauses, such as those limited to investors' 'management, maintenance,

to their territorial limitations,[158] and to specific limitations of dispute settlement clauses.[159] It is thus fairly possible, at least in theory, that a tribunal takes a liberal approach to the general question of applicability, but a strict approach in assessing the contrary indicators, although it is more probable that a tribunal would approach the two questions with the same attitude.[160] However, no matter the approach taken by tribunals, at some instances the indicators are simply too obvious and strong to be circumvented by the means of arbitral discretion.[161]

The biggest problem here is the sharp division of practice in favour of two opposing presumptions. This is best visible in the example of one BIT and its MFN clause being interpreted by different tribunals supporting different presumptions.[162] What is certain, for now, is that when an MFN clause explicitly states that it covers dispute settlement provisions, the MFN-dispute

---

use, enjoyment, or disposal of their investments', cf *Suez, Sociedad General de Aguas de Barcelona SA, and Vivendi Universal SA/AWG v Argentina* (n 120) para 57; with *Ansung Housing Co Ltd v People's Republic of China*, ICSID Case No ARB/14/25, Award (9 March 2017) paras 137–8.

158   cf *Vladimir Berschader & Moïse Berschader v Russia* (n 121) para 185; *ICS Inspection and Control Services Limited (United Kingdom) v Argentina* (n 34) paras 305–9; *ST-AD GmbH (Germany) v Bulgaria* (n 143) paras 394–6; *Beijing Urban Construction Group Co Ltd v Yemen* (n 92) paras 116–21; with *Impregilo SpA v Argentina* (Award) (n 34) para 100; *Telefónica SA v Argentina* (n 35) para 102; and *Le Chèque Déjeuner and CD Holding Internationale v Hungary* (n 138) paras 191–2.

159   cf *RosInvestCo UK Ltd v Russia* (n 137) para 131; *Le Chèque Déjeuner and CD Holding Internationale v Hungary* (n 138) paras 159, 205; with *Señor Tza Yap Shum v The Republic of Peru*, ICSID Case No ARB/07/6, Decision on Jurisdiction and Competence (19 June 2009) para 216; *Austrian Airlines v The Slovak Republic*, UNCITRAL ad hoc arbitration, Final Award (9 October 2009) para 135; *Ivan Peter Busta and James Peter Busta v The Czech Republic*, SCC Case No V 2015/014, Final Award (10 March 2017) paras 166–7.

160   Survey of case law demonstrates that the tribunals that apply the presumption of applicability of MFN clauses to dispute settlement clauses are unlikely to find an indicator of exclusion of such conjunction and to conclude against the applicability. For exceptions, see *Señor Tza Yap Shum v Peru* (n 159) para 216; *Renta 4 SVSA and others v The Russian Federation*, SCC Case No 24/2007, Award on Preliminary Objections (20 March 2009) paras 103–20.

161   *Renta 4 SVSA and others v Russia* (n 160) paras 103–20 (MFN clause limited to the fair and equitable treatment); *Sanum Investments Limited v The Government of the Lao People's Democratic Republic*, PCA Case No 2013-13, Award on Jurisdiction (13 December 2013) paras 357–8 (MFN clause limited to the fair and equitable treatment and protection).

162   The MFN clause in the Argentina-Germany BIT was interpreted to include the dispute settlement clause in *Siemens v Argentina* and *Hochtief v Argentina*, and to the contrary in *Wintershall v Argentina* and *Daimler v Argentina*.

settlement conjunction must be applied.[163] Treaty text should also be given effect when an MFN clause explicitly states that it is not applicable to dispute settlement clauses.[164] Although not unchallenged,[165] these mandatory rules cannot give way to any presumption.

When it comes to silent MFN clauses, presumptions about their reach appear to depend on the arbitrators' support to the jurisdiction/admissibility divide. If the distinction between jurisdiction and admissibility is accepted, and if conditions precedent are qualified as relating to admissibility, then it is possible to presume the applicability of MFN clauses to dispute settlement clauses, but only regarding the conditions of admissibility. In this case, an MFN clause will be applied to the conditions of admissibility, unless it is demonstrated that the treaty parties have intended not to include dispute settlement provisions within the reach of the MFN clause.[166] If the distinction between jurisdiction and admissibility is not accepted, and all elements of dispute settlement clauses are seen as jurisdictional, there is a presumption against the applicability of MFN clauses. In this case, an MFN clause will not be applied to the questions of jurisdiction, unless it is demonstrated that the treaty parties have intended to include dispute settlement provisions within the reach of the MFN clause.[167]

5   Conclusion

The procedural aspects of consensual jurisdictional regulation, ie the conditions of access to international arbitration, have been affected significantly

---

163   *Garanti Koza LLP v Turkmenistan*, ICSID Case No ARB/11/20, Decision on the Objection to Jurisdiction for Lack of Consent (3 July 2013) paras 40–64; *Venezuela US SRL v The Bolivarian Republic of Venezuela*, PCA Case No 2013-34, Interim Award on Jurisdiction (on the Respondent's Objection to Jurisdiction Ratione Voluntatis) (26 July 2016) paras 100–3; *Krederi Ltd v Ukraine*, ICSID Case No ARB/14/17, Award (2 July 2018) para 341.

164   ILC, 'Most-Favoured-Nation Clause' (n 146) para 163.

165   *Garanti Koza LLP v Turkmenistan*, ICSID Case No ARB/11/20, Dissenting Opinion by Laurence Boisson de Chazournes (3 July 2013) (arguing that an MFN clause cannot establish consent to arbitration even if explicitly applicable to dispute settlement provisions); *Venezuela US SRL v The Bolivarian Republic of Venezuela*, PCA Case No 2013-34, Dissenting Opinion of Professor Marcelo G Kohen (26 July 2016) paras 10–24 (arguing that an MFN clause is not applicable to dispute settlement even when referring to the scope of articles comprising dispute settlement provisions).

166   ILC, 'Most-Favoured-Nation Clause' (n 146) paras 167–71. See also Campbell McLachlan, Laurence Shore, and Matthew Weiniger, *International Investment Arbitration: Substantive Principles* (2nd ed, OUP 2017) 352–3.

167   ILC, 'Most-Favoured-Nation Clause' (n 146) para 171.

by the development of arbitrator-made rules. Conditions of access have been detached from party consent and qualified as pertaining to the admissibility of claims, with the effect of relaxing the rigidity of their command. Independent exceptions to conditions precedent have been developed, such as the futility exception and the *Mavrommatis* principle. Local litigation requirements and fork-in-the-road clauses required the development of the criteria governing their application, and tribunals have developed such criteria allowing for their easy satisfaction. Finally, arbitrators have attempted to create a presumption about the (in)applicability of MFN clauses to dispute resolution clauses. The inspiration for such rules came from various sources, like analogies to other spheres of international and domestic law, or policy considerations in international investment law. The inspiration was external to consensual jurisdictional regulation, ie to the jurisdictional rules defined by disputing parties. These rules have been developed as general, prescriptive, arbitration- and treaty-transcending jurisdictional rules supplementing the set of rules provided by virtue of party consent.

CHAPTER 3

Arbitrator-Made Rules and the Substantive Aspects of Consensual Jurisdictional Regulation

1   Introduction

As tribunals have developed rules regulating the conditions of access to international arbitration, so they have developed rules regulating the substantive limits of arbitral jurisdiction. Just as jurisdiction in general, the arbitrator-made rules discussed here have three dimensions, namely temporal, personal, and material (or substantive in the narrow sense). Section 2 addresses the rules with a temporal dimension, namely the non-retroactivity of denial of benefits and the extension of the validity of consent limited by time-bars. Section 3 then discusses the rules affecting the scope of protected investors and investments, namely the Broches test and the presumption of the protection of indirect investments. Section 4 analyses the presumption in favour of jurisdictional bridging, affecting the scope of arbitrable disputes. My approach remains the same as announced in the Introduction.

2   Rules with a Temporal Dimension

This section discusses two arbitrator-made rules with a temporal dimension, namely the non-retroactivity of denial of benefits (1), and the extension of the validity of consent limited by time-bars through the continued act doctrine (2). Strictly speaking, these rules do not concern the temporal jurisdiction of arbitral tribunals, however they are grouped together because they both involve questions of time as the main rationale behind their formation.

2.1   The Non-Retroactivity of Denial of Benefits

Many investment treaties contain denial of benefits clauses, allowing host states to deny protection to investors that, most importantly, do not have a substantial business activity in their home states and are owned or controlled by nationals of third states.[1] Such clauses do not relate to the temporal jurisdiction

---

[1] See generally Yas Banifatemi, 'Taking Into Account Control Under Denial of Benefits Clauses' in Yas Banifatemi (ed), *Jurisdiction in Investment Treaty Arbitration* (Juris 2018) 223; Carlo

of arbitral tribunals in the strict sense, but to other concepts such as the definition of 'investor', ie to personal jurisdiction. However, these clauses have an important temporal aspect: they usually do not expressly state when they can be triggered and whether states can deprive tribunals of jurisdiction retroactively by denying benefits to investors who have already initiated arbitrations.[2] This is a two-fold question: can states trigger denial of benefits clauses after the initiation of arbitration, and if so, do denial of benefits clauses produce effects prospectively only, or also retrospectively?

The starting point of inquiry is the wording of clauses, which can be significant regarding their reach. The Energy Charter Treaty (ECT) limits the reach of its denial of benefits clause to the provisions of substantive protection, and does not cover the arbitration clause.[3] Tribunals have concluded that the triggering of that denial of benefits clause therefore did not affect their jurisdiction but pertained to the questions of merits.[4] When denial of benefits clauses do not contain similar limitations, they affect arbitral competence, which, tribunals have held, can be qualified both as an issue of jurisdiction[5] and of admissibility.[6] However, as it will be demonstrated, the decisions that have addressed the issue of prospective or retrospective effect of denial of benefits clauses reveal that not much help in that respect can be found in the wording and limitations of specific clauses, for which reason tribunals have resorted to objective answers based primarily on policy considerations.

De Stefano, 'Denial of Benefits Clauses in International Investment Agreements: Burden of Proof and Notice to Claimant' (2016) 30 Diritto del Commercio Internazionale 143; Lindsay Gastrell and Paul-Jean Le Cannu, 'Procedural Requirements of "Denial-of-Benefits" Clauses in Investment Treaties: A Review of Arbitral Decisions' (2015) 30 ICSID Rev-FILJ 78.

2 cf India Model BIT (2015) art 35 <https://investmentpolicy.unctad.org/international-investment-agreements/treaty-files/3560/download> accessed 20 August 2020 ('A Party may at any time, including after the institution of arbitration proceedings in accordance with Chapter IV of this Treaty, deny the benefits of this Treaty [...]').

3 Energy Charter Treaty (signed 17 December 1994, entered into force 16 April 1998) 2080 UNTS 95 (ECT) art 17.

4 *Plama Consortium Limited v Republic of Bulgaria*, ICSID Case No ARB/03/24, Decision on Jurisdiction (8 February 2005) paras 146–51.

5 *Ulysseas Inc v The Republic of Ecuador*, UNCITRAL ad hoc arbitration, Interim Award (28 September 2010) para 172; *Pac Rim Cayman LLC v The Republic of El Salvador*, ICSID Case No ARB/09/12, Decision on the Respondent's Jurisdictional Objections (1 June 2012) para 4.4; *Guaracachi America Inc and Rurelec PLC v The Plurinational State of Bolivia*, PCA Case No 2011-17, Award (31 January 2014) para 381; *Bridgestone Licensing Services Inc and Bridgestone Americas Inc v Republic of Panama*, ICSID Case No ARB/16/34, Decision on Expedited Objections (13 December 2017) para 288.

6 *Generation Ukraine Inc v Ukraine*, ICSID Case No ARB/00/9, Award (16 September 2003) para 15.7.

Some tribunals have allowed state respondents to deny benefits to investors after the commencement of arbitration, based on two premises. First, they have noted that the given clauses did not prescribe any time-limits.[7] Second, they have relied on the procedural rules stating that jurisdictional objections must be raised on the first occasion, such as the first submission of memorials by respondents.[8] The argument that by doing so respondent states have unilaterally withdrawn offers to arbitrate after their perfection has been rebutted by the claim that offers are qualified by the possibility of denial of benefits.[9] The holding that a denial of benefits after the initiation of arbitration can deprive the tribunal of jurisdiction supports the retrospective effect of such clauses, because their triggering affects past events. Most importantly, tribunals have observed the function of these clauses in general; as one tribunal maintained:

> The very purpose of the denial of benefits is to give the Respondent the possibility of withdrawing the benefits granted under the BIT to investors who invoke those benefits. As such, it is proper that the denial is 'activated' when the benefits are being claimed.[10]

The other approach, taken in *Ampal v Egypt,* holds that denial of benefits clauses cannot be triggered after the initiation of arbitration to deprive the tribunal of jurisdiction. The argument goes that arbitral jurisdiction should be assessed as per the time of seizure.[11] The Tribunal relied on the practice of the ICJ,[12] but also on the provisions of the ICSID Convention, which provide that 'no party may withdraw its consent unilaterally'.[13] According to this approach,

---

[7] *Ulysseas Inc v Ecuador* (n 5) para 172; *Pac Rim Cayman LLC v El Salvador* (n 5) para 4.83.

[8] *Ulysseas Inc v Ecuador* (n 5) para 172; *Pac Rim Cayman LLC v El Salvador* (n 5) para 4.85; *Guaracachi America Inc and Rurelec PLC v Bolivia* (n 5) para 382. See also *Empresa Eléctrica del Ecuador Inc v Republic of Ecuador,* ICSID Case No ARB/05/9, Award (2 June 2009) para 71.

[9] *Pac Rim Cayman LLC v El Salvador* (n 5) para 4.90; *Guaracachi America Inc and Rurelec PLC v Bolivia* (n 5) paras 371–5; *Bridgestone Licensing Services Inc and Bridgestone Americas Inc v Panama* (n 5) para 288. See also *Ulysseas Inc v Ecuador* (n 5) para 173 ('the protection afforded by the BIT is subject during the life of the investment to the possibility of a denial of the BIT's advantages by the host State').

[10] *Guaracachi America Inc and Rurelec PLC v Bolivia* (n 5) para 376.

[11] *Ampal-American Israel Corp and others v Arab Republic of Egypt,* ICSID Case No ARB/12/11, Decision on Jurisdiction (1 February 2016) paras 167–72.

[12] ibid para 171.

[13] ibid para 168; Convention on the Settlement of Investment Disputes Between States and Nationals of Other States (signed 18 March 1965, entered into force 14 October 1966) 575 UNTS 159 (ICSID Convention) art 25(1).

denial of benefits clauses have only prospective effect and their triggering after the initiation of arbitration cannot invalidate previously established jurisdiction.

The prospective effect of denial of benefits clauses has also been endorsed by the tribunals that have analysed such clauses as questions of merits in the context of the ECT. An early example is the *Plama v Bulgaria* decision,[14] which has been widely followed.[15] It has been argued that these decisions must be distinguished from non-ECT decisions, because the limitation of the ECT's denial of benefits clause to the substantive protection provisions is decisive for its exclusive prospective effect.[16] While it is true that the difference in the limitations of clauses has been used to distinguish decisions as precedents,[17] that does not seem to be the decisive argument in the resolution of the question of their prospective or retrospective effect. Already in *Plama* the Tribunal noted that this question could not be resolved by consulting the wording of the clause only.[18] The Tribunal turned to the object and purpose of the ECT and built the well-known narrative on the legitimate expectations of investors.[19] But as it is usual with references to the object and purpose, this was a gateway for the introduction of the Tribunal's policy considerations, which is visible in its assertion that an investor must be informed before investing about denial of benefits.[20] Furthermore, the Tribunal addressed other questions regarding the prospective/retrospective effect dilemma: it acknowledged, although on a separate note, that conferring the right on the respondent state to invalidate arbitral jurisdiction by denying benefits to the investor would make the state 'the judge in its own cause',[21]

---

14   *Plama Consortium Limited v Bulgaria* (n 4) paras 159–65.
15   *Hulley Enterprises Limited (Cyprus) v The Russian Federation*, PCA Case No AA 226, Interim Award on Jurisdiction and Admissibility (30 November 2009) para 457; *Liman Caspian Oil BV and NCL Dutch Investment BV v Republic of Kazakhstan*, ICSID Case No ARB/07/14, Award (22 June 2010) paras 224–7; *Khan Resources Inc, Khan Resources BV, and CAUC Holding Company Ltd v The Government of Mongolia and MonAtom LLC*, PCA Case No 2011-09, Decision on Jurisdiction (25 July 2012) paras 425–31; *Anatolie Stati and others v The Republic of Kazakhstan*, SCC Case No V 116/2010, Award (19 December 2013) para 745; *Masdar Solar & Wind Cooperatief UA v Kingdom of Spain*, ICSID Case No ARB/14/1, Award (16 May 2018) para 239.
16   Banifatemi (n 1) 247–57; Gastrell and Le Cannu (n 1) 94–5.
17   See, for example, *Ampal-American Israel Corp and others v Egypt* (n 11) paras 128–9.
18   *Plama Consortium Limited v Bulgaria* (n 4) para 159. See also *Khan Resources Inc, Khan Resources BV, and CAUC Holding Company Ltd v Mongolia and MonAtom LLC* (n 15) para 425.
19   *Plama Consortium Limited v Bulgaria* (n 4) paras 160–2.
20   ibid para 161.
21   ibid para 149.

and it rejected the argument that the mere existence of a denial of benefits clause in the ECT would suffice to inform investors of possible denial of benefits.[22] Furthermore, the engagement of the ECT and non-ECT case law in substance is mutual: the decisions that have endorsed the retrospective effect of denial of benefits clauses in the context of jurisdictional objections have not distinguished the issues relating to jurisdiction from those relating to the merits; their support for the retrospective effect, therefore, engages substantive investor protections as well.

Therefore, tribunals have not merely interpreted differently worded denial of benefits clauses in different streams. Despite the attempts of ECT and non-ECT tribunals at mutual exclusion, both have engaged in the creation of a rule governing the application of denial of benefits clauses in general, although advocating in favour of two opposite solutions. The independent input added by tribunals interacts with party-provided jurisdictional rules. This is most obvious when tribunals hold either that offers to arbitrate cannot be revoked after being perfected, or that such offers were qualified by the possibility of denial of benefits from the beginning. Tribunals rely on policy considerations, such as whether investors could expect denial of benefits and deprivation of arbitral jurisdiction,[23] and whether states need an opportunity to track the status of investors.[24] The regulatory deficiency regarding the prospective/retrospective effect dilemma in the domain of party-provided jurisdictional rules has provided regulatory space for the arbitral rule-creation. I believe that there is now an established rule of non-retroactivity of denial of benefits, although it remains to be seen whether a common product of the ECT and non-ECT cases would be accepted in practice.

---

22   ibid para 163.
23   cf ibid para 161 ('A putative investor therefore requires reasonable notice before making any investment in the host state whether or not that host state has exercised its right under Article 17(1) ECT'); with *Guaracachi America Inc and Rurelec PLC v Bolivia* (n 5) para 383 ('one cannot say that such a denial will come as a total surprise for the investor, since the BIT is not secret and we are dealing in this case with an investor who has opted to use an investment vehicle controlled by a company of a third country, which has no substantial business activities in the territory of the Contracting Party under whose laws it is constituted or organized').
24   *Guaracachi America Inc and Rurelec PLC v Bolivia* (n 5) para 379 ('the fulfilment of the aforementioned requirements is not static and can change from one day to the next, which means that it is only when a dispute arises that the respondent State will be able to assess whether such requirements are met and decide whether it will deny the benefits of the treaty in respect of that particular dispute').

2.2 The Extension of the Validity of Consent and the Continued Act Doctrine

The validity of offers to arbitrate can be limited by time-bars.[25] For example, the former North American Free Trade Agreement (NAFTA) limited the investor's right to submit claim to arbitration to three years 'from the date on which the investor first acquired, or should have first acquired, knowledge of the alleged breach and knowledge that the investor has incurred loss or damage'.[26] The question arises whether the continued act doctrine can extend the validity of consent beyond such limits.[27] The doctrine is well known in the sphere of the substantive law of state responsibility.[28] Whether an act qualifies as continuing depends on the relevant substantive obligation with which it interacts.[29] Therefore, per definition this doctrine does not touch upon the jurisdiction of international courts and tribunals, at least not directly.[30]

Applying the continuing act doctrine and extending the NAFTA time-bar, the Tribunal in *UPS v Canada* declared:

> The generally applicable ground for our decision is that [...] continuing courses of conduct constitute continuing breaches of legal obligations and renew the limitation period accordingly. This is true generally in the

---

[25] It is assumed here that time-bars are jurisdictional requirements, but discussion can be led over their qualification as pertaining to jurisdiction or admissibility. See *Resolute Forest Products Inc v Government of Canada*, PCA Case No 2016-13, Decision on Jurisdiction and Admissibility (30 January 2018) paras 83–4.

[26] North American Free Trade Agreement (signed 17 December 1992, entered into force 1 January 1994) 32 ILM 289 (NAFTA) art 1116(2). See also Agreement Between the United States of America, the United Mexican States, and Canada (signed 30 November 2018 and 10 December 2019, entered into force 1 July 2020) art 14.D.5(1)(c) (four years).

[27] See generally Sadie Blanchard, 'State Consent, Temporal Jurisdiction, and the Importation of Continuing Circumstances Analysis into International Investment Arbitration' (2011) 10 Washington University Global Studies L Rev 419.

[28] Art 14(2) in ILC, 'Responsibility of States for Internationally Wrongful Acts', *Yearbook of the International Law Commission 2001*, vol II (Part Two) (UN 2007) 59 ('The breach of an international obligation by an act of a State having a continuing character extends over the entire period during which the act continues and remains not in conformity with the international obligation.').

[29] Commentary to art 14, para 4 in ibid 60.

[30] However, the ILC notes the use of this doctrine by some human rights bodies in the establishment of jurisdiction, in the situations where an act commenced before but continued after the entry into force of a human rights instrument. See Commentary to art 14, paras 9-11 in ibid 60–1.

law, and Canada has provided no special reason to adopt a different rule here.[31]

The Tribunal held that this premise was supported by the *Feldman v Mexico* decision,[32] but it also stressed that such a proposition was 'true generally in the law'.[33] The generalised premise allowed the Tribunal to rule that the claims whose submission exceeded the three-year limit were not time-barred, albeit holding that it could take into account only the losses that were incurred during the three-year period.[34] In sum, by relying on a generalised premise, the Tribunal affected the application of Article 1116(2) of the NAFTA, arguably contrary to its explicit wording which referred to the investor's 'first knowledge'.[35] However, the Tribunal did attempt to address this problem, by distinguishing cases in which the acts ended and thus the knowledge about the loss was present at an earlier point.[36]

---

31 *United Parcel Service of America Inc v Government of Canada*, ICSID Case No UNCT/02/1, Award on the Merits (24 May 2007) para 28.

32 For the incorrect reliance on this decision by the *UPS v Canada* Tribunal, see Blanchard (n 27) 466–7.

33 *United Parcel Service of America Inc v Canada* (n 31) para 28.

34 ibid para 30. One view analogises the approach taken in *UPS v Canada* to the US continued tort doctrine: Pedro J Martinez-Fraga and C Ryan Reetz, 'The Status of the Limitations Period Doctrine in Public International Law: Devising a Functional Analytical Framework for Investors and Host-States' (2017) 4 McGill J Disp Resol 105, 118–9.

35 See *Mondev International Ltd v United States of America*, ICSID Case No ARB(AF)/99/2, Award (11 October 2002) para 87 (rejecting the time-bar objection on the ground that the claims were limited to local court decisions, which fell within the time-limit, but noting: 'If it had mattered, however, the Tribunal would not have accepted Mondev's argument that it could not have had "knowledge of … loss or damage" arising from the actions of the City and BRA prior to the United States court decisions. A claimant may know that it has suffered loss or damage even if the extent or quantification of the loss or damage is still unclear.'). See also *Grand River Enterprises Six Nations Ltd and others v United States of America*, UNCITRAL ad hoc arbitration, Decision on Objections to Jurisdiction (20 July 2006) para 78; and further, for another reading of the NAFTA time-bar, *Resolute Forest Products Inc v Canada* (n 25) para 158 ('Articles 1116(2) and 1117(2) of NAFTA refer to the time when the breach "first" occurred. According to the ordinary meaning of the terms used and the object and purpose of the provision […] whether a breach definitively occurring and known to the claimant prior to the critical date continued in force thereafter is irrelevant.').

36 *United Parcel Service of America Inc v Canada* (n 31) para 29 (distinguishing the *Mondev v USA* decision by holding that 'the dicta [of that decision] relate to a state action that was completed but was subject to challenge in state court', and that 'the state's action was completed and the information about it known – including the fact that the investor would suffer loss from it – before subsequent court action was complete').

As this proposition was made in *UPS v Canada* in principle, so it was rebutted in principle based on policy considerations. The Tribunal in *Spence International Investments and others v Costa Rica* expressly disagreed with the suggested rule and stated:

> While it may be that a continuing course of conduct constitutes a continuing breach, the Tribunal considers that such conduct cannot without more renew the limitation period as this would effectively denude the limitation clause of its essential purpose, namely, to draw a line under the prosecution of historic claims. Such an approach would also encourage attempts at the endless parsing up of a claim into ever finer sub-components of breach over time in an attempt to come within the limitation period. This does not comport with the policy choice of the parties to the treaty. While, from a given claimant's perspective, a limitation clause may be perceived as an arbitrary cut off point for the prosecution of a claim, such clauses are a legitimate legal mechanism to limit the proliferation of historic claims, with all the attendant legal and policy challenges and uncertainties that they bring.[37]

However, the Tribunal conceded that if some acts are separable and independently actionable, they can be separated from the acts that give rise to time-barred claims and retained within jurisdiction.[38] The main value of this decision for the present discussion is the principled rejection of the rule advanced in *UPS v Canada*.

---

[37] *Spence International Investments LLC, Berkowitz, and others v Republic of Costa Rica*, ICSID Case No UNCT/13/2, Interim Award (25 October 2016) para 208. See also *Grand River Enterprises Six Nations Ltd and others v USA* (n 35) para 81 ('this analysis [that time-bars apply separately to each of many similar measures] seems to render the limitations provisions ineffective in any situation involving a series of similar and related actions by a respondent state, since a claimant would be free to base its claim on the most recent transgression, even if it had knowledge of earlier breaches and injuries'); *Corona Materials LLC v Dominican Republic*, ICSID Case No ARB(AF)/14/3, Award on the Respondent's Expedited Preliminary Objections in Accordance with Article 10.20.5 of the DR-CAFTA (31 May 2016) para 192 ('The limitation period clause is written in plain terms and does not contemplate the suspension or "tolling" of the three-year period.'); and *Apotex Inc v The Government of the United States of America*, ICSID Case No UNCT/10/2, Award on Jurisdiction and Admissibility (14 June 2013) paras 325–8 (no tolling of the time-bar by judicial challenge of an administrative act).

[38] *Spence International Investments LLC, Berkowitz, and others v Costa Rica* (n 37) para 210. See also *William Ralph Clayton and others v Government of Canada*, PCA Case No 2009-04, Award on Jurisdiction and Liability (17 March 2015) para 266.

There are two positions therefore in the arbitral rule-creation regarding the ability of the continuing act doctrine to extend the validity of consent. Tribunals clashed in their principled assumptions (or policy-based opinions) on the permissibility of extending time-bars, and by doing so they have arguably omitted to create a more nuanced approach to the problem.[39] Yet, given that the continued act doctrine has also affected time-bars in other branches of international adjudication, the first position should arguably receive a broader acceptance, although requiring considerable refinement.[40]

The continued act doctrine reminds that arbitral rule-making can be limited by the rules of general international law. For example, claimants have relied on this doctrine in the attempt to establish retroactivity of consent covering facts and acts occurring before the entry into force of a treaty.[41] However, this is not possible because of broader issues: even if an offer to arbitrate does not contain any temporal limitations, assuming jurisdiction over treaty disputes concerning facts and acts taking place before the treaty's entry into force would imply the retroactive effect of its substantive provisions.[42] Although the argument exists that if a jurisdictional clause does not make any specific temporal restrictions, there should be no issue in its application to existing disputes, which could have arisen earlier in regard to past events, this reasoning applies only to the extent

---

[39] In the sphere of human rights, a more nuanced approach to the effect of continuing acts on time-bars has been developed, which considers the details of the continuing act in question. See Nick Gallus, *The Temporal Jurisdiction of International Tribunals* (OUP 2017) 96–9.

[40] The rule advanced by the UPS v Canada Tribunal has some echo in general international law. See, in the context of human rights, *Zorica Jovanović v Serbia* App No 21794/08 (ECtHR, 26 March 2013) para 54 ('it has been said that the six-month time-limit does not apply as such to continuing situations [...]; this is because, if there is a situation of an ongoing breach, the time-limit in effect starts afresh each day and it is only once the situation ceases that the final period of six months will run to its end'); and, for a more general view, Gallus (n 39) 92–9. See also *Mobil Investments Canada Inc v Government of Canada*, ICSID Case No ARB/15/6, Decision on Jurisdiction and Admissibility (13 July 2018) para 145–73 (criticising the continuing breach argument and the UPS approach, but relying on the continuing nature of the obligation and finding that the case concerned a fresh breach; notably, the Tribunal stressed that it was not required to decide the correctness of the continuing breach argument).

[41] See, for example, *Impregilo SpA v Islamic Republic of Pakistan*, ICSID Case No ARB/03/3, Decision on Jurisdiction (22 April 2005) para 297; *MCI Power Group LC and New Turbine Inc v Republic of Ecuador*, ICSID Case No ARB/03/6, Award (31 July 2007) paras 56–8.

[42] *Impregilo SpA v Pakistan* (n 41) paras 309–11; *MCI Power Group LC and New Turbine Inc v Ecuador* (n 41) paras 93–4. See also *Spence International Investments LLC, Berkowitz, and others v Costa Rica* (n 37) paras 214–22.

that such clauses can be isolated from the applicable substantive law.[43] The continuing nature of an act, however, requires the involvement of substantive law.[44] Due to the general principle of non-retroactivity of treaties,[45] claimants generally cannot rely on the continued act doctrine to establish jurisdiction over facts and acts that took place before the entry into force of the relevant investment treaty. However, it is established arbitral practice to accept jurisdiction over the parts of continuing acts that took place after entry into force.[46]

3 Rules Expanding the Scope of Protection

Investment treaties define the terms 'investor' and 'investment' and thus regulate the scope of their protection. These definitions also apply to jurisdictional clauses (ie offers to arbitrate) and therefore form an inevitable part of party-provided jurisdictional rules. When it comes to the ICSID framework, the ICSID Convention also contains provisions pertinent to both notions. I discuss here two examples of arbitral law-making relating to the scope of protection, and therefore to the scope of arbitral jurisdiction: the Broches test, pertaining

---

43 *Chevron Corporation (USA) and Texaco Petroleum Corporation (USA) v The Republic of Ecuador*, PCA Case No 34877, Interim Award (1 December 2008) paras 265–8. An often cited authority is *Mavrommatis Palestine Concessions (Greece v UK)* (Judgment) (1924) PCIJ Ser A—No 2, 6, 35 ('The Court is of opinion that, in cases of doubt, jurisdiction based on an international agreement embraces all disputes referred to it after its establishment. [...] The reservation made in many arbitration treaties regarding disputes arising out of events previous to the conclusion of the treaty seems to prove the necessity for an explicit limitation of jurisdiction and, consequently, the correctness of the rule of interpretation enunciated above.'). See further Veijo Heiskanen, '*Entretemps*: Is There a Distinction Between Jurisdiction *Ratione Temporis* and Substantive Protection *Ratione Temporis*?' in Yas Banifatemi (ed), *Jurisdiction in Investment Treaty Arbitration* (Juris 2018) 312 (distinguishing between 'regulatory' and 'compromissory' treaties); and Zachary Douglas, 'When Does an Investment Treaty Claim Arise? An Excursus on the Anatomy of the Cause of Action' in Yas Banifatemi (ed), *Jurisdiction in Investment Treaty Arbitration* (Juris 2018) 345–6 (regarding the link to the scope of consent).

44 See n 29 above; *Mondev International Ltd v USA* (n 35) para 58 ('Whether the act which constitutes the gist of the (alleged) breach has a continuing character depends both on the facts and on the obligation said to have been breached.').

45 Vienna Convention on the Law of Treaties (signed 23 May 1969, entered into force 27 January 1980) 1155 UNTS 331 (VCLT) art 28.

46 *Mondev International Ltd v USA* (n 35) paras 68–75; *Marvin Roy Feldman Karpa v United Mexican States*, ICSID Case No ARB(AF)/99/1, Interim Decision on Preliminary Jurisdictional Issues (6 December 2000) para 62; *Société Générale v The Dominican Republic*, LCIA Case No UN 7927, Award on Preliminary Objections to Jurisdiction (19 September 2008) para 94.

to the definition of 'investor' and affecting the personal aspect of arbitral jurisdiction (1), and the presumption of the protection of indirect investments, affecting the substantive aspect of arbitral jurisdiction (2).

3.1 The Broches Test

The ICSID Convention encourages private investment,[47] and its requirement for the involvement of a 'national of another Contracting State' precludes instituting inter-state arbitrations.[48] The Convention does not preclude access to arbitration regarding investment with any governmental involvement,[49] but the fine line between state-owned companies that can and those that cannot access ICSID arbitration has remained unregulated. An excerpt on the topic from Aron Broches' lectures at the Hague Academy of International Law has become renowned:

> [...] it was recognized in the discussions leading up to the formulation of the Convention that in today's world the classical distinction between private and public investment, based on the source of the capital, is no longer meaningful, if not outdated. There are many companies which combine capital from private and governmental sources and corporations all of whose shares are owned by the government, but which are practically indistinguishable from the completely privately owned enterprise both in their legal characteristics and in their activities. It would seem, therefore, that for purposes of the Convention a mixed economy company or government-owned corporation should not be disqualified as a 'national of another Contracting State' *unless it is acting as an agent for the government or is discharging an essentially governmental function.*[50]

According to Broches, there was a consensus in the drafting process that government-owned companies were not excluded from the scope of the ICSID

---

47   ICSID Convention (n 13) pmbl ('Considering the need for international cooperation for economic development, and the role of private international investment therein;'); 'Report of the Executive Directors on the Convention on the Settlement of Investment Disputes Between States and Nationals of Other States, 1965' (1993) 1 ICSID Reports 23, para 9.
48   ICSID Convention (n 13) art 25; CF Amerasinghe, 'Jurisdiction *Ratione Personae* under the Convention on the Settlement of Investment Disputes between States and Nationals of Other States' (1976) 47 British Yrbk Int'l L 227, 241–2.
49   Christoph H Schreuer and others, *The ICSID Convention: A Commentary* (2nd ed, CUP 2009) 161–2.
50   Aron Broches, 'The Convention on the Settlement of Investment Disputes between States and Nationals of Other States' in Aron Broches, *Selected Essays: World Bank, ICSID, and Other Subjects of Public and Private International Law* (Martinus Nijhoff 1995) 202 (emphasis added).

Convention, and even though this was noted in the preparatory work, '[n]o attempt was made [...] to reduce this common understanding to a legal definition, which would have been a difficult task'.[51] Broches' main contribution, therefore, was the definition of the two exceptions, ie of the cases in which companies would not qualify to access the ICSID mechanism.[52]

The Broches test has been accepted in arbitral practice verbatim.[53] However, its two exceptions seem to have a reverse effect, contributing more to the definition of the wide space in which state-owned companies can be claimants. For example, the Tribunal in *CSOB v Slovakia* held that neither state ownership nor control sufficed to disqualify the Claimant.[54] Furthermore, even acting on behalf of the state or promoting its policies did not suffice to trigger the exceptions, and what mattered was 'the nature of these activities and not their purpose'.[55] A company's reliance on state policies equally did not mean it exercised a governmental function.[56] Finally, even if state policies drove company acts, as in the case of privatization, this alone did not suffice to make such acts governmental.[57] The Tribunal insisted on the concept of the 'nature' of acts.[58] Most importantly, while the Broches test includes two alternative exceptions (acting as a state agent *or* exercising a governmental function), the Tribunal

---

51   ibid. See also Amerasinghe (n 48) 242–3.
52   Interestingly, it appears that Broches both justified such an omission and recognised the objective nature of the negative criteria. See Broches (n 50) 202 (noting: 'Nor was it necessary to do so [to legally define the understanding on the access of government-owned companies to ICSID] because of the consensual character of the Convention as a whole which justified leaving a large measure of discretion to the parties. But this is not to say that in an extreme case the Secretary-General or a Commission or Tribunal, each within the sphere of their own competence, could not review the soundness of the exercise of that discretion.').
53   *Ceskoslovenska Obchodni Banka AS v The Slovak Republic*, ICSID Case No ARB/97/4, Decision of the Tribunal on Objections to Jurisdiction (24 May 1999) para 17; *Flughafen Zürich AG and Gestión e Ingenería IDC SA v Bolivarian Republic of Venezuela*, ICSID Case No ARB/10/19, Award (18 November 2014) para 275; *Beijing Urban Construction Group Co Ltd v Republic of Yemen*, ICSID Case No ARB/14/30, Decision on Jurisdiction (31 May 2017) paras 31, 33. See also Doak Bishop and Margrete Stevens, 'Jurisdiction Ratione Personae – Is There a Standard Definition of an "Investor" in Investment Treaties?' in Yas Banifatemi (ed), *Jurisdiction in Investment Treaty Arbitration* (Juris 2018) 221–2.
54   *Ceskoslovenska Obchodni Banka AS v Slovakia* (n 53) para 18.
55   ibid paras 19–20. See Mark Feldman, 'The Standing of State-Controlled Entities under the ICSID Convention: Two Key Considerations' (2012) 65 Columbia FDI Perspectives; Mark Feldman, 'State-Owned Enterprises as Claimants in International Investment Arbitration' (2016) 31 ICSID Rev-FILJ 24, 34 (criticising the omission to consider the purpose of acts).
56   *Ceskoslovenska Obchodni Banka AS v Slovakia* (n 53) paras 22–3.
57   ibid paras 24–5.
58   See particularly ibid para 21 ('Although these activities were driven by State policies [...] the banking transactions themselves that implemented these policies did not thereby

in *CSOB v Slovakia* considered the governmental nature of an act the decisive criterion.[59] In contrast, the Tribunal in *Beijing Urban Construction Group v Yemen* analysed the two exceptions separately, although it also endorsed the *CSOB*'s 'focus on a context-specific analysis of the commercial function of the investment'.[60]

The inspiration for the rule was thus mainly academic, but analogies have also been made to the law of state responsibility. The Tribunal in *Beijing Urban Construction Group v Yemen* noted that '[t]he *Broches* factors are the mirror image of the attribution rules in Articles 5 and 8 of the ILC's *Articles on State Responsibility*'.[61] Although this analogy can be challenged,[62] it can also be reinforced by the fact that human rights courts apply reminiscent criteria to state-owned companies when examining their capacity to appear as applicants.[63] Because of that 'mirror image', the Broches criteria are used to define the wide space in which state-owned companies can be claimants within the ICSID system, or in the words of the *Beijing* Tribunal, '[t]he *Broches* test lays down

---

lose their commercial nature. They cannot therefore be characterized as governmental in nature.').

59   ibid ('even if one were to conclude that the non-performing assets derived from activities conducted by CSOB as an agent of the State, the measures taken by CSOB to remove them from its books in order to improve its balance and consolidate its financial position in accordance with the provisions of the Consolidation Agreement, must be deemed to be commercial in character').

60   *Beijing Urban Construction Group Co Ltd v Yemen* (n 53) paras 35–44.

61   ibid para 34. See art 5 in ILC, 'State Responsibility' (n 28) 42 ('Conduct of persons or entities exercising elements of governmental authority'); and art 8 in ibid 47 ('Conduct directed or controlled by a State').

62   Arrêt du 29 novembre 2016, Cour d'Appel de Paris, Pôle 1 - Chambre 1 (France) 14/17964 [18] ('Considérant qu'il n'y a pas lieu d'apprécier l'assimilation d'un investisseur à un Etat partie au regard du Projet d'articles invoqué par l'UKRAINE; que ce document énonce, en effet, des règles d'attribution du comportement d'une entité à un Etat afin d'engager la responsabilité de ce dernier pour des faits internationalement illicites; qu'il n'est nullement démontré que ces règles seraient consacrées par la coutume internationale dans le contexte entièrement différent de l'assimilation d'une entité à un Etat afin de la priver d'un droit propre à l'arbitrage en application d'un TBI;').

63   cf *Islamic Republic of Iran Shipping Lines v Turkey* App No 40998/98 (ECtHR, 13 December 2007) para 79 ('The term "governmental organisations", as opposed to "non-governmental organisations" within the meaning of Article 34 [of the ECHR], includes legal entities which participate in the exercise of governmental powers or run a public service under government control. In order to determine whether any given legal person other than a territorial authority falls within that category, account must be taken of its legal status and, where appropriate, the rights that status gives it, the nature of the activity it carries out and the context in which it is carried out, and the degree of its independence from the political authorities [...]').

markers for the non-attribution of State status'.[64] It is not surprising that the Broches test has become invoked by investors in responses to jurisdictional objections to affirm their status as claimants, even outside the ICSID context.[65] Possibly for the same reason, respondents attempt to discredit the Broches test or revise its terms, although so far unsuccessfully.[66]

3.2 Protecting Indirect Investments

A common question is whether investment treaties protect direct investments only, or also those made through intermediaries incorporated in home, host, or third states.[67] Some treaties regulate this explicitly.[68] Others do not, in which case tribunals should determine whether indirect investments qualify for protection, affecting their substantive jurisdiction. This question reveals an

---

[64] *Beijing Urban Construction Group Co Ltd v Yemen* (n 53) para 34.

[65] *China Heilongjiang International Economic & Technical Cooperative Corp and others v Mongolia,* PCA Case No 2010-20, Award (30 June 2017) para 276. To what extent this argument influenced the Tribunal's decision is unclear. See ibid para 418 (noting, among others, that it was 'not persuaded by the Respondent's additional argument that Beijing Shougang and China Heilongjiang acted as "quasi-instrumentalities of the Chinese government"', and that there was no 'evidence in the record to support such a conclusion, or a conclusion that they acted under the Chinese Government's "express instruction to invest abroad in order to serve China's foreign policy goals"'). Scholars have also concluded that the Broches test is unlikely to lead to declining jurisdiction; see Reza Mohtashami and Farouk El-Hosseny, 'State-Owned Enterprises as Claimants before ICSID: Is the Broches Test on the Ebb?' (2016) 3 BCDR Int'l Arb Rev 371, 387.

[66] See *Rumeli Telekom AS and Telsim Mobil Telekomunikasyon Hizmetleri AS v Republic of Kazakhstan,* ICSID Case No ARB/05/16, Award (29 July 2008) paras 293, 296 (where the Respondent argued: '[...] Mr. Broches was writing during the cold war, when, for a multilateral treaty to be effective, he needed to address the peculiarities of genuinely commercial enterprises which happened to be State-owned for political reasons. He did not have in mind the situation in which a State party seized a private company. Respondent therefore submits that the test formulated by Broches has no application in this arbitration.' It also argued, in relation to the second alternative exception of the Broches test, that 'the test is thus whether the entity discharges in general a governmental function and not as suggested by Claimants, whether the particular act in question is of a governmental nature'. These arguments were not addressed by the Tribunal.).

[67] See generally Campbell McLachlan, Laurence Shore, and Matthew Weiniger, *International Investment Arbitration: Substantive Principles* (2nd ed, OUP 2017) 256–8; Panayotis M Protopsaltis, 'The Challenge of the Barcelona Traction Hypothesis: Barcelona Traction Clauses and Denial of Benefits Clauses in BITs and IIAs' (2010) 11 JWIT 561, 567–84; Engela C Schlemmer, 'Investment, Investor, Nationality, and Shareholders' in Peter Muchlinski, Federico Ortino, and Christoph Schreuer (eds), *The Oxford Handbook of International Investment Law* (OUP 2008) 86.

[68] ECT (n 3) art 1(6) ('"Investment" means every kind of asset, owned or controlled *directly or indirectly* by an Investor [...]' [emphasis added]).

important regulatory issue and tribunals have established a firm presumption assisting its resolution.

Tribunals have presumed the protection of indirect investments, so that their exclusion must be demonstrated. This presumption is defended on two grounds. First, tribunals have maintained that the exclusion of indirect investments from treaty protection must be explicit. The Tribunal in *Tza Yap Shum v Peru* held that, unless expressly provided otherwise, BITs cannot be presumed to exclude the protection of indirect investments.[69] The Tribunal observed the BIT's protective purpose,[70] but also expressed the expectation that the exclusion of indirect investments would be explicit.[71] That expectation, as well as the remark that referrals in other treaties to indirect investments (although not considering them decisive) had only illustrative and not normative value,[72] reveals that the Tribunal was led by policy considerations. Although less developed, the same assumption that the exclusion of indirect investments from treaty protections should be explicit can be traced in other arbitral[73] and judicial decisions,[74] which have become relied on as established practice.[75]

---

69 *Señor Tza Yap Shum v The Republic of Peru*, ICSID Case No ARB/07/6, Decision on Jurisdiction and Competence (19 June 2009) para 111 ('en ausencia de lenguaje expreso en el APPRI, no se puede presumir sin más que la intención del mismo es excluir las inversions indirectas de personas naturales cuando estas ejercen la propiedad y en control de las mismas').

70 ibid paras 103–6.

71 ibid para 107.

72 ibid paras 109–10.

73 See, among many others, *Siemens AG v The Argentine Republic*, ICSID Case No ARB/02/8, Decision on Jurisdiction (3 August 2004) para 137; *Ioannis Kardassopoulos v Georgia*, ICSID Case No ARB/05/18, Decision on Jurisdiction (6 July 2007) paras 123–4; *Mobil Corporation, Venezuela Holdings BV, and others v Bolivarian Republic of Venezuela*, ICSID Case No ARB/07/27, Decision on Jurisdiction (10 June 2010) para 165; *Krederi Ltd v Ukraine*, ICSID Case No ARB/14/17, Award (2 July 2018) para 244; *South American Silver Limited (Bermuda) v The Plurinational State of Bolivia*, PCA Case No 2013-15, Award (22 November 2018) paras 295–8; *Mera Investment Fund Limited v Republic of Serbia*, ICSID Case No ARB/17/2, Decision on Jurisdiction (30 November 2018) paras 127–8. See also *Mr Franz Sedelmayer v The Russian Federation*, SCC arbitration, Arbitration Award (7 July 1998) 56–9 (applying the 'control theory' to conclude that the Claimant was a protected investor in respect of indirectly made investments; among others, the Tribunal stated: 'It is a fact that the Treaty does not contain any specific clause providing such application [of the control theory]. On the other hand, there is nothing in the Treaty which excludes the applicability of the said theory.').

74 Arrêt du 11 décembre 2018, Tribunal fédéral, Ire Cour de droit civil (Switzerland) 4A_65/2018 [3.2.1.2.4]; *The Republic of Korea v Mohammad Reza Dayyani and others* [2019] EWHC 3580 (Comm) [72–3].

75 *CEMEX Caracas Investments BV and CEMEX Caracas II Investments BV v Bolivarian Republic of Venezuela*, ICSID Case No ARB/08/15, Decision on Jurisdiction (30 December 2010) paras 156–8.

The second argument in defence of the presumption of the protection of indirect investments holds that reading additional limitations into treaty texts is not permissible. This argument has been put forward by the tribunals that have faced explicit inclusion of indirect investments, but were nevertheless asked to exclude them.[76] The Tribunal in *Enron v Argentina* conceded that enabling the protection of an indefinite chain of investors might not be preferable, but nevertheless gave priority to the treaty text and more specifically state consent.[77]

The development of this presumption relates to the liberalisation of shareholder claims as a specificity of investment law. The Tribunal in *CMS v Argentina*, reacting to the proposition that international law has traditionally precluded shareholder claims regarding the injury done to a company, famously stated:

> The Tribunal therefore finds no bar in current international law to the concept of allowing claims by shareholders independently from those of the corporation concerned, not even if those shareholders are minority or non-controlling shareholders. Although it is true, as argued by the Republic of Argentina, that this is mostly the result of *lex specialis* and specific treaty arrangements that have so allowed, the fact is that *lex specialis* in this respect is so prevalent that it can now be considered the general rule, certainly in respect of foreign investments and increasingly in respect of other matters. To the extent that customary international law or generally the traditional law of international claims might have

---

76   *Ampal-American Israel Corp and others v Egypt* (n 11) paras 342–3; *Waste Management Inc v United Mexican States,* ICSID Case No ARB(AF)/00/3, Award (30 April 2004) para 85. See also *Société Générale v Dominican Republic* (n 46) paras 49–51 (giving priority to the treaty text).

77   *Enron Corporation and Ponderosa Assets LP v The Argentine Republic,* ICSID Case No ARB/01/3, Decision on Jurisdiction (14 January 2004) para 52 ('The Tribunal notes that while investors can claim in their own right under the provisions of the treaty, there is indeed a need to establish a cut-off point beyond which claims would not be permissible as they would have only a remote connection to the affected company. As this is in essence a question of admissibility of claims, the answer lies in establishing the extent of the consent to arbitration of the host State. If consent has been given in respect of an investor and an investment, it can be reasonably concluded that the claims brought by such investor are admissible under the treaty. If the consent cannot be considered as extending to another investor or investment, these other claims should then be considered inadmissible as being only remotely connected with the affected company and the scope of the legal system protecting that investment.'). And further, ibid para 56 ('in the present case the participation of the Claimants was specifically sought and [...] they are thus included within the consent to arbitration given by the Argentine Republic').

followed a different approach – a proposition that is open to debate – then that approach can be considered the exception.[78]

However, at least one tribunal has presumed that indirect investments are not protected and that their inclusion must be demonstrated. The case in question is *Berschader v Russia*. Before engaging in treaty interpretation, and after dismissing the relevance of several decisions advanced by the Claimants, the Tribunal stated that '[i]n the absence of any authority on the point, [...] there can be no presumption that the wording of Article 1.2 [definition of 'investment'] encompasses the kind of indirect investment relied upon in the instant case'.[79] From that point on, the Tribunal sought indicators of inclusion. Although the applicable BIT explicitly covered indirect investments made through intermediaries in third countries, the Tribunal found that there was no indication of the coverage of indirect investments made through intermediaries in the home state,[80] which could not be changed by the BIT's protective purpose.[81] The Tribunal held that the explicit protection of indirect investments made through third-party intermediaries deviated from the general rule that such investments would not be protected, at least at the time of the BIT's conclusion.[82] In contrast, the dissenting arbitrator applied the presumption of the protection of all indirect investments, primarily relying on the protective purpose of the BIT and noting no indicators of their exclusion.[83]

The presumption of the protection of indirect investments seems dominant in practice and therefore it should be seen as a formulated rule. The presumption instructs tribunals to observe indicators of exclusion and respondents to demonstrate that under the terms of the relevant treaty the protection of indirect investment is excluded.

---

78   *CMS Gas Transmission Company v The Republic of Argentina*, ICSID Case No ARB/01/8, Decision of the Tribunal on Objections to Jurisdiction (17 July 2003) para 48 (reference omitted).
79   *Vladimir Berschader & Moïse Berschader v The Russian Federation*, SCC Case No 80/2004, Award (21 April 2006) para 135.
80   ibid paras 136–43.
81   ibid para 144.
82   ibid paras 140–3. cf *HICEE BV v The Slovak Republic*, PCA Case No 2009-11, Partial Award (23 May 2011) paras 110–45 (reaching a similar outcome regarding an indirect investment made via intermediaries in the host state, however strictly through treaty interpretation and relying on additional treaty-related documents).
83   *Vladimir Berschader & Moïse Berschader v The Russian Federation*, SCC Case No 80/2004, Separate Opinion of Arbitrator Todd Weiler (7 April 2006) paras 6–14.

4   Rules Expanding the Scope of Arbitrable Disputes: Example of Jurisdictional Bridging

Jurisdictional clauses often do not define precise limits of arbitrable disputes, and simply refer to 'disputes' or 'all disputes' concerning an investment.[84] An important regulatory question is whether such clauses can serve as general arbitration agreements. Investor-state disputes can be complex, involving both treaty and contract claims. An investor may attempt to arbitrate a contractual dispute with the host state, relying on a jurisdictional clause contained in a BIT. Scholarship has identified this as an interpretative issue concerning the effect of wide treaty jurisdictional clauses on the arbitrability of contract claims (which I term here 'jurisdictional bridging').[85] However, tribunals have approached the issue from a principled perspective and established two opposing presumptions, first against and then in favour of jurisdictional bridging, with the modest dominance of the latter.

The prototypes of the two presumptions can be found in the two SGS cases. On the one hand, the Tribunal in *SGS v Pakistan* held that a jurisdictional clause which referred to 'disputes with respect to investments' was 'descriptive of the *factual subject matter* of the disputes', but did not 'relate to the *legal*

---

[84]   See, for example, Agreement Between the Belgium-Luxembourg Economic Union and Barbados for the Reciprocal Promotion and Protection of Investments (signed 29 May 2009, not in force) art 8(1) ('Any dispute relating to an investment between an investor of one Contracting Party and the other Contracting Party [...]'); Agreement Between the Belgium-Luxembourg Economic Union and the Government of the People's Republic of China on the Reciprocal Promotion and Protection of Investments (signed 6 June 2005, entered into force 1 December 2009) art 8(1) ('When a legal dispute arises between an investor of one Contracting Party and the other Contracting Party [...]'). cf Belgium-Luxembourg Economic Union Model BIT (2019) art 19(A) <https://investmentpolicy.unctad.org/international-investment-agreements/treaty-files/5854/download> accessed 1 September 2020 (limited to breaches of investment treaty protections).

[85]   Stanimir A Alexandrov, 'Breaches of Contract and Breaches of Treaty: The Jurisdiction of Treaty-Based Arbitration Tribunals to Decide Breach of Contract Claims in SGS v. Pakistan and *SGS v. Philippines*' (2004) 5 JWIT 555, 572–6; Emmanuel Gaillard, 'Treaty-Based Jurisdiction: Broad Dispute Resolution Clauses' *NYLJ* (6 October 2005); John P Gaffney and James L Loftis, 'The "Effective Ordinary Meaning" of BITs and the Jurisdiction of Treaty-Based Tribunals to Hear Contract Claims' (2007) 8 JWIT 5; James Crawford, 'Treaty and Contract in Investment Arbitration' (2008) 24 Arb Int'l 351, 361–4; Mary E Footer, 'Umbrella Clauses and Widely-Formulated Arbitration Clauses: Discerning the Limits of ICSID Jurisdiction' (2017) 16 LPICT 87; Alfred Siwy, 'Contract Claims and Treaty Claims' in Crina Baltag (ed), *ICSID Convention after 50 Years: Unsettled Issues* (Kluwer Law International 2017) 218–20.

basis of the claims, or the *cause of action* asserted in the claims'.[86] The Tribunal concluded that 'from that description alone [...] no implication necessarily arises that both BIT and purely contract claims are intended to be covered by the Contracting Parties in Article 9'.[87] The presumption against jurisdictional bridging is evident in the demand for indicators of inclusion of contractual disputes within the scope of the clause. The same approach can be traced in several other decisions dealing with the same issue.[88]

On the other hand, the Tribunal in *SGS v Philippines* held that a jurisdictional clause which referred to 'disputes with respect to investments' was 'not limited by reference to the legal classification of the claim that is made', and therefore *prima facie* covered both treaty and contractual disputes.[89] The Tribunal verified this conclusion by reference to other treaty provisions, which basically amounted to verification that no indicators of exclusion of contractual disputes were present.[90] The Tribunal also relied on the protective purpose of the BIT, supporting offering a choice of forum to investors and considering that 'drawing technical distinctions between causes of action arising under the BIT and those arising under the investment agreement is capable of giving rise to overlapping proceedings and jurisdictional uncertainty'.[91] The Tribunal acknowledged the *SGS v Pakistan* decision, but apart from addressing the issue of coordination between wide jurisdictional treaty clauses and exclusive jurisdiction contractual clauses, it did not address in detail the reasoning applied in that case.[92] The presumption in favour of jurisdictional bridging was evident in *SGS v Philippines* in the demand for indicators of exclusion of contractual

---

86 *SGS Société Générale de Surveillance SA v Islamic Republic of Pakistan,* ICSID Case No ARB/01/13, Decision of the Tribunal on Objections to Jurisdiction (6 August 2003) para 161 (emphasis in the original).

87 ibid. The Tribunal also added: 'Thus, we do not see anything in Article 9 or in any other provision of the BIT that can be read as vesting this Tribunal with jurisdiction over claims resting *ex hypothesi* exclusively on contract.'

88 *Joy Mining Machinery Limited v Arab Republic of Egypt,* ICSID Case No ARB/03/11, Award on Jurisdiction (6 August 2004) para 82; *Consorzio Groupement LESI-DIPENTA v People's Democratic Republic of Algeria,* ICSID Case No ARB/03/08, Award (10 January 2005) paras 25–7.

89 *SGS Société Générale de Surveillance SA v Republic of the Philippines,* ICSID Case No ARB/02/6, Decision of the Tribunal on Objections to Jurisdiction (29 January 2004) para 131.

90 ibid para 132. The Tribunal also advanced two arguments extrinsic to the BIT. First, it pointed out that investments are usually made through contracts. Second, it pointed to the example of the NAFTA, which limited the scope of arbitrable disputes to certain substantive provisions of its investment chapter.

91 ibid para 132(c).

92 ibid paras 133–4.

disputes from the scope of the jurisdictional clause, and the same approach has been taken by other tribunals.[93]

The need for indicators and its unknown origin demonstrate that the permissibility of jurisdictional bridging transcends the domain of treaty interpretation and presents a question of principle. The affirmative answer to that question can have broader effects than allowing for the arbitrability of contract claims. On the one hand, the presumption in favour of jurisdictional bridging can allow investors to bring claims against states for violations of domestic law,[94] customary international law,[95] and possibly even non-investment treaties.[96] On the other hand, the same presumption can serve state interests, by opening the doors for counterclaims against investors. Although the question of the availability of counterclaims in investment arbitration is complex,[97] one of its crucial aspects is the nexus between the scope of consent and the obligations of investors existing outside investment treaties.[98] The tribunals that

---

[93] *Compañiá de Aguas del Aconquija SA and Vivendi Universal v Argentine Republic*, ICSID Case No ARB/97/3, Decision on Annulment (3 July 2002) para 55; *SGS Société Générale de Surveillance SA v The Republic of Paraguay*, ICSID Case No ARB/07/29, Decision on Jurisdiction (12 February 2010) paras 129, 183. See also, for decisions that assumed jurisdictional bridging but focused on the condition of privity between the investor and the host state, *Salini Costruttori SpA and Italstrade SpA v Kingdom of Morocco*, ICSID Case No ARB/00/4, Decision on Jurisdiction (31 July 2001) paras 59–61; *Impregilo SpA v Pakistan* (n 41) paras 211–5.

[94] *Alpha Projektholding GmbH v Ukraine*, ICSID Case No ARB/07/16, Award (8 November 2010) para 243.

[95] *Chevron Corporation (USA) and Texaco Petroleum Corporation (USA) v Ecuador* (n 43) para 209. See also *Cambodia Power Company v Kingdom of Cambodia and Electricité du Cambodge*, ICSID Case No ARB/09/18, Decision on Jurisdiction (22 March 2011) paras 336–7 (finding that contractual arbitration clauses were wide enough to accommodate claims for violation of customary international law). See further Kate Parlett, 'Claims under Customary International Law in ICSID Arbitration' (2016) 31 ICSID Rev-FILJ 434, 453–6.

[96] Berk Demirkol, 'Non-Treaty Claims in Investment Treaty Arbitration' (2018) 31 Leiden JIL 59, 61–8.

[97] See generally Pierre Lalive and Laura Halonen, 'On the Availability of Counterclaims in Investment Treaty Arbitration' in Alexander J Bělohlávek and Naděžda Rozehnalová (eds), *Czech Yearbook of International Law*, vol II (Juris 2011) 141; Thomas Kendra, 'State Counterclaims in Investment Arbitration - A New Lease of Life?' (2013) 29 Arb Int'l 575; Dafina Atanasova, Adrián Martínez Benoit, and Josef Ostřanský, 'The Legal Framework for Counterclaims in Investment Treaty Arbitration' (2014) 31 J Int'l Arb 357; Arnaud de Nanteuil, 'Counterclaims in Investment Arbitration: Old Questions, New Answers?' (2018) 17 LPICT 374.

[98] Crawford (n 85) 364–6; Hege Elisabeth Veenstra-Kjos, 'Counter-Claims by Host States in Investment Dispute Arbitration "without Privity"' in Philippe Kahn and Thomas W Wälde (eds), *New Aspects of International Investment Law* (Martinus Nijhoff 2007) 597.

have denied the availability of counterclaims have taken an approach that can be viewed as rejecting the possibility of jurisdictional bridging.[99] Conversely, the permissibility of jurisdictional bridging seems implied in the acceptance of counterclaims.[100] An affirmative presumption, therefore, facilitates the access to international arbitration in general, although its use in relation to investors is less controversial than when it comes to claims of states.

The externality of these presumptions in relation to treaty interpretation is also visible in comparison with other questions of the scope of consent. For example, a common question is whether narrow jurisdictional clauses, referring to disputes relating to the amount of compensation for expropriation, can be extended to allow arbitrating the issue of the occurrence of expropriation.[101] One group of tribunals has denied the extension, emphasising the ordinary meaning of treaty texts.[102] Others have allowed it, emphasising the context and the object and purpose of treaties.[103] The latter group has also often attempted to reconcile its reasoning with the ordinary meaning of jurisdictional clauses.[104] This brief comparison shows the instances where tribunals have not sought external instruction but focused on internal interpretative elements giving them different priority. That does not mean that tribunals cannot discover regulatory space. For example, tribunals could formulate the presumption that narrow jurisdictional clauses imply jurisdiction over the occurrence of expropriation. If that presumption would not find basis in treaty texts but appear as an external instruction of the interpretative process, it would amount to another arbitrator-made jurisdictional rule.

---

99 *Marco Gavazzi and Stefano Gavazzi v Romania*, ICSID Case No ARB/12/25, Decision on Jurisdiction, Admissibility, and Liability (21 April 2015) para 154.

100 *Urbaser SA and CABB v The Argentine Republic*, ICSID Case No ARB/07/26, Award (8 December 2016) paras 1143–55, 1187. See also *Saluka Investments BV v The Czech Republic*, UNCITRAL ad hoc arbitration, Decision on Jurisdiction over the Czech Republic's Counterclaim (7 May 2004) para 39.

101 See generally August Reinisch, 'How Narrow Are Narrow Dispute Settlement Clauses in Investment Treaties?' (2011) 2 JIDS 115.

102 *Vladimir Berschader & Moïse Berschader v Russia* (Award) (n 79) paras 151–8; *RosInvestCo UK Ltd v The Russian Federation*, SCC Case No V 079/2005, Award on Jurisdiction (October 2007) paras 108–23.

103 *Señor Tza Yap Shum v Peru* (n 69) paras 150–61; *Renta 4 SVSA and others v The Russian Federation*, SCC Case No 24/2007, Award on Preliminary Objections (20 March 2009) paras 52, 55–7; *Sanum Investments Limited v The Government of the Lao People's Democratic Republic*, PCA Case No 2013-13, Award on Jurisdiction (13 December 2013) paras 330–42; *Beijing Urban Construction Group Co Ltd v Yemen* (n 53) paras 78–92.

104 *Señor Tza Yap Shum v Peru* (n 69) para 151; *Renta 4 SVSA and others v Russia* (n 103) paras 27–8; *Sanum Investments Limited v Laos* (n 103) para 329.

5   Conclusion

The substantive aspects of consensual jurisdictional regulation have also been affected by the development of arbitrator-made jurisdictional rules. Arbitrators have developed rules precluding retroactive denial of their jurisdiction through denial of benefits clauses, extending the validity of consent limited by time-bars, extending the scope of protected investors and investments by adopting the Broches test and presuming the protection of indirect investments, and extending the scope of justiciable disputes by presuming the permissibility of jurisdictional bridging. All these developments relax the substantive limits of arbitral jurisdiction. That does not mean that the arbitral regulatory activity has been directed towards facilitating the access to international arbitration exclusively, and Chapter 4 now turns to the examples of arbitral law-making that impose additional jurisdictionala limits, both procedural and substantive.

CHAPTER 4

Arbitrator-Made Rules Imposing Additional Jurisdictional Limits

1   Introduction

Chapters 2 and 3 analysed the arbitrator-made rules that facilitate the access to international arbitration, which operate by assisting the interpretation and application of party-defined jurisdictional rules. In contrast, this chapter focuses on the arbitrator-made rules that hinder the access to international arbitration, which often operate by imposing independent jurisdictional limits, but also assist the interpretation and application of party-provided rules. The emergence of independent rules implies a perceived need for objective limits of the investor-state dispute settlement regime, which are applicable in addition to party-defined jurisdictional limits. Section 2 first addresses the rules restricting the scope of protection, specifically the objective definitions of 'investment' and 'investor', as well as the independent legality requirement. Section 3 then discusses the restriction of the scope of arbitrable disputes by adding the privity requirement to umbrella clauses. Finally, Section 4 analyses the transformation of the abuse of process doctrine from a doctrine of general international law to a specific jurisdictional limitation of the arbitral authority regarding the specific case of investment corporate restructuring. The method in the analysis of case law described in the Introduction continues to apply.

2   Rules Restricting the Scope of Protection

Investment treaties define who qualifies as an 'investor' and what qualifies as an 'investment' and therefore who and what qualifies for their protection. However, it has also become understood that these two notions have objective meanings, implying certain criteria that must be observed in addition to those contained in treaties. I first discuss the objective definition of 'investment' (1), and then I turn to the independent legality requirement (2). Finally, I discuss the emerging objective definition of 'investor' (3).

2.1 The Objective Definition of 'Investment'

The objective definition of 'investment' has emerged in the ICSID context (1), but then spread to other, non-ICSID arbitrations (2).

2.1.1 The ICSID Framework

The trigger for the emergence of an objective definition of 'investment' was the fact that the ICSID Convention limits the jurisdiction of tribunals to 'any legal dispute arising directly out of an investment'.[1] Despite some efforts, the drafting process of that Convention did not provide a definition of the term 'investment'.[2] That omission was considered positive because it allowed the adjustment of the Convention to the developments in forms of investing over time.[3] The definition was left to disputing parties, and more importantly states that become parties to the Convention.[4] However, this has not prevented the controversies about the meaning of the term 'investment' (indeed the central term) within the ICSID framework.[5] The argument has become heated after the development of practice in this respect.

---

[1] Convention on the Settlement of Investment Disputes Between States and Nationals of Other States (signed 18 March 1965, entered into force 14 October 1966) 575 UNTS 159 (ICSID Convention) art 25(1).

[2] Aron Broches, 'The Convention on the Settlement of Investment Disputes between States and Nationals of Other States' in Aron Broches, *Selected Essays: World Bank, ICSID, and Other Subjects of Public and Private International Law* (Martinus Nijhoff 1995) 207–8; Christoph H Schreuer and others, *The ICSID Convention: A Commentary* (2nd ed, CUP 2009) 114–7.

[3] 'ICSID 1984 Annual Report', 9 <https://icsid.worldbank.org/sites/default/files/publications/annual-report/en/1984-ar-final-en.pdf> accessed 28 August 2020.

[4] 'Report of the Executive Directors on the Convention on the Settlement of Investment Disputes Between States and Nationals of Other States, 1965' (1993) 1 ICSID Reports 23, para 27 ('No attempt was made to define the term "investment" given the essential requirement of consent by the parties, and the mechanism through which Contracting States can make known in advance, if they so desire, the classes of disputes which they would or would not consider submitting to the Centre (Article 25(4)).'). See also Julian Davis Mortenson, 'The Meaning of "Investment": ICSID's *Travaux* and the Domain of International Investment Law' (2010) 51 Harvard Int'l LJ 257 (criticising the sharpening of the ICSID notion of investment by tribunals and arguing in favour of deference to state commitments).

[5] See, among many others, Schreuer and others (n 2) 117–9, 128–34; Sebastien Manciaux, 'The Notion of Investment: New Controversies' (2008) 9 JWIT 443; Emmanuel Gaillard, 'Identify or Define? Reflections on the Evolution of the Concept of Investment in ICSID Practice' in Christina Binder and others (eds), *International Investment Law for the 21st Century: Essays in Honour of Christoph Schreuer* (OUP 2009) 403; Pierre-Emmanuel Dupont, 'The Notion of ICSID Investment: Ongoing "Confusion" or "Emerging Synthesis"?' (2011) 12 JWIT 245; Michael Hwang SC and Lee Chengy Fong, 'Definition of "Investment"—A Voice from the Eye of the Storm' (2011) 1 Asian JIL 99; Mavluda Sattorova, 'Defining Investment Under the ICSID Convention and BITs: Of Ordinary Meaning, Telos, and Beyond' (2012) 2 Asian JIL 267; Stephen M Schwebel, 'Does the Consent of the Contracting Parties Govern

The decision that created the famous set of criteria implying an objective definition of 'investment' was the 2001 jurisdictional decision in *Salini v Morocco*.[6] After noting that the ICSID Convention did not define 'investment', the Tribunal stated that 'it would be inaccurate to consider that the requirement that a dispute be *"in direct relation to an investment"* is diluted by the consent of the Contracting Parties', and that 'ICSID case law and legal authors agree that the investment requirement must be respected as an objective condition of the jurisdiction of the Centre'.[7] After noting that there were no criteria developed in practice, the Tribunal stated:

> The doctrine generally considers that investment infers: contributions, a certain duration of performance of the contract and a participation in the risks of the transaction [...] In reading the Convention's preamble, one may add the contribution to the economic development of the host State of the investment as an additional condition.
>
> In reality, these various elements may be interdependent. Thus, the risks of the transaction may depend on the contributions and the duration of performance of the contract. As a result, these various criteria should be assessed globally even if, for the sake of reasoning, the Tribunal considers them individually here.[8]

The Tribunal relied on an academic commentary of arbitral practice.[9] The only other case that it could invoke was *Fedax v Venezuela*.[10] The Tribunal in the latter case noted that it was the very first one to face an objection that the transaction at stake did not qualify as an 'investment' under the ICSID Convention.[11] The *Fedax* Tribunal indeed discussed whether the notion of investment

---

      the Requirement of an "Investment" as Specified in Article 25 of the ICSID Convention?' in Yas Banifatemi (ed), *Jurisdiction in Investment Treaty Arbitration* (Juris 2018) 55.

6   *Salini Costruttori SpA and Italstrade SpA v Kingdom of Morocco*, ICSID Case No ARB/00/4, Decision on Jurisdiction (31 July 2001).

7   ibid para 52 (emphasis in the original).

8   ibid.

9   In particular, relying on Emmanuel Gaillard, 'Centre international pour le reglement des differends relatifs aux investissements (CIRDI)' (1999) 126 Journal du droit international 273, 278–93 (addressing the 1997 *Fedax v Venezuela* decision).

10   *Fedax NV v The Republic of Venezuela*, ICSID Case No ARB/96/3, Decision of the Tribunal on Objections to Jurisdiction (11 July 1997). Another decision rendered before but not mentioned in *Salini*, which recognised the autonomous nature of 'investment' in the ICSID Convention, was *Ceskoslovenska Obchodni Banka AS v The Slovak Republic*, ICSID Case No ARB/97/4, Decision of the Tribunal on Objections to Jurisdiction (24 May 1999) para 68.

11   *Fedax NV v Venezuela* (n 10) para 25.

was met under the Convention independently from the relevant investment treaty, although without analysing any concrete criteria.[12] However, the *Fedax* Tribunal reaffirmed that 'as contemplated by the Convention, the definition of "investment" is controlled by consent of the Contracting Parties'.[13] It distinguished the transaction at stake (promissory notes) from an 'ordinary commercial transaction'.[14] In the very end of its considerations, the *Fedax* Tribunal noted that '[t]he basic features of an investment have been described as involving a certain duration, a certain regularity of profit and return, assumption of risk, a substantial commitment and a significance for the host State's development',[15] relying on the work of Christoph Schreuer.[16] While the *Fedax* Tribunal used these criteria only to verify its previous conclusions, the *Salini* Tribunal formalised them into a clear set of conditions for the establishment of jurisdiction under the ICSID Convention.

Four criteria (contribution, duration, risk, and contribution to the economic development of the host state) have become the famous '*Salini* criteria'. Some tribunals have adopted this test verbatim,[17] but others have modified it by adding new criteria. The Tribunal in *Joy Mining v Egypt* added the condition of 'regularity of profit and return', and qualified the conditions of commitment and contribution to the economic development of the host state as 'substantial' and 'significant' respectively.[18] The Tribunal in *Phoenix Action v Czechia* did not follow the Respondent's reliance on *Salini,* holding that that test had

---

12   ibid paras 25–9.
13   ibid para 31.
14   ibid para 42.
15   ibid para 43.
16   Referring to Christoph Schreuer, 'Commentary on the ICSID Convention' (1996) 11 ICSID Rev-FILJ 318, 372.
17   *Bayindir Insaat Turizm Ticaret Ve Sanayi AS v Islamic Republic of Pakistan,* ICSID Case No ARB/03/29, Decision on Jurisdiction (14 November 2005) para 130; *Jan de Nul NV and Dredging International NV v Arab Republic of Egypt,* ICSID Case No ARB/04/13, Decision on Jurisdiction (16 June 2006) para 91; *Saipem SpA v People's Republic of Bangladesh,* ICSID Case No ARB/05/7, Decision on Jurisdiction and Recommendation on Provisional Measures (21 March 2007) para 99; *Cortec Mining Kenya Limited, Cortec (Pty) Limited, and Stirling Capital Limited v Republic of Kenya,* ICSID Case No ARB/15/29, Award (22 October 2018) paras 298–300.
18   *Joy Mining Machinery Limited v Arab Republic of Egypt,* ICSID Case No ARB/03/11, Award on Jurisdiction (6 August 2004) para 53. See also *Unión Fenosa Gas SA v Arab Republic of Egypt,* ICSID Case No ARB/14/4, Award (31 August 2018) para 6.66 ('these rights satisfy the guidelines provided by the ICSID award in *Salini v. Morocco* (2001) in regard to duration, profit and return, risk and commitment to the development of the Respondent's economy').

to be supplemented.[19] It came up with six criteria: contribution, duration, risk, development of an economic activity in the host state (as opposed to the contribution to economic development), the compliance with the laws of the host state, and the *bona fide* nature of the investment.[20] Although the fourth and fifth criteria were reflected in the applicable BIT, the Tribunal considered them implicit in the ICSID notion and applicable regardless of the specific BIT terms.[21]

Yet another group of tribunals has created a rump *Salini* test consisting of three criteria. One tribunal noted that '[w]ith the evolution of arbitral jurisprudence, the objective definition of the notion of investment now includes only: (i) a contribution, (ii) the receipt of returns and (iii) the assumption of risks'.[22] But the most-represented version of a rump *Salini* test observes contribution, duration, and risk.[23] Finally, the Tribunal in *Abaclat and others v Argentina* rejected the *Salini* test, arguing that a finding that there was an investment under the BIT but which could not be protected under the ICSID Convention would be against the latter's object and purpose, and considering that a contribution that is 'apt to create the value that is protected under the BIT' is the sole criterion under the ICSID Convention.[24]

The tribunals that have formulated a rump *Salini* test had a specific problem with the criterion of the contribution to the development of the host state. Several tribunals have maintained that this should be the effect or

---

19   *Phoenix Action Ltd v The Czech Republic*, ICSID Case No ARB/06/5, Award (15 April 2009) para 82.
20   ibid para 114.
21   ibid para 116.
22   *Isolux Infrastructure Netherlands BV v Kingdom of Spain*, SCC Case No V2013/153, Award (12 July 2016) para 685; translation in *Masdar Solar & Wind Cooperatief UA v Kingdom of Spain*, ICSID Case No ARB/14/1, Award (16 May 2018) para 198.
23   *LESI SpA and ASTALDI SpA v République algérienne démocratique et populaire*, ICSID Case No ARB/05/3, Decision (12 July 2006) para 72(iv); *Victor Pey Casado and President Allende Foundation v Republic of Chile*, ICSID Case No ARB/98/2, Award (8 May 2008) para 233; *Mr Saba Fakes v Republic of Turkey*, ICSID Case No ARB/07/20, Award (14 July 2010) para 110; *Quiborax SA, Non Metallic Minerals SA, and Allan Fosk Kaplún v Plurinational State of Bolivia*, ICSID Case No ARB/06/2, Decision on Jurisdiction (27 September 2012) para 227; *KT Asia Investment Group BV v Republic of Kazakhstan*, ICSID Case No ARB/09/8, Award (17 October 2013) para 173; *Poštová banka as and Istrokapital SE v The Hellenic Republic*, ICSID Case No ARB/13/8, Award (9 April 2015) para 371; *Masdar Solar & Wind Cooperatief UA v Spain* (n 22) para 199; *Krederi Ltd v Ukraine*, ICSID Case No ARB/14/17, Award (2 July 2018) para 237.
24   *Abaclat and others v The Argentine Republic*, ICSID Case No ARB/07/5, Decision on Jurisdiction and Admissibility (4 August 2011) paras 363–5.

consequence of investments, not a condition for their existence.[25] Others have considered that such a requirement is simply difficult to establish.[26] A controversy has also arisen about its relationship with the ICSID framework. Two annulment decisions are instructive in this regard. The Annulment Committee in *Patrick Mitchell v Congo* emphasised the preamble of the ICSID Convention and derived the contribution to the development of the host state as an 'essential' criterion of an investment, although this '[did] not mean that this contribution must always be sizable or successful'.[27] The Committee annulled the Award for the failure to address this issue in its reasoning, and specified that it had to answer the question how the investor 'had concretely assisted' the state.[28] Conversely, in *Malaysian Historical Salvors v Malaysia*, the Annulment Committee did not agree with the Sole Arbitrator's reliance on *Salini* in its entirety,[29] and specifically criticised him for 'exigently interpret[ing] the alleged condition of a contribution to the economic development of the host State so as to exclude small contributions, and contributions of a cultural and historical nature'.[30] The dissenting member of the Committee argued that the contribution to the economic development of the host state was indeed an 'outer limit' and a strict condition of 'investment' under the ICSID Convention, relying on the Convention's context and object and purpose.[31] He also argued that such contribution had to be 'substantial', relying on policy considerations.[32] These examples reveal that despite the alleged treaty basis of the

---

25 *Victor Pey Casado and President Allende Foundation v Chile* (n 23) para 232; *Mr Saba Fakes v Turkey* (n 23) para 111; *Quiborax SA, Non Metallic Minerals SA, and Allan Fosk Kaplún v Bolivia* (n 23) paras 220–5; *KT Asia Investment Group BV v Kazakhstan* (n 23) paras 171–2.
26 *LESI SpA and ASTALDI SpA v Algeria* (n 23) para 72(iv); *Phoenix Action Ltd v Czechia* (n 19) para 85.
27 *Mr Patrick Mitchell v The Democratic Republic of Congo*, ICSID Case No ARB/99/7, Decision on the Application for Annulment of the Award (1 November 2006) paras 27–33.
28 ibid paras 39–41.
29 *Malaysian Historical Salvors Sdn Bhd v The Government of Malaysia*, ICSID Case No ARB/05/10, Decision on the Application for Annulment (16 April 2009) paras 75–81.
30 ibid para 80(b).
31 *Malaysian Historical Salvors Sdn Bhd v The Government of Malaysia*, ICSID Case No ARB/05/10, Annulment Proceedings, Dissenting Opinion of Judge Mohamed Shahabuddeen (19 February 2009) paras 14–32.
32 ibid paras 33–8 (stating at para 34: '[...] the search for the "ordinary meaning" of "investment" sooner or later throws the searcher back on the understanding of the international legal community. The international legal community would have rejected out of hand the idea that any contribution to the economic development of the host State, however miniscule that contribution is, is sufficient to qualify the whole outlay as an "investment" within the meaning of Article 25(1) of the ICSID Convention.').

condition, its inclusion is motivated externally by the policy considerations of arbitrators regarding what amounts to a proper investment.

Some tribunals have not been willing to admit the hard normativity of the *Salini* (or any similar) criteria. One tribunal, deciding before *Salini*, explicitly rejected a similar definition of 'investment' suggested by the Respondent, arguing that its elements 'tend as a rule to be present in most investments, [but] are not a formal prerequisite for the finding that a transaction constitutes an investment as that concept is understood under the [ICSID] Convention'.[33] Almost a decade later, the Tribunal in *Biwater v Tanzania* rejected the *Salini* criteria holing that they 'are not fixed or mandatory as a matter of law'.[34] The Tribunal also had conceptual difficulties with the *Salini* test, holding that it was inflexible and therefore inappropriate for the ICSID context.[35] It argued that

> a more flexible and pragmatic approach to the meaning of "investment" is appropriate, which takes into account the features identified in *Salini*, but along with all the circumstances of the case, including the nature of the instrument containing the relevant consent to ICSID.
>
> [...]
>
> To this end, even if the Republic could demonstrate that any, or all, of the *Salini* criteria are not satisfied in this case, this would not necessarily be sufficient – in and of itself – to deny jurisdiction.[36]

On the facts, the Tribunal concluded that there was an investment, and that 'even if such are required for the purposes of Article 25 of the Convention, the conditions of "*risk*" and "*commitment*" [...] were present'.[37] This stream of practice gave rise to the inductive thinking about the notion of investment under the ICSID Convention,[38] which observes elements that are *characteristic* for an investment, rather than deductive criteria for its qualification.[39] However,

---

33   *Ceskoslovenska Obchodni Banka AS v Slovakia* (n 10) para 90.
34   *Biwater Gauff (Tanzania) Ltd v United Republic of Tanzania*, ICSID Case No ARB/05/22, Award (24 July 2008) para 312.
35   ibid paras 314–5.
36   ibid paras 316, 318.
37   ibid para 320 (emphasis in the original).
38   See also *Toto Costruzioni Generali SpA v The Republic of Lebanon*, ICSID Case No ARB/07/12, Decision on Jurisdiction (11 September 2009) paras 77–87 (endorsing the *Biwater* approach, but practically applying the *Salini* test).
39   cf *Victor Pey Casado and President Allende Foundation v Chile* (n 23) para 232 ('Le présent Tribunal estime pour sa part qu'il existe bien une définition de l'investissement au sens de la Convention CIRDI et qu'il ne suffit pas de relever la présence de certaines des

the argument exists that the distinction between these two streams is only academic, and that they do not imply any differences in practice.[40]

Finally, the fifth group of tribunals has thought that there was no space for reading additional requirements into the ICSID Convention: because that Convention did not define 'investment', only BIT definitions were relevant. While some tribunals have simply proceeded straightforward to treaty definitions,[41] others have emphasised the lack of a definition in the ICSID Convention.[42] Some have deferred to BIT definitions and contractual arrangements.[43] However, these tribunals have not isolated themselves from the broader discourse. One tribunal opined that

> the requirements that were taken into account in some arbitral precedents for purposes of denoting the existence of an investment protected by a treaty (such as the duration and risk of the alleged investment) must be considered as mere examples and not necessarily as elements that are required for its existence.[44]

« caractéristiques » habituelles d'un investissement pour que cette condition objective de la compétence du Centre soit satisfaite.').

40 *Malaysian Historical Salvors Sdn Bhd v The Government of Malaysia*, ICSID Case No ARB/05/10, Award on Jurisdiction (17 May 2007) para 105.

41 *Middle East Cement Shipping and Handling Co SA v Arab Republic of Egypt*, ICSID Case No ARB/99/6, Award (12 April 2002) paras 135–6.

42 *Generation Ukraine Inc v Ukraine*, ICSID Case No ARB/00/9, Award (16 September 2003) para 8.2; *Tokios Tokelės v Ukraine*, ICSID Case No ARB/02/18, Decision on Jurisdiction (29 April 2004) para 73; *MCI Power Group LC and New Turbine Inc v Republic of Ecuador*, ICSID Case No ARB/03/6, Award (31 July 2007) para 159; *Parkerings-Compagniet AS v Republic of Lithuania*, ICSID Case No ARB/05/8, Award (11 September 2007) para 249.

43 *Georg Gavrilović and Gavrilović doo v Republic of Croatia*, ICSID Case No ARB/12/39, Award (26 July 2018) para 192 (deference to the BIT definition); *Caratube International Oil Company LLP and Mr Devincci Salah Hourani v Republic of Kazakhstan*, ICSID Case No ARB/13/13, Award (27 September 2017) para 635 ('where there is an agreement between the parties regarding the existence of an investment, they are generally precluded from later challenging ICSID's jurisdiction based on the alleged absence of an investment'); *Alpha Projektholding GmbH v Ukraine*, ICSID Case No ARB/07/16, Award (8 November 2010) para 314 (deference to the BIT definition). See also *Abaclat and others v Argentina* (n 24) para 364 (although acknowledging the double-barrelled test, prioritising the BIT definition).

44 *MCI Power Group LC and New Turbine Inc v Ecuador* (n 42) para 165. See also *Georg Gavrilović and Gavrilović doo v Croatia* (n 43) para 193 (admitting that the *Salini* criteria can be useful in special circumstances).

The Sole Arbitrator in *Pantechniki v Albania* also took this route. He started by challenging the general understanding of *Salini* in a *Biwater* manner,[45] but then disputed the autonomous meaning of the term 'investment' within the ICSID Convention, especially as a jurisdictional requirement.[46] Admittedly, the Sole Arbitrator supported reaching a consensus on an inherent meaning of the term 'investment' from a policy perspective, but this did not have a clear effect on his final determination.[47]

The practice concerning the objective definition of 'investment' is often criticised for inconsistency.[48] However, I suggest that there is more consistency than it seems at first. It is now a dominant view that the qualification of an investment assumes a double-barrelled test, observing criteria under both the ICSID Convention and the relevant BIT.[49] Furthermore, when it comes to the objective criteria, the *Salini* test dominates. Even the tribunals that have not considered this test decisive have consulted its criteria in drawing their conclusions.[50] It is not surprising, therefore, that these criteria have transcended the ICSID Convention.

2.1.2 Non-ICSID Context

The objective definition of 'investment' has spread from ICSID to non-ICSID arbitrations. Because of the absence of an instrument doubling the notion of investment, only treaty definitions appear relevant in the non-ICSID context. However, a different view has emerged. In *Romak v Uzbekistan*, the Tribunal stressed the need for an inherent meaning of the notion of investment. That meaning was necessary, among other reasons, because the relevant treaty did

---

45 *Pantechniki SA Contractors & Engineers (Greece) v The Republic of Albania*, ICSID Case No ARB/07/21, Award (30 July 2009) para 36.
46 ibid paras 41, 43.
47 ibid paras 46–7.
48 *Mr Saba Fakes v Turkey* (n 23) para 97.
49 See *Global Trading Resource Corp and Globex International Inc v Ukraine*, ICSID Case No ARB/09/11, Award (1 December 2010) para 43 ('it is now beyond argument that there are two independent parameters that must both be satisfied: what the parties have given their consent to, as the foundation for submission to arbitration; and what the Convention establishes as the framework for the competence of any tribunal set up under its provisions'); Schwebel (n 5) 55.
50 See, for example, *Georg Gavrilović and Gavrilović doo v Croatia* (n 43) para 194; *MCI Power Group LC and New Turbine Inc v Ecuador* (n 42) para 165; *Pantechniki SA Contractors & Engineers (Greece) v Albania* (n 45) paras 48–9; *Alpha Projektholding GmbH v Ukraine* (n 43) paras 316–31; *Abaclat and others v Argentina* (n 24) paras 370–1; *CMC Muratori Cementisti CMC Di Ravenna SOC Coop and others v Republic of Mozambique*, ICSID Case No ARB/17/23, Award (24 October 2019) paras 194–5.

not define investments exhaustively,[51] but also because it was necessary to distinguish conceptually between investments and 'purely commercial transactions'.[52] Concerning the latter point, the Tribunal adopted the policy considerations advanced in the *Joy Mining* case,[53] although it also attempted to link the need for distinguishing to the treaty's object and purpose.[54] After reviewing arbitral practice, the Tribunal came up with a set of criteria that could be characterised as a rump *Salini* test:

> The Arbitral Tribunal therefore considers that the term "investments" under the BIT has an inherent meaning (irrespective of whether the investor resorts to ICSID or UNCITRAL arbitral proceedings) entailing a *contribution* that extends over a *certain period of time* and that involves some *risk*.[55]

Although accommodating this conclusion within the narrative of treaty interpretation,[56] the Tribunal clearly engaged in an arbitration-transcending discourse about the objective meaning of 'investment'.[57] The Tribunal even suggested that states can opt-out of the inherent meaning of 'investment' and assign that term whatever meaning they wish, however under the condition that 'the wording of the instrument in question must leave no room for doubt that the intention of the contracting States was to accord to the term "investment" an extraordinary and counterintuitive meaning'.[58]

The endeavour of the *Romak* Tribunal is somehow surprising, given its insistence that it was neither bound by previous decisions nor mandated to develop the law.[59] Perhaps more pragmatic reasons have forced the Tribunal to move

---

51   *Romak SA (Switzerland) v The Republic of Uzbekistan,* PCA Case No AA280, Award (26 November 2009) para 180.
52   ibid para 185.
53   *Joy Mining Machinery Limited v Egypt* (n 18) para 58 ('[...] if a distinction is not drawn between ordinary sales contracts, even if complex, and an investment, the result would be that any sales or procurement contract involving a State agency would qualify as an investment. [...] Yet, those contracts are not investment contracts, except in exceptional circumstances, and are to be kept separate and distinct for the sake of a stable legal order.').
54   *Romak SA (Switzerland) v Uzbekistan* (n 51) para 189.
55   ibid para 207 (emphasis in the original).
56   ibid para 206.
57   See ibid para 207 ('The Arbitral Tribunal is further comforted in its analysis by the reasoning adopted by other arbitral tribunals [...] which consistently incorporates contribution, duration and risk as hallmarks of an "investment." ').
58   ibid para 205.
59   ibid paras 170–1.

in that direction: the Tribunal noted that it would be unreasonable to allow the term 'investment' to change meaning by simple choice of the claimant between ICSID and non-ICSID arbitrations, or to render the choice of ICSID arbitration ineffective by broadening the term's meaning.[60] The Tribunal therefore acknowledged the objective meaning of 'investment' in the ICSID context and admitted the need for harmonisation.

The *Romak* decision was the first step in the objectivization of the term 'investment' independently of any framework regulation. Other non-ICSID tribunals followed, usually applying a rump *Salini*.[61] Some ICSID tribunals referred to an inherent meaning of the term 'investment' itself, rather than the one provided in Article 25(1) of the ICSID Convention.[62] And some ICSID tribunals asserted that this provision referred to the 'ordinary meaning' (ie objective one) of 'investment' existing outside the ICSID Convention.[63] The *Romak* case is the usual point of reference in these ICSID decisions.[64] That is not to say that the practice is absolutely uniform. It is occasionally maintained that outside the ICSID context there is no room for adding another definition of 'investment' and that only BIT definitions apply,[65] especially by domestic courts reviewing arbitral decisions.[66] Yet, the objective definition of 'investment' is a good example of widespread acceptance of an arbitrator-made rule, which is visible in the attitudes of claimants, who are now reluctant to

---

60   ibid paras 194–5. See also *Pantechniki SA Contractors & Engineers (Greece) v Albania* (n 45) para 46.

61   *Professor Christian Doutremepuich and Antoine Doutremepuich v The Republic of Mauritius*, PCA Case No 2018-37, Award on Jurisdiction (23 August 2019) paras 117–8; *Isolux Infrastructure Netherlands BV v Spain* (n 22) paras 683–5; *Nova Scotia Power Incorporated (Canada) v Bolivarian Republic of Venezuela*, ICSID Case No ARB(AF)/11/1, Award (30 April 2014) paras 77–84; *Alps Finance and Trade AG v The Slovak Republic*, UNCITRAL ad hoc arbitration, Award (5 March 2011) paras 239–41.

62   *GEA Group Aktiengesellschaft v Ukraine*, ICSID Case No ARB/08/16, Award (31 March 2011) para 141; *Masdar Solar & Wind Cooperatief UA v Spain* (n 22) para 196.

63   *Mr Saba Fakes v Turkey* (n 23) para 108; *Quiborax SA, Non Metallic Minerals SA, and Allan Fosk Kaplún v Bolivia* (n 23) para 212; *KT Asia Investment Group BV v Kazakhstan* (n 23) para 165.

64   *GEA Group Aktiengesellschaft v Ukraine* (n 62) para 141; *Masdar Solar & Wind Cooperatief UA v Spain* (n 22) para 197; *Quiborax SA, Non Metallic Minerals SA, and Allan Fosk Kaplún v Bolivia* (n 23) para 216; *KT Asia Investment Group BV v Kazakhstan* (n 23) para 165.

65   *AnY Ltd v Czech Republic*, ICSID Case No UNCT/15/1, Award (29 June 2018) paras 139–40.

66   Arrêt du 25 septembre 2008, Cour d'Appel de Paris, 1ère Chambre - Section C (France) 07/04675, 5; Arrêt du 20 septembre 2016, Tribunal fédéral, Ire Cour de droit civil (Switzerland) 4A_616/2015 [3.2.2, 3.4.1]; *The Republic of Korea v Mohammad Reza Dayyani and others* [2019] EWHC 3580 (Comm) [57–9].

challenge its existence.[67] As pointed out by commentators, the objectivity at hand has become systemic, rather than institutional.[68]

2.2 The Independent Legality Requirement

Many investment treaties limit the scope of protected investments with the requirement that they are established in accordance with the law of the host state (legality requirements).[69] The specific question addressed here is whether in the absence of a legality requirement in the applicable treaty, such a requirement exists independently of the treaty text, and if so whether it presents a jurisdictional limit? I argue that the answer is affirmative.

The first step in the formation of the independent legality requirement was the recognition of the need to deny protection to illegally made investments and of the regulatory space exposed by the absence of explicit legality requirements. In *Inceysa v El Salvador*, involving an explicit legality requirement in the BIT, the Tribunal opined that the inclusion of such clauses in BITs was 'a clear manifestation of said international public policy, which demonstrates the clear and obvious intent of the signatory States to exclude from its protection investments made in violation of the internal laws of each of them'.[70] These clauses followed 'international public policies designed to sanction illegal acts and their resulting effects'.[71] The Tribunal noted that 'respect for the law is a matter of public policy [...] in any civilized country' and that 'there is a meta-positive provision that prohibits attributing effects to an act done illegally'.[72] The international public policy was also cited in *Plama v Bulgaria*.

---

67   See, for example, *Quiborax SA, Non Metallic Minerals SA, and Allan Fosk Kaplún v Bolivia* (n 23) para 213; *KT Asia Investment Group BV v Kazakhstan* (n 23) para 164.
68   Perry S Bechky, '*Salini*'s Nature: Arbitrators' Duty of Jurisdictional Policing' (2018) 17 LPICT 145, 158–9.
69   See generally Rahim Moloo and Alex Khachaturian, 'The Compliance with the Law Requirement in International Investment Law' (2011) 34 Fordham Int'l LJ 1473; Stephan W Schill, 'Illegal Investments in Investment Treaty Arbitration' (2012) 11 LPICT 281; Thomas Obersteiner, '"In Accordance with Domestic Law" Clauses: How International Investment Tribunals Deal with Allegations of Unlawful Conduct of Investors' (2014) 31 J Int'l Arb 265; Michael Polkinghorne and Sven-Michael Volkmer, 'The Legality Requirement in Investment Arbitration' in Yas Banifatemi (ed), *Jurisdiction in Investment Treaty Arbitration* (Juris 2018) 65.
70   *Inceysa Vallisoletana SL v Republic of El Salvador*, ICSID Case No ARB/03/26, Award (2 August 2006) para 246.
71   ibid para 247.
72   ibid para 248. See also ibid para 252 ('not to exclude Inceysa's investment from the protection of the BIT would be a violation of international public policy, which this Tribunal cannot allow').

The applicable ECT did not contain an explicit legality requirement, but the Tribunal held that 'the substantive protections of the ECT cannot apply to investments that are made contrary to law'.[73] After surveying case law, the Tribunal held that granting protection to the investment under the ECT would 'be contrary to the basic notion of international public policy – that a contract obtained by wrongful means (fraudulent misrepresentation) should not be enforced by a tribunal'.[74] These questions were discussed as part of the merits, because of the lack of a jurisdictional limitation in the ECT.[75] The central value of these decisions is the acknowledgment of the international public policy as the carrier of the requirement that an investor must act legally in establishing his investment, and of the regulatory space exposed by the absence of explicit legality clauses. This suggestion has also been affirmed in the context of contractual arbitrations.[76]

The second step was the formalisation of the independent legality requirement as a jurisdictional condition. In the absence of an explicit legality requirement in the relevant treaty, imposing such a requirement as a jurisdictional limit seems problematic, for which reason scholars argue that the legality of an investment can be discussed only as a matter of admissibility[77] or merits.[78] Nevertheless, tribunals have done so. The Tribunal in *Phoenix Action v Czechia* included a legality requirement in the objective definition of 'investment', or more precisely the definition of a *protected* investment.[79] Despite the fact that the relevant BIT contained an explicit legality requirement, the Tribunal stated:

> In the Tribunal's view, *States cannot be deemed to offer access to the ICSID dispute settlement mechanism to investments made in violation of their laws.* If a State, for example, restricts foreign investment in a sector of its

---

[73] *Plama Consortium Limited v Republic of Bulgaria*, ICSID Case No ARB/03/24, Award (27 August 2008) paras 138–9.

[74] ibid para 143. See also *Blusun SA, Jean-Pierre Lecorcier, and Michael Stein v Italian Republic*, ICSID Case No ARB/14/3, Award (27 December 2016) para 264; *Yukos Universal Limited (Isle of Man) v The Russian Federation*, PCA Case No AA 227, Final Award (18 July 2014) paras 1349–52.

[75] *Plama Consortium Limited v Republic of Bulgaria*, ICSID Case No ARB/03/24, Decision on Jurisdiction (8 February 2005) para 229.

[76] *World Duty Free Company Limited v The Republic of Kenya*, ICSID Case No ARB/00/7, Award (4 October 2006) paras 138–57.

[77] Moloo and Khachaturian (n 69) 1489; Obersteiner (n 69) 275.

[78] Schill (n 69) 322–3.

[79] *Phoenix Action Ltd v Czechia* (n 19) para 114.

economy and a foreign investor disregards such restriction, the investment concerned cannot be protected under the ICSID/BIT system. These are illegal investments according to the national law of the host State and cannot be protected through an ICSID arbitral process. *And it is the Tribunal's view that this condition – the conformity of the establishment of the investment with the national laws – is implicit even when not expressly stated in the relevant BIT.* This position of the Tribunal has also been adopted in the case of *Plama*, where the Tribunal was faced with the silence of the relevant treaty on the necessary conformity of a protected investment with the laws of the host country.[80]

For the Tribunal, manifestly illegal investments would lead to the denial of jurisdiction, although it also conceded that the fact of illegality can be discovered only on the merits or considered better addressed at that stage.[81] The Tribunal did not clearly distinguish between the establishment and performance of an investment. It held that the legality requirement pertained 'to the access to the substantive provisions', which 'can be denied through a decision on the merits', but 'if it is manifest that the investment has been *performed* in violation of the law, it is in line with judicial economy not to assert jurisdiction'.[82] While the Tribunal did not elaborate on the procedural consequences of the distinction between the establishment and performance of an investment, its reasoning implies that illegality in the establishment of an investment is in any event a jurisdictional obstacle.

The Tribunal in *Hamester v Ghana*, also facing a BIT with an explicit legality requirement,[83] endorsed the reasoning of *Phoenix*:

> An investment will not be protected if it has been created in violation of national or international principles of good faith; by way of corruption, fraud, or deceitful conduct; or if its creation itself constitutes a misuse of the system of international investment protection under the ICSID Convention. It will also not be protected if it is made in violation of the host State's law [...] *These are general principles that exist independently of specific language to this effect in the Treaty.*[84]

---

80 ibid para 101 (emphasis added).
81 ibid para 102.
82 ibid para 104 (emphasis added).
83 *Gustav F W Hamester GmbH & Co KG v Republic of Ghana*, ICSID Case No ARB/07/24, Award (18 June 2010) para 126.
84 ibid paras 123–4 (emphasis added). See also *SAUR International SA v Republic of Argentina*, ICSID Case No ARB/04/4, Decision on Jurisdiction and Liability (6 June 2012) para 308

Regarding the reach of the legality requirement, the Tribunal held that 'on the wording of this BIT, the legality of the creation of the investment is a jurisdictional issue; the legality of the investor's conduct during the life of the investment is a merits issue', but that 'the broader principle of international law [...] does not change this analysis of [the BIT legality requirement], and in particular its distinction between legality at different stages of the investment'.[85] The Tribunal thus gave priority to the BIT terms over the arbitrator-made law, and rightly so. In the absence of an explicit clause, however, there is no reason for not applying the same distinction between illegally *made* (precluding jurisdiction) and *operated* investments (pertaining to merits). The rationale is the same: illegally made investments could never qualify for protection (thus precluding jurisdiction *ratione materiae*). Nevertheless, the question whether an implied legality requirement concerns jurisdiction or merits remains blurred.[86] Recently, the Tribunal in *Cortec v Kenya* held: 'It is accepted jurisprudence that in order to be protected an investment has to be in accordance with the laws of the host State and made in good faith. This requirement can be analyzed at the jurisdictional or the merits level.'[87] The Tribunal then dismissed claims for the lack of jurisdiction because of the illegality of the investment.[88]

These steps have formulated the arbitrator-made legality requirement. There is a growing understanding that investments that are not made in compliance with domestic laws of host states cannot be protected under

('Le fait que l'APRI entre la France et l'Argentine mentionne ou non l'exigence que l'investisseur agisse conformément à la législation interne ne constitue pas un facteur pertinent. La condition de ne pas commettre de violation grave de l'ordre juridique est une condition tacite, propre à tout APRI, car en tout état de cause, il est incompréhensible qu'un État offre le bénéfice de la protection par un arbitrage d'investissement si l'investisseur, pour obtenir cette protection, a agit à l'encontre du droit.' [reference omitted]).

85   *Gustav F W Hamester GmbH & Co KG v Ghana* (n 83) para 127.
86   Note the debate about whether any legality requirement, explicit or implicit, relates to jurisdiction or admissibility/merits. cf Zachary Douglas, 'The Plea of Illegality in Investment Treaty Arbitration' (2014) 29 ICSID Rev-FILJ 155 (illegal conduct of an investor is never a question of jurisdiction); and Andrew Newcombe, 'Investor Misconduct: Jurisdiction, Admissibility or Merits?' in Chester Brown and Kate Miles (eds), *Evolution in Investment Treaty Law and Arbitration* (CUP 2011) 187 (illegality as a question of admissibility); with Thomas Roe, 'Illegality and Jurisdiction in Investment Arbitration' (2016) 2 Turkish Commercial L Rev 17 (illegality as a question of jurisdiction in the case of explicit clauses).
87   *Cortec Mining Kenya Limited, Cortec (Pty) Limited, and Stirling Capital Limited v Kenya* (n 17) para 260.
88   ibid para 333 (holding, among other reasons, that '[t]he *explicit* language to the effect that protected investments must be made "in accordance with the laws of Kenya" is therefore unnecessary to secure the objects and purpose of the BIT' [emphasis in the original]).

investment treaties in principle, even if that assumes leaving the terms of clear treaty provisions and entering the sphere of meta rules.[89] This development is indeed conceptual, because it rebuts the paradigm of investment law that imposes obligations on states exclusively.[90] Furthermore, tribunals are capable and willing to translate that general understanding into a rule governing their jurisdiction. Despite the attempts to embed the arbitrator-made rule in treaty terms,[91] tribunals readily reach to policy considerations, therefrom formulating an independent jurisdictional rule.

Again, arbitral practice has not been uniform. Some tribunals have criticised the inclusion of a legality requirement in the objective definition of 'investment', arguing that the applicability of such a requirement to investments depends on the will of BIT parties.[92] These tribunals have taken a rather technical view, arguing that the question whether something qualifies as an investment is different from the question whether that investment is protected. Other tribunals have maintained that legality requirements cannot be imported into BITs.[93] This formalistic opinion, however, loses much of its strength in light of the widespread understanding that illegal investments do not qualify for international protection.

---

89 See also *Yaung Chi Oo Trading Pte Ltd v Government of the Union of Myanmar*, ASEAN Case No ARB/01/1, Award (31 March 2003) para 58 (stating, in the context of a requirement for an investment to be approved in writing and registered, that 'Article 11 goes beyond *the general rule* that for a foreign investment to enjoy treaty protection it must be lawful under the law of the host State' [emphasis added]); *Ioannis Kardassopoulos v Georgia*, ICSID Case No ARB/05/18, Decision on Jurisdiction (6 July 2007) para 182 ('"Protection of investments" under a BIT is obviously not without some limits. It does not extend, for instance, to an investor making an investment in breach of the local laws of the host State.'); *Rumeli Telekom AS and Telsim Mobil Telekomunikasyon Hizmetleri AS v Republic of Kazakhstan*, ICSID Case No ARB/05/16, Award (29 July 2008) para 319 ('Indeed, in order to receive the protection of a bilateral investment treaty, the disputed investments have to be in conformity with the host State laws and regulations.').

90 See, in this direction, Jorge E Viñuales, 'Investor Diligence in Investment Arbitration: Sources and Arguments' (2017) 32 ICSID Rev-FILJ 346, 367–8.

91 *Plama Consortium Limited v Bulgaria* (Award) (n 73) para 139 (mentioning the objective of the ECT to contribute to the rule of law); *Cortec Mining Kenya Limited, Cortec (Pty) Limited, and Stirling Capital Limited v Kenya* (n 17) para 333(a) (referring to the 'text and purpose' of the BIT and the ICSID Convention).

92 *Mr Saba Fakes v Turkey* (n 23) paras 112–4; *Quiborax SA, Non Metallic Minerals SA, and Allan Fosk Kaplún v Bolivia* (n 23) para 226.

93 *Capital Financial Holdings Luxembourg SA v Republic of Cameroon*, ICSID Case No ARB/15/18, Award (22 June 2017) paras 464–8; *Bear Creek Mining Corporation v Republic of Perú*, ICSID Case No ARB/14/21, Award (30 November 2017) para 320.

2.3　*The Objective Definition of 'Investor'*

The ICSID Convention allows for the settlement of disputes between 'a Contracting State [...] and a national of another Contracting State',[94] and provides details about the meaning of the phrase 'national of another Contracting State'.[95] The Convention thus sets some outer limits on the notion of investor that cannot be exceeded by party arrangements, similarly to the objective definition of 'investment'.[96] Investment treaties normally refer to the treatment by a contracting party of investors of the other contracting party.[97] The question arises whether an omission of the mention of a foreign element allows for the protection of both domestic and foreign investors. It appears the answer is 'no', thanks to the arbitral recognition of the issue as a regulatory deficiency and the development of the objective foreign element in practice.

The first occasion on which a tribunal added the foreign element to a definition of 'investor' was in *Bayview Irrigation District and others v Mexico*, a case initiated by a group of domestic investors within the US against Mexico for alleged transboundary damage.[98] The NAFTA, as the applicable treaty, did not limit the definitions of 'investor' and 'investment' with a foreign element, and its dispute settlement clause provided that '[a]n investor of a Party may submit to arbitration under this Section a claim [against] another Party [...]'.[99] Technically, the Claimants satisfied these criteria. However, the scope of the NAFTA's investment chapter was limited to 'measures adopted or maintained by a Party relating to: (a) investors of another Party; (b) investments of investors of another Party in the territory of the Party [...]'.[100] This was a sufficient basis for rejecting the claims on the grounds of substantive jurisdiction. However,

---

[94]　ICSID Convention (n 1) art 25(1).
[95]　ibid art 25(2).
[96]　Broches (n 2) 207; CF Amerasinghe, 'Jurisdiction *Ratione Personae* under the Convention on the Settlement of Investment Disputes between States and Nationals of Other States' (1976) 47 British Yrbk Int'l L 227, 244.
[97]　See, for example, Agreement Between the Belgium-Luxembourg Economic Union and the Government of the People's Republic of China on the Reciprocal Promotion and Protection of Investments (signed 6 June 2005, entered into force 1 December 2009) art 3(1) ('Each Contracting Party shall accord to investments and activities associated with such investments by the investors of the other Contracting Party treatment not less favourable than that accorded to the investments and associated activities by its own investors.').
[98]　*Bayview Irrigation District and others v United Mexican States*, ICSID Case No ARB(AF)/05/1, Award (19 June 2007).
[99]　North American Free Trade Agreement (signed 17 December 1992, entered into force 1 January 1994) 32 ILM 289, art 1116(1).
[100]　ibid art 1101(1).

the Tribunal took another route. It turned to the definition of 'investor' and the question whether a cross-border investment is required for protection. It concluded that, although such wording was not explicit, 'NAFTA Chapter XI in fact refers to "foreign investment" and that it regulates "foreign investors" and "investments of foreign investors of another Party"'.[101] This conclusion could be made by the reliance on the treaty text, which the Tribunal did in part to confirm its views.[102] But the Tribunal's main considerations concerned the different status of domestic and foreign investors in relation to host states and the familiarity with local laws in general. It endorsed the statement of the US Government which read:

> The aim of international investment agreements is the protection of foreign investments, and the investor who make them. This is as true with respect to the investment provisions of free trade agreements (FTAs) as it is for agreements devoted exclusively to investment protection, such as bilateral investment treaties (BITs). NAFTA Chapter Eleven is no different in this regard.[103]

The Tribunal concluded 'that in order to be an "investor" within the meaning of NAFTA Art. 1101 (a), an enterprise must make an investment in another NAFTA State, and not in its own'.[104] The value of this reasoning is that the Tribunal addressed the rationale behind investment protection agreements in general. That was the source of the foreign element in the notion of investor, not the text of the NAFTA.

In 2017 the Singapore High Court (SGHC) faced a more clear-cut scenario in a set-aside proceeding. Annex 1 to the Protocol on Finance and Investment of the Southern African Development Community (SADC) did not distinguish between domestic and foreign investors, which led an arbitral tribunal to conclude that arbitration under that Annex was open to both domestic and foreign investors.[105] The SGHC disagreed, and held that Annex 1 was meant to protect foreign investors only. The Court inferred such purpose of the Annex 1 from a number of provisions which attempted to improve the position of the SADC region as a whole as an investment destination, but also from the

---

101   *Bayview Irrigation District and others v Mexico* (n 98) paras 87–96.
102   ibid para 105.
103   ibid paras 97–100.
104   ibid para 101.
105   *Kingdom of Lesotho v Swissbourgh Diamond Mines (Pty) Limited and others* [2017] SGHC 195 [324].

fact that it provided for *international* arbitration (before the SADC Tribunal or ICSID or ad hoc tribunals).[106]

The SGHC addressed conceptual considerations as well. It stated that its conclusion was supported by the requirement of the exhaustion of local remedies in the same Annex, which protected state sovereignty in relation to foreign investors.[107] Notably, the mechanisms that allow individuals and companies to bring claims against their own states, like human rights courts, do so with the requirement of the exhaustion of local remedies. However, the SGHC rejected a parallel with a human rights case heard before the SADC Tribunal, which affirmed jurisdiction over a claim by a plaintif against his own state. The Court distinguished the objectives of the SADC Treaty from Annex 1, as if the latter had nothing to do with the SADC framework.[108] The jurisdiction of the SADC Tribunal regulated by its Protocol was different from the jurisdiction defined in Annex 1, because it was 'not confined to disputes concerning specific subject-matter or persons suing in a particular capacity', while arbitration under the latter instrument was 'limited exclusively to persons suing in a particular capacity (*ie*, as investors) and to disputes with a specific subject-matter (*ie*, concerning a host State's obligations in relation to an admitted investment)'.[109] The SGHC asserted that it was not led by comparative considerations,[110] but it engaged a broad narrative, presuming the limitation to foreigners:

> The fact that Annex 1 does not *expressly* confine its terms to foreign investors is not so compelling as to outweigh the clear context, object and purpose of Annex 1. On the contrary, it is difficult to believe that if SADC Member States did intend to confer treaty protections on domestic investors, which would trigger broad-ranging and significant legal consequences (not least the *de facto* creation of a new tier to the judicial system for domestic investors), they would have neglected to provide for and regulate these consequences expressly. That is far less plausible than the alternative, *ie*, the SADC Member States did not intend to trigger such consequences although they did not expressly say so. The definition of "investment" in Annex 1 is one which, if applied to nationals, would invariably include every national who had ever purchased property, acquired company shares or acquired licences to exploit natural resources

---

106 ibid [331].
107 ibid [332].
108 ibid [335(a)].
109 ibid [335(b)–6].
110 ibid [338].

(amongst others). Extending treaty protections to nationals would constitute a significant intrusion into the sovereignty and freedoms of each Member State. Indeed, it seems quite extraordinary to conclude as such in the absence of clear and explicit language. Construing Annex 1 in such a way contradicts the principle that treaties must be interpreted with due recognition to the interests of the negotiating States and their sovereignty [...][111]

The objective definition of 'investor' therefore involves a rudimentary element of foreignness. Most of treaties contain provisions to the same effect, which makes the objective definition usually redundant. To what extent the foreign element will be defended in concrete cases is a more complex question. One should only mention the debates concerning the piercing of corporate veil of investors who formally qualify as foreign but substantively arguably do not,[112] and the permissibility of claims by dual nationals (of home and host states) outside the ICSID context.[113] These issues exceed the scope of this study. It suffices to observe that extreme cases, which do not involve an explicit foreign element, reveal the objective nature of that element and its applicability by virtue of an arbitrator-made jurisdictional rule.

3   Rules Restricting the Scope of Arbitrable Disputes: Example of Umbrella Clauses

Umbrella clauses oblige states to observe the obligations they have entered into with respect to investments.[114] They involve many questions, such as the

---

111   ibid [333] (emphasis in the original).
112   Tribunals have been asked many times to pierce the corporate veil of companies to discover the true investor, which has mostly been rejected. This can be seen as a failure of rule-formation, which was sought by states as respondents. See, for the precedent, *Tokios Tokelės v Ukraine* (n 42) paras 24–71.
113   See *Serafín García Armas and Karina García Gruber v The Bolivarian Republic of Venezuela*, PCA Case No 2013-3, Decision on Jurisdiction (15 December 2014) paras 159–75; and Javier García Olmedo, 'Claims by Dual Nationals under Investment Treaties: Are Investors Entitled to Sue Their Own States?' (2017) 8 JIDS 695. The ICSID Convention explicitly excludes dual nationals of home and host states as claimants: ICSID Convention (n 1) art 25(2)(a). If the exclusion of dual nations as claimants would be extended beyond ICSID on treaty-independent terms, that could be seen as another example of arbitral rule-creation.
114   For example, Agreement Between the Belgium-Luxembourg Economic Union and Barbados for the Reciprocal Promotion and Protection of Investments (signed 29 May

governmental and non-governmental character of the covered conduct[115] and their reach to different commitments.[116] I focus here on the specific issue of privity. The question is whether umbrella clauses imply the condition of privity and cover only contracts concluded between states and investors, or whether they cover contracts concluded through affiliates as well. While some treaties provide textual guidance on this point,[117] others do not,[118] which demonstrates a regulatory deficiency allowing for arbitral law-making.

As a preliminary remark, it is questionable whether the condition of privity is a jurisdictional issue. One can argue that alleging a contractual breach (as a fact) and invoking an umbrella clause (as the cause of action) would suffice to establish jurisdiction of a tribunal, provided that disputes arising from the umbrella clause are arbitrable.[119] The reach of the umbrella clause would be a substantive question, and the finding that it does not cover the contract whose breach the investor invokes would lead to the dismissal of the claim on the merits.[120] But tribunals regularly address the reach of umbrella clauses as a jurisdictional question, including the condition of privity.[121] Regardless of one's view on these issues, practice has established the pertinence of the condition of privity to jurisdiction.

2009, not in force) art 2(4) ('Each Contracting Party shall observe any obligation it may have entered into with regard to investments of nationals or companies of the other Contracting Party.').

115 cf Thomas W Wälde, 'The "Umbrella" Clause in Investment Arbitration: A Comment on Original Intentions and Recent Cases' (2005) 6 JWIT 183, 235–6 (arguing that umbrella clauses concern breaches of contracts by sovereign conduct only); with Stephan W Schill, 'Enabling Private Ordering: Function, Scope and Effect of Umbrella Clauses in International Investment Treaties' (2009) 18 Minn J Int'l L 1, 37–47 (arguing that umbrella clauses concern breaches of contracts regardless of the nature of state conduct).

116 cf *SGS Société Générale de Surveillance SA v Islamic Republic of Pakistan*, ICSID Case No ARB/01/13, Decision of the Tribunal on Objections to Jurisdiction (6 August 2003) para 166; with *SGS Société Générale de Surveillance SA v Republic of the Philippines*, ICSID Case No ARB/02/6, Decision of the Tribunal on Objections to Jurisdiction (29 January 2004) paras 115–8.

117 Energy Charter Treaty (signed 17 December 1994, entered into force 16 April 1998) 2080 UNTS 95 (ECT) art 10(1) ('Each Contracting Party shall observe any obligations it has entered into with an Investor or an Investment of an Investor of any other Contracting Party.').

118 See n 114 above.

119 cf ECT (n 117) art 26(3)(c) (excluding the arbitrability of disputes arising from the umbrella clause in respect of certain states).

120 *Nissan Motor Co Ltd (Japan) v The Republic of India*, PCA Case No 2017-37, Decision on Jurisdiction (29 April 2019) para 284.

121 See nn 131–136 below.

From the state perspective, the condition of privity in umbrella clauses often seems obvious, because they normally refer to obligations entered into by the state. Accordingly, some tribunals have denied the possibility of invoking contractual obligations entered into by state affiliates, with more[122] or less discussion.[123] At first sight, some decisions seem to have allowed triggering umbrella clauses without the privity of contract, however one should avoid jumping to conclusions. Their focus has been on the law of state responsibility concerning attribution, attempting to attribute the obligations of affiliates to states.[124] Regardless of the correctness of that approach, what it effectively does is find a route for binding the state, which does not rebut but rather affirms the condition of privity.[125]

The true force of the condition of privity is better visible from the investor perspective. Because many umbrella clauses refer to obligations 'with respect to investments', they do not necessarily require contracts to be concluded by investors themselves. At first, arbitral practice was contradictory: some tribunals have not seen a problem in relying on contractual rights of investors' affiliates,[126] while others have assumed the condition of privity without offering any explanation.[127] One tribunal opined that 'provided that these obligations have

---

[122] *Gustav F W Hamester GmbH & Co KG v Ghana* (n 83) paras 342–9; *EDF (Services) Limited v Romania*, ICSID Case No ARB/05/13, Award (8 October 2009) paras 314–20.

[123] *Impregilo SpA v Islamic Republic of Pakistan*, ICSID Case No ARB/03/3, Decision on Jurisdiction (22 April 2005) para 223.

[124] *Eureko BV v Republic of Poland*, ad hoc arbitration, Partial Award (19 August 2005) paras 115–34; *Noble Ventures Inc v Romania*, ICSID Case No ARB/01/11, Award (12 October 2005) paras 68–86. See also *Bosh International Inc and B&P Ltd Foreign Investments Enterprise v Ukraine*, ICSID Case No ARB/08/11, Award (25 October 2012) para 246; *SGS Société Générale de Surveillance SA v Pakistan* (n 116) para 166.

[125] cf Nick Gallus, 'An Umbrella Just for Two? BIT Obligations Observance Clauses and the Parties to a Contract' (2008) 24 Arb Int'l 157, 162–9 (for the arguments in support of applying the rules of attribution); with Shotaro Hamamoto, 'Parties to the "Obligations" in the Obligations Observance ("Umbrella") Clause' (2015) 30 ICSID Rev-FILJ 449, 463–4 (arguing that what is decisive are not the rules of attribution but the representation of the state by a separate entity); and James Crawford, 'Treaty and Contract in Investment Arbitration' (2008) 24 Arb Int'l 351, 369 ('the question of the scope of a commitment to arbitrate made by the State is a matter of interpretation and has nothing to do with attribution').

[126] *CMS Gas Transmission Company v The Argentine Republic*, ICSID Case No ARB/01/8, Award (12 May 2005) paras 132, 298–9; *Sempra Energy International v Argentine Republic*, ICSID Case No ARB/02/16, Award (28 September 2007) para 241. See also *Enron Corporation and Ponderosa Assets LP v Argentine Republic*, ICSID Case No ARB/01/3, Award (22 May 2007) para 152.

[127] *Azurix Corp v The Argentine Republic*, ICSID Case No ARB/01/12, Award (14 July 2006) para 384; *Siemens AG v The Argentine Republic*, ICSID Case No ARB/02/8, Award (6 February 2007) para 204.

been entered "with regard" to investments, they may have been entered with persons or entities other than foreign investors themselves, so that an undertaking by the host State with a subsidiary [...] is not in principle excluded'.[128] Again, such generalised pronouncements on the reach of umbrella clauses should be distinguished from the assessment of concrete facts establishing privity.[129]

Yet, the condition of privity was fully addressed only in the decisions that insisted on its imposition. The Annulment Committee in *CMS v Argentina* was the first to express doubts about unrestricted reading of an umbrella clause. The Committee held, among others, that '[c]onsensual obligations are not entered into *erga omnes* but with regard to particular persons', and that 'the performance of such obligations or requirements occurs with regard to, and as between, obligor and obligee'.[130] The Tribunal in *Burlington v Ecuador* went further. Although it firstly dismissed the alleged general rule of privity established in *CMS*,[131] it arrived at the same solution. The Tribunal advanced two main arguments. First, that 'the obligation of one subject is generally seen in correlation with the right of another', and that '[a]n obligation entails a party bound by it and another one benefiting from it, in other words, entails an obligor and an obligee'.[132] Second, the Tribunal held that every obligation must be analysed in light of its governing law, however it did not examine the Ecuadorian law as the governing law of the contracts.[133] The central argument,

---

128   *Continental Casualty Company v The Argentine Republic*, ICSID Case No ARB/03/9, Award (5 September 2008) para 297.

129   See *EDF International SA, SAUR International SA, and León Participaciones Argentinas SA v Argentine Republic*, ICSID Case No ARB/03/23, Award (11 June 2012) para 942 (seemingly not requiring privity, but noting that the concession agreement 'makes explicit mention of shareholders').

130   *CMS Gas Transmission Company v Argentine Republic*, ICSID Case No ARB/01/8, Decision of the Ad Hoc Committee on the Application for Annulment of the Argentine Republic (25 September 2007) para 95(b). See also ibid para 95(c) ('The effect of the umbrella clause is not to transform the obligation which is relied on into something else; the content of the obligation is unaffected, as is its proper law. If this is so, it would appear that the *parties* to the obligation (*i.e.*, the persons bound by it and entitled to rely on it) are likewise not changed by reason of the umbrella clause.' [emphasis in the original]).

131   *Burlington Resources Inc v Republic of Ecuador*, ICSID Case No ARB/08/5, Decision on Jurisdiction (2 June 2010) para 195. The Tribunal emphasised that the *CMS* Annulment Committee annulled the award for the lack of sufficient reasons, and not for the manifest excess of powers.

132   *Burlington Resources Inc v Republic of Ecuador*, ICSID Case No ARB/08/5, Decision on Liability (14 December 2012) para 214.

133   ibid paras 214–5. The Tribunal shifted the burden on the Claimant to argue that the Ecuadorian law would allow enforcement by non-signatories of contracts, which the Claimant did not pursue.

therefore, in both *CMS* and *Burlington* was the conceptual understanding of an obligation, which led to restricting the reach of umbrella clauses. Moreover, the *Burlington* Tribunal, in light of its aspiration to contribute to the development of investment law, engaged in a broader discourse on the privity requirement in umbrella clauses, and found that the majority of ICSID decisions supported the imposition of that requirement.[134] Another tribunal, despite finding an explicit privity requirement in the relevant clause, engaged in a similar analysis and found that such a requirement was generally accepted in case law.[135]

There is a strong case, therefore, for implying the condition of privity in umbrella clauses, although the practice is not uniform. For example, one tribunal maintained that an umbrella clause went 'beyond the simple direct contractual relationship between the investor and the host State, because such provision establishes that the State shall comply with the obligations undertaken "… *related to investments by investors of the other Contracting Party* …".[136] But a strong example of arbitral law-making is visible in the common willingness of tribunals to fill what they see as a regulatory gap in umbrella clauses with their theoretical views on the process of obliging, and to imply an additional jurisdictional requirement in treaty texts.

4   Abuse of Process as a Jurisdictional Limit *in Statu Nascendi*

The final example of arbitral law-making that I discuss in this study is the doctrine of abuse of process as a developing jurisdictional limit. The doctrine is well-known in international law, and in its essence it instructs that no legal process can be used in bad faith and contrary to its purpose.[137] The main value

---

134   ibid paras 221–33.
135   *WNC Factoring Ltd (United Kingdom) v The Czech Republic*, PCA Case No 2014-34, Award (22 February 2017) paras 312–41.
136   *Supervisión y Control SA v The Republic of Costa Rica*, ICSID Case No ARB/12/4, Award (18 January 2017) para 287 (emphasis in the original).
137   The concept of abuse of process is generally seen as part of the broader concept of abuse of rights, which is in turn a reflection of the principle of good faith in the exercise of rights. See, for the doctrine of abuse of rights, Bin Cheng, *General Principles of Law as Applied by International Courts and Tribunals* (Stevens & Sons 1953) 121–36; Sir Gerald Fitzmaurice, 'The Law and Procedure of the International Court of Justice, 1954-9: General Principles and Sources of International Law' (1959) 35 British Yrbk Int'l L 183, 207–16; and, for the abuse of rights/process doctrine in investment arbitration, Jorun Baumgartner, *Treaty Shopping in International Investment Law* (OUP 2016) 202–5; Eric De Brabandere, ' "Good Faith", "Abuse of Process" and the Initiation of Investment Treaty Claims' (2012) 3 JIDS 609, 618–9. But see John P Gaffney, ' "Abuse of Process" in Investment Treaty Arbitration'

of this doctrine is that it allows tribunals to find claims inadmissible if they are abusive.[138] As a doctrine of a general significance in international law, it has been employed in investment arbitrations numerous times. The usual example of an abusive conduct is the restructuring of an investment for the sake of bringing the investor under the protection of an investment treaty and gaining access to international arbitration in respect of a foreseeable dispute.[139] I will not address many questions that arise in this scenario, such as how an abusive restructuring should be identified.[140] What I am interested in is the arbitral translation of the abuse of process doctrine into a jurisdictional rule tailored for the specific scenario of investment restructuring aimed at accessing international arbitration.

There are two routes for transforming the abuse of process doctrine into a jurisdictional rule. The first route targets the definition of 'investment'. The Tribunal in *Phoenix v Czechia* held that 'States cannot be deemed to offer access to the ICSID dispute settlement mechanism to investments not made in good faith'.[141] Discussing the meaning of the good faith principle in general, it stated that '[n]obody shall abuse the rights granted by treaties, and more generally, every rule of law includes an implied clause that it should not be abused'.[142] The Tribunal even formulated this as its own duty:

> The Tribunal has to prevent an abuse of the system of international investment protection under the ICSID Convention, in ensuring that only investments that are made in compliance with the international principle of good faith and do not attempt to misuse the system are protected.[143]

The Tribunal thus included the good faith element in the definition of protected 'investment'.[144] On the facts, the Tribunal found that '[t]he unique goal

---

(2010) 11 JWIT 515, 523–4 (finding the translation of the abuse of rights doctrine into the concept of abuse of process difficult in the context of investment treaty arbitration).

138   De Brabandere (n 137) 619–20; Hervé Ascensio, 'Abuse of Process in International Investment Arbitration' (2014) 13 Chinese JIL 763, 784.

139   I focus on this scenario, although many other scenarios can also be qualified as abuse of process. See Emmanuel Gaillard, 'Abuse of Process in International Arbitration' (2017) 32 ICSID Rev-FILJ 17, 19–27; Ascensio (n 138) 767–77.

140   See, for a discussion on the applicable test, Duncan Watson and Tom Brebner, 'Nationality Planning and Abuse of Process: A Coherent Framework' (2018) 33 ICSID Rev-FILJ 302.

141   *Phoenix Action Ltd v Czechia* (n 19) para 106.

142   ibid para 107.

143   ibid para 113.

144   ibid para 114.

of the "investment" was to transform a pre-existing domestic dispute into an international dispute subject to ICSID arbitration under a bilateral investment treaty'.[145] Because the investment was made solely for the purpose of gaining access to arbitration, and thus not in good faith, it was not protected and the Tribunal declined jurisdiction.[146] Support for this type of reasoning can be found elsewhere,[147] although practice is not uniform and some tribunals have explicitly opposed adding the good faith element to the objective definition of 'investment'.[148]

The second route is more straightforward: finding an abuse of process leads directly to denial of jurisdiction. Abuse of process appears as a stand-alone jurisdictional limitation, without intermediary concepts such as the objective definition of 'investment'. Some tribunals have started from the *Phoenix* decision, but have not discussed the abuse of process doctrine as part of the broader issue of the existence of a protected investment.[149] Others have made general statements that they had to examine the allegation of abuse of right/process in order to verify whether they had jurisdiction.[150] The application of the abuse of process doctrine can be complex, especially when it comes to the relevant facts, which often require engaging other legal concepts too.[151] But what matters here are the considerations about the status of the abuse of process doctrine. Although some tribunals have explicitly endorsed the *Phoenix* reasoning, they have not focused on the objective definition of 'investment', and the arbitral focus on abuse of process as such makes a direct translation of that doctrine into a jurisdictional limit.

---

145   ibid para 142.
146   ibid paras 143–5.
147   Arrêt du 7 février 2017, Cour d'Appel de Paris, Pôle 1 - Chambre 1 (France) 14/21103, 4 (in the context of the definition of 'investor', noting 'que le bénéfice de la protection du Traité ne peut, dès lors, lui [investor] être refusé que s'il est démontré que l'incorporation au Canada est purement fictive ou procède d'un abus de droit').
148   *Mr Saba Fakes v Turkey* (n 23) paras 112–3; *Quiborax SA, Non Metallic Minerals SA, and Allan Fosk Kaplún v Bolivia* (n 23) para 226.
149   *Cementownia 'Nowa Huta' SA v Republic of Turkey*, ICSID Case No ARB(AF)/06/2, Award (17 September 2009) para 154; *ST-AD GmbH (Germany) v The Republic of Bulgaria*, PCA Case No 2011-06, Award on Jurisdiction (18 July 2013) para 423; *Transglobal Green Energy LLC and Transglobal Green Panama SA v Republic of Panama*, ICSID Case No ARB/13/28, Award (2 June 2016) paras 102, 118.
150   *Mobil Corporation, Venezuela Holdings BV, and others v Bolivarian Republic of Venezuela*, ICSID Case No ARB/07/27, Decision on Jurisdiction (10 June 2010) para 185.
151   See Baumgartner (n 137) 219–22 (discussing the distinction between temporal jurisdiction and abuse of process).

Abuse of process in the context of corporate restructuring is a developing arbitrator-made jurisdictional rule, and its development is surrounded by open questions. On the one hand, the *Phoenix* Tribunal included the good faith requirement in the objective definition of 'investment', which is already in itself an example of arbitral law-making.[152] On the other, the involvement of the notion of abuse of process is not theoretically settled. It can be objected that if there is no right to access international arbitration in the first place, there is nothing capable of being abused. It has been therefore suggested that investors who restructure their investments can be seen as acting in bad faith, but not as committing an abuse of process.[153] It has been argued in turn that investors are actually abusing a general right to arbitration, in order to acquire their own specific right to arbitration.[154] Because offers to arbitrate in investment treaties are addressed to those qualifying as investors, I would argue that by restructuring their investments investors abuse that qualification itself. Investors do not abuse offers to arbitrate that are already applicable to them, but restructure their investments to qualify as addressees of such offers. This discussion, however, seems academic, because none of these arguments denies that in these circumstances jurisdiction should be declined.

Arbitral law-making is visible in the view that the arbitral authority to adjudicate needs to be limited. It is obvious that abuse of process is still based on a doctrine of general international law. But the need to characterise its consequences as jurisdictional evidences a perceived need for a stronger rule, existing independently of general doctrines and governing the authority to adjudicate of arbitral tribunals. Yet, because arbitral law-making in respect of either of the two routes is not as widespread as to be considered firmly established (and tribunals still apply abuse of process as a doctrine leading to the inadmissibility of claims),[155] one can only see a sketch of a possible future jurisdictional rule.[156]

---

152   See s 2.1 above.
153   De Brabandere (n 137) 619–20.
154   Yuka Fukunaga, 'Abuse of Process under International Law and Investment Arbitration' (2018) 33 ICSID Rev-FILJ 181, 194–7.
155   *Philip Morris Asia Limited v The Commonwealth of Australia*, PCA Case No 2012-12, Award on Jurisdiction and Admissibility (17 December 2015) para 588. But see *Pac Rim Cayman LLC v The Republic of El Salvador*, ICSID Case No ARB/09/12, Decision on the Respondent's Jurisdictional Objections (1 June 2012) para 2.10 (considering the jurisdiction/admissibility divide in the context of abuse of process 'a distinction without a difference').
156   See in this respect Gaillard, 'Abuse of Process' (n 139) 37 ('Where certain types of conduct generate a sense of unease, they are first addressed through the application of general principles such as "abuse of rights" or "good faith". Over time, new legal rules will emerge that are specifically designed to tackle particular types of procedural conduct. One would

5 Conclusion

This chapter concludes the analysis of the practical examples of arbitral law-making. I showed that, besides crafting rules relaxing the procedural and substantive aspects of arbitral jurisdiction defined by disputing parties, tribunals have also created rules imposing additional jurisdictional limits. The latter often impose limits independently of party-defined jurisdictional rules. Tribunals have limited the scope of investment protection by developing the objective definitions of 'investment' and 'investor', as well as the independent legality requirement. Tribunals have also limited the scope of arbitrable disputes by creating the privity condition as a default rule in the application of umbrella clauses. Finally, tribunals have initiated the translation of the abuse of process doctrine, as a well-known doctrine of general international law, into a specific jurisdictional rule limiting the arbitral authority to adjudicate in the specific scenario of investment restructuring.

expect the same development to take place in the field of international arbitration with respect to abuse of process.').

CHAPTER 5

Towards a New Jurisdictional Framework of Investment Treaty Arbitration

1   Introduction

The activity of arbitral tribunals discussed in Chapters 2 to 4 can be considered part of arbitral interpretations of treaty provisions and an ordinary event in the exercise of the judicial function. From this perspective, what I call 'arbitrator-made rules' belongs to a corpus of interpretations of various treaty provisions and cannot have any heavier legal value than that of persuasive arbitral decisions.[1] In my opinion, the discussed activity requires a stronger appreciation. Tribunals add input into interpretive exercises, and they do so by formulating premises in general and prescriptive terms. What is their character? What are the implications of the fact that in the application of treaty provisions tribunals also apply presumptions, default rules, and standards? My answer to these questions is that the discussed activity of arbitral tribunals amounts to law-making and should be given a pertinent place in the process of jurisdictional regulation. This de facto existing situation is constantly ignored due to the traditional premise that states, or for that matter disputing parties, are law-makers whereas tribunals are law-appliers. Any form of arbitral self-regulation in jurisdictional matters, according to these traditional canons, is inconceivable. In opposition to the traditional views, the realities of practice demand an acknowledgment of the regulatory character of arbitral practice.

The argument of this chapter is that the regulatory function of arbitral tribunals relating to their jurisdiction should be recognised and integrated into the jurisdictional framework of investment treaty arbitration. To have a clear overview of the area of the tribunals' regulatory competence and its boundaries, I sketch a two-layered model of jurisdictional regulation in investment treaty arbitration. Besides the basic rules provided by virtue of party consent (which can be dubbed for the present purposes *primary rules*), I identify another layer of jurisdictional rules (hereinafter *secondary rules*), which is developed

---

1   See particularly Frédéric G Sourgens, 'By Equal Contest of Arms: Jurisdictional Proof in Investor-State Arbitrations' (2013) 38 North Carolina J Int'l L & Com Reg 875, 877–80 (criticising legal scholarship for overemphasising the development of 'formal legal rules' and for attempting to deduce such rules from arbitral interpretations of jurisdictional clauses).

by arbitral tribunals in the application of primary rules. As seen in previous chapters, primary rules frequently contain regulatory deficiencies, rendering them non-self-executing, in the sense of lacking sufficient detail to allow for their direct application. They often require an additional level of regulation, providing regulatory space for tribunals, which tribunals have filled and thus enabled their application.

Section 2 first addresses the impetus behind the production of jurisdictional rules in arbitral practice. Section 3 then sketches a two-layered model of jurisdictional regulation, while Section 4 addresses some of its challenges. Section 5 places the sketched model within a broader context of the international legal order, addressing the function of arbitral tribunals as global governors and the increasingly accepted regulatory function of international courts and tribunals.

2   The Impetus of Arbitral Jurisdictional Regulation

The first step towards accepting arbitrator-made jurisdictional rules is the recognition of the rationale motivating their production. I therefore first discuss the impetus of arbitral jurisdictional regulation, and I do so in two stages: I firstly dismiss the ability of the common criticisms of investment arbitration to offer an explanation of the driving force behind arbitral jurisdictional regulation (1), and then I offer an alternative explanation of such force in a new view on party consent as the primary but not the only means of jurisdictional regulation (2).

2.1   *Traditional Concerns about Investment Arbitration*
Traditional critiques of investment treaty arbitration focus on interpretative outcomes. The pressure of the litigating parties in the arbitral process (investor v state) might lead to re-balancing the protection of interests as set out by two states in a BIT.[2] Even in the normative sense, both theory[3] and practice[4] sometimes instruct tribunals to resolve jurisdictional issues by balancing the

---

2   Alex Mills, 'The Balancing (and Unbalancing?) Of Interests in International Investment Law and Arbitration' in Zachary Douglas, Joost Pauwelyn, and Jorge E Viñuales (eds), *The Foundations of International Investment Law: Bringing Theory into Practice* (OUP 2014) 445–8.
3   Sourgens, 'By Equal Contest of Arms' (n 1).
4   *Abaclat and others v The Argentine Republic*, ICSID Case No ARB/07/5, Decision on Jurisdiction and Admissibility (4 August 2011) para 584 (bypassing the local litigation requirement because of the prevailing Claimants' interest to access arbitration).

interests (or arguments) at stake. These perspectives shift the focus on interpretative outcomes, and do not offer an explanation of more nuanced activities of arbitral tribunals, such as the production of rules assisting jurisdictional determinations. I survey the three most common criticisms: that investment arbitration is dominated by commercial law approaches (1), that it is a one-sided system favouring investors (2), and that its practice is affected by arbitral bias in favour of investors (3).

2.1.1 Commercial Law Approaches

A chronic problem of the system of investment treaty arbitration is that it is often equated with commercial arbitration.[5] The idea of 'international arbitration' as a sufficiently defined and independent category, together with some common driving forces behind the two systems like international money flows and increasing globalisation, is central for the establishment of that link.[6] But because of the critically different foundations of the two regimes, their principal link persists in the sociological sense, because the actors (primarily arbitrators and counsels) in the field of investment arbitration often come from the commercial sphere,[7] which can leave a mark in their work.[8]

What are these commercial approaches, then? While it would be certainly hard to define a single 'commercial approach' to arbitration, it is fruitful to look

---

5 See ch 1, s 2.4.3.
6 Bernardo M Cremades and David JA Cairns, 'The Brave New World of Global Arbitration' (2002) 3 JWIT 173; Alec Stone Sweet and Florian Grisel, *The Evolution of International Arbitration: Judicialization, Governance, Legitimacy* (OUP 2017) 66–78. See also, on the unification of the investment treaty- and contract-based arbitration fields, Charles N Brower and Shashank P Kumar, 'Investomercial Arbitration: Whence Cometh It? What Is It? Whither Goeth It?' (2015) 30 ICSID Rev-FILJ 35.
7 Thomas W Wälde, 'The Specific Nature of Investment Arbitration' in Philippe Kahn and Thomas W Wälde (eds), *New Aspects of International Investment Law* (Martinus Nijhoff 2007) 54; Stephan W Schill, 'W(h)ither Fragmentation? On the Literature and Sociology of International Investment Law' (2011) 22 EJIL 875, 880, 888; Sergio Puig, 'Social Capital in the Arbitration Market' (2014) 25 EJIL 387, 401–2; Joost Pauwelyn, 'The Rule of Law without the Rule of Lawyers? Why Investment Arbitrators Are from Mars, Trade Adjudicators from Venus' (2015) 109 AJIL 761, 773; Malcolm Langford, Daniel Behn, and Runar Hilleren Lie, 'The Revolving Door in International Investment Arbitration' (2017) 20 JIEL 301, 307, fn 35.
8 Moshe Hirsch, 'The Sociology of International Investment Law' in Zachary Douglas, Joost Pauwelyn, and Jorge E Viñuales (eds), *The Foundations of International Investment Law: Bringing Theory into Practice* (OUP 2014) 148–58 (arguing that investment tribunals are reluctant to rely on human rights law because of the socio-cultural distance between the two legal communities). But see, on a positive transfer of skills between the two areas, Charles N Brower, 'W(h)ither International Commercial Arbitration?' (2008) 24 Arb Int'l 181, 191–4.

at a few of its frequently alleged features. First, arbitrators from the commercial sphere might be inclined to focus on or analogise to a contractual relationship between disputing parties, not paying much attention to the public international law context.[9] It is true that in some cases jurisdictional determinations seem like simple reading of treaty clauses and their application to facts. But when facing regulatory deficiencies, it is hard to claim that arbitrators tend to stick to the relationship between disputing parties. Inspiration is always external. For example, creating the futility exception, tribunals have drawn an analogy to the law of diplomatic protection.[10] The Broches test in the identification of state-owned companies as private investors resembles the identification of state-owned companies as non-governmental under the ECHR,[11] while the inspiration can also reach to sources of the substantive international law.[12] Regulatory deficiencies prevent isolating bilateral relationships as self-sufficient jurisdictional frameworks.[13] A related but very different question is whether investment tribunals should look into the practice of commercial arbitrations and draw analogies from there in search for inspiration, however that question is outside the scope of this work.

Second, arbitrators coming from the commercial sphere might focus on the monetary losses of investors, as opposed to the administrative (or simply public) law review of state conduct.[14] Although this issue might pertain more to the questions of merits, it also has some relevance for the questions of jurisdiction. For example, tribunals expressing a sharp view on the distinction between treaty and contract claims can bear in mind their role as reviewers of state

---

[9]   Anthea Roberts, 'Clash of Paradigms: Actors and Analogies Shaping the Investment Treaty System' (2013) 107 AJIL 45, 77; Julie A Maupin, 'Public and Private in International Investment Law: An Integrated Systems Approach' (2014) 54 Virginia J Int'l L 367, 394–7.
[10] *Ambiente Ufficio SpA and others v The Argentine Republic*, ICSID Case No ARB/08/9, Decision on Jurisdiction and Admissibility (8 February 2013) paras 597–607. See further ch 2, s 3.1.1.
[11] cf *Beijing Urban Construction Group Co Ltd v Republic of Yemen*, ICSID Case No ARB/14/30, Decision on Jurisdiction (31 May 2017) paras 31–6; with *Islamic Republic of Iran Shipping Lines v Turkey* App No 40998/98 (ECtHR, 13 December 2007) paras 78–81.
[12] *Beijing Urban Construction Group v Yemen* (n 11) para 34 (arguing that the Broches test mirrors Articles 5 and 8 of the ILC Articles on State responsibility). See further ch 3, s 3.1.
[13] See further, for a variety of sources of inspiration of investment tribunals's reasoning, Valentina Vadi, *Analogies in International Investment Law and Arbitration* (CUP 2016) 88–110; and ibid ch 4.
[14] See in this regard Stone Sweet and Grisel (n 6) 230–2 (arguing that investment arbitration is closer to commercial arbitration than to public law review mechanisms, because arbitrators are empowered to award damages for losses and not to invalidate unlawful state acts).

conduct against international standards of treatment.[15] On some occasions tribunals have arguably focused on the losses of investors when regulating jurisdictional questions, for instance maintaining that jurisdictional treaty clauses allow arbitrating contract claims altogether.[16] However, one or the other focus does not address the need for law-making. In the given example, the regulatory question is whether compromissory clauses should be presumed limited to the treaty in which they are contained. The answer can surely be motivated by the said criticism, but eventually has to be implemented through a premise on the nexus between the clause and the substantive law.[17] The need for such a premise itself is a regulatory deficiency, which is where the entire problem of arbitral law-making only begins.

Third, it is said that commercial arbitration concerns the interests of disputing parties only, which justifies procedural confidentiality, in opposition to public law adjudication, which concerns public interests and therefore requires transparency.[18] There is a striking difference between commercial and investment arbitrations in this regard, and although still some traces of confidentiality exist, investment arbitrations are now dominantly public.[19] Yet, assuming that investment arbitrations are indeed dominantly confidential and lack the pressure and other effects that publicity and the participation of non-disputing actors might bring, this does not address arbitral law-making. The publicity of proceedings can indeed bring additional elements influencing arbitral re-balancing of the interests under a BIT.[20] But again, this can be the

---

15 *Compañiá de Aguas del Aconquija SA and Vivendi Universal v Argentine Republic*, ICSID Case No ARB/97/3, Decision on Annulment (3 July 2002) paras 94–115; *SGS Société Générale de Surveillance SA v Islamic Republic of Pakistan*, ICSID Case No ARB/01/13, Decision of the Tribunal on Objections to Jurisdiction (6 August 2003) para 161; *Impregilo SpA v Islamic Republic of Pakistan*, ICSID Case No ARB/03/3, Decision on Jurisdiction (22 April 2005) paras 255–62.

16 *SGS Société Générale de Surveillance SA v Republic of the Philippines*, ICSID Case No ARB/02/6, Decision of the Tribunal on Objections to Jurisdiction (29 January 2004) para 132(c).

17 See, for an analysis of the nexus, ibid paras 132(a), (d) (regarding the applicable law and the relevance of contracts in making an investment); and ibid paras 132(b), (e) (regarding the lack of limitations in the definition of dispute).

18 Brower (n 8) 186–7, 194–5; Roberts, 'Clash of Paradigms' (n 9) 48. The use of commercial arbitration rules, providing for confidentiality, has been criticised as particularly inappropriate in investment disputes; see Giuditta Cordero Moss, 'Commercial Arbitration and Investment Arbitration: Fertile Soil for False Friends?' in Christina Binder and others (eds), *International Investment Law for the 21st Century: Essays in Honour of Christoph Schreuer* (OUP 2009) 791–6.

19 Karl-Heinz Böckstiegel, 'Commercial and Investment Arbitration: How Different Are They Today?' (2012) 28 Arb Int'l 577, 586–7.

20 Mills (n 2) 448–51.

case only when it comes to the weighting of the stakes at hand in the interpretation of treaty provisions. When facing a regulatory deficiency, there is nothing in the publicity of proceedings or the lack of it preventing an arbitral tribunal from reaching for a legal concept in another field of law, or finding inspiration elsewhere, in search of solutions. One can argue that a deficit of voices in a process can substantially affect the creativity of arbitral reasoning, but that does not say anything about the need itself for inspiration. Besides their inaccuracy when it comes to the contemporary investment arbitration practice, the criticisms of confidentiality do not contribute to the discussion about arbitral law-making.

There is one aspect of commercial approaches that is useful for the present discussion, but not fully satisfactory: adopting a commercial arbitration point of view, with the belief of serving disputing parties only, can induce arbitrators to neglect the interpretive interests of states parties to investment treaties, which ultimately gives arbitral tribunals more law-making opportunities.[21] On the one hand, this suggestion is useful because it identifies a gateway for the introduction of arbitral law-making. On the other hand, it is not fully satisfactory for two reasons: first, as maintained in this study, dispute-centrism in the delegation of the authority to adjudicate is not alien to public international law; second, the presence of an opportunity for law-making is important but not the sole issue. What constitutes the driving force behind law-making remains questionable.

2.1.2   One-Sided System

Investment treaty arbitration is often characterised as a 'one-sided' system. This can be defined in two ways. First, the system allows only one side in the investor-state relationship (the investor) to vindicate its rights.[22] This is a clear consequence of the fact that investment treaties dominantly provide for investor rights only (without imposing any obligations),[23] which means that only

---

21 Anthea Roberts, 'Power and Persuasion in Investment Treaty Interpretation: The Dual Role of States' (2010) 104 AJIL 179, 184.
22 See, for a critique, Mehmet Toral and Thomas Schultz, 'The State, a Perpetual Respondent in Investment Arbitration? Some Unorthodox Considerations' in Michael Waibel and others (eds), *The Backlash Against Investment Arbitration* (Kluwer 2010) 577. And, for broader, systemic effects, Martti Koskenniemi, 'It's Not the Cases, It's the System' (2017) 18 JWIT 343.
23 But see, for examples of treaties imposing obligations on investors, Supplementary Act A/SA.3/12/08 Adopting Community Rules on Investment and the Modalities for Their Implementation with ECOWAS (signed 19 December 2008, entered into force 19 January 2009) arts 11-18; Reciprocal Investment Promotion and Protection Agreement Between

investors appear as claimants in arbitrations. There is more to this aspect of one-sidedness: the purpose of international investment law and arbitration as a defined branch of law and a protective regime is to protect foreign investments.[24] In such an environment the interests of other stakeholders and their representation are said to be unfairly ignored,[25] especially if the sustainable economic development of states and local communities is considered the ultimate purpose of investment treaties.[26]

This asymmetry has been rebutted from a theoretical point of view by Thomas Wälde on the basis that host states have an advantage over investors as their sovereigns,[27] but also as treaty masters.[28] This proposition appears correct in principle, but it does not assist with the question whether the one-sidedness of investment arbitration guides tribunals in practice. Translated into my quest for an explanation of arbitral law-making, the question is whether the one-sided character of investment arbitration inclines tribunals to supplement the substance of jurisdictional frameworks towards the enhancement of investor protection exclusively.

---

the Government of the Kingdom of Morocco and the Government of the Federal Republic of Nigeria (signed 3 December 2016, not in force) arts 14, 17-21, 24.

24 See, for the acknowledgment of such purpose usually relying on treaty objectives, *SGS Société Générale de Surveillance SA v Philippines* (n 16) para 116; *Renta 4 SVSA and others v The Russian Federation*, SCC Case No 24/2007, Award on Preliminary Objections (20 March 2009) para 56; *Señor Tza Yap Shum v The Republic of Peru*, ICSID Case No ARB/07/6, Decision on Jurisdiction and Competence (19 June 2009) para 187; *The Republic of Ecuador v Occidental Exploration & Production Co* [2007] EWCA Civ 656 [28]; and in a domestic law, see *The Kyrgyz Republic v Stans Energy Corp and Kutisay Mining LLC* [2017] EWHC 2539 (Comm) [124–31].

25 Ilija Mitrev Penusliski, 'A Dispute Systems Design Diagnosis of ICSID' in Michael Waibel and others (eds), *The Backlash Against Investment Arbitration* (Kluwer 2010) 520–5; Gus Van Harten, 'Five Justifications for Investment Treaties: A Critical Discussion' (2010) 2 Trade, Law and Development 19, 33–4.

26 See, for the acknowledgement in case law, *Malaysian Historical Salvors Sdn Bhd v The Government of Malaysia*, ICSID Case No ARB/05/10, Award on Jurisdiction (17 May 2007) paras 66–8; *Malaysian Historical Salvors Sdn Bhd v The Government of Malaysia*, ICSID Case No ARB/05/10, Annulment Proceedings, Dissenting Opinion of Judge Mohamed Shahabuddeen (19 February 2009) para 2; *Mr Patrick Mitchell v The Democratic Republic of Congo*, ICSID Case No ARB/99/7, Decision on the Application for Annulment of the Award (1 November 2006) para 28; *Alps Finance and Trade AG v The Slovak Republic*, UNCITRAL ad hoc arbitration, Award (5 March 2011) para 226.

27 Wälde, 'Specific Nature' (n 7) 55.

28 Thomas W Wälde, 'Procedural Challenges in Investment Arbitration under the Shadow of the Dual Role of the State: Asymmetries and Tribunals' Duty to Ensure, Pro-Actively, the Equality of Arms' (2010) 26 Arb Int'l 3, 15–8.

I have argued elsewhere that investment treaty arbitration demonstrates a rivalry between legalistic and teleological ideals, approaching state obligations from the points of view of state consent and the protective purpose of investment law in the international community, respectively.[29] This rivalry is evident in the sphere of jurisdictional determinations where the two ideals are used in the formulation of decisive arguments.[30] They form the bases of 'pro-state' (legalistic) and 'pro-investor' (teleological) decisive arguments and, eventually, interpretative outcomes.[31] Certainly, a good amount of arbitral law-making has been openly directed towards enhancing the protection of investors, like presuming the applicability of MFN clauses to dispute resolution clauses,[32] and presuming the protection of indirect investments.[33] However, accepting the one-sidedness of investment arbitration as a fact of the international legal life,[34] there is nothing in that feature of the system preventing tribunals from reaching 'anti-investor' interpretative outcomes and building rules along the same lines. In fact, investment tribunals have often done so; examples are the doctrine of abuse of process,[35] the independent legality requirement,[36] and the objective definition of 'investment',[37] among others, which are clearly directed at controlling investors' conduct and limiting the access to international arbitration.

The second aspect of one-sidedness is more specific, and it alleges that investment treaty arbitration favours the interests of strong companies against capital demanding and importing states.[38] This argument has evolved

---

29 Relja Radović, 'Inherently Unneutral Investment Treaty Arbitration: The Formation of Decisive Arguments in Jurisdictional Determinations' (2018) 2018 J Disp Resol 143.
30 ibid 157–71.
31 ibid 171–82.
32 See, for example, *Emilio Agustín Maffezini v The Kingdom of Spain*, ICSID Case No ARB/97/7, Decision of the Tribunal on Objections to Jurisdiction (25 January 2000) paras 54–5; *Gas Natural SDG SA v The Argentine Republic*, ICSID Case No ARB/03/10, Decision of the Tribunal on Preliminary Questions on Jurisdiction (17 June 2005) para 49; *Hochtief AG v The Argentine Republic*, ICSID Case No ARB/07/31, Decision on Jurisdiction (24 October 2011) para 68. See further ch 2, s 4.
33 See, for example, *Señor Tza Yap Shum Shum v Peru* (n 24) para 106; *Vladimir Berschader & Moïse Berschader v The Russian Federation*, SCC Case No 80/2004, Separate Opinion of Arbitrator Todd Weiler (7 April 2006) paras 6, 14. See further ch 3, s 3.2.
34 Wälde, 'Procedural Challenges' (n 28) 15–6 (attributing this asymmetry to the function of reviewing governmental conduct, which is also present in human rights adjudication).
35 See ch 4, s 4.
36 See ch 4, s 2.2.
37 See ch 4, s 2.1.
38 See generally Muthucumaraswamy Sornarajah, 'Power and Justice in Foreign Investment Arbitration' (1997) 14 J Int'l Arb 103.

together with the growth of transnational corporations: from the initial suggestion that the system benefits developed over developing countries, to the context of a neo-liberal movement in which companies are frequently seen as stronger players than states.[39] Despite their generality, and moreover despite their empirical rebuttal,[40] these concerns are alleged to have brought about concrete changes in the jurisdictional structure of investment arbitration. The concept of 'arbitration without privity' is said to be a direct product of neo-liberal tendencies,[41] followed by the urges for further expansion of arbitral jurisdiction in favour of investors.[42] Such arguments should be taken with caution. As argued in Chapter 1, 'arbitration without privity' was not quite an innovation in international law.[43] The question to be asked here is how the arbitral work on jurisdictional determinations is affected by one-sidedness. The arguments alleging arbitral excessiveness, however, face a major problem preventing drawing convincing conclusions regarding arbitral law-making, insofar as they rely heavily on outcomes rather than nuances and the means of arbitral work. They do not observe something close to what I call here arbitral jurisdictional regulation. Additionally, as mentioned above, tribunals have often limited the access to international arbitration.

2.1.3   Biased Arbitrators and 'Adventurism' in Jurisdictional Determinations

A related criticism claims that arbitrators adjudicating investment disputes are biased in favour of foreign investors, which can be reflected in jurisdictional determinations. This claim can be deconstructed as follows. First, a limited circle of actors dominates investment arbitration, both as arbitrators and counsels.[44] Second, their interest in maintaining their business brings about

---

39 See M Sornarajah, *Resistance and Change in the International Law on Foreign Investment* (CUP 2015) 10–9.

40 Susan D Franck, 'Development and Outcomes of Investment Treaty Arbitration' (2009) 50 Harvard Int'l LJ 435; Susan D Franck, 'Conflating Politics and Development? Examining Investment Treaty Arbitration Outcomes' (2014) 55 Virginia J Int'l L 13; and, for a critique of the former, Gus Van Harten, 'Fairness and Independence in Investment Arbitration: A Critique of "Development and Outcomes of Investment Treaty Arbitration"' *ITN Quarterly* (December 2010) 7.

41 Sornarajah, 'Power and Justice' (n 38) 126–39; Sornarajah, *Resistance* (n 39) 139–43.

42 Muthucumaraswamy Sornarajah, 'Toward Normlessness: The Ravage and Retreat of Neo-Liberalism in International Investment Law' in Karl P Sauvant (ed), *Yearbook on International Investment Law & Policy 2009-2010* (OUP 2010) 619–24; M Sornarajah, 'A Coming Crisis: Expansionary Trends in Investment Treaty Arbitration' in Karl P Sauvant (ed), *Appeals Mechanism in International Investment Disputes* (OUP 2008) 51–61.

43 See ch 1, s 3.1.2.

44 See generally Puig (n 7); and Langford, Behn, and Hilleren Lie (n 7).

perceived bias in favour of claimants, ie foreign investors.[45] Third, some argue that support for the allegations of perceived bias can be found empirically.[46] Fourth, it is questionable whether institutional aspects of the regime, such as the ICSID framework, are biased to a certain extent.[47] Fifth, bias in favour of foreign investors, either perceived or real, inclines towards expansionism or adventurism in jurisdictional determinations.[48]

In opposition, it is argued that allegations of systemic bias in investment arbitration are not supported by either theory or evidence.[49] One can add to this the recognition of a schism between pro-investor and pro-state arbitrators, each appearing favourable to their respective group of prospective clients and advocating corresponding views.[50] Furthermore, the expectation of an arbitrator to appear balanced, reasonable, neutral, or to aim to present the system as coherent and functional, might be another driving factor in

---

45   See generally Gus Van Harten, *Investment Treaty Arbitration and Public Law* (OUP 2007) 167–75 (on the 'dependency of arbitrators on prospective claimants'); Gus Van Harten, 'Perceived Bias in Investment Treaty Arbitration' in Michael Waibel and others (eds), *The Backlash Against Investment Arbitration* (Kluwer 2010) 433, 445.

46   Gus Van Harten, 'Arbitrator Behaviour in Asymmetrical Adjudication: An Empirical Study of Investment Treaty Arbitration' (2012) 50 Osgoode Hall LJ 211; Gus Van Harten, 'Arbitrator Behaviour in Asymmetrical Adjudication (Part Two): An Examination of Hypotheses of Bias in Investment Treaty Arbitration' (2016) 53 Osgoode Hall LJ 540. See also, for the behaviour of individual arbitrators and leaders of expansive interpretations, Gus Van Harten, 'Leaders in the Expansive and Restrictive Interpretation of Investment Treaties: A Descriptive Study of ISDS Awards to 2010' (2018) 29 EJIL 507.

47   For an empirical, albeit older, analysis and rebuttal of this suggestion, see Susan D Franck, 'The ICSID Effect? Considering Potential Variations in Arbitration Awards' (2011) 51 Virginia J Int'l L 825.

48   See Van Harten, *Public Law* (n 45) 167–75; Chen Huiping, 'The Expansion of Jurisdiction by ICSID Tribunals: Approaches, Reasons and Damages' (2011) 12 JWIT 671, 683–4; Sornarajah, *Resistance* (n 39) 136–47; Sornarajah, 'Toward Normlessness' (n 42) 618 (attributing the inclination to expansionism to neo-liberal values).

49   William W Park, 'Arbitrator Integrity' in Michael Waibel and others (eds), *The Backlash against Investment Arbitration* (Kluwer 2010) 213–6; Daphna Kapeliuk, 'The Repeat Appointment Factor: Exploring Decision Patterns of Elite Investment Arbitrators' (2010) 96 Cornell L Rev 47; Susan D Franck and Lindsey E Wylie, 'Predicting Outcomes in Investment Treaty Arbitration' (2015) 65 Duke LJ 459; Susan D Franck, 'Empirically Evaluating Claims About Investment Treaty Arbitration' (2007) 86 North Carolina L Rev 1, 50; Charles N Brower and Stephan W Schill, 'Is Arbitration a Threat or a Boon to the Legitimacy of International Investment Law?' (2009) 9 Chicago JIL 471, 489–95. See also Catherine A Rogers, 'The Politics of International Investment Arbitrators' (2013) 12 Santa Clara J Int'l L 223, 248–53 (arguing that Van Harten's thesis on arbitral expansionism is not peculiar to the arbitral environment).

50   Sornarajah, 'Toward Normlessness' (n 42) 599, 618, 638–9.

decision-making.[51] These considerations argue that state interests are not left without defenders in the arbitral process, and that tribunals are not inclined towards adventurism.

Allegations of arbitral bias are directly connected to jurisdictional determinations.[52] Their problem, however, is the same as with the arguments about one-sidedness: they emphasise the results instead of the means. Despite the occasional criticisms of the reliance on outcomes, the scholarly attempts to approach the reasoning of arbitral tribunals from an empirical perspective have continued to focus on interpretive (as opposed to final) outcomes.[53] Furthermore, as biases are defined in sharper terms than one-sidedness, their link to outcomes should be stronger too. This has led some authors to rebut the allegations of bias relying, among other things, on the success rate of jurisdictional objections.[54] If those findings are correct, one cannot speak of a systemic impact of biases on jurisdictional determinations, and that can be even less so when it comes to arbitral law-making. Accepted as true, arbitral biases would impose a pro-investor objective in jurisdictional rulings, setting out a pro-investor law-making agenda. There is no proof of such practice, as seen in Chapters 2 to 4. The trajectory from arbitral attitudes to jurisdictional determinations suggested by the allegations of pro-investor bias, therefore, does not offer a satisfactory explanation of the driving force of arbitral jurisdictional regulation.

2.2   *A Fresh Start: Changing Perspectives on Party Consent*

This section offers an explanation of the impetus behind arbitral jurisdictional regulation in the shift from a 'hard' to 'soft' perspective on party consent in investment arbitration, and possibly in international adjudication more generally. The perception of the principal role played by consent has shifted from that of consent as a guardian of state sovereignty to that of consent as the primary means of jurisdictional regulation. While the two functions should not be mutually exclusive, the true dilemma concerns the *principal* function of consent. The soft perspective has evolved in parallel with the growth

---

51   Mills (n 2) 451–5; Kapeliuk (n 49) 83, 90.
52   See n 48 above.
53   Van Harten, 'Arbitrator Behaviour' (n 46) 225–8 (classifying resolutions of jurisdictional issues as expansive, restrictive, or non-classifiable); Van Harten, 'Arbitrator Behaviour (Part Two)' (n 46) 549–54 (using the same classification in regard to substantive issues).
54   See Franck, 'Empirically Evaluating Claims' (n 49) 48–55; and, for a summary of overall success rates, Susan D Franck, 'International Investment Arbitration: Winning, Losing and Why' (2009) 7 Columbia FDI Perspectives.

of international adjudication, which is supported by the preservation of the hard perspective on consent in those fields of international dispute settlement that have not witnessed a significant growth. I first address the hard (1) and then the soft perspective on consent (2), followed by an analysis of the specific framework of investor-state dispute resolution (3).

2.2.1   Hard Perspective

Sovereignty is difficult to define, at least in legal terms. This does not prevent its frequent mention: critics of the investment arbitral practice, for example, often invoke eroded sovereignty as their core concern.[55] Respondent states also often invoke sovereignty in their defences,[56] which is occasionally followed by tribunals in their reasoning.[57] Nevertheless, such mentions of sovereignty do not reveal much of its concrete legal meaning. The lack of its concrete meaning might reflect the long-established principle that sovereignty should not have a direct effect on international legal rules, especially those governing the jurisdiction of international courts and tribunals.[58]

Sovereignty is still important, and perhaps can be defined from another angle, through an inductive process. Jorge Viñuales sees sovereignty as a

---

[55]   Sornarajah, *Resistance* (n 39) 138 (erosion of sovereignty through jurisdictional expansionism); Mary Bottari and Lori Wallach, *NAFTA's Threat to Sovereignty and Democracy: The Record of NAFTA Chapter 11 Investor-State Cases 1994-2005* (Public Citizen 2005); Chen (n 48) 686–7; Julia Hueckel, 'Rebalancing Legitimacy and Sovereignty in International Investment Agreements' (2012) 61 Emory LJ 601, 610–4. Sornarajah also talks about the 'surrender of sovereign rights' of states through investment treaties; see Sornarajah, *Resistance* (n 39) 159.

[56]   See, for example, *Amco Asia Corp and others v The Republic of Indonesia*, ICSID Case No ARB/81/1, Award on Jurisdiction (25 September 1983) para 12(i); *Methanex Corporation v The United States of America*, UNCITRAL ad hoc arbitration, Partial Award (7 August 2002) para 103; *Vladimir Berschader & Moïse Berschader v The Russian Federation*, SCC Case No 80/2004, Award (21 April 2006) paras 53, 203; *Cambodia Power Company v Kingdom of Cambodia and Electricité du Cambodge*, ICSID Case No ARB/09/18, Decision on Jurisdiction (22 March 2011) para 323.

[57]   See, for example, *Wintershall Aktiengesellschaft v Argentine Republic*, ICSID Case No ARB/04/14, Award (8 December 2008) para 160(3); *Daimler Financial Services AG v Argentine Republic*, ICSID Case No ARB/05/1, Award (22 August 2012) para 193.

[58]   See H Lauterpacht, 'Restrictive Interpretation and the Principle of Effectiveness in the Interpretation of Treaties' (1949) 26 British Yrbk Int'l L 48, 56–67 (challenging the restrictive approach to treaty interpretation, which is alleged to relate to state sovereignty, both in principle and in practice); and particularly ibid 65–6 (the same regarding jurisdictional determinations); *Oil Platforms (Islamic Republic of Iran v United States of America)* (Preliminary Objection) (Separate Opinion of Judge Higgins) (1996) ICJ Rep 847, para 35 (noting that there are no rules instructing restrictive or liberal interpretation of jurisdictional clauses).

mosaic, instead of a unified concept.[59] That mosaic consists of many legal concepts which altogether position the state within the international legal order. The consensualism of international adjudication can be seen as part of such mosaic: it is clearly related to the idea of sovereignty,[60] yet it can be defined in legal terms and positioned within the coordinate system of international legal norms.[61] Because the principle of consensualism, together with other legal concepts of international law, is permeated by an idea that does not bear a precise legal meaning, it can be seen as one of many family resemblances of state sovereignty.[62]

My argument is that the hard perspective on consent relies excessively on the concept of state sovereignty. Sovereignty is used in this context as a political and highly symbolic category.[63] Take the example of the concept of exhaustion of local remedies in diplomatic protection. That legal concept has been a barrier between two legal worlds—domestic and international.[64] A barrier was necessary precisely because of the symbolic exit of a dispute from the domestic to the inter-sovereign sphere, where only sovereigns were able to address claims against each other.[65] Allowing private persons to directly address international claims against states was, as it later turned out, technically possible with an appropriate jurisdictional link, but not acceptable from a symbolic point of view. It is thus not surprising that the arguments in favour of restoring a similar legal concept in the field of investment arbitration are made through the symbolic prism of sovereignty.[66]

---

59   Jorge E Viñuales, 'Sovereignty in Foreign Investment Law' in Zachary Douglas, Joost Pauwelyn, and Jorge E Viñuales (eds), *International Investment Law: Bringing Theory into Practice* (OUP 2014) 319–24.
60   See ch 1, s 2.1.
61   See ch 1, s 2.3.
62   See, for the famous concept in philosophy, Ludwig Wittgenstein, *Philosophical Investigations* (GEM Anscombe tr, 3rd ed, Basil Blackwell 1967) 32.
63   See generally Jens Bartelson, *Sovereignty as Symbolic Form* (Routledge 2014).
64   See James R Crawford and Thomas D Grant, 'Local Remedies, Exhaustion Of' in Rüdiger Wolfrum (ed), *The Max Planck Encyclopedia of Public International Law*, vol 6 (OUP 2012) 895–7.
65   *Mavrommatis Palestine Concessions (Greece v UK)* (Judgment) (1924) PCIJ Ser A—No 2, 6, 12 ('Once a State has taken up a case on behalf of one of its subjects before an international tribunal, in the eyes of the latter the State is sole claimant.').
66   See, for example, George K Foster, 'Striking a Balance Between Investor Protections and National Sovereignty: The Relevance of Local Remedies in Investment Treaty Arbitration' (2011) 49 Columbia J Transnat'l L 201, 267 (supporting the encouragement of recourse to local remedies in arbitral practice).

A hard perspective on consent is preserved in the practice of the ICJ. The importance of the consensualism of international adjudication as 'a well-established principle of international law' is emphasised when necessary to defend third states from having their rights and obligations determined in a litigation process of which they are not part.[67] This is essentially just another reaffirmation of the sovereignist premise that states' rights and obligations stem from their 'own free will'.[68] The notion of sovereignty behind the notion of consent instructs the latter's practical effects. For example, when in doubt how to qualify certain questions, the ICJ has resorted to the principle of consensualism, arguing that any procedural limitation included in a jurisdictional clause limits party consent and raises jurisdictional questions.[69] The symbolism of sovereignty plays a bigger part than it seems at first: whether an issue pertains to jurisdiction or admissibility does not imply any significant consequences in the context of the ICJ; yet, the Court's resolution of the problem defers to the principle that parties define its jurisdiction. States as sovereigns, it follows, are the sole governors of the conditions under which they can be litigated.

A hard perspective on consent is reasonable in the inter-state adjudication context. States are the traditional law-makers in international law and their principal focus has been the regulation of their mutual relations. The ICJ can reach to various rules and concepts of legally regulated inter-state relations in the construction of state consent.[70] The known framework of inter-state legal relations allows the Court even to hypothesize in the establishment of procedural doctrines.[71] In doing so, the Court stays in the domain of the state-created

---

67 *Monetary Gold Removed from Rome in 1943 (Italy v France, UK, and USA)* (Preliminary Question) (1954) ICJ Rep 19, 32; *East Timor (Portugal v Australia)* (Judgment) (1995) ICJ Rep 90, para 34.

68 *The Case of the ss 'Lotus' (France v Turkey)* (Judgment) (1927) PCIJ Ser A—No 10, 4, 18.

69 *Armed Activities on the Territory of the Congo (New Application: 2002) (Democratic Republic of the Congo v Rwanda)* (Jurisdiction and Admissibility) (2006) ICJ Rep 6, para 88.

70 See, for example, *Factory at Chorzów (Germany v Poland)* (Claim for Indemnity) (Jurisdiction) (1927) PCIJ Ser A—No 9, 4, 21 (stating the principles of state responsibility, and consequently implying jurisdiction over the questions of reparations); *Application of the Convention on the Prevention and Punishment of the Crime of Genocide (Bosnia and Herzegovina v Yugoslavia)* (Preliminary Objections) (1996) ICJ Rep 595, paras 17–24 (discussing the questions of state continuity and succession in regard to the Genocide Convention); and, regarding the exercise of jurisdiction, *Interhandel (Switzerland v United States of America)* (Preliminary Objections) (1959) ICJ Rep 6, 27 (observing the requirement of the exhaustion of domestic remedies as 'a well-established rule of customary international law' concerning diplomatic protection).

71 For example, the *Mavrommatis* doctrine, which allows the Court some flexibility in jurisdictional determinations, is based on the hypothesis that the applicant state could

law which is also directly applicable between disputing parties. The sufficiency and non-excess of the traditional sphere of inter-state law allows for not disturbing the hard perspective on consent as a guardian of sovereignty.

The principle of consensualism in this context guards sovereignty as a political concept. Sovereignty can be invoked as an inspiration in the interpretation of jurisdictional rules, while the direct source of the legal rules governing the jurisdiction of international courts and tribunals is strictly limited to the will of states as disputing parties. In practice, this hard perspective on consent means that apart from interpretation, an international tribunal does not have any right or possibility to supplement the rules governing its jurisdiction.

2.2.2   Soft Perspective

In contrast to the hard perspective on consent, the practice of investment arbitral tribunals demonstrates a soft perspective. The principle of consensualism seems, to a certain extent, untied from the political symbol of sovereignty. The principle is liberated from the symbolic instruction of sovereignty in its application. In my view, this liberation from political and symbolic ideals, which permits tribunals to see consent more pragmatically as a pure legal concept, creates the driving force behind arbitral jurisdictional regulation.

There are two factors explaining this shift of perspectives. The first one is the investor-state *jurisdictional relationship*. Arguably, the departure from the chains of sovereignty has resulted from the development of an inclusive public international law, which observes interests of not only states but also private persons.[72] The principle of consensualism in its original form might have represented one of many family resemblances of the idea of sovereignty, but in practice it engages primarily disputing parties delegating the authority to adjudicate.[73] Once international law accepted private persons as possible litigants, the principle engaged them too. The notion of sovereignty behind consent has been lost. A dispute is property of both of its parties in equal shares, and one party should not be discriminated against by permeating the idea of sovereignty behind consent to the advantage of the other party, only because of the

---

remedy a procedural defect in its application by filing a new one. See, for the precedent, *Mavrommatis Palestine Concessions* (n 65) 34; and, for practical application, *Bosnia and Herzegovina v Yugoslavia* (n 70) para 26.

72 Tillmann Rudolf Braun, 'Globalization: The Driving Force in International Investment Law' in Michael Waibel and others (eds), *The Backlash Against Investment Arbitration* (Kluwer 2010) 502–5.

73 See ch 1, s 2.2.

statehood of that other party.[74] Practical application of this view is visible in practice.[75]

Another important aspect of jurisdictional relationships is their usual incompleteness. No matter how detailed rules governing the jurisdiction of a court or tribunal are, new and unregulated questions will always appear. This is visible already in the context of the ICJ, and the Court often must search extensively for the applicable legal rules to resolve jurisdictional questions, but as seen above the Court has an entire corpus of the traditional inter-state law at its disposal.[76] In contrast, investment tribunals face a more difficult task, because private-public claims and jurisdictional relationships are not the traditional issues governed by international law.[77] Investor-state relationships require special regulation, which was initiated in modern investment treaties. Facing an issue that is not regulated by the given jurisdictional framework (for example, a BIT and the ICSID Convention), investment tribunals must look elsewhere. This is the point where analogies, personal understandings and beliefs, legal knowledge, and so on come into play. Where references to the traditional rules of international law fail to resolve jurisdictional questions, it is reasonable that the symbolic value of sovereignty fades away.

The second factor is the perceived *regularity,* in the sense of dealing with everyday matters on an everyday basis. The judicialization of international law has increased states' referrals to international courts and tribunals, however one cannot ignore the fact that inter-state adjudication is still exceptional compared to individual-state (private-public) international adjudication by

---

74 See further in this direction, although in the context of the tension between deference to the state and equality of arms, Wälde, 'Procedural Challenges' (n 28) 11–4.

75 *Millicom International Operations BV and Sentel GSM SA v The Republic of Senegal,* ICSID Case No ARB/08/20, Decision on Jurisdiction of the Arbitral Tribunal (16 July 2010) para 65 ('Moreover, there is nothing extraordinary about the rule [offer of arbitration in the relevant BIT] to the extent that it implies nothing else for the State involved except to agree to submit itself to an arbitration proceeding under the aegis of ICSID by independent arbitrators, in a proceeding during which it shall have every opportunity to defend its positions.'). See also *Amco Asia Corp and others v Indonesia* (n 56) para 14(i) (albeit in a contractual context, facing an argument for restrictive interpretation of the jurisdictional clause due to state sovereignty, and stating that an arbitration agreement should not be interpreted either restrictively or liberally).

76 See s 2.2.1 above.

77 Traditionally, prior to the emergence of modern special regimes such as human rights and investment laws, private interests have been internationalised by the attachment to their states of origin. See, regarding foreign investors' claims and diplomatic protection, Rudolf Dolzer and Christoph Schreuer, *Principles of International Investment Law* (2nd ed, OUP 2012) 232; and Andrew Newcombe and Lluís Paradell, *Law and Practice of Investment Treaties: Standards of Treatment* (Kluwer 2009) 3–7.

numbers. This is understandable: inter-state litigation often forms part of broader political differences, it can have serious consequences on the life of the international community, and it requires coordination of both legal and political considerations.[78] Investment arbitrations can also be significant and high-profile, but their standard setting is meant to resolve the issues of treatment as common in the field of foreign investment. They form part (the most important part, some would argue) and ensure the stability of the legal framework governing foreign investments.[79] This is a consequence of the depoliticization of investor-state disputes.[80] In this context the concept of sovereignty does not have much to offer and party consent remains nothing but a source of jurisdictional rules.

These factors reveal a new, soft perspective on the principle of consensualism, where party consent is seen as nothing more than the primary means of jurisdictional regulation. BITs, the ICSID Convention, counteroffers made by investors—in short, all the sources injecting the substance to arbitration agreements—provide the rules establishing a tribunal, defining its mandate and the applicable procedure. And nothing else. Most importantly, the disappearance of the idea of sovereignty behind the principle of consensualism, and the liberation from its instruction, lifts the perceived restrictions on tribunals regarding the ability to fill jurisdictional regulatory deficiencies. The elimination of such deficiencies becomes the cardinal condition for the successful work of a tribunal.

2.2.3 The Specific Framework of Investor-State Dispute Settlement

The investor-state dispute settlement framework provides an excellent opportunity for the implementation of the soft perspective on consent and filling jurisdictional regulatory deficiencies. I address two aspects of such opportunity: substantive, regarding the absence of detailed jurisdictional rules (1), and procedural, regarding mainly the ad hoc nature of this dispute settlement regime (2).

---

[78] Bart L Smit Duijzentkunst and Sophia LR Dawkins, 'Arbitrary Peace? Consent Management in International Arbitration' (2015) 26 EJIL 139, 168 ('To achieve a peaceful outcome, it is not enough for parties to offer initial consent to arbitration; tribunals need to maintain the consent of the parties throughout the arbitration process and the implementation phase of the award.').

[79] Stephan W Schill, 'Private Enforcement of International Investment Law: Why We Need Investor Standing in BIT Dispute Settlement' in Michael Waibel and others (eds), *The Backlash Against Investment Arbitration* (Kluwer 2010) 31–3.

[80] Ibrahim FI Shihata, 'Towards a Greater Depoliticization of Investment Disputes: The Roles of ICSID and MIGA' (1986) 1 ICSID Rev-FILJ 1.

2.2.3.1 Substantive Opportunities for Law-Making

Chapters 2 to 4 showed a significant practice of rule-development by arbitral tribunals. Arguably, such practice would be absent, or at least present to a lesser extent, should investment treaties and other instruments provide more detailed jurisdictional rules. Investment treaties are often said to be minimalist in terms of regulation, and frequently vague and ambiguous.[81] This problem has been discussed extensively in the context of treaty interpretation. It can be argued that states deliberately leave definitions in BITs vague and ambiguous for a variety of reasons, from allowing evolution in the meaning of terms, to the inability to agree on more precise terms.[82] It can also be argued that an endless inquiry into the intentions of treaty parties is inappropriate: if the delegation of the authority to adjudicate comes from disputing parties, as maintained in this study, an investor accepting an offer to arbitrate accepts it with all its imperfections and should be able to rely on them. When it comes to solving concrete issues, the vagueness and ambiguities of treaty provisions are usually considered problematic.[83] However, it is also possible to view them as opportunities, which 'enable a court or tribunal to engage in judicial law- or policy-making'.[84] These opportunities for asserting the true, correct, precise, definitive, or whatever else meaning of provisions, lead to the establishment of tribunals' 'semantic authority'.[85]

Structurally, vague and ambiguous legal provisions, the absence of clear and precise norms, and the questions of their interactions, grant international adjudicators certain legal discretion.[86] This leads to a greater independence of international adjudicators from norm-creators, which are still primarily

---

[81] But see Anne van Aaken, 'International Investment Law Between Commitment and Flexibility: A Contract Theory Analysis' (2009) 12 JIEL 507, 527–31 (discussing vague treaty terms as a possible device for securing flexibility of investment treaties, which suits states).

[82] Mills (n 2) 455–6.

[83] Andreas Kulick, 'From Problem to Opportunity? An Analytical Framework for Vagueness and Ambiguity in International Law' in Andreas von Arnauld and Kerstin von der Decken (eds), *German Yearbook of International Law*, vol 59 (Duncker & Humblot 2016) 273–4.

[84] ibid 274–5.

[85] ibid 277. For the concept of 'semantic authority' as 'an actor's capacity to influence and shape meanings as well as the ability to establish its communications as authoritative reference points in legal discourse', see Ingo Venzke, *How Interpretation Makes International Law: On Semantic Change and Normative Twists* (OUP 2012) 62–4.

[86] Robert O Keohane, Andrew Moravcsik, and Anne-Marie Slaughter, 'Legalized Dispute Resolution: Interstate and Transnational' (2000) 54 Int'l Org 457, 461–2. For the extent of interpretive discretion see Roberts, 'Power and Persuasion' (n 21) 185 ('The zone of interpretive discretion of investment tribunals may be understood as the interpretive powers explicitly or implicitly delegated to them minus the formal and informal powers retained by treaty parties to influence their interpretations, including through dialogue.' [with

states.[87] At the same time, this gives them the opportunity to establish new norms. It is the framework of private-public adjudication itself that makes such adjudicative discretion, because of the transfer of the decision-making power from the original norm-creators to third-party adjudicators. That framework, it has been argued, is crucially different from the traditional inter-state adjudication model, in which states retain the gatekeeping functions and control over dispute settlement processes.[88] Furthermore, if international law has traditionally accommodated inter-state relations, the adjudication of private-public relationships can incline adjudicators to focus on the development of the law in that particular context, released from the duty to follow traditional concepts of general international law.[89]

I wish to be sharper in my terms: the practice of investment tribunals has not faced vague and ambiguous treaty provisions only, but also regulatory deficiencies meaning the absence of rules addressing the jurisdictional question at stake. Jurisdictional regulation is specific: while the substantive standards of investor protection allow for broader spectra of interpretations addressing emerging issues,[90] the establishment of the authority to adjudicate requires precise rules and thus gaps are identified with more ease. If interpretation presents an opportunity for asserting new norms, such opportunity is even greater in the case of regulatory gaps.

2.2.3.2 *Procedural Opportunities for Law-Making*

The procedural features of the investor-state dispute settlement regime also give opportunities for remedying regulatory deficiencies by tribunals. Factors like a low control of states over adjudicators (ie independence), the direct access of private persons to international adjudication, and the assurance of enforcement, are considered decisive for the possibility of developing jurisprudence, precedents, and new norms.[91] Investment arbitration is an example

---

reference to Alec Stone Sweet, 'Constitutionalism, Rights, and Judicial Power' in Daniele Caramani (ed), *Comparative Politics* (OUP 2008) 228–9]).
87 Keohane, Moravcsik, and Slaughter (n 86) 461–2.
88 See generally Keohane, Moravcsik, and Slaughter (n 86).
89 See also in this direction Radović, 'Inherently Unneutral' (n 29) 155–6.
90 For example, the substantive standards of protection are considered more likely to be influenced by the rule of systemic integration in treaty interpretation, despite some difficulties in applying that rule in investment law generally; see Rumiana Yotova, 'Systemic Integration: An Instrument for Reasserting the State's Control in Investment Arbitration?' in Andreas Kulick (ed), *Reassertion of Control over the Investment Treaty Regime* (CUP 2016) 193–207.
91 Keohane, Moravcsik, and Slaughter (n 86) 459–70, 479.

where these factors are fully met: states select (usually) one out of three arbitrators,[92] investors can institute arbitrations directly, normally without the need to exhaust domestic remedies, and awards are enforceable domestically, either directly[93] or through a limited domestic judicial control.[94] The last factor, however, should be taken cautiously, because local courts can review the jurisdiction of arbitral tribunals outside the ICSID context. In my view, the crucial factor here is the direct access of investors, who by initiating arbitrations set the agenda of tribunals and raise regulatory issues as an impulse to act.[95]

Another important consideration is the ad hoc character of the system. As often pointed out, the system provides neither a doctrine of precedent, nor any other sort of obligation of tribunals to follow previous awards and judgments.[96] There is no controlling authority capable of conducting an exhaustive and uniform analysis of arbitral rulings. Admittedly, jurisdictional determinations are peculiar, insofar as they are subject to a limited control, which is however also decentralised and certainly not uniform.[97] Investment arbitration arguably presents a prototype of an ad hoc system, lacking any legal component imposing uniformity and inter-dependence between adjudicating bodies.

Despite the ad hoc structure, tribunals prefer to appear systematised and to that effect they rely on previous decisions, pursuing consistency.[98] Such references are not limited to the investment sector, and investment tribunals eagerly rely on the practice of the ICJ,[99] of course only when possible

---

[92] It is also notable that the other nominating party in this scenario, an investor as a private person, does not have the interpretive interests of treaty-masters.

[93] Convention on the Settlement of Investment Disputes Between States and Nationals of Other States (signed 18 March 1965, entered into force 14 October 1966) 575 UNTS 159 (ICSID Convention) art 54.

[94] Convention on the Recognition and Enforcement of Foreign Arbitral Awards (signed 10 June 1958, entered into force 7 June 1959) 330 UNTS 38 (New York Convention) art v.

[95] See in this respect Keohane, Moravcsik, and Slaughter (n 86) 462, 468–70. See also ibid 481 ('The key to the dynamics of transnational dispute resolution is access.').

[96] See ss 3.2.2–3.2.3 below.

[97] ICSID annulment committees are also constituted on an ad hoc basis. Non-ICSID awards can be set aside or denied recognition and/or enforcement by domestic courts, which can have different policies on the intensity of their review; see William Laurence Craig, 'Uses and Abuses of Appeal from Awards' (1988) 4 Arb Int'l 174.

[98] See Jeffery P Commission, 'Precedent in Investment Treaty Arbitration: A Citation Analysis of a Developing Jurisprudence' (2007) 24 J Int'l Arb 129; Ole Kristian Fauchald, 'The Legal Reasoning of ICSID Tribunals – An Empirical Analysis' (2008) 19 EJIL 301, 333–43.

[99] See in this regard Hirsch (n 8) 165–7 ('This pattern is linked to the concepts of social status and reference groups in sociological literatures.').

because the practice of that court does not pertain much to investment disputes.[100] At this point, the influence of audiences on arbitral decision-making and motivation of decisions should be considered.[101] The audiences in investment arbitration are not uniform.[102] They can have cardinally different attitudes towards concrete issues, but what they probably want to see is the implementation of their views as part of the investment law system. The main thought in the minds of the readers of arbitral decisions is not 'what are the rules of international law', but 'what are the rules of international investment law and arbitration'. Therefore, what is at stake here is the ad hoc nature of the system (perceived separately from the mainstream public international law litigation), rather than of arbitrations. The apprehension of investment arbitration as a separate system provides a perceived opportunity to create norms crafted specifically for that regime. In other words, arbitral jurisdictional regulation can be seen as part of a broader process of system-formation.[103]

3 A Two-Layered Model of Jurisdictional Regulation in Investment Treaty Arbitration

I now turn to sketching a model of jurisdictional regulation in investment treaty arbitration consisting of two layers and providing two types of rules: primary (1) and secondary (2). I maintain that such division of jurisdictional regulation already de facto exists in practice but that it has not been recognised,

---

100 Alain Pellet, 'The Case Law of the ICJ in Investment Arbitration' (2013) 28 ICSID Rev-FILJ 223, 239–40 (observing that investment tribunals are more likely to refer to the ICJ jurisprudence when dealing with procedural and general international law issues).

101 See generally Ingo Venzke, 'Judicial Authority and Styles of Reasoning: Self-Presentation between Legalism and Deliberation' in Joanna Jemielniak, Laura Nielsen, and Henrik Palmer Olsen (eds), *Establishing Judicial Authority in International Economic Law* (CUP 2016) 240.

102 For the 'investment arbitration community' as a 'social group, comprised of lawyers, arbitrators, and scholars specializing in investment arbitration', see Hirsch (n 8) 146–8. See also, for the 'epistemic community of international lawyers and scholars' shaping investment law, Jeswald W Salacuse, 'The Emerging Global Regime for Investment' (2010) 51 Harvard Int'l LJ 427, 465–6.

103 See in this respect Alec Stone Sweet, Michael Yunsuck Chung, and Adam Saltzman, 'Arbitral Lawmaking and State Power: An Empirical Analysis of Investor–State Arbitration' (2017) 8 JIDS 579, 584–5 (discussing various notions of precedent and concluding that under an advanced one 'the duty to pursue doctrinal coherence is owed to the regime itself, not just to the contracting states and disputing parties').

especially regarding the second layer, consisted of arbitrator-made jurisdictional rules.[104]

3.1 *Primary Rules*

Primary rules of jurisdictional regulation are the main means of empowering international arbitral tribunals to adjudicate. They are the starting point in every assessment of the existence and the limits of that empowerment. Primary rules are direct products of party consent, or more precisely of the common will of disputing parties. They derive from all the provisions manifesting the will of disputing parties, such as those in investment treaties, ICSID Convention, investor acceptances, direct arbitration agreements etc. They have been addressed earlier in this study.[105]

Primary rules are usually imposed by states, because treaty dispute settlement clauses function as offers and adhesion contracts towards investors. But the contribution of investor acceptances perfecting arbitration agreements should not be underestimated. At the moment of acceptance, a treaty dispute settlement clause transforms into an arbitration agreement. From the arbitration perspective, only at that moment primary rules gain normativity. It therefore follows that investors trigger the binding force of primary rules, not states. From the moment of acceptance, states are not able to change the content of their offers.[106] This is significant from the investor perspective, given the importance of the scope of consent and the related issue of jurisdictional bridging for the availability of counterclaims.[107] Furthermore, investors can make counteroffers to states and negotiate with them the details of arbitration agreements, amending initial jurisdictional arrangements.[108]

---

104 See also Dolores Bentolila, *Arbitrators as Lawmakers* (Kluwer 2017) 231–2. Bentonila recognises the arbitrator-created 'power-conferring rules that regulate international arbitration'. However, that analysis differs from the present one. First, it examines arbitral law-making in commercial and investment arbitration altogether, as a common field of international arbitration. Second, it does not accommodate arbitrator-created rules within a specific legal system such as international law, and it does not specify their relationship and interaction with the norms created by virtue of consensual law-making.

105 See ch 1, s 3.3.

106 See ch 1, s 3.2.1.

107 See ch 3, s 4.

108 See, for example, *Burlington Resources Inc v Republic of Ecuador*, ICSID Case No ARB/08/5, Decision on Counterclaims (7 February 2017) paras 60–1 (where counterclaims were allowed because of the parties' subsequent agreement to that effect); *Lao Holdings NV and Sanum Investments Limited v Lao People's Democratic Republic*, ICSID Case Nos ARB(AF)/16/2 and ADHOC/17/1, Procedural Order No 2 (23 October 2017) para 31 (where the parties agreed on the consolidation of two cases and thus reached a special agreement on the scope of arbitrable disputes); *Cargill Incorporated v Republic of Poland*, UNCITRAL ad hoc

3.2 *Secondary Rules*

Secondary rules of jurisdictional regulation are created by arbitral tribunals in practice, and they assist the interpretation and application of primary rules. I first define them (1), and then I address the questions of arbitral practice as a source of law (2) and the practical application of secondary rules (3). The idea of creating additional jurisdictional rules is not unchallenged,[109] and therefore their justification is emphasised.

3.2.1   Defining Secondary Rules

Practice shows that primary rules are often not self-executory. They contain deficiencies and require assistance in their application. Arbitral tribunals have for that purpose developed a number of tools, which I define here as secondary rules of jurisdictional regulation. I identify three types of secondary rules: presumptions, default rules, and standards. This classification is made in accordance with the function of secondary rules in relation to primary rules.

Presumptions direct the interpretation of primary rules regarding their applicability. For example, tribunals have been asked to determine whether MFN clauses are applicable to dispute resolution clauses within BITs, and whether BITs protect indirect investments and thus confer jurisdiction to arbitral tribunals over a broader circle of investors. As seen in Chapters 2 and 3, arbitral tribunals have answered these questions by adopting premises dictating the process of treaty interpretation by specifying the indicators that should be sought. In practice, the tribunals that have supported the general applicability of MFN clauses to dispute settlement provisions, have shifted the burden of proof (or rather argumentation) to the party arguing to the contrary, and *vice versa*.[110] The same has been the case with indirect investments.[111] Presumptions leave open the possibility of different application of a primary rule, subject to convincing arguments.

Default rules fill gaps in primary rules. For example, some tribunals have been willing to give effect to umbrella clauses only subject to the condition of privity, ie that the contract whose protection is sought via an umbrella clause

---

arbitration, Final Award (29 February 2008) paras 20–2 (where the parties changed the procedural rules by virtue of a subsequent agreement).

109   Oscar M Garibaldi, 'Jurisdictional Errors: A Critique of the North American Dredging Company Case' in David D Caron and others (eds), *Practising Virtue: Inside International Arbitration* (OUP 2015) 168 (criticising the introduction of presumptions in favour of or against jurisdiction as well as of additional rules that affect the application of original jurisdictional rules as a structural error).

110   See ch 2, s 4.

111   See ch 3, s 3.2.

is concluded directly between the investor and the host state (to the exclusion of investors' and states' affiliates).[112] An umbrella clause can possibly provide otherwise, but in the absence of a detailed primary rule the default secondary rule applies. Another example concerns the independent legality requirement. Primary rules may require investments to comply with domestic laws to be protected and gain access to international arbitration. But very often such a requirement is lacking in the domain of primary rules. Tribunals have considered that that requirement should be a default rule, ie that every investor seeking access to arbitration must ensure that he has observed local laws in establishing the investment.[113]

Standards set out the criteria for the implementation of primary rules. The best example is the objective definition of 'investment': given that Article 25(1) of the ICSID Convention limits the jurisdiction of arbitral tribunals to disputes 'arising directly out of an investment' without defining the term 'investment', tribunals have come up with the *Salini* test.[114] Some non-ICSID tribunals have also supported the creation of a secondary standard, and established a default rule requiring an objective definition outside the ICSID framework.[115] Faced with the arguments that certain conditions precedent, such as local litigation requirements, need not be fulfilled, tribunals have analysed the futility exception and what it means to be 'futile'.[116] Some primary rules require secondary standards for verifying their positive application, ie that they have been complied with: fork-in-the-road clauses and local litigation requirements require comparing the identity of international and local claims, and arbitrators have developed relevant tests.[117] One of the biggest controversies in practice was the distinction between jurisdiction and admissibility.[118] This primarily concerns the application of conditions precedent and the applicable procedure as well as the finding a tribunal makes in the operative part of its award, but it can also affect the rigidity of the primary rules' command.[119] Standards have a default element: they can be deviated from by a primary rule.[120] What distinguishes

---

112 See ch 4, s 3.
113 See ch 4, s 2.2.
114 See ch 4, s 2.1.1.
115 See ch 4, s 2.1.2.
116 See ch 2, s 3.1.1.
117 See ch 2, ss 3.1.3 and 3.2.
118 See ch 2, s 2.1.
119 See ch 2, ss 2.2 and 2.3.
120 See, concerning futility exceptions, India Model BIT (2015) art 15(1) <https://investment-policy.unctad.org/international-investment-agreements/treaty-files/3560/download> accessed 20 August 2020 (requiring that 'there are no available domestic legal remedies capable of reasonably providing any relief').

them is that standards do not define jurisdictional limits as default rules do, but rather the conditions under which pre-defined limits should be implemented.

It is obvious that secondary rules cannot regulate arbitral jurisdiction on their own. They cannot create the authority to adjudicate from scratch. Graph 3 presents a diagram of the relationship between primary and secondary jurisdictional rules, and of the process of application of the latter to the former. It shows that the power to adjudicate is still defined by virtue of party consent through primary rules, which are in turn assisted by arbitrator-made (secondary) rules. The latter are made and applied in the process of interpretation and application of primary rules. Yet, secondary rules cannot be regarded as usual products of interpretative processes, because they are injected as supplementary input aimed to assist the process of interpretation and application of primary rules. Furthermore, secondary jurisdictional rules are distinguishable from other factors, like facts, that are relevant in jurisdictional determinations, because they are subject to legal argumentation and not to proof in the strict meaning. In Frédéric Sourgens' words, secondary rules are governed by the 'jurisdictional proof' whose burden is not on disputing parties only, but on the tribunal too.[121] Questions of secondary jurisdictional rules can be and in practice have been raised by tribunals on their own initiative,[122] which complies with the principle of *jura novit curia*, ie that the law is within the judicial knowledge of tribunals.[123]

---

[121] See Sourgens, 'By Equal Contest of Arms' (n 1) 923ff. Sourgens starts from the ICJ's preponderance standard, and suggests that a tribunal can raise jurisdictional issues on its own initiative, but 'is not free to establish jurisdiction beyond the parties' submissions, but instead must "interact" with the parties to do so'; this of course does not mean that a tribunal is bound verbatim to such submissions: ibid 924–5.

[122] See, regarding the objective definition of 'investment', *Phoenix Action Ltd v The Czech Republic*, ICSID Case No ARB/06/5, Award (15 April 2009) para 82 (rejecting the arguments of both parties and supplementing the test on its own initiative); *Krederi Ltd v Ukraine*, ICSID Case No ARB/14/17, Award (2 July 2018) paras 235–8 (applying a rump *Salini* test on its own initiative).

[123] It can be debated whether the principle of *jura novit curia* applies in international arbitrations, but support for such an argument can be made even in regard to arbitrator-made law. See *Glamis Gold Ltd v United States of America*, UNCITRAL ad hoc arbitration, Award (8 June 2009) para 8 ('to the degree that the parties to the dispute do not raise what the tribunal regards to be a particularly relevant authority, the tribunal should bring such an authority to the attention of the parties and provide them an opportunity to comment'); and generally Friedrich Rosenfeld, 'Iura Novit Curia in International Law' in Franco Ferrari and Giuditta Cordero-Moss (eds), *Iura Novit Curia in International Arbitration* (Juris 2018) 425.

TOWARDS A NEW JURISDICTIONAL FRAMEWORK

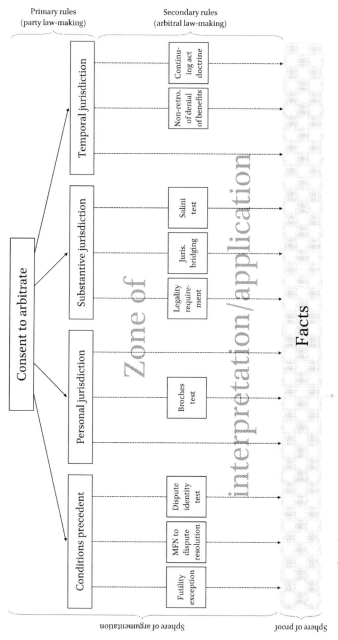

GRAPH 3   The relationship between primary and secondary jurisdictional rules

3.2.2 Practice as a Source of Law

It is often said that the practice of arbitral tribunals is not a source of law formally, but it does play such a role factually.[124] Arbitral law-making can be seen from two perspectives. The first perspective, which can be called *negative* or *indirect* law-making, recalls that states as treaty-makers draft treaty provisions in reaction to arbitral interpretations of the law.[125] This perspective is not in the focus of the present discussion. The second perspective, which can be dubbed *positive* or *direct* and which is crucial in this study, observes the arbitral establishment of new norms, which are in turn directly applied.

The question of direct arbitral law-making is controversial. Arbitral tribunals are not given a mandate to legislate but to resolve disputes, while the principal legislators in the field are states as treaty-makers.[126] Because tribunals clearly lack legal empowerment to create law, it is usually said that their decisions de facto achieve that effect.[127] A modest version of this argument claims that arbitrators create law through interpretation, by giving precise meaning to treaty provisions, possibly deviating from the intentions of the states concerned.[128] I wish to make a sharper argument: arbitrators make proper rules

---

124 See generally, in respect of general international law, Alan Boyle and Christine Chinkin, *The Making of International Law* (OUP 2007) 266–9, 293–300.

125 See Eric De Brabandere, 'Arbitral Decisions as a Source of International Investment Law' in Tarcisio Gazzini and Eric De Brabandere (eds), *International Investment Law: The Sources of Rights and Obligations* (Brill 2012) 282–6; and Catharine Titi, 'The Arbitrator as a Lawmaker: Jurisgenerative Processes in Investment Arbitration' (2013) 14 JWIT 829, 843–7.

126 De Brabandere (n 125) 248.

127 ibid 249; Lucy Reed, 'The *De Facto* Precedent Regime in Investment Arbitration: A Case for Proactive Case Management' (2010) 25 ICSID Rev-FILJ 95; August Reinisch, 'The Role of Precedent in ICSID Arbitration' in Christian Klausegger and others (eds), *Austrian Arbitration Yearbook 2008* (Beck/Stämpfli/Manz 2008) 495; Gabrielle Kaufmann-Kohler, 'Arbitral Precedent: Dream, Necessity or Excuse?' (2007) 23 Arb Int'l 357, 361; Tai-Heng Cheng, 'Precedent and Control in Investment Treaty Arbitration' (2006) 30 Fordham Int'l LJ 1014, 1030–1. cf Zachary Douglas, 'Can a Doctrine of Precedent Be Justified in Investment Treaty Arbitration?' (2010) 25 ICSID Rev-FILJ 104, 105 (criticising the distinction between *de jure* and *de facto* precedents); Pellet (n 100) 229 ('I think that there is no rule of precedent either *de jure* or *de facto*'). For the difficulties in accommodating the use of arbitral precedent in the orthodox doctrine of sources of international law, see generally Patrick M Norton, 'The Role of Precedent in the Development of International Investment Law' (2018) 33 ICSID Rev-FILJ 280. The phenomenon of informal precedent is by no means limited to investment arbitration; see Gilbert Guillaume, 'The Use of Precedent by International Judges and Arbitrators' (2011) 2 JIDS 5.

128 Stephan W Schill, 'Sources of International Investment Law: Multilateralization, Arbitral Precedent, Comparativism, Soft Law' in Samantha Besson and Jean D'Aspremont (eds), *The Oxford Handbook on the Sources of International Law* (OUP 2017) 1105–6; Titi (n 125) 833–8.

governing their jurisdiction. I acknowledge that such law-making takes place within interpretive processes. However, secondary jurisdictional rules are not interpretative *products,* but rather *inputs* into interpretive exercises, and are meant to assist the interpretation and application of primary rules.

This can be put in different terms. Every legal text requires interpretation before its actual application.[129] An interpreter can exercise more or less creativity, and many debates can be had over the question what it means to be 'creative' in the first place. I take such activities for fact; I do not challenge them. What I aim to identify are specific points in arbitral reasoning which (i) formulate general premises, and (ii) are detached from treaty terms, constructed through analogies, derived from policy considerations, general legal knowledge, or even personal beliefs and values. Such generalised and prescriptive premises resemble—and form—independent rules of law. In other words, I look for the instances of independent supplementing action, as opposed to the considerations of the terms of the relevant primary rules.

The crucial question here is not whether arbitrators can create independent rules of law, but rather whether they do so in practice. There is no doubt that investment tribunals refer extensively to previous decisions on similar (or sometimes identical) legal issues.[130] That phenomenon has always raised important questions: do arbitrators create law by virtue of their decisions, and if so how? There are two approaches to answering these questions. The first approach can be labelled *standardisation*. One opinion is that arbitral practice can produce some sort of international custom, or at least contribute to the determination of its content.[131] However, this argument can be rebutted on

---

[129] See generally Venzke, *Interpretation* (n 85) 1ff.

[130] See generally Commission (n 98); Fauchald (n 98) 333–43; Schill, 'Sources' (n 128) 1103–6; Vadi (n 13) 92–6; Cheng (n 127) 1030–44. See also Stephan W Schill, 'System-Building in Investment Treaty Arbitration and Lawmaking' in Armin von Bogdandy and Ingo Venzke (eds), *International Judicial Lawmaking: On Public Authority and Democratic Legitimation in Global Governance* (Springer 2012) 156 (identifying different modes of the use of precedent in investment arbitration). But see Christoph Schreuer and Matthew Weiniger, 'A Doctrine of Precedent?' in Peter Muchlinski, Federico Ortino, and Christoph Schreuer (eds), *The Oxford Handbook of International Investment Law* (OUP 2008) 1191–5 (noting that when invoking previous decisions, tribunals often rebut the applicability of a theory of binding precedent).

[131] *International Thunderbird Gaming Corporation v The United Mexican States,* UNCITRAL ad hoc arbitration, Separate Opinion of Thomas Wälde (1 December 2005) para 16; Andreas F Lowenfeld, 'Investment Agreements and International Law' (2003) 42 Columbia J Transnat'l L 123, 129; Kaufmann-Kohler (n 127) 377; José E Alvarez, 'A BIT on Custom' (2009) 42 NYU J Int'l L & Pol 17, 45–8; W Michael Reisman, 'Canute Confronts the Tide: States versus Tribunals and the Evolution of the Minimum Standard in Customary International Law' (2015) 30 ICSID Rev-FILJ 616, 622–3. See also Norton (n 127) 299–301 (on the ability of

both formalistic and substantive grounds.[132] Besides that, standardisation can be achieved relying on the theory of *jurisprudence constante,* which suggests that a chain of consistent decisions becomes authoritative for future tribunals facing the same issues.[133] The other approach to arbitral law-making can be labelled *competition.* It has been suggested that international investment arbitration should be viewed as common law, encouraging conflicting decisions on the same issue to compete with each other for the title of the most persuasive (as opposed to binding) precedent.[134] Looking from this perspective, '[d]isagreement between tribunals [...] is a sign of healthy development'.[135] Although arbitral tribunals and ICSID annulment committees at times invoke the first approach, and specifically the theory of *jurisprudence constante,*[136] I share the opinion that the second—common law—approach factually dominates arbitral practice.[137] As seen in Chapters 2 to 4, tribunals indeed tend to create an atmosphere of competition. That condition should be changed.

Giving precedential value to previous decision complies with the general international law view that judicial decisions are not formal but can be material sources of law.[138] Generally, the question whether the theory of precedent is justified in investment arbitration is popular, but the overall attitude

---

the investment arbitral practice to influence the development of customary law through an inductive process); Stephan W Schill, 'From Sources to Discourse: Investment Treaty Jurisprudence as the New Custom?' (2011) <www.biicl.org/files/5630_stephan_schill.pdf> accessed 15 July 2018 (on arbitral precedent taking the function of the traditional customary law).

132 Formally, custom is formed from *state* practice. Substantively, it is questionable whether arbitral practice can achieve the consistency and stability necessary for a custom. See Frédéric G Sourgens, 'Law's Laboratory: Developing International Law on Investment Protection as Common Law' (2014) 34 Northwestern J Int'l L & Business 181, 190–2; Frédéric Gilles Sourgens, *A Nascent Common Law: The Process of Decisionmaking in International Legal Disputes between States and Foreign Investors* (Brill Nijhoff 2015) 256–63.

133 Andrea K Bjorklund, 'Investment Treaty Arbitral Decisions as *Jurisprudence Constante*' in Colin B Picker, Isabella D Bunn, and Douglas W Arner (eds), *International Economic Law: The State and Future of the Discipline* (Hart 2008) 265.

134 Sourgens, 'Law's Laboratory' (n 132) 223–45.

135 ibid 245. See also generally Sourgens, *Common Law* (n 132).

136 See, for example, *Enron Creditors Recovery Corp and Ponderosa Assets LP v The Argentine Republic,* ICSID Case No ARB/01/3, Decision on the Application for Annulment of the Argentine Republic (30 July 2010) para 66; *Daimler Financial Services AG v Argentina* (n 57) para 91.

137 See Sourgens, 'Law's Laboratory' (n 132) 228–31 (reaching the same conclusion, but for the reason that previous decisions are used in defining the problem in question).

138 See Sir Gerald G Fitzmaurice, 'Some Problems Regarding the Formal Sources of International Law' in Martti Koskenniemi (ed), *Sources of International Law* (Ashgate 2000) 72–7 (taking as settled that case law is a material source of law in every legal system,

is that such a theory is not necessary in the field.[139] What results from such an attitude is the idea of a 'persuasive precedent': decisions are 'precedential' because of their persuasiveness, and not because of some rule of law awarding them such status.[140] As I will discuss when I turn to the practical application of the proposed model, I do not find such a criterion fully convincing. What matters here is the fact that arbitral decisions are widely followed as precedents or in streams.[141] An important part of that usage, which I believe has been neglected, is the fact that these precedents are often used as sources of generalised premises, forming rules governing jurisdiction.

Why do I call the products of arbitral practice 'rules' or 'norms'? To answer this question, it is not necessary to analyse general qualities of these notions. A more fruitful path is to discuss the role played by the rules at hand. First of all, they interact with the primary rules that empower investment tribunals to resolve disputes, by assisting the application and interpretation of party-provided jurisdictional rules. Because the rules that empower individuals and entities to adjudicate must be distinguished from the rules that determine rights and obligations,[142] arbitrator-made secondary rules pertaining to the implementation of primary empowering rules must fall within that same category. In Hart's words, these are specific 'rules of adjudication', which determine judicial powers to rule on breaches of rights and obligations.[143] It is not hard to observe this point in practice: when a tribunal says that the applicability of MFN clauses to jurisdictional clauses, the protection of indirect investments, or the permissibility of jurisdictional bridging, should be presumed, it essentially says that its authority to adjudicate

---

arguing that arbitral and judicial decisions cannot be seen as 'no more than' a material source of international law, but that they in reality have a more direct effect).

139   Douglas, 'Precedent' (n 127) 110 (countering heavy reliances on previous decisions in general); Alvarez (n 131) 46 (dismissing the need for 'formal precedential value'); Sourgens, 'Law's Laboratory' (n 132) 234 (arguing that the common law approach to investment arbitration does not require qualifying arbitral decisions as formal sources of international law).

140   Sourgens, 'Law's Laboratory' (n 132) 239–46. But see RY Jennings, 'The Judiciary, International and National, and the Development of International Law' (1996) 45 Int'l & Comp LQ 1, 6–12 (discussing the grey zone between precedent and *res judicata*).

141   See n 130 above. After many repetitions, tribunals do not perceive a duty to refer to specific precedents; see *Cortec Mining Kenya Limited, Cortec (Pty) Limited, and Stirling Capital Limited v Republic of Kenya*, ICSID Case No ARB/15/29, Award (22 October 2018) para 271 ('*It is well established in arbitral law* that the "origin of funds" issue is not a valid objection.' [emphasis added]).

142   HLA Hart, *The Concept of Law* (3rd ed, OUP 2012) 96–7.

143   ibid.

should be presumed. That presumption directs the further interpretative work with the aim to determine the precise scope of jurisdiction before moving to the merits. Therefore, tribunals do not merely render jurisdictional determinations, but also supplement the rules of adjudication, ie the rules empowering them to decide investment disputes.

Second, previous decisions are used in subsequent cases in a deductive, not inductive, process. It has been argued that the main benefit of the reliance on previous decisions is the definition, or filtering, of the relevant questions.[144] By discussing previous decisions, which are usually submitted by the parties, tribunals narrow down possible interpretations and choices, formulating the precise questions before them and the factors to be weighed in their assessment.[145] That is certainly the case from the point of view of the parties and their counsel, especially throughout the conduct of cases.[146] However, this is not the only benefit of relying on previous decisions. Chapters 2 to 4 reveal that tribunals use previous decisions in support of the rules to be applied as inputs to treaty interpretations. To use an already mentioned example: tribunals do not rely on previous decisions to conclude that possible interpretations of an MFN clause offer two solutions—in favour of or against its applicability to a dispute resolution clause. That choice is implicit in the arguments of the parties. Tribunals invoke previous decisions addressing the same issue to inquire whether such applicability should be presumed or not. That is the abstract nature of arbitral practice that implies top-down direction of its application. That is why arbitral reasonings formulate rules.

What is the source of normativity of arbitrator-made rules? I consult Kelsen here, who argues that the validity of a norm is always derived from a higher norm.[147] From the top-down perspective on the validation process, the higher

---

144   Sourgens, 'Law's Laboratory' (n 132) 209–15. This suggestion largely motivates Sourgens' proposal that investment arbitration should be seen as common law, as an 'inductive paradigm' as opposed to the 'deductive paradigm' of the civil law tradition; see ibid 224–31. See also Sourgens, *Common Law* (n 132) 286–305.

145   See, for example, *Brandes Investment Partners LP v The Bolivarian Republic of Venezuela*, ICSID Case No ARB/08/3, Award (2 August 2011) para 31 ('[… the Tribunal is not precluded] from considering the substance of decisions rendered by other arbitral tribunals, and the arguments of the Parties based on those decisions, to the extent that those decisions may shed light on the issue to be decided at this stage of the proceeding').

146   See particularly Sourgens, 'Law's Laboratory' (n 132) 209–15.

147   Hans Kelsen, *General Theory of Law and State* (Harvard University Press 1945) 110ff. See also, for Kelsen's tracing of the basic norm of international law, Hans Kelsen, *Principles of International Law* (Rinehart & Company 1952) 417–8. In contrast, another suggested route does not seek to validate arbitrator-created rules in a specific legal order such as international law and its sources, but holds that these rules possess 'intrinsic legality'

norm in question is the empowerment to settle disputes, which is a power to create individual norms. More precisely, I refer to the power of tribunals to resolve jurisdictional questions, ie to make final and binding determinations of the limits of their own jurisdiction.[148] Now, the general norm-creating function of investment tribunals appears as a 'free rider' in the execution of its individual norm-creation empowerment. Free riding is possible, because general norms find their expression in the creation of individual norms. General norms are—to use sharp language for the sake of the argument—meaningless. To become truly binding, they must be individualised. Just as a prohibition of expropriation contained in a BIT becomes truly binding by an arbitral finding of its violation and an order of compensation as a remedy, an arbitral-made rule that, for example, the application of an MFN clause to a dispute resolution clause should be presumed, becomes truly binding by an arbitral finding of jurisdiction in a particular case. Precisely this trajectory of normativity, which has perhaps a non-positivist sound but is essentially reflected in Kelsen's claim that creation of one norm is application of another,[149] makes room for arbitral law-making, when such an activity appears necessary.[150]

A bottom-up perspective also supports admitting the force of arbitrator-made jurisdictional rules. When a jurisdictional determination is based on a jurisdictional clause plus an arbitrator-made premise, both party- and arbitrator-made rules function as pertinent general norms. Given that the creation of individual norms in the form of jurisdictional determinations amounts to the application of general norms, there is no justification for not admitting the normative force of arbitrator-made jurisdictional rules.

I am aware that this argument could encounter resistance from the proponents of 'hard' positivism in international law, with the objection that arbitrators are not empowered to create law and that that should be the end of the matter. But international law does not support such strong claims. If international law has never truly developed proper 'rules of recognition',[151] which is evidenced in the never-ending discussions on the sources of international

---

within the arbitration community and within a special arbitral legal system; see Bentolila (n 104) 242–53.
148   See ch 1, s 4.3.2.
149   Kelsen, *Principles* (n 147) 303–4. Kelsen makes this claim by rebutting the assumption that tribunals cannot have any law-creating, but only law-applying function.
150   Because the power to adjudicate is conferred on arbitral tribunals by virtue of what I call here primary jurisdictional rules, such primary rules will always be superior to secondary, arbitrator-made rules, and will prevail in a case of conflict.
151   Hart (n 142) 214.

law[152] and the always topical issues of judicial law-making,[153] free riding in relation to the arbitral power to create individual norms (ie the decision-making power), which I suggest here, should not be disqualified by the formalistic division between law-creation and law-application. Furthermore, the lack of clear boundaries between law-creation and law-application in international law provides for an increased mixture of Hart's 'rules of recognition' and 'rules of adjudication', whose inherent overlap has been recognised from the beginning.[154]

3.2.3 Practical Application and the Doctrine of Evolutive Jurisdictional Regulation

Arbitral practice continues to insist on the individualisation of every jurisdictional clause.[155] Because investment arbitrations are ad hoc and based on different treaties, the insistence seems justified, and tribunals often emphasise the possibility of deviating from previous practice.[156] However, this tendency seems prompted by the fear of the appearance of neglecting the dispute settlement mandate.[157] Contrary to such practice, arbitrators should not refrain from

---

152 See generally Fitzmaurice, 'Some Problems' (n 138) 57; Hugh Thirlway, *The Sources of International Law* (OUP 2014) ch 1.
153 Scholars have also attempted to accommodate judicial law-making within the framework of Article 38(1)(d) of the ICJ Statute, to an extent also relying on the above-suggested trajectory from general norms to their individualisation in judicial decisions; see Mohamed Shahabuddeen, *Precedent in the World Court* (CUP 1996) 76–83 (distinguishing previous decisions that are used as subsidiary sources in the determination of the law, from new decisions that give effect to the law determined relying on such earlier decisions, but in effect amount to new rules created by the Court). For judicial law-making in international law, see generally Armin von Bogdandy and Ingo Venzke (eds), *International Judicial Lawmaking: On Public Authority and Democratic Legitimation in Global Governance* (Springer 2012).
154 Because adjudicators recognise the substance of the law by enforcing it. This is precisely the trajectory of normativity addressed above. See Hart (n 142) 97.
155 See, for example, *AES Corporation v The Argentine Republic,* ICSID Case No ARB/02/17, Decision on Jurisdiction (26 April 2005) paras 24–5.
156 ibid para 30 ('Each tribunal remains sovereign and may retain, as it is confirmed by ICSID practice, a different solution for resolving the same problem; but decisions on jurisdiction dealing with the same or very similar issues may at least indicate some lines of reasoning of real interest;').
157 See, for example, *Romak SA (Switzerland) v The Republic of Uzbekistan,* PCA Case No AA280, Award (26 November 2009) para 171 ('Ultimately, the Arbitral Tribunal has not been entrusted, by the Parties or otherwise, with a mission to ensure the coherence or development of "arbitral jurisprudence." The Arbitral Tribunal's mission is more mundane, but no less important: to resolve the present dispute between the Parties in a reasoned and persuasive manner, irrespective of the unintended consequences that this

generalising jurisdictional questions and engaging in arbitration-transcending discourses on the appropriate rules governing their jurisdiction.

It is a commonplace that investment treaties, including jurisdictional clauses, comprise standardised parts, often based on a model,[158] such as the requirements of local litigation, exhaustion of local remedies, prior negotiation, MFN and umbrella clauses, and so on. They use modelled phrases defining arbitrable disputes, such as 'all disputes' or 'disputes concerning the amount of compensation for expropriation'. Of course, different details remain possible, and due regard to specificities of different texts must be given.[159] But what is actually standardised and modelled in these clauses and forms their essence is their function: local litigation clauses require investors to first resort to domestic courts; the exhaustion of local remedies requires them to use all available domestic remedies; prior negotiation clauses require negotiating with the host state before initiating arbitration, and so on. What engages tribunals in a debate regarding the application of a type of treaty clause, and consequently creates their consistent or conflicting, but in any case interacting, practice, is its function. The arbitral invocation of previous decisions interpreting *other* but *functionally same* jurisdictional clauses to prove a point seems reasonable in this context and indeed is often done in practice.[160]

This brings me to the central question of my argument: what decisions should be followed? As already mentioned, both theory and practice maintain that persuasiveness is the only criterion awarding decisions the precedential value.[161] Putting the theory on one side, that has indeed been the practice of arbitral tribunals: previous decisions are often compared, and some of them

---

Arbitral Tribunal's analysis might have on future disputes in general.'); *Gas Natural SDG SA v Argentina* (n 32) para 36 ('The Tribunal wishes to emphasize that it has rendered its decision independently, without considering itself bound by any other judgments or arbitral awards.'); *Joy Mining Machinery Limited v Arab Republic of Egypt*, ICSID Case No ARB/03/11, Award on Jurisdiction (6 August 2004) para 80 ('However, this Tribunal is not called upon to sit in judgment on the views of other tribunals. It is only called to decide this dispute in the light of its specific facts and the law, beginning with the jurisdictional objections.').

158   See also Vadi (n 13) 92–3 (noting that this phenomenon 'facilitates borrowing' of arbitral reasonings); Schill, 'System-Building' (n 130) 154 (arguing that such similarities, along with other factors, result in a 'treaty-overarching regime for international investment relations').

159   James Crawford, 'Similarity of Issues in Disputes Arising under the Same or Similarly Drafted Investment Treaties' in Yas Banifatemi (ed), *Precedent in International Arbitration* (Juris 2008) 100–1.

160   See n 130 above.

161   See n 140 above and the accompanying text.

given precedence because of their 'persuasiveness'. However, that practice is unconvincing, because it essentially amounts to cherry-picking. As seen in Chapters 2 to 4, investment tribunals have often formed opposing streams of practice, criticising one another, and supporting previous decisions which confirm their preferred view. The criterion of 'persuasiveness' is nothing else but a gateway for a free choice of previous decisions in support of the decision-maker's view. Such choice is inappropriate in the sphere of rules. An arbitrator does not simply choose between two, more or less convincing, interpretations of the same or similarly worded jurisdictional provisions, but which legal rule should be applied as an independent input.

Therefore, the reliance on previous decisions must be led by more objective criteria. If international law-making indeed can be seen as a broader, communicative process, than usually thought in a formalistic sense (and I will come back to this shortly, when discussing arbitral impulses for legal change),[162] there is no justification for isolating selected decisions only because they are 'persuasive' to a two-member majority. There is also no justification for siding with one stream of practice only to dismiss the relevance of the 'others' on same subjective grounds. What makes a precedent the law is not the precedent itself, but the subsequent practice accepting its authority. Arbitral tribunals should therefore consider all relevant evidence of the development of secondary rules, including conflicting considerations, and distil the applicable rule. I am not saying that tribunals must survey *all* decisions on the issue, but they should at least address a sample of decisions sufficient to reveal all known considerations in the public discourse. Most importantly, they should observe a variety of voices as part of the *evolution* of the jurisdictional framework of investment treaty arbitration. State and public reactions to previous practice, sending signals about the content of arbitrator-made law, cannot be left out of this context and previous decisions should not be addressed in isolation from them. Certainly, whether the application of a secondary rule is persuasive is an important question, which should be addressed in every case. But if the majority of voices considers, or at least if a dominant opinion is, that Rule 1 should be preferred over Rule 2, there is not much justification for applying Rule 2.[163] In

---

162   W Michael Reisman, 'International Lawmaking: A Process of Communication' in Martti Koskenniemi (ed), *Sources of International Law* (Ashgate 2000) 501.
163   See in this respect *Cargill Incorporated v Poland* (n 108) para 224; *Saipem SpA v People's Republic of Bangladesh*, ICSID Case No ARB/05/7, Decision on Jurisdiction and Recommendation on Provisional Measures (21 March 2007) para 67; *Noble Energy Inc and Machalapower Cia Ltda v The Republic of Ecuador and Consejo Nacional de Electricidad*, ICSID Case No ARB/05/12, Decision on Jurisdiction (5 March 2008) para 50; *Duke Energy Electroquil Partners & Electroquil SA v Republic of Ecuador*, ICSID Case No ARB/04/19,

other words, there is no room for the 'sovereignty' of arbitral tribunals allowing for an arbitrary choice of the applicable secondary rule.[164]

The objectivization of the criteria finds support in international law. It is well established in international law, and indeed international courts and tribunals often state, that 'like cases should be decided alike', unless there are strong reasons for deviation.[165] The ICJ often holds that 'it will not depart from its settled jurisprudence unless it finds very particular reasons to do so',[166] and that the question that should be asked is whether in a particular case 'there is cause not to follow the reasoning and conclusions of earlier cases'.[167] The crucial pillar in this approach is the settled or consistent case law, also called *jurisprudence constante*.[168] There is nothing unusual in such a heavy reliance on practice: it is well established that previous decisions can be used to find

---

Award (18 August 2008) para 117; and *Burlington Resources Inc v Republic of Ecuador*, ICSID Case No ARB/08/5, Decision on Jurisdiction (2 June 2010) para 100. These Tribunals made practically the same statement, with insignificant variations in the wording: 'It [the Tribunal] believes that, subject to compelling contrary grounds, it has a duty to adopt solutions established in a series of consistent cases. It also believes that, subject to the specifics of a given treaty and of the circumstances of the actual case, it has a duty to seek to contribute to the harmonious development of investment law and thereby to meet the legitimate expectations of the community of States and investors towards certainty of the rule of law.' (reference omitted). It is only worth noting that the *Duke* Tribunal stated that 'it has a duty to consider' (instead of 'adopt') established solutions. It appears that the same statement has also been made elsewhere.

164 cf statement at n 156.
165 *Suez, Sociedad General de Aguas de Barcelona SA, and Vivendi Universal SA v The Argentine Republic*, ICSID Case No ARB/03/19, and *AWG Group v The Argentine Republic*, UNCITRAL arbitration, Decision on Liability (30 July 2010) para 189; *Daimler Financial Services AG v Argentina* (n 57) para 52.
166 *Application of the Convention on the Prevention and Punishment of the Crime of Genocide (Croatia v Serbia)* (Preliminary Objections) (2008) ICJ Rep 412, para 53.
167 *Land and Maritime Boundary between Cameroon and Nigeria (Cameroon v Nigeria: Equatorial Guinea intervening)* (Preliminary Objections) (1998) ICJ Rep 275, para 28.
168 *Suez, Sociedad General de Aguas de Barcelona SA, and Vivendi Universal SA/AWG Group v Argentina* (Liability) (n 165) para 189 ('[...] a recognized goal of international investment law is to establish a predictable, stable legal framework for investments, a factor that justifies tribunals in giving due regard to previous decisions on similar issues. Thus, absent compelling reasons to the contrary, a tribunal should always consider heavily solutions established in a series of consistent cases.'); *Daimler Financial Services AG v Argentina* (n 57) para 52 ('This latter consideration [whether cases should be distinguished] will weigh more or less heavily depending upon: a) how "like" the prior and present cases are, having regard to all relevant considerations; b) the degree to which a clear *jurisprudence constante* has emerged in respect of a particular legal issue; and c) the Tribunal's independent estimation of the persuasiveness of prior tribunals' reasoning.').

the law,[169] which is also the main rationale for including 'judicial decisions' in Article 38(1) of the PCIJ/ICJ Statute. The question is what is the effect of previous decisions in specific cases. It has been convincingly noted that they 'shift[] the burden of argumentation by demanding a reasoned justification for departing from established precedent', and 'the more investment treaty tribunals align themselves with a certain line of jurisprudence, the more difficult it becomes for parties and tribunals to meet that burden and to deviate from prior practice'.[170]

The comparison of jurisdictional questions at issue and in previous decisions must be led by the essence—function—of both primary and secondary rules, and not by the ultimate interpretive outcomes.[171] The 'like cases' that should be observed, treated, and 'decided alike', I submit, are not textual specificities of applicable treaties, but the essential function of each and every primary rule. Two essentially the same primary rules should be accompanied by the same secondary rule. The textual specificities in primary rules should be consulted in the second place, in order to verify whether they instruct deviation from the relevant secondary rule. And if such deviation is indeed instructed, the secondary rule must give way to the supremacy of the text of the primary rule.

This approach to finding and applying relevant secondary rules can be called 'evolutive jurisdictional regulation', because it tracks the development and acceptance of secondary rules. It must be taken as a doctrine, not a rule of law, due to a broader problem. It is often said that there is no rule of binding precedent in international law, which combined with the ad hoc nature of international arbitration disqualifies any form of arbitral law-making.[172] The actual problem with a hypothetical requirement that tribunals observe precedents in international law is not the lack of a rule of precedent, but that such a

---

169   See Shahabuddeen (n 153) 9–12 (identifying three ways of using precedents: 'such a system may authorise the judge to consider previous decisions as part of the general legal material from which the law may be ascertained; or, it may oblige him to decide the case in the same way as a previous case unless he can give a good reason for not doing so; or, still yet, it may oblige him to decide it in the same way as the previous case even if he can give a good reason for not doing so').
170   Schill, 'Sources' (n 128) 1104–5.
171   Tribunals make a cardinal error when analysing the existence of *jurisprudence constante* through the lens of outcomes, because that inevitably leads to the conclusion that practice is not consistent. See, for an example of such error, *European American Investment Bank AG (Austria) v The Slovak Republic,* PCA Case No 2010-17, Award on Jurisdiction (22 October 2012) paras 436–7.
172   De Brabandere (n 125) 253–7; Stone Sweet and Grisel (n 6) 132–3.

rule is not possible at all, because there is no framework regulation capable of regulating international courts and tribunals horizontally. That is why I argue in favour of a doctrine instructing tribunals to observe previous practice. Such a doctrine is not a doctrine of sources of law in the strict sense, but of arbitral reasoning. Tracing the evolution of rules of law throughout arbitral practice should not be prevented by formalistic arguments. The precedential character of arbitral decisions is often disqualified on the grounds that they are binding between disputing parties only and cannot be binding generally on other states.[173] That issue is irrelevant here for several reasons: first, secondary rules are not developed in the binding, operative part of decisions; second, what is at stake are procedural norms, or rules of adjudication, which do not establish rights and obligations; third, secondary rules do not even confer the basic power (or obligation, if one prefers that label) to adjudicate, but only assist the implementation of such power once it has been granted explicitly.

It remains to be asked whether such a use of arbitrator-made jurisdictional rules relying on evolutive jurisdictional regulation is disturbed by the duty of tribunals to reach their own conclusions on the law, its interpretation and application in each and every case.[174] Implicitly, this argument holds that a tribunal cannot decide in one direction because previous case law instructs so, considering the possibility that the tribunal might not agree with that direction. But this argument is misleading. The tribunal is faced with a much simpler choice: it either agrees or it disagrees with the previously developed (evolved) law. If it disagrees, that should form an 'impulse for change' (to which I will come back shortly). However, for a law-changing action the tribunal needs well-substantiated reasons. This is an opportunity to test whether the tribunal has serious doubts about previous practice (and thus created secondary rules), or creates disagreements for some other reasons. Besides, arguments about the arbitral duty to reach independent legal conclusions idealize the image of an arbitrator as an independent, uninfluenced, and almost isolated decision-maker, which is hardly imaginable in practice.[175]

---

173 De Brabandere (n 125) 253–4; Schreuer and Weiniger (n 130) 1190.
174 cf the statement made by a number of tribunals at n 163 above with *Burlington Resources Inc v Ecuador* (Jurisdiction) (n 163) para 100 ('Arbitrator Stern does not analyze the arbitrator's role in the same manner, as she considers it her duty to decide each case on its own merits, independently of any apparent jurisprudential trend.'); De Brabandere (n 125) 286 (arguing that a reliance on previous decisions can be made only as a result of an independent assessment by tribunals).
175 See Irene M Ten Cate, 'The Costs of Consistency: Precedent in Investment Treaty Arbitration' (2013) 51 Columbia J Transnat'l L 418, 459, 472 (arguing that 'there are compelling reasons to place a strong value on the independent judgment of the tribunal

4 Some Challenges of the Proposed Model

The above-sketched two-layered model of jurisdictional regulation raises several important questions. Is the proposed model flexible enough to allow a dynamic development of secondary rules (1), and if so would it cause problems regarding the application of treaties (2)? Can the application of the proposed system be controlled (3)? Does the procedural confidentiality imperil the feasibility of the proposed model (4)? Finally, does the proposed model encourage arbitral excessiveness in jurisdictional determinations and does it allow for stabilisation of practice (5)? These questions are now addressed.

4.1 *The Development of Secondary Rules and the 'Impulse for Change'*

Is the proposed model flexible enough to allow a dynamic development of secondary rules? Questions of legal change have always troubled international law in general.[176] On the one hand, the need for legal change is inevitable, even in the context of international adjudication. Mohamed Shahabuddeen has noted that the ICJ will 'follow them [precedents] unless they can be distinguished on valid grounds or shown to be clearly wrong, or, possibly, where they no longer meet the new conditions of the evolving international community'.[177] The needs of the international community therefore change, but also one should not overlook the possibility that a previously established legal rule is simply wrong. On the other hand, international courts and tribunals have preferred distinguishing cases over admitting a change.[178] This also holds true in the specific context of investment arbitration.[179] International courts and tribunals appear generally reluctant to admit legal change in its true meaning.

---

appointed pursuant to the parties' agreement, as opposed to the collective wisdom of tribunals that have decided similar disputes in the past'; but noting the impossibility of arbitral isolation in decision-making and supporting consulting previous decisions).

176   See, among many others, Sir Hersch Lauterpacht, *The Function of Law in the International Community* (reprint, OUP 2011) 253–67.
177   Shahabuddeen (n 153) 12.
178   For the ICJ, see ibid 110–1.
179   See, for example, in the context of the MFN-dispute resolution conjunction, *National Grid plc v The Argentine Republic*, UNCITRAL ad hoc arbitration, Decision on Jurisdiction (20 June 2006) para 91; *Suez, Sociedad General de Aguas de Barcelona SA, and InterAguas Servicios Integrales del Agua SA v The Argentine Republic*, ICSID Case No ARB/03/17, Decision on Jurisdiction (16 May 2006) para 63; *Suez, Sociedad General de Aguas de Barcelona SA, and Vivendi Universal SA v The Argentine Republic*, ICSID Case No ARB/03/19, and *AWG Group Ltd v The Argentine Republic*, UNCITRAL arbitration, Decision on Jurisdiction (3 August 2006) para 65. See also Pellet (n 100) 229–40.

To make the proposed model work, it is necessary to allow legal change. This is required by the mere idea of formalising the regulatory role of arbitral tribunals. A legal change requires admitting that circumstances and/or needs of the international community have changed,[180] or that a previously established rule is clearly wrong.[181] These admissions can be made under several conditions: first, that arbitrators observe a broader range of circumstances than that of a specific case; second, that prior practice and other voices are observed in terms of dominant or prevailing views, especially in a temporal dimension as trends; and third, that tribunals are willing to declare the inadequacy of previously developed secondary rules, either in their essence or because of the changed circumstances and/or needs.

The possibility of legal change, therefore, does not depend on the firmness of the established practice, but rather on the requirements for departure. In my view, what is required for departure from previously established practice (and therefore for a change of a secondary rule) is advanced arbitral reasoning. It is already recognised in arbitral practice that a departure from a trend should be well-justified and reasoned.[182] No more is required for the proposed model. An advanced reasoning in this context means listening to more voices than disputing parties, which send signals about the content of secondary rules within a broader discourse than a concrete dispute.[183] For quite a while

---

180 For example, states by drafting new treaties and issuing specific communications, as well as various other voices in the investment law community, can signal to arbitrators their policies and views on the appropriateness of secondary rules.
181 cf Thomas Schultz, 'Against Consistency in Investment Arbitration' in Zachary Douglas, Joost Pauwelyn, and Jorge E Viñuales (eds), *The Foundations of International Investment Law: Bringing Theory into Practice* (OUP 2014) 297 (arguing that the possibility that some rules of investment law have been set wrongly, could imply that their inconsistent application would do less harm).
182 See in that respect *Glamis Gold Ltd v USA* (n 123) para 8 ('regardless of whether the particular line of reasoning was argued to the tribunal, it is our view that the tribunal should indicate its reasons for departing from a major trend of previous reasoning'); *International Thunderbird Gaming Corporation v Mexico* (Wälde Separate Opinion) (n 131) para 16 ('A deviation from well and firmly established jurisprudence requires an extensively reasoned justification.') and ibid para 129 ('WTO, ICJ and in particular investment treaty jurisprudence shows the importance to tribunals of not "confronting" established case law by divergent opinion – except if it is possible to clearly distinguish and justify in-depth such divergence.'); and the statement adopted by a number of tribunals at n 163.
183 See in this respect Federico Ortino, 'Legal Reasoning of International Investment Tribunals: A Typology of Egregious Failures' (2012) 3 JIDS 31 (identifying minimalism as a problem in arbitral reasoning); Guillermo Aguilar Alvarez and W Michael Reisman, 'How Well Are Investment Awards Reasoned?' in Guillermo Aguilar Alvarez

already, international lawyers discuss the substantive aspects of international law-making: that law-making is not only a formal adoption of a treaty or an expression of the opinion that something is a custom (both by states exclusively), but a broader process engaging all actors who can influence the content of the law.[184] The proposed model provides an excellent opportunity for giving effect to this view. In this respect, I consult the scholars who characterise law-making in international law as a communicative process. In that process, tribunals do not communicate to disputing parties only, but to a much bigger audience (and also *vice versa*), while their communications form part of a broader regulatory discourse or 'functional' law-making.[185] Therefore arbitrators should be expected to listen to previous tribunals, academics, states, civil society, and other relevant actors expressing views about jurisdictional questions, and in return to write decisions not for the satisfaction of disputing parties only, but as a functional part of a broader discourse about the jurisdictional framework of investment arbitration. Arbitral tribunals have a specific position in this context, insofar as arbitral communication with the investment law community is authoritative and at the same time it enforces the rules created in practice.[186]

Only when listening to such various voices, can a tribunal find an 'impulse for change'. A presumption can change,[187] a default rule can disappear an a

---

and W Michael Reisman (eds), *The Reasons Requirement in International Investment Arbitration* (Martinus Nijhoff 2008) 29 (arguing that because of the far-reaching effects of investment awards, the reasons requirement could be stricter than in commercial arbitration).

184 See generally Boyle and Chinkin (n 124) ch 2.
185 See generally Reisman, 'International Lawmaking' (n 162); and particularly ibid 503.
186 McDougal and Reisman argued that international law-making (or prescription, as they maintain) includes communicating to the targeted audience and creating their corresponding expectations in respect of three elements: policy content, authority signal, and control intention. Arbitral decisions as communications meet these criteria. Besides stating the content of secondary rules, arbitral tribunals do so with a direct and judicial authority towards disputing parties, and with an indirect and epistemic authority towards the investment law community. Furthermore, arbitral tribunals communicate with disputing parties and the investment law community by giving effect to secondary jurisdictional rules, thus not only signalling, but actually exercising the control intention. See Myres S McDougal and W Michael Reisman, 'The Prescribing Function in World Constitutive Process: How International Law Is Made' (1980) 6 Yale Studies in World Public Order 249, 250.
187 Arguably, after the initial impetus towards a wide acceptance of the applicability of MFN clauses to dispute settlement clauses, the development of arbitral practice has reversed that presumption. See ch 2, s 4.2.

new one can emerge,[188] and a standard can be modified.[189] What is required when it comes to these changes is that a tribunal must justify the existence of a regulatory space and of the convincing reasons for adopting a new rule: what circumstances have changed from those surrounding a previously established rule? Or what discovery implies the incorrectness of an existing rule? These are the minimum expectations for diverting from the established practice. So far, tribunals have been able to change what in reality represents true jurisdictional rules, often with a cardinal effect on the success of claims, without proper justifications and full reasons for such action.[190]

Indeed, if the difference between creating and determining the law is only in the degree, and not in the kind,[191] an 'impulse for change' would require a proportionally higher degree of arbitral diligence than the tendency to follow the existing law. A diligent tribunal would firstly identify a regulatory space, as opposed to expressing minor disagreements with previous trends, and secondly, draft a well-reasoned jurisdictional decision capable of convincing the investment law community that a new rule better addresses the issue and better fits in the current circumstances, and that it should be followed in subsequent cases. Because the reaffirmation of the existing rules is crucial for their survival, the cessation of the enforcement of a rule would facilitate the accommodation of a new one.[192] Finally, the openness towards the community would

---

188 See, for example, although in a contractual arbitration context, *World Duty Free Company Limited v The Republic of Kenya*, ICSID Case No ARB/00/7, Award (4 October 2006) para 157 ('In light of domestic laws and international conventions relating to corruption, and in light of the decisions taken in this matter by courts and arbitral tribunals, this Tribunal is convinced that bribery is contrary to the international public policy of most, if not all, States or, to use another formula, to transnational public policy. Thus, claims based on contracts of corruption or on contracts obtained by corruption cannot be upheld by this Arbitral Tribunal.'). Further on the development of the legality requirement, see ch 4, s 2.2.

189 For the emergence and subsequent modification of the *Salini* criteria in the objective definition of 'investment', see ch 4, s 2.1.1.

190 See, for example, *H&H Enterprises Investments Inc v The Arab Republic of Egypt*, ICSID Case No ARB/09/15, Award (6 May 2014) paras 363–70 (in the context of a fork-in-the-road clause, rejecting the 'triple identity' test and adopting the 'fundamental basis of the claim' test, without examining the suitability, advantages, and possible shortcomings of the latter).

191 RY Jennings, 'General Course on Principles of International Law' (1967) 121 Recueil des Cours 323, 341.

192 Reisman, 'International Lawmaking' (n 162) 507 ('the communication of control intention must be continuous throughout the life of the prescription').

lead to reinforcing the arbitral law-making role, because it is the audience (ie disputing parties and the investment law community) that grants tribunals the law-making authority.[193]

4.2 The Relationship between Primary and Secondary Rules Regarding Legal Change

The proposed model of two-layered jurisdictional regulation can be contested on the ground that any legal change in the domain of secondary rules would impact drastically on the application of investment treaties, contrary to the principle of legal certainty and possibly against the intentions of their parties. For example, a presumption can emerge reversing the way treaty provisions were read and interpreted. This argument basically defends treaties as static instruments and aims to preserve the original intentions of states parties, against the dynamic layer of secondary jurisdictional rules.

At the outset, radical changes in the domain of secondary rules should not be frequent, but rather exceptional. When they do occur, the real problem is not the change in the application of treaties caused by a secondary rule, but the fact that treaties themselves were not capable of answering a jurisdictional question. For example, if arbitrators have created a presumption in favour of the applicability of MFN clauses to dispute resolution, that development was caused by the fact that tribunals faced a new jurisdictional question which was not regulated in treaties.[194] And if that presumption was later reversed, that development has taken a long time, observing many voices and considerations, and eventually settling at a position that could hardly be said to ignore the wishes of states as treaty drafters and respondents.[195]

When it comes to more subtle and modest changes, they are more expectable. The standard of the objective definition of 'investment' has been advanced and enforced in a number of variations,[196] as were the standards of futility[197] and identity of claims.[198] One can be more or less satisfied with the justifications given for each of these variations, but they do not cause earthquakes in the world of investment arbitration. Such variations are subject to detailed

---

193   ibid 506 ('It is the audience, whether or not its members realize it, that endows the prescriber with the authority that renders his communications prescription.'). See also, for the link between judicial decision-making and audiences, Venzke, 'Judicial Authority' (n 101) 240.
194   See ch 2, s 4.2.1.
195   See ch 2, s 4.2.2.
196   See ch 4, s 2.1.1.
197   See ch 2, s 3.1.1.
198   See ch 2, ss 3.1.3 and 3.2.

academic analyses, which often accept them as different but legitimate approaches to treaty application. Within the layer of secondary rules, these variations can be envisaged as subsequent changes, instead of co-existing alternatives that cause uncertainty.

Two further arguments are particularly worth mentioning in this context. The first one is the inapplicability of the principle of contemporaneity to the jurisdictional questions addressed by secondary rules. This principle, which instructs an interpreter to observe the meaning of treaty terms in light of the circumstances and rules of international law existing at the time of the conclusion of the treaty, is generally important.[199] However, the principle is simply meaningless in the context of secondary jurisdictional rules, because they exist due to, first, the novelty of raised questions, and second, the failure of treaty terms to provide direct answers.[200] The application of that principle to the issues governed by secondary rules can even lead to absurd results, such as allowing states to manipulate the investors' reliance on treaties by subsequently

---

199 *Rights of Nationals of the United States of America in Morocco (France v United States of America)* (Judgment) (1952) ICJ Rep 176, 189; Sir Gerald Fitzmaurice, 'The Law and Procedure of the International Court of Justice, 1951-54: General Principles and Sources of Law' (1953) 30 British Yrbk Int'l L 1, 5–6; Sir Gerald Fitzmaurice, 'The Law and Procedure of the International Court of Justice 1951-4: Treaty Interpretation and Other Treaty Points' (1957) 33 British Yrbk Int'l L 203, 212. But see Epaminontas E Triantafilou, 'Contemporaneity and Evolutive Interpretation under the Vienna Convention on the Law of Treaties' (2017) 32 ICSID Rev-FILJ 138, 139–51 (challenging a broad definition of the principle by distinguishing the questions of interpretation and application of treaties, and disputing the principle's link to the concept of inter-temporal law).

200 When used in this context, the principle of contemporaneity often leads to mere restatements of the initial interpretive questions; see *Daimler Financial Services AG v Argentina* (n 57) paras 220–1; *ICS Inspection and Control Services Limited (United Kingdom) v The Republic of Argentina,* PCA Case No 2010-9, Decision on Jurisdiction (10 February 2012) paras 289–90 (both Tribunals, facing a failure of the parties to submit any evidence of the intentions of the states parties to the relevant BITs regarding the applicability of MFN clauses to dispute resolution clauses, stated that that issue was 'entirely unexplored' in the early 1990s; both Tribunals found the principle of contemporaneity useful to inquire into certain 'soft law' instruments dealing with the notion of 'treatment', however its application could not produce decisive arguments and the Tribunals had to turn back to the textual interpretation of the BITs). Conversely, where a treaty provision answers the interpretive question, the principle of contemporaneity is of no use; see *Garanti Koza LLP v Turkmenistan,* ICSID Case No ARB/11/20, Decision on the Objection to Jurisdiction for Lack of Consent (3 July 2013) paras 55–7 (faced with the argument that in the 1990s the parties to the BIT could not foresee the idea of applying MFN clauses to dispute resolution, the Tribunal responded that the principle of contemporaneity could not affect the reading of the MFN clause, which explicitly allowed its application to the jurisdictional clause).

changing domestic legal environments.[201] Finally, from an extreme technical perspective, an arbitration agreement is concluded only upon the acceptance of an offer to arbitrate, implying that the meanings, circumstances, and rules to be observed under this principle are contemporary with the initiation of arbitration.

On the other side of the spectrum of interpretative principles, the doctrine of the evolutive interpretation of treaties fully supports the proposed model. Indeed, the intention of treaty parties can presumably be not to fix the meaning of treaty terms, but to allow it to evolve.[202] That presumption arises primarily where generic terms are used,[203] but some tribunals have been willing to extend the presumption to non-generic treaty provisions, relying on the object and purpose of the treaty.[204] What is decisive is the long and continuous duration of a treaty regime.[205] That is why this interpretative doctrine is particularly important when it comes to protective and other objective regimes, such as human rights treaties,[206] international trade and environmental laws.[207]

---

201 *Urbaser SA and CABB v The Argentine Republic*, ICSID Case No ARB/07/26, Decision on Jurisdiction (19 December 2012) para 149. The problems caused by such application of the principle of contemporaneity in the resolution of jurisdictional questions can be seen in the *Wintershall* award, where the Tribunal, sitting in 2008 and facing a dispute that emerged in the early 2000s, discussed whether foreign investors could settle disputes before domestic courts in 1991 and 1993 (when the BIT was signed and entered into force respectively), in the context of a local litigation requirement. See *Wintershall Aktiengesellschaft v Argentina* (n 57) para 129. See further Epaminontas E Triantafilou, 'Contemporaneity and Its Limits in Treaty Interpretation' in David D Caron and others (eds), *Practising Virtue: Inside International Arbitration* (OUP 2015) 474–6 (arguing that the *Wintershall* Tribunal did not apply the principle of contemporaneity, but simply applied the treaty to the facts existing at the time of its conclusion).

202 *Dispute regarding Navigational and Related Rights (Costa Rica v Nicaragua)* (Judgment) (2009) ICJ Rep 213, para 64.

203 *Aegean Sea Continental Shelf (Greece v Turkey)* (Judgment) (1978) ICJ Rep 3, para 77.

204 *Iron Rhine Arbitration (Belgium/Netherlands)*, PCA Case No 2003-02, Award of the Arbitral Tribunal (24 May 2005) para 80.

205 *Aegean Sea Continental Shelf* (n 203) para 77; *Costa Rica v Nicaragua* (n 202) para 66; *Iron Rhine Arbitration* (n 204) paras 81–2.

206 For the 'living instrument' doctrine in the interpretation of the ECHR, as developed in the ECtHR practice, see *Tyrer v The United Kingdom* App No 5856/72 (ECtHR, 25 April 1978) para 31; and *Loizidou v Turkey* App No 15318/89 (ECtHR, 23 March 1995) paras 71–2. In the latter decision, the ECtHR held that this doctrine applied equally to the matters of substantive protection and jurisdiction.

207 WTO, *United States: Import Prohibition of Certain Shrimp and Shrimp Products—Report of the Appellate Body* (12 October 1998) WT/DS58/AB/R [129–30]; Robert Howse, 'The Appellate Body Rulings in the *Shrimp/Turtle* Case: A New Legal Baseline for the Trade and Environment Debate' (2002) 27 Columbia J Envt'l L 489, 518–9.

Given that international investment law and arbitration qualify as a protective regime,[208] the protective purpose written down in treaty texts requires actuality, and implies that jurisdictional rules should follow current circumstances. In fact, some tribunals have already followed this view: faced with the argument that an older investment treaty could not make an offer to foreign investors to arbitrate, because the offer-acceptance theory had emerged in investment law only after its conclusion, one tribunal affirmed the existence of an offer relying on modern practices and the treaty's objective of investment protection.[209] In sum, if the use of generic and open-ended terms in investment treaties implies the acceptance of their evolution,[210] it can be argued with an equal force that insufficient regulation of certain jurisdictional questions in the sphere of primary rules implies the acceptance of the evolution of secondary rules and their effect.

4.3   *Control Mechanisms*

Can the compliance with the proposed model be controlled? The lack of a control mechanism in investment arbitration, particularly in a hierarchical form, is commonly seen as an obstacle to arbitral law-making.[211] That problem is more visible in the merits sphere, because in the jurisdictional sphere a limited control exists, either in the form of annulment of ICSID awards,[212] or in the form of refusal of recognition/enforcement and setting aside of non-ICSID awards by domestic courts.[213] This is an important facilitating factor for the proposed model.

The compliance with the two-layered model of jurisdictional regulation can be controlled and secured by ICSID annulment committees and domestic courts. Tribunals have expressed an expectation from control mechanisms to

---

208   See ch 1, s 2.4.2.
209   *Hesham Talaat M Al-Warraq v The Republic of Indonesia,* UNCITRAL ad hoc arbitration, Award on Respondent's Preliminary Objections to Jurisdiction and Admissibility of the Claims (21 June 2012) paras 81–3.
210   Triantafilou, 'Contemporaneity and Evolutive Interpretation' (n 199) 168. See also ibid 160 ('It is difficult to imagine that the meaning of entire legal instruments, which are expressly intended to serve broad and lasting policies with respect to ever-changing concepts such as "investments", are meant to remain "frozen in time" in the general sense [...]').
211   Beata Gessel-Kalinowska vel Kalisz and Konrad Czech, 'The Role of Precedent in Investment Treaty Arbitration' in Barton Legum (ed), *The Investment Treaty Arbitration Review* (3rd ed, Law Business Research 2018) 175.
212   ICSID Convention (n 93) art 52(1).
213   New York Convention (n 94) art V(1); UNCITRAL Model Law on International Commercial Arbitration of 1985, with amendments as adopted in 2006, art 34(2) <https://uncitral.un.org/sites/uncitral.un.org/files/media-documents/uncitral/en/19-09955_e_ebook.pdf> accessed 4 April 2021.

answer difficult jurisdictional questions.[214] However, control mechanisms cannot resolve jurisdictional questions initially, but only in the second instance when controlling arbitral decisions. As a matter of general approach, I argue that when decisions are challenged before control mechanisms regarding the issues involving secondary rules, annulment committees and courts should review the methodology applied by arbitral tribunals in jurisdictional determinations. Specifically, they should verify whether tribunals have conducted a comprehensive analysis of previous practice on the issue and correctly distilled the applicable secondary rule. When it comes to the questions of legal change, control mechanisms should verify whether a change is sufficiently reasoned and justified, in terms of identifying a regulatory space and providing convincing reasons for the adoption of a new secondary rule. Control mechanisms can also contribute to the content of secondary rules by addressing the state of arbitral practice and advancing arguments on the development of secondary rules.

Control mechanisms should invalidate the improper application and creation of secondary rules by tribunals, but to this end different control mechanisms require different improvements. When it comes to the ICSID context, annulment committees must start treating the disregard of secondary rules as a 'manifest' excess of powers. Because the task of arbitral tribunals is to find and apply the relevant secondary rule, a failure to do so qualifies as a 'manifest' excess of powers.[215] The requirement that an excess of powers must be 'manifest' for annulment is often seen as an important limitation of the ICSID annulment system.[216] What I call secondary rules has usually been seen as varieties in treaty interpretations and therefore connotes details outside the reach of annulment committees. But if secondary rules are viewed as rules

---

214   SGS *Société Générale de Surveillance SA v Philippines* (n 16) para 97. cf *MCI Power Group LC and New Turbine Inc v Republic of Ecuador*, ICSID Case No ARB/03/6, Decision on Annulment (19 October 2009) para 24 ('The annulment mechanism is not designed to bring about consistency in the interpretation and application of international investment law. The responsibility for ensuring consistency in the jurisprudence and for building a coherent body of law rests primarily with the investment tribunals.').

215   See *Compañiá de Aguas del Aconquija SA and Vivendi Universal v Argentina* (n 15) paras 93–115 (the Committee identified the 'fundamental basis of a claim' as the relevant standard for distinguishing between treaty and contract claims, and because the Tribunal failed to give effect to that distinction and exercise jurisdiction over treaty claims, the Committee concluded that the Tribunal manifestly exceeded its powers).

216   *Impregilo SpA v Argentine Republic*, ICSID Case No ARB/07/17, Decision of the ad hoc Committee on the Application for Annulment (24 January 2014) para 128 ('it is clear that not every excess of powers could result in an annulment of an award issued under the ICSID Convention').

of jurisdictional regulation, ie as proper law, a failure of their observance and application, or an improper attempt at their creation, could not escape being qualified as a 'manifest' excess of powers. A straightforward consequence is that a disregard or an improper creation of a secondary rule must be sanctioned. Furthermore, the ICSID Convention also allows annulment for the failure to state the reasons.[217] Given that the implementation of the proposed model is suggested by means of a doctrine of arbitral reasoning, the control of compliance is also possible on this ground. Whether a tribunal has properly distilled the applicable secondary rule, or whether it has properly engaged in the creation of a new one, can therefore be controlled both as a matter of excess of powers and as a matter of sufficient reasoning.

Domestic courts usually do not face the limitation that the excess of powers must be manifest for setting aside or denying recognition/enforcement, and therefore they can exercise a more prudential jurisdictional review with the effect of an easier accommodation of the proposed model.[218] However, domestic courts must improve their engagement with arbitral practice. Although styles of judicial reasoning differ among different domestic systems, which exceeds the scope of this study, domestic courts seem overall reluctant to address arbitral practice extensively.[219] The crucial pillar of the proposed model is arbitral practice, and therefore domestic courts should engage arbitral practice more extensively in their reasonings. Given that arbitral decisions are usually reviewed by prominent domestic courts, this should not be a difficult task.

Therefore, I maintain that the application of the proposed model can be controlled even through the existing mechanisms of limited review of jurisdictional determinations. But one should not ignore the prospective development of appellate mechanisms. The idea of their establishment is old, but has gained momentum only more recently with the attempts to establish an investment court system.[220] The model advanced by the EU provides for an

---

217 ICSID Convention (n 93) art 52(1)(e).
218 See ch 1, s 4.3.3.
219 Relja Radović, 'Arbitral Jurisdictional Regulation in Investment Treaty Arbitration and Domestic Courts' (2021) JIDS (forthcoming).
220 For older ideas and problems regarding the establishment of an appellate mechanism, see Barton Legum, 'Options to Establish an Appellate Mechanism for Investment Disputes' in Karl P Sauvant (ed), *Appeals Mechanism in International Investment Disputes* (OUP 2008) 231. For newer developments in this direction and current challenges, see, among many others, Freya Baetens, 'Keeping the Status Quo or Embarking on a New Course? Setting Aside, Refusal of Enforcement, Annulment and Appeal' in Andreas Kulick (ed), *Reassertion of Control over the Investment Treaty Regime* (CUP 2016) 114–26; Freya Baetens, 'Judicial Review of International Adjudicatory Decisions: A Cross-Regime Comparison of Annulment and Appellate Mechanisms' (2017) 8 JIDS 432.

appellate tribunal which can modify or reverse arbitral awards in respect of jurisdiction on the same grounds as provided for annulment in the ICSID Convention (most importantly, manifest excess of powers).[221] Because this model refers to the grounds enumerated in Article 52(1) of the ICSID Convention, first instance awards can presumably also be modified or reversed for the failure to state the reasons. In terms of substance, control should be conducted as suggested in the previous paragraphs, because the grounds for review remain the same as within the ICSID system. Furthermore, given the explicit empowerment of appellate tribunals to modify or reverse first instance awards, they can contribute more directly to the law-making of secondary jurisdictional rules, by expressing their view on the correct secondary rule. Finally, from an institutional perspective, appellate bodies can strengthen and streamline the control of the implementation of the proposed model.

4.4 *Transparency and the Availability of the Law-Making Material*

There is a striking difference between investment and commercial arbitrations regarding transparency, which has been significantly advanced in the investment sector.[222] But because some investment arbitrations are still confidential, it is sometimes argued that this precludes arbitral law-making.[223] Besides being seen as an obstacle to a system of precedent in general, some traces of confidentiality in the context of the proposed model would imply that tribunals do not have a clear overview of the relevant law-making material when searching for the relevant secondary rule.

Confidentiality, if present, indeed raises challenges for the proposed model, but they are surmountable. First, confidentiality is a chronic difficulty of investment arbitration, and being recognised as such, it is fought systematically.[224]

---

[221] Comprehensive Economic and Trade Agreement between Canada and the European Union (signed 30 October 2016, not in force) art 8.28(2)(c); EU-Vietnam Investment Protection Agreement (signed 30 June 2019, not in force) art 3.54(1)(c); EU-Singapore Investment Protection Agreement (signed 19 October 2018, not in force) art 3.19(1)(c). These provisions refer to Article 52(1) of the ICSID Convention. Other grounds for appeal, mentioned specifically in these treaties, are errors in the application or interpretation of the applicable law and manifest errors in the appreciation of the facts which includes the appreciation of domestic law.

[222] See s 2.1.1 above.

[223] Gessel-Kalinowska vel Kalisz and Czech (n 211) 174.

[224] For some efforts to fight the confidentiality of investor-state disputes, see United Nations Convention on Transparency in Treaty-based Investor-State Arbitration (signed 10 December 2014, entered into force 18 October 2017); UNCITRAL Rules on Transparency in Treaty-based Investor-State Arbitration (in force 1 April 2014); ICSID, 'Proposals for Amendment of the ICSID Rules' (February 2020) Working Paper #4, vol 1, 64–5, r 62(3)

Second, once confidential decisions become exceptional, which is arguably already the case,[225] they should not present an obstacle for the functioning of the proposed model. Arguably, confidential decisions are not valid law-making material. As argued above, to engage in a law-making process, tribunals must observe broader discourses and draft decisions in a manner that engages them in such broader discourses.[226] Arbitral reasoning must be advanced and cannot be addressed to disputing parties only. Without the engagement in a broader communicative process, awards do not have the law-making capacity. Confidentiality evidences the inability of engagement. In short, overlooking confidential decisions would not harm decision- and law-making by the tribunals that are able and willing to engage in a broader communicative process and discourses.[227] What can be problematic in this suggestion is that disputing parties retain the ultimate control over the decisions' access to public discourses, and therefore over their law-making effect, however that is an unavoidable cost due to the authority of the principle of consensualism.[228]

4.5 The Risk of Excessiveness and the Prospect of Stabilisation of Practice

Can the recognition of the arbitral regulatory role encourage the excessiveness in jurisdictional determinations and the formation of secondary rules along those lines? Arbitrators are often accused of expansionism and 'adventurism', allegedly resulting in extensions of their jurisdiction.[229] In that sense, the consistency of arbitral practice is arguably undesirable, insofar as occasional excesses would do less harm to the international community than persistent

---

<https://icsid.worldbank.org/sites/default/files/amendments/WP_4_Vol_1_En.pdf> accessed 1 September 2020 (proposing presumed consent for publication of awards).

[225] See data tracking known investment treaty arbitrations at UNCTAD, Investment Policy Hub, Investment Dispute Settlement Navigator <https://investmentpolicy.unctad.org/investment-dispute-settlement> accessed 1 September 2020. See also Emilie M Hafner-Burton and David G Victor, 'Secrecy in International Investment Arbitration: An Empirical Analysis' (2016) 7 JIDS 161 (criticising the ICSID system for encouraging secrecy, but empirically finding that the majority of 'secret' cases ended in settlement or discontinuance).

[226] See s 4.1 above.

[227] See also, in the same direction, Thomas Wälde, 'Confidential Awards as Precedent in Arbitration: Dynamics and Implication of Award Publication' in Yas Banifatemi (ed), *Precedent in International Arbitration* (Juris 2008) 113 (arguing that awards outside the public domain and debate cannot have a precedential effect in investment arbitration).

[228] ICSID Convention (n 93) art 48(5) ('The Centre shall not publish the award without the consent of the parties.').

[229] See s 2.1.3 above.

practices violating purported jurisdictional limits.[230] I do not share this view, because consistency is a necessary pre-condition for assessing which rules and practices are wrong and for what reasons. Putting on one side subjective dissatisfactions with outcomes in specific cases, it would be difficult to characterise specific practices as objectively expansionary in the absence of their consistent application. I do not claim that practice should be absolutely uniform, but at least some degree of consistency is necessary to disclose the full regulatory effects of secondary rules.[231] Another question is who decides what is right or wrong, expansionary, restrictive or ideally neutral. If international law-making includes various communicating actors,[232] there is no justification for vesting the power of judgment to only one and limited circle of actors, namely states. The coordination of primary and secondary rules in the proposed model is meant to accommodate various voices in a broader discourse on the jurisdictional framework of investment arbitration. Finally, the importance of consistency is amplified regarding the application of jurisdictional rules, because they involve a higher degree of precision and clarity than substantive protections.[233]

Crucially, I maintain that the proposed model offers no more opportunities for expansionism than the current setting which does not recognise the regulatory function of arbitral tribunals in jurisdictional matters. To the contrary, the burden of the law-making role, manifested in the awareness that jurisdictional determinations produce effects beyond individual arbitrations, can be expected to restrain arbitrators from making easy decisions that some authors would characterise as 'adventuristic'. Mainstream jurisdictional questions that have been addressed extensively show that, although some early decisions

---

230 Schultz (n 181) (assuming that some rules of investment law are bad, their inconsistent application would do less harm than consistent); Mark Feldman, 'Investment Arbitration Appellate Mechanism Options: Consistency, Accuracy, and Balance of Power' (2017) 32 ICSID Rev-FILJ 528, 531–4 (consistency does not ensure accuracy in treaty interpretation); Ten Cate (n 175) 457–9 (consistency undermines accuracy in decision-making).

231 See, for example, *Plama Consortium Limited v Republic of Bulgaria*, ICSID Case No ARB/03/24, Decision on Jurisdiction (8 February 2005) para 224 (departing from the case law that allowed the application of MFN clauses to dispute resolution clauses, the Tribunal noted that the previous precedent was 'perhaps understandable', because it faced an 'exceptional' jurisdictional issue; the same principled answer to the application of MFN clauses to dispute settlement clauses would produce more radical effects in different scenarios, and the Tribunal advanced a new rule).

232 See s 4.1 above.

233 Julian Arato, Chester Brown, and Federico Ortino, 'Parsing and Managing Inconsistency in Investor-State Dispute Settlement' (2020) 21 JWIT 336.

could be called expansionary, the growth of practice tends to have a stabilising effect in terms of producing more nuanced approaches and fixing their drawbacks.[234] The same can be expected with the proposed model, even more so due to the encouragement of communication of arbitral tribunals as part of a broader discourse on the jurisdictional framework of investment arbitration.

A different question is whether the consistency and stabilisation of practice are possible and desirable from the point of view of the structure of investment law. First, it is often said that the fragmented architecture of investment law, consisting of more than 3000 separate investment treaties, does not allow for a true consistency.[235] When it comes to jurisdictional matters, this objection can be rebutted by the observance of the essential function of jurisdictional primary rules used in investment treaties.[236] Second, the non-uniformity of investment law has motivated the acknowledgment at the UNCITRAL Working Group III that consistency should not be an objective in itself, and the arguments about its possible undesirability.[237] While I acknowledge that different treaties can include different jurisdictional primary rules for specific reasons, I argue that the development of a consistent and predictable body of secondary rules would serve the interests of states too.[238] If states disagree with certain secondary rules and their effects, the proposed model allows states to both influence their content by sending signals to arbitrators about the desirability of specific secondary rules, and to draft different treaty provisions derogating from the existing secondary rules.

---

[234] In the context of the application of MFN clauses to dispute resolution clauses, one argument holds that a general view generated in practice is that such application is possible in regard to admissibility but not jurisdiction; see, for example, Stephan W Schill, *The Multilateralization of International Investment Law* (CUP 2009) 151. Although this proposition can be challenged, the application of MFN clauses to dispute resolution is a good example of the evolution of practice. Only after facing various jurisdictional questions, and after seeing the effects of previous rulings reflected in demands for further jurisdictional extensions, can tribunals 'correct' the rules governing the MFN-dispute resolution conjunction.

[235] Gessel-Kalinowska vel Kalisz and Czech (n 211) 174–5; Ten Cate (n 175) 422.

[236] See s 3.2.3 above.

[237] UNCITRAL, 'Report of Working Group III (Investor-State Dispute Settlement Reform) on the Work of Its Thirty-Fourth Session (Vienna, 27 November–1 December 2017)' (26 February 2018) UN Doc A/CN.9/930/Add.1/Rev.1, paras 11, 17–9.

[238] See *ADC Affiliate Limited and ADC & ADMC Management Limited v The Republic of Hungary*, ICSID Case No ARB/03/16, Award of the Tribunal (2 October 2006) para 293 ('cautious reliance on certain principles developed in a number of those [previous] cases, as persuasive authority, may advance the body of law, which in turn may serve predictability in the interest of both investors and host States').

5   The Two-Layered Model of Jurisdictional Regulation and the International Legal Order

The final question addressed here is how the proposed model fits within broader developments in the international legal order, which, although not revolutionary, have brought significant changes to the perception of its functioning. I address two such developments, namely the concept of global governance and its relevance to the law-making function of arbitrators (1), and a wider acceptance of judicial law-making in international law (2).

5.1   *Investment Arbitration and Global Governance*

Investment treaty arbitration forms part of a broader regime governing international investment flows.[239] Hence the suggestion that those who control investment arbitration at the same time control, at least to a certain extent, the regime governing international investments.[240] In other words, those who govern investment arbitration also engage in global governance.[241] Investment arbitration involves different actors, the most important being states, investors, and arbitrators (excluding other stakeholders such as local communities, the general public, and non-governmental organisations). The extent of their control over the regime can be assessed by observing their practical abilities to influence the functioning of the regime and individual arbitrations. Arguably, all three main categories of actors exercise more or less control over the investment dispute settlement regime, rebutting the traditional view that the global governance in this matter belongs mainly to states.[242]

---

239   Zachary Douglas, *The International Law of Investment Claims* (CUP 2009) 1–6; Schill, *Multilateralization* (n 234) 5–6; Schill, 'Private Enforcement' (n 79) 30–3.

240   Stephan W Schill, 'International Investment Law and Comparative Public Law—An Introduction' in Stephan W Schill (ed), *International Investment Law and Comparative Public Law* (OUP 2010) 18 (arbitral decision-making affecting the whole system).

241   Benedict Kingsbury and Stephan Schill, 'Investor-State Arbitration as Governance: Fair and Equitable Treatment, Proportionality and the Emerging Global Administrative Law' (2009) New York University Public Law and Legal Theory Working Papers, Paper 146; Schill, 'Introduction' (n 240) 17–23; Stephan W Schill and Vladislav Djanic, 'International Investment Law and Community Interests' in Eyal Benvenisti and Georg Nolte (eds), *Community Interests Across International Law* (OUP 2018) 225–7 (investment law as governance of the global economy).

242   See in this respect Rosalyn Higgins, 'International Law and the Reasonable Need of Governments to Govern. Inaugural Lecture, London School of Economics and Political Science 22nd November, 1982' in Rosalyn Higgins, *Themes and Theories: Selected Essays, Speeches, and Writings in International Law*, vol 2 (OUP 2009) 784 ('It is manifest that there are a variety of international actors contributing to the development of international law, and in turn affected by it—international organizations, individuals, multinational

States claim the biggest share in the governance of the investment dispute settlement regime. This belongs to them, it is often assumed, because of their statehood and mastership over treaties.[243] States decide freely if and to what kind of adjudication they will consent. But as I argued earlier, the principle of consensualism does not grant states the exclusivity of jurisdictional regulation, but only an opportunity to initiate jurisdictional relationships.[244] Jurisdictional relationships are most often initiated by offers in investment treaties alongside the regulation of substantive protections, which motivates the claim for an exclusive state governance over international investment law and arbitration.[245] It is often argued that states require regulatory space and must have a clear overview of the area of free conduct.[246] The same objection can be advanced regarding the proposed model: states determine to what extent and under what conditions substantive protections are arbitrable at the international level, which would be endangered by the power of arbitrators to create jurisdictional rules. However, the proposed model aims to safeguard the regulatory space of states, by establishing the priority of primary over secondary rules. Only knowing the exact relationship between party- and arbitrator-made law, can states draft treaties with the effect of implicitly accepting or explicitly derogating from secondary jurisdictional rules.

Investors are on the opposite side of the governance spectrum. Per default, they accept offers made by states, and they usually do not contribute substantially to the formation of primary rules. However, occasionally they get an opportunity to have a bigger say in the rule-formation.[247] Another aspect of the investors' control over the regime concerns the fact that investors put the system in motion by instituting arbitrations, set the agenda of arbitral tribunals, and advance legal arguments before them.[248] Still, to the extent that investors

---

corporations and others. But states are still the most important of the actors in the international legal system, and their sovereignty is at the heart of this system.').

[243] See, in respect of the proposal to structure investment treaties as 'triangular treaties', Anthea Roberts, 'Triangular Treaties: The Extent and Limits of Investment Treaty Rights' (2015) 56 Harvard Int'l LJ 353, 363–4 (adopting the basic premise that states are masters of treaties).

[244] See ch 1, s 2.1.

[245] See generally Roberts, 'Triangular Treaties' (n 243).

[246] For the problem of regulatory space appearing in international economic law, see generally Markus Wagner, 'Regulatory Space in International Trade Law and International Investment Law' (2014) 36 Univ Penn JIL 1.

[247] See n 108 above.

[248] See in this respect Keohane, Moravcsik, and Slaughter (n 86) 462–6 (analysing different levels of access among international courts, which determines to what extent non-state actors can set their agenda).

have so far been able to influence the governance of investment arbitration, the proposed model would not bring any significant changes in that respect.

Arbitrators are somewhere in between, but their governing role over the investment arbitration regime is central for the present discussion. By authorising arbitral tribunals to settle investor-state disputes, authority is conferred on arbitrators. The question is whether the conferral of the law-making power on arbitral tribunals, alongside the adjudicative, is legitimate.[249] Questions of legitimacy relating to international courts and tribunals are complex and the present study cannot address all of them.[250] However, the assignment of the law-making role to arbitral tribunals increases the need for the legitimisation of their work,[251] which makes it necessary to answer at least two important questions: first, whether investment tribunals fulfil the expectations of their mandators when creating rules of law (as opposed to dry dispute settlement); and second, whether that activity is legitimate from the sociological and external perspectives.

Because every arbitration is based on party consent, the normative legitimacy of the arbitral work should not raise difficulties, at least initially.[252] Problems can arise in another respect. Yuval Shany has proposed a model for assessing the effectiveness of international courts and tribunals, which inquires whether a judicial body is achieving its goals defined by its mandators.[253] This study maintains that the authority to adjudicate is defined by disputing parties, so the question is what goal accompanies that definition. International courts and tribunals can have different 'normative goals', such as the settlement of concrete disputes or the development of the law, but that does not mean that one necessarily excludes the other.[254] Even if investment tribunals are not in charge of a single regulatory regime, an expectation of

---

[249] The concept of legitimacy in its core meaning refers to the justification of authority; see Rüdiger Wolfrum, 'Legitimacy of International Law from a Legal Perspective: Some Introductory Considerations' in Rüdiger Wolfrum and Volker Röben (eds), *Legitimacy in International Law* (Springer 2008) 6–7.

[250] See generally Harlan Grant Cohen and others, 'Legitimacy and International Courts – A Framework' in Nienke Grossman and others (eds), *Legitimacy and International Courts* (CUP 2018) 1.

[251] ibid 28 ('The less authority a body claims or asserts, the less justification it needs to do so legitimately.').

[252] See the discussion about primary jurisdictional rules in s 3.1 above. For the foundation of normative legitimacy in consent, see Wolfrum (n 249) 7–9; Andrea K Bjorklund, 'The Legitimacy of the International Centre for Settlement of Investment Disputes' in Nienke Grossman and others (eds), *Legitimacy and International Courts* (CUP 2018) 271–2.

[253] Yuval Shany, *Assessing the Effectiveness of International Courts* (OUP 2014) ch 1.

[254] Grant Cohen and others (n 250) 15–6.

clarification and development of the law is present, although not as tribunals' primary task.[255] Investment tribunals are often seen as having a dispute resolution role exclusively,[256] which can seem supported by the theory of delegation of the authority to adjudicate advocated in this study.[257] However, it is difficult to imagine a tribunal being entrusted with a dispute resolution task without any expectation to contribute to the clarification and development of the law. The goal of law development can be implicit and does not need an explicit formulation.[258] As regards the achievement of that goal, it is clear that arbitral practice forms part of the 'body of investment law',[259] and that prior decisions are used extensively to determine the content of legal rules.[260] Coming back to the topic of this book, tribunals have created additional rules remedying regulatory deficiencies of party-defined rules. Regardless of one's judgment about the merits of such rules, by doing so tribunals effectively fulfil the expectation to clarify and develop the law.

What appears more challenging are the sociological and external aspects of legitimacy, ie aspects dealing with the beliefs that arbitrators can conduct regulatory work, specifically of those not directly engaged in the system.[261] The attitudes of broader audiences are particularly important because the law-making process advocated here is the one of communication.[262] The critical notions are belief or trust in the system and its reliability, and consequently the question arises whether arbitrators are improving these virtues. The consistency of practice has been considered crucial for the establishment of legitimacy of investment arbitration, from both theoretical and sociological perspectives.[263] The truth is that not only disputing parties, but also indirect

---

255 ibid 24–5.
256 Bjorklund, 'Legitimacy' (n 252) 253. ('ICSID's goal is providing a neutral forum for dispute settlement.').
257 See ch 1, s 2.2.1.
258 Shany, *Effectiveness* (n 253) 19.
259 Schill, 'W(h)Ither Fragmentation' (n 7) 880.
260 See n 130 above.
261 For definitions of 'sociological' and 'external' legitimacy, see Grant Cohen and others (n 250) 4–5. See also Allen Buchanan and Robert O Keohane, 'The Legitimacy of Global Governance Institutions' in Rüdiger Wolfrum and Volker Röben (eds), *Legitimacy in International Law* (Springer 2008) 25.
262 See s 4.1 above.
263 Katharina Diel-Gligor, *Towards Consistency in International Investment Jurisprudence: A Preliminary Ruling System for ICSID Arbitration* (Brill 2017) 117–27. See also Susan D Franck, 'The Legitimacy Crisis in Investment Treaty Arbitration: Privatizing Public International Law Through Inconsistent Decisions' (2005) 73 Fordham L Rev 1521 (inconsistent decisions damaging the legitimacy of the system).

actors and the public at large build their perceptions about the legitimacy of a legal system based on how the law is applied.[264] Leaving the discussion about the validity of the ideal of consistency on one side, the proposed model of two-layered jurisdictional regulation would undoubtedly help the consolidation of arbitral practice, and prospectively improve the perceptions of broader audiences about arbitral work. This would ultimately enhance the legitimacy of the arbitral regulatory activity.

The final issue relates to the desirability of the arbitral entitlement to a bigger part in global governance by means of jurisdictional regulation. This issue is sensitive because it involves difficult policy questions. The first one is whether arbitrators would promote global investment flows if they are given the power of jurisdictional regulation.[265] Arguably, that would indeed be the case, although no assurances can be made: at times arbitrators have taken rather limiting approaches to the access of investors to international arbitration, although this can also be seen as a positive development aimed at establishing clear boundaries of the investment law regime.[266] The second question is whether investments have become so important globally as to require an independent existence of their legal regime, justifying a (partial) transfer of the regulatory role from states to non-state actors. This question pertains to the understanding of some legal regimes as global public goods, and probably will not obtain definite answers in the near future.[267] These questions remain to be answered by someone else, and I only note that if the answers turn out positive, the theory of international adjudication would welcome them prepared. The shift in the characterisation of adjudicators from agents to trustees,[268] the recognition of the benefit of judicial independence

---

264 Diel-Gligor (n 263) 120–7.
265 Nienke Grossman, 'The Normative Legitimacy of International Courts' (2013) 86 Temple L Rev 61, 103 (arguing that, to be normatively legitimate, international courts and tribunals 'must promote the purposes of the normative regimes they are charged with interpreting and applying').
266 See generally ch 4.
267 See ch 1, s 2.4.1. But see, for a prospective positive answer, Schill and Djanic (n 241) 224 (arguing that investment law advances the community interest in increasing investment flows).
268 Karen J Alter, 'Agents or Trustees? International Courts in Their Political Context' (2008) 14 European J Int'l Relations 33, 35 ('Principals choose to delegate to Trustees, as opposed to Agents, when the point of delegation is to harness the authority of the Trustee so as to enhance the legitimacy of political decision-making. Trustees are (1) selected because of their personal reputation or professional norms, (2) given independent authority to make decisions according to their best judgment or professional criteria, and (3) empowered to act on behalf of a beneficiary.').

with limited control of the mandate providers,[269] as well as the possible trust of law-makers in adjudicators to supplement incomplete treaty regimes,[270] would accommodate the conferral of the regulatory role on investment arbitrators. Finally, it should be borne in mind that the proposed model of two-layered jurisdictional regulation does not aim to transfer the jurisdictional regulatory role from disputing parties to arbitrators in its entirety, but only partially, with a strong emphasis on the supremacy of consensual jurisdictional regulation. For these reasons, even if the above-mentioned questions remain unanswered, the proposed model should not be dismissed. To the contrary, it should be encouraged, primarily because it already de facto functions to some extent in practice. A solution for those seeking to reassert control over investment arbitration might be in an increased engagement in the system, rather than in restraining its functioning.[271]

5.2 Trends towards Accepting Judicial Regulation in International Adjudication

The proposed model of two-layered jurisdictional regulation in investment treaty arbitration would not be alone in formalising the regulatory role of adjudicatory bodies in international law. It fits within a broader movement acknowledging the law-making role of international courts and tribunals. The development of international law by adjudicatory bodies was recognised in legal scholarship relatively early.[272] The increased judicialization of international law has amplified the significance of international courts and tribunals in the international legal order, and therefore their function in the development of international law.[273]

---

269   Laurence R Helfer and Anne-Marie Slaughter, 'Why States Create International Tribunals: A Response to Professors Posner and Yoo' (2005) 93 California L Rev 899, 904 ('Independent tribunals act as trustees to enhance the credibility of international commitments in specific multilateral contexts.').
270   For the incomplete contracts analogy, albeit with some difficulties, in the context of the WTO dispute resolution, see Joel P Trachtman, 'The Domain of WTO Dispute Resolution' (1999) 40 Harvard Int'l LJ 333, 346–50.
271   Diane A Desierto, 'State Controls over Available Remedies in Investor-State Arbitration' in Andreas Kulick (ed), *Reassertion of Control over the Investment Treaty Regime* (CUP 2016) 259 (arguing that some states have been able to reassert control by enhanced engagement in investment arbitrations).
272   See, for example, Sir Hersch Lauterpacht, *The Development of International Law by the International Court* (Stevens & Sons 1958).
273   See generally Philippe Sands, 'Reflections on International Judicialization' (2016) 27 EJIL 885.

Well-established judicial bodies, such as the ICJ[274] and the ECtHR,[275] openly talk about something that can be called a semi- or quasi-binding force of their decisions in terms of law-making. One can argue that these approaches reflect institutional arrangements, in the sense that these courts follow previous decisions for the sake of internal consistency and maintaining their reputation, and not for the sake of law-development alone. But it would be hard to argue that decisions of these courts do not have broader law-making effects. The ICJ practice is cited as authoritative by virtually all international courts and tribunals.[276] A similar phenomenon appears with the ECtHR practice, and because this is a 'regime-specific' court,[277] its treaty- or regime-transcending law-making effects become apparent.[278]

In the field of international economic law, the dispute settlement mechanism of the World Trade Organization (WTO) has developed a somewhat stronger form of judicial law-making. The Appellate Body's reports have a de facto vertical *stare decisis* effect towards future panels, which has been developed for either conceptual considerations of predictability of the system or more practical considerations, like the threat of having findings reversed.[279] Although it can be debated whether this development reflects the specific

---

[274] See text to nn 166–167 above. But note that the ICJ has been cautious not to vest on itself a direct legislative role; see *Legality of the Threat or Use of Nuclear Weapons* (Advisory Opinion) (1996) ICJ Rep 226, para 18 ('It is clear that the Court cannot legislate, and, in the circumstances of the present case, it is not called upon to do so. [...] The contention that the giving of an answer to the question posed would require the Court to legislate is based on a supposition that the present *corpus juris* is devoid of relevant rules in this matter. The Court could not accede to this argument; it states the existing law and does not legislate. This is so even if, in stating and applying the law, the Court necessarily has to specify its scope and sometimes note its general trend.').

[275] *Chapman v The United Kingdom* App No 27238/95 (ECtHR, 18 January 2001) para 70 ('The Court considers that, while it is not formally bound to follow any of its previous judgments, it is in the interests of legal certainty, foreseeability and equality before the law that it should not depart, without good reason, from precedents laid down in previous cases.').

[276] The reliance on the practice of the ICJ is a widespread phenomenon in international law. In the context of investment arbitration, Moshe Hirsch explains this phenomenon from the sociological perspective with the concepts of social status and reference groups; see Hirsch (n 8) 165–7.

[277] Grant Cohen and others (n 250) 23–4 (defining regime-specific courts as those embedded within a particular regime, which in this case is the ECHR).

[278] For example, for the use of ECtHR precedents in the practice of the Inter-American Court of Human Rights, see Gerald L Neuman, 'Import, Export, and Regional Consent in the Inter-American Court of Human Rights' (2008) 19 EJIL 101, 109.

[279] Meredith Crowley and Robert Howse, 'US–Stainless Steel (Mexico)' (2010) 9 World Trade Rev 117, 122–9.

structure of the WTO dispute resolution mechanism (such as the existence of appeal and the different character of adjudicators at the two levels), the point that matters here is very simple: it has become recognised that judicial activity determines the reliability of the WTO system, and for that reason it is given a wider, law-making effect.

The recognition of judicial law-making is broad and has entered virtually all spheres of international law. The International Criminal Court thus 'may apply principles and rules of law as interpreted in its previous decisions'.[280] Earlier criminal tribunals have established a vertical *stare decisis* effect of appellate decisions.[281] Although outside the scope of this study,[282] these examples show that judicial law-making is more of a fact than a policy choice and requires recognition for the sake of proper functioning of the international legal order.

The fact that the given examples involve a higher level of institutionalisation than investment arbitration should not disqualify the latter from the trend. Modern international arbitration exercises the judicial function because, as with international courts, the task of arbitral tribunals is to settle international disputes by an independent determination of facts and application of the law.[283] As long as investment tribunals are meant to interpret and apply international investment law for the purpose of settling investment disputes, there is no reason for distinguishing between them and standing courts as regards their law-making capacity. One can argue about the lack of institutional capacities on the part of arbitral tribunals (in comparison to standing courts),[284] but as seen in previous sections, that should not be a major concern for the functioning of the law-making model advanced in this study. Law-making as a communicative process and the system of adjudication in international law

---

[280] Rome Statute of the International Criminal Court (signed 17 July 1998, entered into force 1 July 2002) 2187 UNTS 90, art 21(2).

[281] See *Prosecutor v Zlatko Aleksovski* (Judgment) ICTY-95-14/1-A (24 March 2000) para 113 ('The Appeals Chamber considers that a proper construction of the Statute requires that the *ratio decidendi* of its decisions is binding on Trial Chambers [...]').

[282] As stated in the Introduction, the concept of international adjudication is understood in this study as more akin to civil adjudication in domestic legal systems, whose central notion is a dispute between parties over their rights and obligations. Accordingly, I have not dealt with international criminal courts and tribunals.

[283] Chittharanjan F Amerasinghe, 'International Arbitration: A Judicial Function?' in Rüdiger Wolfrum, Maja Seršić, and Trpimir M Šošić (eds), *Contemporary Developments in International Law: Essays in Honour of Budislav Vukas* (Brill 2015) 687–9.

[284] It can be objected that the system of investment arbitration lacks institutional devices capable of consolidating arbitral practice, such as appellate mechanisms, or that the circle of individuals serving as arbitrators is too broad to allow unification of arbitral practices.

are both dispersed, and by default involve a variety of actors and voices. The key to successful law-making is in their inclusion in the law-making process, rather than exclusion by means of conferring the exclusivity of regulation on a single entity. Last but not least, the current movement towards the institutionalisation of investor-state dispute settlement, in the form of establishing either an appellate body, a network of similar investment courts, or one multilateral investment court, should be seen as a good opportunity for the implementation of the proposed model.[285]

6   Conclusion

Arbitral work on jurisdictional determinations includes not only black letter approaches to the application of party-defined jurisdictional rules, but also the making of rules remedying regulatory deficiencies in party-defined rules. The filling of regulatory deficiencies has been driven by the shift from a hard to a soft perspective on party consent. The proposed model of two-layered jurisdictional regulation aims to define clear boundaries of competences in jurisdictional regulation and to enable clear coordination between the two sets of rules. To that end, however, the regulatory role played by arbitral tribunals must be recognised. In sum, I argue that the jurisdictional framework of investment arbitration consists of (i) primary rules, which are created by virtue of party consent, and (ii) secondary rules, which are created in arbitral practice. Primary rules confer the power to adjudicate, while secondary rules operate in the interpretation and application of primary rules. Primary rules remain superior to secondary rules and should always prevail in the event of a conflict. This proposal reaffirms the principle of consensualism, because it allows disputing parties to implicitly agree or explicitly disagree with secondary rules. The model allows states and investors to deviate from secondary rules by regulating the relevant issue in the sphere of primary rules, on the one hand, and to engage in the making of secondary rules by sending signals to arbitrators about their appropriateness, on the other. The proposed model is feasible within the existing structure of investment arbitration, and even more so in an institutionalised one, and its implementation does not require any hard steps, such as renegotiation of treaties or amending arbitration rules. All that is required is a more prudential approach in drafting arbitral decisions and exercising control over them, and the acceptance of the reality on the part of states and investors.

---

285   See UNCITRAL, 'Report of Working Group III (Investor-State Dispute Settlement Reform) on the Work of Its Thirty-Eighth Session (Vienna, 14–18 October 2019)' (23 October 2019) UN Doc A/CN.9/1004, para 25.

Final Conclusions

This book started from the question to what extent party consent defines jurisdictional rules in investment treaty arbitration. I find that the principle of consensualism is eroded in this field by the rise of arbitral jurisdictional regulation. But contrary to the mainstream thought, I do not find that erosion in terms of how consensual bonds between disputing parties are established, but in the degree to which disputing parties define the authority to adjudicate of investment arbitral tribunals.

This study first inquired into the process of jurisdictional regulation in investment treaty arbitration. As shown in Chapter 1, the principle of consensualism is inherently related to the lack of a central regulatory authority in international law. The definition of the authority to adjudicate at the international level is possible only by consent of disputing parties. The definition of the authority to adjudicate, meaning drawing the limits of the jurisdiction of international courts and tribunals, is therefore the main function of the principle of consensualism. Consensualism therefore governs the process of jurisdictional regulation in international law, by conferring the exclusive power to regulate jurisdictional limits on disputing parties. Specific views on investment arbitration, such as a global public good, as a protective regime, or through the lens of commercial arbitration, can introduce new considerations relating to party consent and jurisdictional regulation in practice, but cannot affect the principle of consensualism as the foundation of the process of jurisdictional regulation.

Investment treaty arbitration follows the general international law pattern that jurisdictional relationships form contractual relationships between disputing parties. This has been implemented relying on the theory of offer and acceptance. However, party-provided definitions of the authority to adjudicate usually do not amount to a comprehensive regulation of jurisdictional questions. On the trajectory from party-provided jurisdictional rules to concrete jurisdictional determinations many questions can emerge, which often evidence regulatory deficiencies in the domain of party-defined jurisdictional rules. Such deficiencies can appear at several stages of jurisdictional examinations, such as those conducted by administrative organs of arbitral institutions, arbitral tribunals, ICSID annulment committees, and domestic courts. Arbitral tribunals remain the principal jurisdictional examiners and therefore they have most of the opportunities to discover such deficiencies. Regulatory deficiencies require some action on the part of arbitral tribunals to enable rendering concrete jurisdictional determinations. That is where another problem emerges: the power of arbitral tribunals to decide the questions of their own jurisdiction does not allow them to define new rules, but only to interpret the given set of party-provided jurisdictional rules.

Despite this background, arbitral tribunals have engaged in jurisdictional law-making. Arbitrators have formulated rules directing the interpretation and application of party-provided jurisdictional rules, but also imposing independent jurisdictional limits. Chapter 2 addressed the arbitrator-made rules that relax the conditions of access to international arbitration defined in the domain of consensual jurisdictional regulation. Arbitrators have generated rules affecting the rigidity of the conditions of access (qualifying them as related to the admissibility of claims rather than jurisdiction), and providing avenues for their bypassing (the futility exception, the *Mavrommatis* principle, liberal criteria for the satisfaction of local litigation requirements, and strict criteria for the triggering of fork-in-the-road clauses). They have also created presumptions in favour and against the applicability of MFN clauses to dispute resolution clauses, although practice remains divided on this issue. In a nutshell, they have either presumed that MFN clauses covered jurisdictional clauses so that their interpretation had to observe possible indicators of exclusion, or that MFN clauses did not cover jurisdictional clauses, so that their interpretation had to observe possible indicators of inclusion. This issue, however, is complex insofar as it involves the arbitral acceptance or rejection of the jurisdiction/admissibility dichotomy in the context of conditions of access.

Chapter 3 turned to the arbitrator-made rules that relax the substantive aspects of arbitral jurisdiction defined in the domain of consensual jurisdictional regulation. Tribunals have built rules precluding retroactive denial of their jurisdiction by one disputing party (non-retroactivity of denial of benefits), extending the validity of consent limited by time-bars (continued act doctrine), extending the scope of protected investors and investments (the Broches test and the presumption of the protection of indirect investments), and extending the scope of arbitrable disputes (the presumption in favour of jurisdictional bridging). The first two operate as default rules in the absence of party-defined rules. The Broches test can be seen as a standard that instructs when an investor should not qualify for the access to the ICSID mechanism. Finally, the two mentioned presumptions set interpretative directions: they presume the protection of indirect investments and the permissibility of jurisdictional bridging, so that treaty interpretations should observe if there are any indicators of their exclusion.

In contrast, Chapter 4 found the examples of arbitral law-making that hinder the access to investment arbitration by introducing additional jurisdictional limits. Tribunals have limited the scope of protection of investors and investments (the objective definitions of these notions and the independent legality requirement), limited the scope of arbitrable disputes (the condition of privity in the application of umbrella clauses), and translated the abuse of process doctrine into a jurisdictional rule limiting their authority. The objective definition of 'investment' can be seen as a standard instructing the qualification for the access to ICSID, but that definition also creates an independent default rule when observed outside the ICSID context. The objective definition of 'investor', the independent legality requirement, and the abuse of process doctrine equally function as default rules imposing jurisdictional limits independently of treaty texts. The privity requirement in the application of umbrella clauses also functions as a default rule, but it does not present an independent requirement, because it operates in the interpretation and application of treaty-provided umbrella clauses.

Chapters 2 to 4 demonstrate that investment treaty arbitration has witnessed the rise of the arbitral regulatory activity in jurisdictional matters. The analysed practice shows that arbitral tribunals have attempted to resolve regulatory deficiencies in given sets of jurisdictional rules in general and prescriptive terms. The proposed solutions have been applied in streams of practices, gaining normativity and the character of a legal rule. The inspiration for thus created jurisdictional rules has been external to party-provided rules: tribunals have drawn analogies to other fields of law, relied on policy considerations, personal beliefs and values, and similar. This has led tribunals to create conflicting streams of practice, advocating in favour of opposing rules, and entering debates about their appropriateness. Tribunals praise and criticise the rules adopted by other tribunals; they rely on previous decisions as authoritative sources and they disdainfully ignore them. In any event, they engage in law-making, attempting to create arbitration-transcending rules governing the questions of jurisdiction.

The development of arbitral jurisdictional regulation cannot be explained by reference to the mainstream criticisms of investment treaty arbitration. In Chapter 5, I reviewed the three main suspects: commercial law approaches to investment arbitration, the one-sidedness of the regime, and alleged arbitral biases. These criticisms cannot find the driving force behind arbitral jurisdictional regulation. In order to find such force, I suggested that the perspective on the principle of consensualism has shifted, and that consent is now seen only as the primary means of jurisdictional regulation, liberated from the political and symbolic concept of sovereignty which has surrounded it in the inter-state context. This liberation, together with the investment arbitration framework, motivates arbitral law-making as a secondary means of jurisdictional regulation.

The development of such arbitral regulatory activity has significant ramifications regarding the principle of consensualism. The bigger the extent of arbitral jurisdictional regulation, the smaller the share of consensual jurisdictional regulation in the definition of the authority to adjudicate. In other words, the development of arbitrator-made jurisdictional rules proves the hypothesis of this study true, namely that the strength of the principle of consensualism is inversely proportional to the extent of arbitral jurisdictional regulation. This correlation appears straightforward by observing *who* defines the authority to adjudicate. It also holds true by observing the *function* of arbitrator-made jurisdictional rules: they either direct the interpretation and application of party-provided jurisdictional rules, or impose independent limits on arbitral jurisdiction. Overall, the principle of consensualism, which confers on disputing parties the authority to define the limits of arbitral jurisdiction, is eroded by the rise of arbitral jurisdictional regulation. I note that this conclusion is limited to the field of investment treaty arbitration, but as already indicated in the Introduction, given the general relevance of consensualism in international adjudication, similar phenomena might be present elsewhere. Further research, therefore, can examine to what extent other international courts and tribunals have engaged in a regulatory activity in jurisdictional matters and to what extent that development has affected their jurisdictional structures.

Turning back to the topic of this study, the rise of arbitral jurisdictional regulation is not surprising. It has appeared due to regulatory deficiencies in party-provided jurisdictional frameworks. This book did not seek to eliminate the opportunities for arbitral tribunals to engage in law-making but it suggested the integration of the arbitral law-making function in the jurisdictional framework of investment treaty arbitration. In Chapter 5, I sketched a two-layered model of jurisdictional regulation in investment treaty arbitration, consisting of primary rules (which are defined by disputing parties) and secondary rules (which are developed by arbitral tribunals). The two layers of rules can be easily coordinated, because the model establishes the primacy of party-provided over arbitrator-made jurisdictional rules, but allows the application of the latter as proper law in the event of the silence of the former. Furthermore, I argued in favour of evolutive jurisdictional regulation, as a doctrine of arbitral reasoning. Tribunals are instructed to observe various voices and signals over time which influence the content of secondary rules and to engage in the making of secondary rules as a communicative process. Some challenges of this model can be raised by reference to the issues of legal change, its effect on the operation of treaties, the existence of control mechanisms, the availability of law-making material, and the risk of excessiveness and prospect of stabilisation of practice, but they are surmountable and do not present greater difficulties. Overall, the proposed model would improve legal certainty when it comes to the development and application of secondary rules in the event of silence of primary rules.

Now is the time to think about the consensualism of investment treaty arbitration in the future. I argue that the proposed model of two-layered jurisdictional regulation can restore the principle of consensualism from its perceived erosion. The normative embeddedness of that principle in the foundations of the international legal order does not suffice to eliminate the challenges of its validity raised by the fact of arbitral jurisdictional regulation. In contrast, the recognition of the arbitral law-making function and the integration of arbitral jurisdictional regulation in the jurisdictional structure of investment treaty arbitration can resolve this tension. This would give all the actors a full overview of the law-making competences and the existing rules, as well as allow disputing parties to implicitly agree or explicitly disagree with secondary rules. States and investors can deviate from secondary rules by establishing specific rules in investment treaties or elsewhere. They can also engage in the making of secondary rules by sending signals about their appropriateness, which in turn should be recognised by arbitrators in a communicative law-making process. The consensualism of investment treaty arbitration cannot be rebuilt by keeping a layer of unknown and unpredictable rules in secrecy, but only by admitting the realities of practice and actively engaging with them.

Bibliography

Abi-Saab G, *Les Exceptions préliminaires dans la procédure de la Cour internationale* (Pedone 1967).

Aguilar Alvarez G and Reisman WM, 'How Well Are Investment Awards Reasoned?' in Guillermo Aguilar Alvarez and W Michael Reisman (eds), *The Reasons Requirement in International Investment Arbitration* (Martinus Nijhoff 2008).

Alexandrov SA, 'Breaches of Contract and Breaches of Treaty: The Jurisdiction of Treaty-Based Arbitration Tribunals to Decide Breach of Contract Claims in *SGS v. Pakistan* and *SGS v. Philippines*' (2004) 5 JWIT 555.

Alexandrov SA, 'The Compulsory Jurisdiction of the International Court of Justice: How Compulsory Is It?' (2006) 5 Chinese JIL 29.

Alter KJ, 'Agents or Trustees? International Courts in Their Political Context' (2008) 14 European J Int'l Relations 33.

Alvarez JE, 'A BIT on Custom' (2009) 42 NYU J Int'l L & Pol 17.

Alvarez JE, 'Is Investor-State Arbitration "Public"?' (2016) 7 JIDS 534.

Alvarez JE, 'The Public International Law Regime Governing International Investment' (2009) 344 Recueil des Cours 193.

Amerasinghe CF, 'International Arbitration: A Judicial Function?' in Rüdiger Wolfrum, Maja Seršić, and Trpimir M Šošić (eds), *Contemporary Developments in International Law: Essays in Honour of Budislav Vukas* (Brill 2015).

Amerasinghe CF, 'Jurisdiction *Ratione Personae* under the Convention on the Settlement of Investment Disputes between States and Nationals of Other States' (1976) 47 British Yrbk Int'l L 227.

Amerasinghe CF, *International Arbitral Jurisdiction* (Brill 2011).

Amerasinghe CF, *Jurisdiction of International Tribunals* (Kluwer Law International 2003).

Amerasinghe CF, *Jurisdiction of Specific International Tribunals* (Martinus Nijhoff 2009).

Andreeva Y, 'Interpreting Consent to Arbitration as a Unilateral Act of State: A Case Against Conventions' (2011) 27 Arb Int'l 129.

Arato J, Brown C, and Ortino F, 'Parsing and Managing Inconsistency in Investor-State Dispute Settlement' (2020) 21 JWIT 336.

Ascensio H, 'Abuse of Process in International Investment Arbitration' (2014) 13 Chinese JIL 763.

Atanasova D, Martínez Benoit A, and Ostřanský J, 'The Legal Framework for Counterclaims in Investment Treaty Arbitration' (2014) 31 J Int'l Arb 357.

Audit M and Forteau M, 'Investment Arbitration without BIT: Toward a Foreign Investment Customary Based Arbitration?' (2012) 29 J Int'l Arb 581.

Baetens F, 'Keeping the Status Quo or Embarking on a New Course? Setting Aside, Refusal of Enforcement, Annulment and Appeal' in Andreas Kulick (ed), *Reassertion of Control over the Investment Treaty Regime* (CUP 2016).

Baetens F, 'Judicial Review of International Adjudicatory Decisions: A Cross-Regime Comparison of Annulment and Appellate Mechanisms' (2017) 8 JIDS 432.

Baltag C, 'The ICSID Convention: A Successful Story – The Origins and History of the ICSID' in Crina Baltag (ed), *ICSID Convention after 50 Years: Unsettled Issues* (Kluwer Law International 2017).

Banifatemi Y (ed), *Jurisdiction in Investment Treaty Arbitration* (Juris 2018).

Banifatemi Y, 'Taking Into Account Control Under Denial of Benefits Clauses' in Yas Banifatemi (ed), *Jurisdiction in Investment Treaty Arbitration* (Juris 2018).

Bartelson J, *Sovereignty as Symbolic Form* (Routledge 2014).

Bassiouni MC, 'A Functional Approach to General Principles of International Law' (1990) 11 Michigan J Int'l L 768.

Baumgartner J, *Treaty Shopping in International Investment Law* (OUP 2016).

Bechky PS, '*Salini*'s Nature: Arbitrators' Duty of Jurisdictional Policing' (2018) 17 LPICT 145.

Becker MA, 'The Dispute That Wasn't There: Judgments in the Nuclear Disarmament Cases at the International Court of Justice' (2017) 6 Cambridge Int'l LJ 4.

Bentolila D, *Arbitrators as Lawmakers* (Kluwer 2017).

Bernardini P, 'International Commercial Arbitration and Investment Treaty Arbitration: Analogies and Differences' in David D Caron and others (eds), *Practising Virtue: Inside International Arbitration* (OUP 2015).

Bishop D and Stevens M, 'Jurisdiction Ratione Personae – Is There a Standard Definition of an "Investor" in Investment Treaties?' in Yas Banifatemi (ed), *Jurisdiction in Investment Treaty Arbitration* (Juris 2018).

Bjorklund AK, 'Are Arbitrators (Judicial) Activists?' (2018) 17 LPICT 49.

Bjorklund AK, 'Contract without Privity: Sovereign Offer and Investor Acceptance' (2001) 2 Chicago JIL 183.

Bjorklund AK, 'Investment Treaty Arbitral Decisions as *Jurisprudence Constante*' in Colin B Picker, Isabella D Bunn, and Douglas W Arner (eds), *International Economic Law: The State and Future of the Discipline* (Hart 2008).

Bjorklund AK, 'The Legitimacy of the International Centre for Settlement of Investment Disputes' in Nienke Grossman and others (eds), *Legitimacy and International Courts* (CUP 2018).

Bjorklund AK, 'The Public Interest in International Investment Law' in August Reinisch, Mary E Footer, and Christina Binder (eds), *International Law and... Select Proceedings of the European Society of International Law* (Hart 2016).

Blanchard S, 'State Consent, Temporal Jurisdiction, and the Importation of Continuing Circumstances Analysis into International Investment Arbitration' (2011) 10 Washington University Global Studies L Rev 419.

Böckstiegel K-H, 'Commercial and Investment Arbitration: How Different Are They Today?' (2012) 28 Arb Int'l 577.

Bodansky D, 'What's in a Concept? Global Public Goods, International Law, and Legitimacy' (2012) 23 EJIL 651.

Boisson de Chazournes L, 'The Principle of *Compétence de la Compétence* in International Adjudication and Its Role in an Era of Multiplication of Courts and Tribunals' in Mahnoush H Arsanjani and others (eds), *Looking to the Future: Essays on International Law in Honor of W. Michael Reisman* (Martinus Nijhoff 2011).

Born G, 'A New Generation of International Adjudication' (2012) 61 Duke LJ 775.

Bottari M and Wallach L, *NAFTA's Threat to Sovereignty and Democracy: The Record of NAFTA Chapter 11 Investor-State Cases 1994-2005* (Public Citizen 2005).

Boyle A and Chinkin C, *The Making of International Law* (OUP 2007).

Braun TR, 'Globalization: The Driving Force in International Investment Law' in Michael Waibel and others (eds), *The Backlash Against Investment Arbitration* (Kluwer 2010).

Brilmayer L, 'From "Contract" to "Pledge": The Structure of International Human Rights Agreements' (2007) 77 British Yrbk Int'l L 163.

Broches A, 'Bilateral Investment Protection Treaties and Arbitration of Investment Disputes' in Aron Broches, *Selected Essays: World Bank, ICSID, and Other Subjects of Public and Private International Law* (Martinus Nijhoff 1995).

Broches A, 'The Convention on the Settlement of Investment Disputes: Some Observations on Jurisdiction' (1966) 5 Columbia J Transnat'l L 263.

Broches A, 'The Convention on the Settlement of Investment Disputes between States and Nationals of Other States' in Aron Broches, *Selected Essays: World Bank, ICSID, and Other Subjects of Public and Private International Law* (Martinus Nijhoff 1995).

Brower CN and Kumar SP, 'Investomercial Arbitration: Whence Cometh It? What Is It? Whither Goeth It?' (2015) 30 ICSID Rev-FILJ 35.

Brower CN and Schill SW, 'Is Arbitration a Threat or a Boon to the Legitimacy of International Investment Law?' (2009) 9 Chicago JIL 471.

Brower CN, 'W(h)ither International Commercial Arbitration?' (2008) 24 Arb Int'l 181.

Brown C, 'The Inherent Powers of International Courts and Tribunals' (2006) 76 British Yrbk Int'l L 195.

Brown C, *A Common Law of International Adjudication* (OUP 2007).

Brownlie I, 'The Justiciability of Disputes and Issues in International Relations' (1967) 42 British Yrbk Int'l L 123.

Buchanan A and Keohane RO, 'The Legitimacy of Global Governance Institutions' in Rüdiger Wolfrum and Volker Röben (eds), *Legitimacy in International Law* (Springer 2008).

Caron DD, 'The Interpretation of National Foreign Investment Laws as Unilateral Acts Under International Law' in Mahnoush H Arsanjani and others (eds), *Looking to the Future: Essays on International Law in Honor of W. Michael Reisman* (Martinus Nijhoff 2011).

Charlotin D and Peterson LE, 'The Merck v. Ecuador Award (Part One): Arbitrators Wave Away Jurisdictional Objections – Including on Exhaustion – and Warn That Non-Compliance With Interim Orders Could Aggravate Treaty Breach' (*Investment Arbitration Reporter*, 27 March 2018) <www.iareporter.com/articles/the-merck-v-ecuador-award-part-one-arbitrators-wave-away-ecuadors-jurisdictional-objections-including-on-exhaustion-and-warn-that-ecuadors-non-compliance-with-interim-orders/> accessed 3 January 2019.

Chen H, 'The Expansion of Jurisdiction by ICSID Tribunals: Approaches, Reasons and Damages' (2011) 12 JWIT 671.

Cheng B, *General Principles of Law as Applied by International Courts and Tribunals* (Stevens & Sons 1953).

Cheng T-H, 'Precedent and Control in Investment Treaty Arbitration' (2006) 30 Fordham Int'l LJ 1014.

Choudhury B, 'International Investment Law as a Global Public Good' (2013) 17 Lewis & Clark L Rev 481.

Ciurtin H, 'Paradoxes of (Sovereign) Consent: On the Uses and Abuses of a Notion in International Investment Law' in Crina Baltag (ed), *ICSID Convention after 50 Years: Unsettled Issues* (Kluwer Law International 2017).

Commission JP, 'Precedent in Investment Treaty Arbitration: A Citation Analysis of a Developing Jurisprudence' (2007) 24 J Int'l Arb 129.

Cordero Moss G, 'Commercial Arbitration and Investment Arbitration: Fertile Soil for False Friends?' in Christina Binder and others (eds), *International Investment Law for the 21st Century: Essays in Honour of Christoph Schreuer* (OUP 2009).

Craig WL, 'Uses and Abuses of Appeal from Awards' (1988) 4 Arb Int'l 174.

Craig WL, Park WW, and Paulsson J, *International Chamber of Commerce Arbitration* (3rd ed, Oceana 2000).

Crawford J, 'International Protection of Foreign Direct Investments: Between Clinical Isolation and Systematic Integration' in Rainer Hofmann and Christian J Tams (eds), *International Investment Law and General International Law: From Clinical Isolation to Systemic Integration?* (Nomos 2011).

Crawford J, 'Similarity of Issues in Disputes Arising under the Same or Similarly Drafted Investment Treaties' in Yas Banifatemi (ed), *Precedent in International Arbitration* (Juris 2008).

Crawford J, 'Sovereignty as a Legal Value' in James Crawford and Martti Koskenniemi (eds), *The Cambridge Companion to International Law* (CUP 2012).

Crawford J, 'The Legal Effect of Automatic Reservations to the Jurisdiction of the International Court' (1980) 50 British Yrbk Int'l L 63.

Crawford J, 'Treaty and Contract in Investment Arbitration' (2008) 24 Arb Int'l 351.

Crawford JR and Grant TD, 'Local Remedies, Exhaustion Of' in Rüdiger Wolfrum (ed), *The Max Planck Encyclopedia of Public International Law* (OUP 2012).

Cremades BM and Cairns DJ, 'The Brave New World of Global Arbitration' (2002) 3 JWIT 173.

Crowley M and Howse R, 'US–Stainless Steel (Mexico)' (2010) 9 World Trade Rev 117.

Cuniberti G, *Rethinking International Commercial Arbitration: Towards Default Arbitration* (Edward Elgar 2017).

Daly B, Goriatcheva E, and Meighen H, *A Guide to the PCA Arbitration Rules* (OUP 2014).

De Brabandere E, ' "Good Faith", "Abuse of Process" and the Initiation of Investment Treaty Claims' (2012) 3 JIDS 609.

De Brabandere E, 'Arbitral Decisions as a Source of International Investment Law' in Tarcisio Gazzini and Eric De Brabandere (eds), *International Investment Law: The Sources of Rights and Obligations* (Brill 2012).

De Brabandere E, *Investment Treaty Arbitration as Public International Law: Procedural Aspects and Implications* (CUP 2014).

De Luca A and others, 'Responding to Incorrect Decision-Making in Investor-State Dispute Settlement: Policy Options' (2020) 21 JWIT 374.

De Nanteuil A, 'Counterclaims in Investment Arbitration: Old Questions, New Answers?' (2018) 17 LPICT 374.

De Stefano C, 'Denial of Benefits Clauses in International Investment Agreements: Burden of Proof and Notice to Claimant' (2016) 30 Diritto del Commercio Internazionale 143.

Demirkol B, 'Does an Investment Treaty Tribunal Need Special Consent for Mass Claims?' (2013) 2 Cambridge Int'l LJ 612.

Demirkol B, 'Non-Treaty Claims in Investment Treaty Arbitration' (2018) 31 Leiden JIL 59.

Desierto DA, 'State Controls over Available Remedies in Investor-State Arbitration' in Andreas Kulick (ed), *Reassertion of Control over the Investment Treaty Regime* (CUP 2016).

Diallo O, *Le consentement des parties à l'arbitrage international* (Presses Universitaires de France 2010).

Diel-Gligor K, *Towards Consistency in International Investment Jurisprudence: A Preliminary Ruling System for ICSID Arbitration* (Brill 2017).

Dolzer R and Myers T, 'After *Tecmed*: Most-Favored-Nation Clauses in Investment Protection Agreements' (2004) 19 ICSID Rev-FILJ 49.

Dolzer R and Schreuer C, *Principles of International Investment Law* (2nd ed, OUP 2012).

Dörr O and Schmalenbach K (eds), *Vienna Convention on the Law of Treaties: A Commentary* (Springer 2012).

Douglas Z, 'Can a Doctrine of Precedent Be Justified in Investment Treaty Arbitration?' (2010) 25 ICSID Rev-FILJ 104.

Douglas Z, 'The Hybrid Foundations of Investment Treaty Arbitration' (2003) 74 British Yrbk Int'l L 151.

Douglas Z, 'The MFN Clause in Investment Arbitration: Treaty Interpretation Off the Rails' (2011) 2 JIDS 97.

Douglas Z, 'The Plea of Illegality in Investment Treaty Arbitration' (2014) 29 ICSID Rev-FILJ 155.

Douglas Z, 'When Does an Investment Treaty Claim Arise? An Excursus on the Anatomy of the Cause of Action' in Yas Banifatemi (ed), *Jurisdiction in Investment Treaty Arbitration* (Juris 2018).

Douglas Z, *The International Law of Investment Claims* (CUP 2009).

Dumberry P, 'The Emergence of the Concept of "General Principle of International Law" in Investment Arbitration Case Law' (2020) 11 JIDS 194.

Dupont P-E, 'The Notion of ICSID Investment: Ongoing "Confusion" or "Emerging Synthesis"?' (2011) 12 JWIT 245.

Earnest DL, 'The Duty of Arbitrators to Delimitate between Jurisdiction and Admissibility in Investor-State Arbitration: A Developed Consensus or an Enduring Lacuna?' (2018) 17 LPICT 135.

Elkins Z, Guzman AT, and Simmons BA, 'Competing for Capital: The Diffusion of Bilateral Investment Treaties, 1960 – 2000' (2006) 60 Int'l Org 811.

Fauchald OK, 'The Legal Reasoning of ICSID Tribunals – An Empirical Analysis' (2008) 19 EJIL 301.

Feldman M, 'Investment Arbitration Appellate Mechanism Options: Consistency, Accuracy, and Balance of Power' (2017) 32 ICSID Rev-FILJ 528.

Feldman M, 'State-Owned Enterprises as Claimants in International Investment Arbitration' (2016) 31 ICSID Rev-FILJ 24.

Feldman M, 'The Standing of State-Controlled Entities under the ICSID Convention: Two Key Considerations' (2012) 65 Columbia FDI Perspectives.

Feldman MB, 'The Annulment Proceedings and the Finality of ICSID Arbitral Awards' (1987) 2 ICSID Rev-FILJ 85.

Fitzmaurice SG, 'The Law and Procedure of the International Court of Justice, 1951-4: Questions of Jurisdiction, Competence and Procedure' (1958) 34 British Yrbk Int'l L 1.

Fitzmaurice SG, 'The Law and Procedure of the International Court of Justice, 1954-9: General Principles and Sources of International Law' (1959) 35 British Yrbk Int'l L 183.

Fitzmaurice SG, 'The Law and Procedure of the International Court of Justice, 1951-54: General Principles and Sources of Law' (1953) 30 British Yrbk Int'l L 1.

Fitzmaurice SG, 'The Law and Procedure of the International Court of Justice 1951-4: Treaty Interpretation and Other Treaty Points' (1957) 33 British Yrbk Int'l L 203.

Fitzmaurice SGG, 'Some Problems Regarding the Formal Sources of International Law' in Martti Koskenniemi (ed), *Sources of International Law* (Ashgate 2000).

Fontanelli F and Tanzi A, 'Jurisdiction and Admissibility in Investment Arbitration: A View from the Bridge at the Practice' (2017) 16 LPICT 3.

Fontanelli F, *Jurisdiction and Admissibility in Investment Arbitration: The Practice and the Theory* (Brill 2018).

Footer ME, 'Umbrella Clauses and Widely-Formulated Arbitration Clauses: Discerning the Limits of ICSID Jurisdiction' (2017) 16 LPICT 87.

Foster GK, 'Striking a Balance Between Investor Protections and National Sovereignty: The Relevance of Local Remedies in Investment Treaty Arbitration' (2011) 49 Columbia J Transnat'l L 201.

Franck SD and Wylie LE, 'Predicting Outcomes in Investment Treaty Arbitration' (2015) 65 Duke LJ 459.

Franck SD, 'Conflating Politics and Development? Examining Investment Treaty Arbitration Outcomes' (2014) 55 Virginia J Int'l L 13.

Franck SD, 'Development and Outcomes of Investment Treaty Arbitration' (2009) 50 Harvard Int'l LJ 435.

Franck SD, 'Empirically Evaluating Claims About Investment Treaty Arbitration' (2007) 86 North Carolina L Rev 1.

Franck SD, 'International Investment Arbitration: Winning, Losing and Why' (2009) 7 Columbia FDI Perspectives.

Franck SD, 'The ICSID Effect? Considering Potential Variations in Arbitration Awards' (2011) 51 Virginia J Int'l L 825.

Franck SD, 'The Legitimacy Crisis in Investment Treaty Arbitration: Privatizing Public International Law Through Inconsistent Decisions' (2005) 73 Fordham L Rev 1521.

Freyer DH and Herlihy D, 'Most-Favored-Nation Treatment and Dispute Settlement in Investment Arbitration: Just How "Favored" Is "Most-Favored"?' (2005) 20 ICSID Rev-FILJ 58.

Fukunaga Y, 'Abuse of Process under International Law and Investment Arbitration' (2018) 33 ICSID Rev-FILJ 181.

Gaffney JP and Loftis JL, 'The "Effective Ordinary Meaning" of BITs and the Jurisdiction of Treaty-Based Tribunals to Hear Contract Claims' (2007) 8 JWIT 5.

Gaffney JP, ' "Abuse of Process" in Investment Treaty Arbitration' (2010) 11 JWIT 515.

Gaillard E, 'Abuse of Process in International Arbitration' (2017) 32 ICSID Rev-FILJ 17.

Gaillard E, 'Centre international pour le reglement des differends relatifs aux investissements (CIRDI)' (1999) 126 Journal du droit international 273.

Gaillard E, 'Identify or Define? Reflections on the Evolution of the Concept of Investment in ICSID Practice' in Christina Binder and others (eds), *International Investment Law for the 21st Century: Essays in Honour of Christoph Schreuer* (OUP 2009).

Gaillard E, 'Some Notes on the Drafting of ICSID Arbitration Clauses' (1988) 3 ICSID Rev-FILJ 136.

Gaillard E, 'Treaty-Based Jurisdiction: Broad Dispute Resolution Clauses' *NYLJ* (6 October 2005).

Gallus N, 'An Umbrella Just for Two? BIT Obligations Observance Clauses and the Parties to a Contract' (2008) 24 Arb Int'l 157.

Gallus N, *The Temporal Jurisdiction of International Tribunals* (OUP 2017).

García Olmedo J, 'Claims by Dual Nationals under Investment Treaties: Are Investors Entitled to Sue Their Own States?' (2017) 8 JIDS 695.

Garcia Sanchez GJ, 'The Blurring of the Public/Private Distinction or the Collapse of a Category? The Story of Investment Arbitration' (2018) 18 Nevada LJ 489.

García-Salmones Rovira M, *The Project of Positivism in International Law* (OUP 2013).

Garibaldi OM, 'Jurisdictional Errors: A Critique of the North American Dredging Company Case' in David D Caron and others (eds), *Practising Virtue: Inside International Arbitration* (OUP 2015).

Gastrell L and Le Cannu P-J, 'Procedural Requirements of "Denial-of-Benefits" Clauses in Investment Treaties: A Review of Arbitral Decisions' (2015) 30 ICSID Rev-FILJ 78.

Gazzini T, *Interpretation of International Investment Treaties* (Hart 2016).

Gessel-Kalinowska vel Kalisz B and Czech K, 'The Role of Precedent in Investment Treaty Arbitration' in Barton Legum (ed), *The Investment Treaty Arbitration Review* (3rd ed, Law Business Research 2018).

Grant Cohen H and others, 'Legitimacy and International Courts – A Framework' in Nienke Grossman and others (eds), *Legitimacy and International Courts* (CUP 2018).

Grossman N, 'The Normative Legitimacy of International Courts' (2013) 86 Temple L Rev 61.

Guillaume G, 'The Use of Precedent by International Judges and Arbitrators' (2011) 2 JIDS 5.

Guzman AT, 'Against Consent' (2012) 52 Virginia J Int'l L 747.

Guzman AT, 'Why LDCs Sign Treaties That Hurt Them: Explaining the Popularity of Bilateral Investment Treaties' (1997) 38 Virginia J Int'l L 639.

Hafner-Burton EM and Victor DG, 'Secrecy in International Investment Arbitration: An Empirical Analysis' (2016) 7 JIDS 161.

Hai Yen T, *The Interpretation of Investment Treaties* (Brill 2014).

Hamamoto S, 'Parties to the "Obligations" in the Obligations Observance ("Umbrella") Clause' (2015) 30 ICSID Rev-FILJ 449.

Hart HLA, *The Concept of Law* (3rd ed, OUP 2012).

Hegel G, *Elements of the Philosophy of Right* (CUP 1991).

Heiskanen V, 'Comment on Andrea Marco Steingruber's Remarks on Veijo Heiskanen's Note "*Ménage à Trois?* Jurisdiction, Admissibility and Competence in Investment Treaty Arbitration"' (2014) 29 ICSID Rev-FILJ 669.

Heiskanen V, '*Entretemps*: Is There a Distinction Between Jurisdiction Ratione Temporis and Substantive Protection Ratione Temporis?' in Yas Banifatemi (ed), *Jurisdiction in Investment Treaty Arbitration* (Juris 2018).

Heiskanen V, 'Forbidding *Dépeçage*: Law Governing Investment Treaty Arbitration' (2009) 32 Suffolk Transnat'l L Rev 367.

Heiskanen V, '*Ménage à Trois?* Jurisdiction, Admissibility and Competence in Investment Treaty Arbitration' (2014) 29 ICSID Rev-FILJ 231.

Helfer LR and Slaughter A-M, 'Why States Create International Tribunals: A Response to Professors Posner and Yoo' (2005) 93 California L Rev 899.

Helfer LR, 'Nonconsensual International Lawmaking' (2008) 2008 Univ Illinois L Rev 71.

Hepburn J, 'Domestic Investment Statutes in International Law' (2018) 112 AJIL 658.

Higgins R, 'International Law and the Reasonable Need of Governments to Govern. Inaugural Lecture, London School of Economics and Political Science 22nd November, 1982' in Rosalyn Higgins, *Themes and Theories: Selected Essays, Speeches, and Writings in International Law*, vol 2 (OUP 2009).

Hirsch M, 'The Sociology of International Investment Law' in Zachary Douglas, Joost Pauwelyn, and Jorge E Viñuales (eds), *The Foundations of International Investment Law: Bringing Theory into Practice* (OUP 2014).

History of the ICSID Convention, vol I (ICSID 1970).

History of the ICSID Convention, vol II–1 (ICSID 1968).

History of the ICSID Convention, vol II–2 (ICSID 1968).

Hobér K, '*Res Judicata* and *Lis Pendens* in International Arbitration' (2014) 366 Recueil des Cours 99.

Hobér K, *International Commercial Arbitration in Sweden* (OUP 2011).

Hollis DB, 'Why State Consent Still Matters—Non-State Actors, Treaties, and the Changing Sources of International Law' (2005) 23 Berkeley J Int'l L 137.

Howse R, 'The Appellate Body Rulings in the Shrimp/Turtle Case: A New Legal Baseline for the Trade and Environment Debate' (2002) 27 Columbia J Envt'l L 489.

Hueckel J, 'Rebalancing Legitimacy and Sovereignty in International Investment Agreements' (2012) 61 Emory LJ 601.

Hwang SC M and Fong LC, 'Definition of "Investment"—A Voice from the Eye of the Storm' (2011) 1 Asian JIL 99.

Jennings R, 'General Course on Principles of International Law' (1967) 121 Recueil des Cours 323.

Jennings R, 'The Judiciary, International and National, and the Development of International Law' (1996) 45 Int'l & Comp LQ 1.

Jennings SR, 'Reflections on the Term "Dispute"' in Ronald St John Macdonald (ed), *Essays in Honour of Wang Tieya* (Martinus Nijhoff 1994).

Junngam N, 'An MFN Clause and BIT Dispute Settlement: A Host State's Implied Consent to Arbitration by Reference' (2010) 15 UCLA J Int'l L & For Aff 399.

Kabra R, 'Has *Abaclat v Argentina* Left the ICSID with a 'Mass'Ive Problem?' (2015) 31 Arb Int'l 425.

Kalderimis D, 'Investment Treaty Arbitration as Global Administrative Law: What This Might Mean in Practice' in Chester Brown and Kate Miles (eds), *Evolution in Investment Treaty Law and Arbitration* (CUP 2011).

Kapeliuk D, 'The Repeat Appointment Factor: Exploring Decision Patterns of Elite Investment Arbitrators' (2010) 96 Cornell L Rev 47.

Kaufmann-Kohler G, 'Arbitral Precedent: Dream, Necessity or Excuse?' (2007) 23 Arb Int'l 357.

Kaufmann-Kohler G, 'Interpretation of Treaties: How Do Arbitral Tribunals Interpret Dispute Settlement Provisions Embodied in Investment Treaties?' in Loukas A Mistelis and Julian DM Lew (eds), *Pervasive Problems in International Arbitration* (Kluwer Law International 2006).

Kaul I and Mendoza RU, 'Advancing the Concept of Public Goods' in Inge Kaul and others (eds), *Providing Global Public Goods: Managing Globalization* (OUP 2003).

Kawano M, 'The Role of Judicial Procedures in the Process of the Pacific Settlement of International Disputes' (2009) 346 Recueil des Cours 9.

Kelsen H, *General Theory of Law and State* (Harvard University Press 1945).

Kelsen H, *Principles of International Law* (Rinehart & Company 1952).

Kendra T, 'State Counterclaims in Investment Arbitration - A New Lease of Life?' (2013) 29 Arb Int'l 575.

Keohane RO, Moravcsik A, and Slaughter A-M, 'Legalized Dispute Resolution: Interstate and Transnational' (2000) 54 Int'l Org 457.

Kingsbury B and Schill S, 'Investor-State Arbitration as Governance: Fair and Equitable Treatment, Proportionality and the Emerging Global Administrative Law' (2009) New York University Public Law and Legal Theory Working Papers, Paper 146.

Kjos HE, *Applicable Law in Investor–State Arbitration: The Interplay Between National and International Law* (OUP 2013).

Koskenniemi M, 'It's Not the Cases, It's the System' (2017) 18 JWIT 343.

Koskenniemi M, *From Apology to Utopia: The Structure of International Legal Argument* (CUP 2005).

Krisch N, 'The Decay of Consent: International Law in an Age of Global Public Goods' (2014) 108 AJIL 1.

Kulick A, 'From Problem to Opportunity? An Analytical Framework for Vagueness and Ambiguity in International Law' in Andreas von Arnauld and Kerstin von der Decken (eds), *German Yearbook of International Law*, vol 59 (Duncker & Humblot 2016).

Lalive P and Halonen L, 'On the Availability of Counterclaims in Investment Treaty Arbitration' in Alexander J Bělohlávek and Naděžda Rozehnalová (eds), *Czech Yearbook of International Law*, vol II (Juris 2011).

Lamm V, *Compulsory Jurisdiction in International Law* (Edward Elgar 2014).

Langford M, Behn D, and Hilleren Lie R, 'The Revolving Door in International Investment Arbitration' (2017) 20 JIEL 301.

Lauterpacht H, 'Restrictive Interpretation and the Principle of Effectiveness in the Interpretation of Treaties' (1949) 26 British Yrbk Int'l L 48.

Lauterpacht SH, *Private Law Sources and Analogies of International Law (with Special Reference to International Arbitration)* (Longmans 1927, reprint Lawbook Exchange 2013).

Lauterpacht SH, *The Development of International Law by the International Court* (Stevens & Sons 1958).

Lauterpacht SH, *The Function of Law in the International Community* (reprint, OUP 2011).

Legum B, 'Options to Establish an Appellate Mechanism for Investment Disputes' in Karl P Sauvant (ed), *Appeals Mechanism in International Investment Disputes* (OUP 2008).

Lim C and Elias O, *The Paradox of Consensualism in International Law* (Brill 1998).

Lindsnaes B, 'The Global and the Regional Outlook: How Can Global Public Goods Be Advanced from a Human Rights Perspective?' in Erik André Andersen and Birgit Lindsnaes (eds), *Towards New Global Strategies: Public Goods and Human Rights* (Martinus Nijhoff 2007).

Lowenfeld AF, 'Investment Agreements and International Law' (2003) 42 Columbia J Transnat'l L 123.

Manciaux S, 'The Notion of Investment: New Controversies' (2008) 9 JWIT 443.

Mann F, 'The Proper Law of Contracts Concluded by International Persons' (1959) 35 British Yrbk Int'l L 34.

Martinez-Fraga PJ and Reetz CR, 'The Status of the Limitations Period Doctrine in Public International Law: Devising a Functional Analytical Framework for Investors and Host-States' (2017) 4 McGill J Disp Resol 105.

Maupin JA, 'Public and Private in International Investment Law: An Integrated Systems Approach' (2014) 54 Virginia J Int'l L 367.

Mavroidis PC, 'Free Lunches? WTO as Public Good, and the WTO's View of Public Goods' (2012) 23 EJIL 731.

McDougal MS and Reisman WM, 'The Prescribing Function in World Constitutive Process: How International Law Is Made' (1980) 6 Yale Studies in World Public Order 249.

McLachlan C, Shore L, and Weiniger M, *International Investment Arbitration: Substantive Principles* (2nd ed, OUP 2017).

McNair, Lord, *The Law of Treaties* (Clarendon Press 1961).

McWhinney E, 'Judicial Settlement of Disputes: Jurisdiction and Justiciability' (1990) 221 Recueil des Cours 9.

Mills A, 'Antinomies of Public and Private at the Foundations of International Investment Law and Arbitration' (2011) 14 JIEL 469.

Mills A, 'The Balancing (and Unbalancing?) Of Interests in International Investment Law and Arbitration' in Zachary Douglas, Joost Pauwelyn, and Jorge E Viñuales (eds), *The Foundations of International Investment Law: Bringing Theory into Practice* (OUP 2014).

Mills A, 'The Public–Private Dualities of International Investment Law and Arbitration' in Chester Brown and Kate Miles (eds), *Evolution in Investment Treaty Law and Arbitration* (CUP 2011).

Mitrev Penusliski I, 'A Dispute Systems Design Diagnosis of ICSID' in Michael Waibel and others (eds), *The Backlash Against Investment Arbitration* (Kluwer 2010).

Mohtashami R and El-Hosseny F, 'State-Owned Enterprises as Claimants before ICSID: Is the Broches Test on the Ebb?' (2016) 3 BCDR Int'l Arb Rev 371.

Moloo R and Khachaturian A, 'The Compliance with the Law Requirement in International Investment Law' (2011) 34 Fordham Int'l LJ 1473.

Mortenson JD, 'The Meaning of "Investment": ICSID's Travaux and the Domain of International Investment Law' (2010) 51 Harvard Int'l LJ 257.

Mosler H, 'Political and Justiciable Legal Disputes: Revival of an Old Controversy?' in Bin Cheng and ED Brown (eds), *Contemporary Problems of International Law: Essays in Honour of Georg Schwarzenberger on His Eightieth Birthday* (Stevens & Sons 1988).

Mullen S and Whitsitt E, 'ICSID and Legislative Consent to Arbitrate: Questions of Applicable Law' (2017) 32 ICSID Rev-FILJ 92.

Nash Leich M, 'Contemporary Practice of the United States Relating to International Law' (1985) 79 AJIL 431.

Neuman GL, 'Import, Export, and Regional Consent in the Inter-American Court of Human Rights' (2008) 19 EJIL 101.

Newcombe A and Paradell L, *Law and Practice of Investment Treaties: Standards of Treatment* (Kluwer 2009).

Newcombe A, 'Investor Misconduct: Jurisdiction, Admissibility or Merits?' in Chester Brown and Kate Miles (eds), *Evolution in Investment Treaty Law and Arbitration* (CUP 2011).

Nolan MD and Sourgens FG, 'Limits of Consent – Arbitration Without Privity and Beyond' in MÁ Fernández-Ballesteros and David Arias (eds), *Liber Amicorum Bernardo Cremades* (La Ley 2010).

Norton PM, 'The Role of Precedent in the Development of International Investment Law' (2018) 33 ICSID Rev-FILJ 280.

Obadia E and Nitschke F, 'Institutional Arbitration and the Role of the Secretariat' in Chiara Giorgetti (ed), *Litigating International Investment Disputes: A Practitioner's Guide* (Brill 2014).

Obersteiner T, '"In Accordance with Domestic Law" Clauses: How International Investment Tribunals Deal with Allegations of Unlawful Conduct of Investors' (2014) 31 J Int'l Arb 265.

Orakhelashvili A, 'The Concept of International Judicial Jurisdiction: A Reappraisal' (2003) 3 LPICT 501.

Ortino F, 'Legal Reasoning of International Investment Tribunals: A Typology of Egregious Failures' (2012) 3 JIDS 31.

Oxman BH, 'Complementary Agreements and Compulsory Jurisdiction' (2001) 95 AJIL 277.

Paine J, 'International Adjudication as a Global Public Good?' (2018) 29 EJIL 1223.

Palestini L, 'Forget About Mavrommatis and Judicial Economy: The Alleged Absence of a Dispute in the Cases Concerning the Obligations to Negotiate the Cessation of the Nuclear Arms Race and Nuclear Disarmament' (2017) 8 JIDS 557.

Palevičienė S, 'Consent to Arbitration and the Legacy of the *SPP v. Egypt* Case' (2014) 7 Baltic J Law & Politics 149.

Palmer VV, *The Paths to Privity: A History of Third Party Beneficiary Contracts at English Law* (Austin & Winfield 1992).

Paparinskis M, 'MFN Clauses and International Dispute Settlement: Moving beyond *Maffezini* and *Plama*?' (2011) 26 ICSID Rev-FILJ 14.

Park WW, 'Arbitrator Integrity' in Michael Waibel and others (eds), *The Backlash against Investment Arbitration* (Kluwer 2010).

Parlett K, 'Claims under Customary International Law in ICSID Arbitration' (2016) 31 ICSID Rev-FILJ 434.

Paulsson J, 'Arbitration Without Privity' (1995) 10 ICSID Rev-FILJ 232.

Paulsson J, 'Jurisdiction and Admissibility' in Gerald Aksen (ed), *Global Reflections on International Law, Commerce and Dispute Resolution: Liber Amicorum in Honour of Robert Briner* (ICC 2005).

Paulsson J, 'The Tipping Point' in Meg Kinnear and others (eds), *Building International Investment Law: The First 50 Years of ICSID* (Kluwer 2016).

Pauwelyn J, 'Rational Design or Accidental Evolution? The Emergence of International Investment Law' in Zachary Douglas, Joost Pauwelyn, and Jorge E Viñuales (eds), *The Foundations of International Investment Law: Bringing Theory into Practice* (OUP 2014).

Pauwelyn J, 'The Rule of Law without the Rule of Lawyers? Why Investment Arbitrators Are from Mars, Trade Adjudicators from Venus' (2015) 109 AJIL 761.

Pellet A, 'The Case Law of the ICJ in Investment Arbitration' (2013) 28 ICSID Rev-FILJ 223.

Pérez Aznar F, 'Local Litigation Requirements in International Investment Agreements: Their Characteristics and Potential in Times of Reform in Latin America' (2016) 17 JWIT 536.

Peterson LE, 'Venezuela Sees a New BIT Claim – By Another Oil Services Provider That Suffered Expropriation in 2009' (*Investment Arbitration Reporter*, 20 December 2016) <www.iareporter.com/articles/venezuela-sees-a-new-bit-claim/> accessed 15 October 2018.

Pinsolle P, 'Jurisdictional Review of ICSID Awards' (2004) 5 JWIT 613.

Polasek M, 'The Threshold for Registration of a Request for Arbitration under the ICSID Convention' (2011) 5 Disp Resol Int'l 177.

Polkinghorne M and Volkmer S-M, 'The Legality Requirement in Investment Arbitration' in Yas Banifatemi (ed), *Jurisdiction in Investment Treaty Arbitration* (Juris 2018).

Potestà M, 'The Interpretation of Consent to ICSID Arbitration Contained in Domestic Investment Laws' (2011) 27 Arb Int'l 149.

Protopsaltis PM, 'The Challenge of the Barcelona Traction Hypothesis: Barcelona Traction Clauses and Denial of Benefits Clauses in BITs and IIAs' (2010) 11 JWIT 561.

Proulx V-J, 'The World Court's Jurisdictional Formalism and Its Lost Market Share: The Marshall Islands Decisions and the Quest for a Suitable Dispute Settlement Forum for Multilateral Disputes' (2017) 30 Leiden JIL 925.

Puig S and Brown C, 'The Secretary-General's Power to Refuse to Register a Request for Arbitration under the ICSID Convention' (2012) 27 ICSID Rev-FILJ 172.

Puig S, 'No Right Without a Remedy: Foundations of Investor-State Arbitration' (2014) 35 Univ Penn J Int'l L 829.

Puig S, 'Social Capital in the Arbitration Market' (2014) 25 EJIL 387.

Radi Y, 'The Application of the Most-Favoured-Nation Clause to the Dispute Settlement Provisions of Bilateral Investment Treaties: Domesticating the "Trojan Horse"' (2007) 18 EJIL 757.

Radović R, 'Arbitral Jurisdictional Regulation in Investment Treaty Arbitration and Domestic Courts' (2021) JIDS (forthcoming).

Radović R, 'Between Rights and Remedies: The Access to Investment Treaty Arbitration as a Substantive Right of Foreign Investors' (2019) 10 JIDS 42.

Radović R, 'Inherently Unneutral Investment Treaty Arbitration: The Formation of Decisive Arguments in Jurisdictional Determinations' (2018) 2018 J Disp Resol 143.

Radović R, 'Problematizing *Abaclat's* Mass Claims Investment Arbitration Using Domestic Class Actions' (2017) 4 McGill J Disp Resol 1.

Radović R, 'Screening Powers in Investment Arbitration: Questions of Legal Change and Legitimacy' in Freya Baetens (ed), *Legitimacy of Unseen Actors in International Adjudication* (CUP 2019).

Reed L, 'The *De Facto* Precedent Regime in Investment Arbitration: A Case for Proactive Case Management' (2010) 25 ICSID Rev-FILJ 95.

Reinisch A, 'How Narrow Are Narrow Dispute Settlement Clauses in Investment Treaties?' (2011) 2 JIDS 115.

Reinisch A, 'Jurisdiction and Admissibility in International Investment Law' (2017) 16 LPICT 21.

Reinisch A, 'The Role of Precedent in ICSID Arbitration' in Christian Klausegger and others (eds), *Austrian Arbitration Yearbook 2008* (Beck/Stämpfli/Manz 2008).

Reisman WM, 'Canute Confronts the Tide: States versus Tribunals and the Evolution of the Minimum Standard in Customary International Law' (2015) 30 ICSID Rev-FILJ 616.

Reisman WM, 'International Lawmaking: A Process of Communication' in Martti Koskenniemi (ed), *Sources of International Law* (Ashgate 2000).

Reisman WM, 'The Breakdown of the Control Mechanism in ICSID Arbitration' (1989) 1989 Duke LJ 739.

Roberts A, 'Clash of Paradigms: Actors and Analogies Shaping the Investment Treaty System' (2013) 107 AJIL 45.

Roberts A, 'Power and Persuasion in Investment Treaty Interpretation: The Dual Role of States' (2010) 104 AJIL 179.

Roberts A, 'Triangular Treaties: The Extent and Limits of Investment Treaty Rights' (2015) 56 Harvard Int'l LJ 353.

Roe T, 'Illegality and Jurisdiction in Investment Arbitration' (2016) 2 Turkish Commercial L Rev 17.

Rogers CA, 'The Politics of International Investment Arbitrators' (2013) 12 Santa Clara J Int'l L 223.

Romano CP, 'The Shift From the Consensual to the Compulsory Paradigm in International Adjudication: Elements for a Theory of Consent' (2007) 39 Int'l L & Politics 791.

Romano CP, Alter KJ, and Shany Y, 'Mapping International Adjudicative Bodies, the Issues, and Players' in Cesare PR Romano, Karen J Alter, and Yuval Shany (eds), *The Oxford Handbook of International Adjudication* (OUP 2014).

Rosenfeld F, 'Arbitral Praeliminaria – Reflections on the Distinction between Admissibility and Jurisdiction after *BG v. Argentina*' (2016) 29 Leiden JIL 137.

Rosenfeld F, '*Iura Novit Curia* in International Law' in Franco Ferrari and Giuditta Cordero-Moss (eds), Iura Novit Curia *in International Arbitration* (Juris 2018).

Rosentreter D, *Article 31(3)(c) of the Vienna Convention on the Law of Treaties and the Principle of Systemic Integration in International Investment Law and Arbitration* (Nomos 2015).

Salacuse JW, 'The Emerging Global Regime for Investment' (2010) 51 Harvard Int'l LJ 427.

Salles LE, 'Jurisdiction' in William A Schabas and Shannonbrooke Murphy (eds), *Research Handbook on International Courts and Tribunals* (Edward Elgar 2017).

Sands P, 'Reflections on International Judicialization' (2016) 27 EJIL 885.

Santacroce FG, 'Navigating the Troubled Waters between Jurisdiction and Admissibility: An Analysis of Which Law Should Govern Characterization of Preliminary Issues in International Arbitration' (2017) 33 Arb Int'l 539.

Sattorova M, 'Defining Investment Under the ICSID Convention and BITs: Of Ordinary Meaning, Telos, and Beyond' (2012) 2 Asian JIL 267.

Schill S and Briese R, ' "If the State Considers": Self-Judging Clauses in International Dispute Settlement' in Armin von Bogdandy and Rüdiger Wolfrum (eds), *Max Planck Yearbook of United Nations Law*, vol 13 (Martinus Nijhoff 2009).

Schill SW and Djanic V, 'International Investment Law and Community Interests' in Eyal Benvenisti and Georg Nolte (eds), *Community Interests Across International Law* (OUP 2018).

Schill SW, 'Crafting the International Economic Order: The Public Function of Investment Treaty Arbitration and Its Significance for the Role of the Arbitrator' (2010) 23 Leiden JIL 401.

Schill SW, 'Enabling Private Ordering: Function, Scope and Effect of Umbrella Clauses in International Investment Treaties' (2009) 18 Minn J Int'l L 1.

Schill SW, 'From Sources to Discourse: Investment Treaty Jurisprudence as the New Custom?' (2011) <www.biicl.org/files/5630_stephan_schill.pdf> accessed 15 July 2018.

Schill SW, 'Illegal Investments in Investment Treaty Arbitration' (2012) 11 LPICT 281.

Schill SW, 'International Investment Law and Comparative Public Law—An Introduction' in Stephan W Schill (ed), *International Investment Law and Comparative Public Law* (OUP 2010).

Schill SW, 'Private Enforcement of International Investment Law: Why We Need Investor Standing in BIT Dispute Settlement' in Michael Waibel and others (eds), *The Backlash Against Investment Arbitration* (Kluwer 2010).

Schill SW, 'Sources of International Investment Law: Multilateralization, Arbitral Precedent, Comparativism, Soft Law' in Samantha Besson and Jean D'Aspremont (eds), *The Oxford Handbook on the Sources of International Law* (OUP 2017).

Schill SW, 'System-Building in Investment Treaty Arbitration and Lawmaking' in Armin von Bogdandy and Ingo Venzke (eds), *International Judicial Lawmaking: On Public Authority and Democratic Legitimation in Global Governance* (Springer 2012).

Schill SW, 'The Jurisprudence of Investment Treaty Tribunals: Between Public Good and Common Concern' in Tullio Treves, Francesco Seatzu, and Seline Trevisanut (eds), *Foreign Investment, International Law and Common Concerns* (Routledge 2014).

Schill SW, 'W(h)Ither Fragmentation? On the Literature and Sociology of International Investment Law' (2011) 22 EJIL 875.

Schill SW, *The Multilateralization of International Investment Law* (CUP 2009).

Schlag P, 'Rules and Standards' (1985) 33 UCLA L Rev 379.

Schlemmer EC, 'Investment, Investor, Nationality, and Shareholders' in Peter Muchlinski, Federico Ortino, and Christoph Schreuer (eds), *The Oxford Handbook of International Investment Law* (OUP 2008).

Schmitt C, *Political Theology: Four Chapters on the Concept of Sovereignty* (University of Chicago Press 2005).

Schreuer C and Weiniger M, 'A Doctrine of Precedent?' in Peter Muchlinski, Federico Ortino, and Christoph Schreuer (eds), *The Oxford Handbook of International Investment Law* (OUP 2008).

Schreuer C, 'Belated Jurisdictional Objections in ICSID Arbitration' (2010) 7(1) TDM <www.transnational-dispute-management.com/article.asp?key=1533> accessed 30 October 2018.

Schreuer C, 'Calvo's Grandchildren: The Return of Local Remedies in Investment Arbitration' (2005) 4 LPICT 1.

Schreuer C, 'Commentary on the ICSID Convention' (1996) 11 ICSID Rev-FILJ 318.

Schreuer C, 'Consent to Arbitration' in Peter Muchlinski, Federico Ortino, and Christoph Schreuer (eds), *The Oxford Handbook of International Investment Law* (OUP 2008).

Schreuer C, 'From ICSID Annulment to Appeal Half Way Down the Slippery Slope' (2011) 10 LPICT 211.

Schreuer C, 'Jurisdiction and Applicable Law in Investment Treaty Arbitration' (2014) 1 McGill J Disp Resol 1.

Schreuer C, 'Travelling the BIT Route: Of Waiting Periods, Umbrella Clauses and Forks in the Road' (2004) 5 JWIT 231.

Schreuer CH and others, *The ICSID Convention: A Commentary* (2nd ed, CUP 2009).

Schultz T, 'Against Consistency in Investment Arbitration' in Zachary Douglas, Joost Pauwelyn, and Jorge E Viñuales (eds), *The Foundations of International Investment Law: Bringing Theory into Practice* (OUP 2014).

Schwebel SM, 'Does the Consent of the Contracting Parties Govern the Requirement of an "Investment" as Specified in Article 25 of the ICSID Convention?' in Yas Banifatemi (ed), *Jurisdiction in Investment Treaty Arbitration* (Juris 2018).

Scobbie IG, 'The Theorist as Judge: Hersch Lauterpacht's Concept of the International Judicial Function' (1997) 8 EJIL 264.

Shahabuddeen M, *Precedent in the World Court* (CUP 1996).

Shany Y, 'Jurisdiction and Admissibility' in Cesare PR Romano, Karen J Alter, and Yuval Shany (eds), *The Oxford Handbook of International Adjudication* (OUP 2014).

Shany Y, *Assessing the Effectiveness of International Courts* (OUP 2014).

Shany Y, *Questions of Jurisdiction and Admissibility before International Courts* (CUP 2016).

Shihata IF, 'Towards a Greater Depoliticization of Investment Disputes: The Roles of ICSID and MIGA' (1986) 1 ICSID Rev-FILJ 1.

Shihata IF, *The Power of the International Court to Determine Its Own Jurisdiction: Compétence de la Compétence* (Springer 1965).

Siwy A, 'Contract Claims and Treaty Claims' in Crina Baltag (ed), *ICSID Convention after 50 Years: Unsettled Issues* (Kluwer Law International 2017).

Smit Duijzentkunst BL and Dawkins SL, 'Arbitrary Peace? Consent Management in International Arbitration' (2015) 26 EJIL 139.

Söderlund C and Burova E, 'Is There Such a Thing as Admissibility in Investment Arbitration?' (2018) 33 ICSID Rev-FILJ 525.

Sornarajah M, 'A Coming Crisis: Expansionary Trends in Investment Treaty Arbitration' in Karl P Sauvant (ed), *Appeals Mechanism in International Investment Disputes* (OUP 2008).

Sornarajah M, 'Power and Justice in Foreign Investment Arbitration' (1997) 14 J Int'l Arb 103.

Sornarajah M, 'Toward Normlessness: The Ravage and Retreat of Neo-Liberalism in International Investment Law' in Karl P Sauvant (ed), *Yearbook on International Investment Law & Policy 2009-2010* (OUP 2010).

Sornarajah M, *Resistance and Change in the International Law on Foreign Investment* (CUP 2015).

Sornarajah M, *The International Law on Foreign Investment* (3rd ed, CUP 2010).

Sornarajah M, *The International Law on Foreign Investment* (CUP 1994).

Sourgens FG, 'By Equal Contest of Arms: Jurisdictional Proof in Investor-State Arbitrations' (2013) 38 North Carolina J Int'l L & Com Reg 875.

Sourgens FG, 'Law's Laboratory: Developing International Law on Investment Protection as Common Law' (2014) 34 Northwestern J Int'l L & Business 181.

Sourgens FG, *A Nascent Common Law: The Process of Decisionmaking in International Legal Disputes between States and Foreign Investors* (Brill Nijhoff 2015).

Spiermann O, *International Legal Argument in the Permanent Court of International Justice: The Rise of the International Judiciary* (CUP 2005).

Steinbach A, 'The Trend towards Non-Consensualism in Public International Law: A (Behavioural) Law and Economics Perspective' (2016) 27 EJIL 643.

Steiner H, 'Working Rights' in Matthew H Kramer, NE Simmonds, and Hillel Steiner, *A Debate Over Rights: Philosophical Enquiries* (OUP 1998).

Steingruber AM, '*Abaclat and Others v Argentine Republic:* Consent in Large-Scale Arbitration Proceedings' (2012) 27 ICSID Rev-FILJ 237.

Steingruber AM, 'Some Remarks on Veijo Heiskanen's Note "*Ménage à Trois?* Jurisdiction, Admissibility and Competence in Investment Treaty Arbitration"' (2014) 29 ICSID Rev-FILJ 675.

Steingruber AM, *Consent in International Arbitration* (OUP 2012).

Stern B, 'ICSID Arbitration and the State's Increasingly Remote Consent: Apropos the Maffezini Case' in Steve Charnovitz, Debra P Steger, and Peter Van den Bossche (eds), *Law in the Service of Human Dignity: Essays in Honour of Florentino Feliciano* (CUP 2005).

Stern B, 'Un coup d'arrêt à la marginalisation du consentement dans l'arbitrage international (A propos de l'arrêt de la Cour d'appel de Paris du 1er juin 1999)' (2000) 2000 Revue de l'Arbitrage 403.

Stone Sweet A and Grisel F, *The Evolution of International Arbitration: Judicialization, Governance, Legitimacy* (OUP 2017).

Stone Sweet A, Yunsuck Chung M, and Saltzman A, 'Arbitral Lawmaking and State Power: An Empirical Analysis of Investor–State Arbitration' (2017) 8 JIDS 579.

Strong S, 'Mass Procedures in *Abaclat v. Argentine Republic* – Are They Consistent with the International Investment Regime?' in Marianne Roth and Michael Geistlinger (eds), *Yearbook on International Arbitration*, vol 3 (NWV Verlag 2013).

Swarabowicz M, 'Identity of Claims in Investment Arbitration: A Plea for Unity of the Legal System' (2017) 8 JIDS 280.

Tanzi AM, 'On Judicial Autonomy and the Autonomy of the Parties in International Adjudication, with Special Regard to Investment Arbitration and ICSID Annulment Proceedings' (2020) 33 Leiden JIL 57.

Ten Cate IM, 'The Costs of Consistency: Precedent in Investment Treaty Arbitration' (2013) 51 Columbia J Transnat'l L 418.

Thirlway H, *The Sources of International Law* (OUP 2014).

Timmer LJ, 'Manifest Excess of Powers as a Ground for the Annulment of ICSID Awards' (2013) 14 JWIT 775.

Titi C, 'The Arbitrator as a Lawmaker: Jurisgenerative Processes in Investment Arbitration' (2013) 14 JWIT 829.

Tomuschat C, 'What Is "General International Law"?' in *Guerra y Paz: 1945-2009. Obra homenaje al Dr. Santiago Torres Bernárdez* (Universidad Del País Vasco 2010).

Toral M and Schultz T, 'The State, a Perpetual Respondent in Investment Arbitration? Some Unorthodox Considerations' in Michael Waibel and others (eds), *The Backlash Against Investment Arbitration* (Kluwer 2010).

Trachtman JP, 'The Domain of WTO Dispute Resolution' (1999) 40 Harvard Int'l LJ 333.

Triantafilou EE, 'Contemporaneity and Evolutive Interpretation under the Vienna Convention on the Law of Treaties' (2017) 32 ICSID Rev-FILJ 138.

Triantafilou EE, 'Contemporaneity and Its Limits in Treaty Interpretation' in David D Caron and others (eds), *Practising Virtue: Inside International Arbitration* (OUP 2015).

Vadi V, *Analogies in International Investment Law and Arbitration* (CUP 2016).

Van Aaken A, 'Control Mechanisms in International Investment Law' in Zachary Douglas, Joost Pauwelyn, and Jorge E Viñuales (eds), *The Foundations of International Investment Law: Bringing Theory into Practice* (OUP 2014).

Van Aaken A, 'International Investment Law Between Commitment and Flexibility: A Contract Theory Analysis' (2009) 12 JIEL 507.

Van Harten G and Loughlin M, 'Investment Treaty Arbitration as a Species of Global Administrative Law' (2006) 17 EJIL 121.

Van Harten G, 'Arbitrator Behaviour in Asymmetrical Adjudication (Part Two): An Examination of Hypotheses of Bias in Investment Treaty Arbitration' (2016) 53 Osgoode Hall LJ 540.

Van Harten G, 'Arbitrator Behaviour in Asymmetrical Adjudication: An Empirical Study of Investment Treaty Arbitration' (2012) 50 Osgoode Hall LJ 211.

Van Harten G, 'Fairness and Independence in Investment Arbitration: A Critique of "Development and Outcomes of Investment Treaty Arbitration"' *ITN Quarterly* (December 2010) 7.

Van Harten G, 'Five Justifications for Investment Treaties: A Critical Discussion' (2010) 2 Trade, Law and Development 19.

Van Harten G, 'Leaders in the Expansive and Restrictive Interpretation of Investment Treaties: A Descriptive Study of ISDS Awards to 2010' (2018) 29 EJIL 507.

Van Harten G, 'Perceived Bias in Investment Treaty Arbitration' in Michael Waibel and others (eds), *The Backlash Against Investment Arbitration* (Kluwer 2010).

Van Harten G, 'The Public-Private Distinction in the International Arbitration of Individual Claims against the State' (2007) 56 Int'l & Comp LQ 371.

Van Harten G, *Investment Treaty Arbitration and Public Law* (OUP 2007).

Van Houtte H and McAsey B, '*Abaclat and Others v Argentine Republic:* ICSID, the BIT and Mass Claims' (2012) 27 ICSID Rev-FILJ 231.

Vandevelde KJ, 'A Brief History of International Investment Agreements' (2005) 12 UC Davis J Int'l L & Policy 157.

Vandevelde KJ, *Bilateral Investment Treaties: History, Policy, and Interpretation* (OUP 2010).

Veenstra-Kjos HE, 'Counter-Claims by Host States in Investment Dispute Arbitration "without Privity"' in Philippe Kahn and Thomas W Wälde (eds), *New Aspects of International Investment Law* (Martinus Nijhoff 2007).

Venzke I, 'Judicial Authority and Styles of Reasoning: Self-Presentation between Legalism and Deliberation' in Joanna Jemielniak, Laura Nielsen, and Henrik Palmer Olsen (eds), *Establishing Judicial Authority in International Economic Law* (CUP 2016).

Venzke I, *How Interpretation Makes International Law: On Semantic Change and Normative Twists* (OUP 2012).

Vesel S, 'Clearing a Path Through a Tangled Jurisprudence: Most-Favored-Nation Clauses and Dispute Settlement Provisions in Bilateral Investment Treaties' (2007) 32 Yale J Int'l L 125.

Viñuales JE, 'Investor Diligence in Investment Arbitration: Sources and Arguments' (2017) 32 ICSID Rev-FILJ 346.

Viñuales JE, 'Sovereignty in Foreign Investment Law' in Zachary Douglas, Joost Pauwelyn, and Jorge E Viñuales (eds), *International Investment Law: Bringing Theory into Practice* (OUP 2014).

Von Bogdandy A and Venzke I (eds), *International Judicial Lawmaking: On Public Authority and Democratic Legitimation in Global Governance* (Springer 2012).

Wagner M, 'Regulatory Space in International Trade Law and International Investment Law' (2014) 36 Univ Penn JIL 1.

Waibel M, 'International Investment Law and Treaty Interpretation' in Rainer Hofmann and Christian J Tams (eds), *International Investment Law and General International Law: From Clinical Isolation to Systemic Integration?* (Nomos 2011).

Waibel M, 'Investment Arbitration: Jurisdiction and Admissibility' in Marc Bungenberg and others (eds), *International Investment Law: A Handbook* (CH Beck/Hart/Nomos 2015).

Waibel M, 'Putting the MFN Genie Back in the Bottle' (2018) 112 AJIL 60.

Wälde T, 'Confidential Awards as Precedent in Arbitration: Dynamics and Implication of Award Publication' in Yas Banifatemi (ed), *Precedent in International Arbitration* (Juris 2008).

Wälde TW, 'Interpreting Investment Treaties: Experiences and Examples' in Christina Binder and others (eds), *International Investment Law for the 21st Century: Essays in Honour of Christoph Schreuer* (OUP 2009).

Wälde TW, 'Procedural Challenges in Investment Arbitration under the Shadow of the Dual Role of the State: Asymmetries and Tribunals' Duty to Ensure, Pro-Actively, the Equality of Arms' (2010) 26 Arb Int'l 3.

Wälde TW, 'The "Umbrella" Clause in Investment Arbitration: A Comment on Original Intentions and Recent Cases' (2005) 6 JWIT 183.

Wälde TW, 'The Specific Nature of Investment Arbitration' in Philippe Kahn and Thomas W Wälde (eds), *New Aspects of International Investment Law* (Martinus Nijhoff 2007).

Wang G, 'Consent in Investor–State Arbitration: A Critical Analysis' (2014) 13 Chinese JIL 335.

Wass J, 'Jurisdiction by Estoppel and Acquiescence in International Courts and Tribunals' (2015) 86 British Yrbk Int'l L 155.

Watson D and Brebner T, 'Nationality Planning and Abuse of Process: A Coherent Framework' (2018) 33 ICSID Rev-FILJ 302.

Weeramantry JR, *Treaty Interpretation in Investment Arbitration* (OUP 2012).

Weiniger M, 'Jurisdiction Challenges in BIT Arbitrations – Do You Read a BIT by Reading a BIT or by Reading into a BIT?' in Loukas A Mistelis and Julian DM Lew (eds), *Pervasive Problems in International Arbitration* (Kluwer Law International 2006).

Werner J, 'The Trade Explosion and Some Likely Effects on International Arbitration' (1997) 14 J Int'l Arb 5.

Widdows K, 'What Is an Agreement in International Law?' (1980) 50 British Yrbk Int'l L 117.

Williams QC DA, 'Jurisdiction and Admissibility' in Peter Muchlinski, Federico Ortino, and Christoph Schreuer (eds), *The Oxford Handbook of International Investment Law* (OUP 2008).

Wittgenstein L, *Philosophical Investigations* (GEM Anscombe tr, 3rd edn, Basil Blackwell 1967).

Wolfrum R, 'Legitimacy of International Law from a Legal Perspective: Some Introductory Considerations' in Rüdiger Wolfrum and Volker Röben (eds), *Legitimacy in International Law* (Springer 2008).

Wong J, 'The Application of Most-Favored-Nation Clauses to Dispute Resolution Provisions in Bilateral Investment Treaties' (2008) 3 AJWH 171.

Wordsworth S and Brown C, 'A Re-Run of *Siemens, Wintershall* and *Hochtief* on Most-Favoured-Nation Clauses: *Daimler Financial Services AG v Argentine Republic*' (2015) 30 ICSID Rev-FILJ 365.

Yotova R, 'Systemic Integration: An Instrument for Reasserting the State's Control in Investment Arbitration?' in Andreas Kulick (ed), *Reassertion of Control over the Investment Treaty Regime* (CUP 2016).

Zeiler G, 'Jurisdiction, Competence, and Admissibility of Claims in ICSID Arbitration Proceedings' in Christina Binder and others (eds), *International Investment Law for the 21st Century: Essays in Honour of Christoph Schreuer* (OUP 2009).

Table of Cases

ICJ/PCIJ

Aegean Sea Continental Shelf (Greece v Turkey) (Judgment) (1978) ICJ Rep 3
Alleged Violations of Sovereign Rights and Maritime Spaces in the Caribbean Sea (Nicaragua v Colombia) (Preliminary Objections) (2016) ICJ Rep
Ambatielos (Greece v United Kingdom) (Merits: Obligation to Arbitrate) (1953) ICJ Rep 10
Anglo-Iranian Oil Co (UK v Iran) (Individual Opinion of President McNair) (1952) ICJ Rep 93
Application of the Convention on the Prevention and Punishment of the Crime of Genocide (Bosnia and Herzegovina v Serbia and Montenegro) (Judgment) (2007) ICJ Rep 43
Application of the Convention on the Prevention and Punishment of the Crime of Genocide (Bosnia and Herzegovina v Yugoslavia) (Preliminary Objections) (1996) ICJ Rep 595
Application of the Convention on the Prevention and Punishment of the Crime of Genocide (Croatia v Serbia) (Judgment) (2015) ICJ Rep 3
Application of the Convention on the Prevention and Punishment of the Crime of Genocide (Croatia v Serbia) (Preliminary Objections) (2008) ICJ Rep 412
Application of the International Convention on the Elimination of All Forms of Racial Discrimination (Georgia v Russian Federation) (Preliminary Objections) (Judgment) (2011) ICJ Rep 70
Arbitral Award of 31 July 1989 (Guinea-Bissau v Senegal) (Judgment) (1991) ICJ Rep 53
Armed Activities on the Territory of the Congo (New Application: 2002) (Democratic Republic of the Congo v Rwanda) (Jurisdiction and Admissibility) (Judgment) (2006) ICJ Rep 6
Border and Transborder Armed Actions (Nicaragua v Honduras) (Jurisdiction and Admissibility) (1988) ICJ Rep 69
Case of the SS 'Wimbledon' (UK, France, Italy, Japan, and Poland intervening v Germany) (Judgment) (1923) PCIJ Ser A—No 1, 15
Certain Norwegian Loans (France v Norway) (Judgment) (1957) ICJ Rep 9
Certain Norwegian Loans (France v Norway) (Separate Opinion of Sir Hersch Lauterpacht) (1957) ICJ Rep 9, 34
Continental Shelf (Libyan Arab Jamahiriya/Malta) (Application to Intervene) (1984) ICJ Rep 3

Corfu Channel (United Kingdom of Great Britain and Northern Ireland v Albania) (Preliminary Objection) (Dissenting Opinion by Judge ad hoc Daxner) (1948) ICJ Rep 15

Corfu Channel (United Kingdom of Great Britain and Northern Ireland v Albania) (Preliminary Objection) (Judgment) (1948) ICJ Rep 15

Customs Régime Between Germany and Austria (Protocol of March 19th, 1931) (Advisory Opinion) (1931) PCIJ Ser A/B—No 41, 37

Customs Régime Between Germany and Austria (Protocol of March 19th, 1931) (Dissenting Opinion of M Adatci, Mr Kellogg, Baron Rolin-Jaequemyns, Sir Cecil Hurst, M Schücking, Jonkheer van Eysinga, and M Wang) (1931) PCIJ Ser A/B—No 41, 74

Delimitation of the Maritime Boundary in the Gulf of Maine Area (Canada/United States of America) (Judgment) (1984) ICJ Rep 246

Dispute regarding Navigational and Related Rights (Costa Rica v Nicaragua) (Judgment) (2009) ICJ Rep 213

East Timor (Portugal v Australia) (Judgment) (1995) ICJ Rep 90

Factory at Chorzów (Germany v Poland) (Claim for Indemnity) (Jurisdiction) (1927) PCIJ Ser A—No 9, 4

Fisheries Jurisdiction (Germany v Iceland) (Merits) (1974) ICJ Rep 175

Fisheries Jurisdiction (Spain v Canada) (Jurisdiction) (1998) ICJ Rep 432

Fisheries Jurisdiction (United Kingdom v Iceland) (Merits) (1974) ICJ Rep 3

Haya de la Torre (Colombia v Peru) (Judgment) (1951) ICJ Rep 71

Interhandel (Switzerland v United States of America) (Preliminary Objections) (Dissenting Opinion of Sir Hersch Lauterpacht) (1959) ICJ Rep 6, 95

Interhandel (Switzerland v United States of America) (Preliminary Objections) (1959) ICJ Rep 6

Interpretation of Peace Treaties with Bulgaria, Hungary and Romania (First Phase) (Advisory Opinion) (1950) ICJ Rep 65

Interpretation of the Greco-Turkish Agreement of 1 December 1926 (Final Protocol, Article IV) (Advisory Opinion) (1928) PCIJ Ser B—No 16, 4

Jurisdictional Immunities of the State (Germany v Italy: Greece intervening) (Dissenting Opinion of Judge Cançado Trindade) (2012) ICJ Rep 179

LaGrand (Germany v US) (Judgment) (2001) ICJ Rep 466

Land and Maritime Boundary between Cameroon and Nigeria (Cameroon v Nigeria: Equatorial Guinea intervening) (Preliminary Objections) (1998) ICJ Rep 275

Legal Consequences of the Construction of a Wall in the Occupied Palestinian Territory (Advisory Opinion) (2004) ICJ Rep 136

Legality of the Threat or Use of Nuclear Weapons (Advisory Opinion) (1996) ICJ Rep 226

TABLE OF CASES 251

Legality of Use of Force (Serbia and Montenegro v Belgium) (Preliminary Objections) (Separate Opinion of Judge ad hoc Kreća) (2004) ICJ Rep 371

Legality of Use of Force (Yugoslavia v Belgium) (Provisional Measures) (1999) ICJ Rep 124

Maritime Delimitation and Territorial Questions (Qatar v Bahrain) (Jurisdiction and Admissibility) (1994) ICJ Rep 112

Mavrommatis Palestine Concessions (Greece v UK) (Judgment) (1924) PCIJ Ser A—No 2, 6

Military and Paramilitary Activities in and against Nicaragua (Nicaragua v United States of America) (Jurisdiction and Admissibility) (1984) ICJ Rep 392

Military and Paramilitary Activities in and against Nicaragua (Nicaragua v United States of America) (Merits) (1986) ICJ Rep 14

Monetary Gold Removed from Rome in 1943 (Italy v France, UK, and USA) (Preliminary Question) (1954) ICJ Rep 19

Nottebohm Case (Liechtenstein v Guatemala) (Preliminary Objection) (1953) ICJ Rep 111

Nuclear Tests (Australia v France) (Judgment) (1974) ICJ Rep 253

Nuclear Tests (New Zealand v France) (Judgment) (1974) ICJ Rep 457

Obligations concerning Negotiations relating to Cessation of the Nuclear Arms Race and to Nuclear Disarmament (Marshall Islands v United Kingdom) (Judgment) (2016) ICJ Rep

Oil Platforms (Islamic Republic of Iran v United States of America) (Preliminary Objection) (Separate Opinion of Judge Higgins) (1996) ICJ Rep 847

Reparation for Injuries Suffered in the Service of the United Nations (Advisory Opinion) (1949) ICJ Rep 174

Right of Passage over Indian Territory (Portugal v India) (Preliminary Objections) (1957) ICJ Rep 125

Rights of Minorities in Upper Silesia (Minority Schools) (Germany v Poland) (Judgment) (1928) PCIJ Ser A—No 15, 4

Rights of Nationals of the United States of America in Morocco (France v United States of America) (Judgment) (1952) ICJ Rep 176

Serbian Loans (France v The Kingdom of the Serbs, Croats, and Slovenes) (Judgment) (1929) PCIJ Ser A—No 20, 5

South West Africa Cases (Ethiopia v South Africa; Liberia v South Africa) (Preliminary Objections) (1962) ICJ Rep 319

Status of Eastern Carelia (Advisory Opinion) (1923) PCIJ Ser B—No 5, 7

The Case of the ss 'Lotus' (France v Turkey) (Judgment) (1927) PCIJ Ser A—No 10, 4

The Electricity Company of Sofia and Bulgaria (Belgium v Bulgaria) (Preliminary Objection) (Separate Opinion by M Anzilotti) (1939) PCIJ Ser A/B—No 77, 86

United States Diplomatic and Consular Staff in Tehran (United States of America v Iran) (Judgment) (1980) ICJ Rep 3

ICSID-Administered Arbitrations

AnY Ltd v Czech Republic, ICSID Case No UNCT/15/1, Award (29 June 2018)
AnY Ltd v Czech Republic, ICSID Case No UNCT/15/1, Decision on Jurisdiction (9 February 2017)
Abaclat and others v The Argentine Republic, ICSID Case No ARB/07/5, Decision on Jurisdiction and Admissibility (4 August 2011)
Abaclat and others v The Argentine Republic, ICSID Case No ARB/07/5, Dissenting Opinion of Georges Abi-Saab (4 August 2011)
ADC Affiliate Limited and ADC & ADMC Management Limited v The Republic of Hungary, ICSID Case No ARB/03/16, Award of the Tribunal (2 October 2006)
AES Corporation v The Argentine Republic, ICSID Case No ARB/02/17, Decision on Jurisdiction (26 April 2005)
Alex Genin, Eastern Credit Limited Inc, and AS Baltoil v The Republic of Estonia, ICSID Case No ARB/99/2, Award (25 June 2001)
Almasryia for Operating & Maintaining Touristic Construction Co LLC v State of Kuwait, ICSID Case No ARB/18/2, Award on the Respondent's Application under Rule 41(5) of the ICSID Arbitration Rules (1 November 2019)
Alpha Projektholding GmbH v Ukraine, ICSID Case No ARB/07/16, Award (8 November 2010)
Ambiente Ufficio SpA and others v The Argentine Republic, ICSID Case No ARB/08/9, Decision on Jurisdiction and Admissibility (8 February 2013)
Amco Asia Corp and others v The Republic of Indonesia, ICSID Case No ARB/81/1, Award on Jurisdiction (25 September 1983)
American Manufacturing & Trading Inc v Republic of Zaire, ICSID Case No ARB/93/1, Award (21 February 1997)
Ampal-American Israel Corp and others v Arab Republic of Egypt, ICSID Case No ARB/12/11, Decision on Jurisdiction (1 February 2016)
Ansung Housing Co Ltd v People's Republic of China, ICSID Case No ARB/14/25, Award (9 March 2017)
Apotex Inc v The Government of the United States of America, ICSID Case No UNCT/10/2, Award on Jurisdiction and Admissibility (14 June 2013)
Asian Agricultural Products Ltd v Republic of Sri Lanka, ICSID Case No ARB/87/3, Final Award (27 June 1990)
Azurix Corp v The Argentine Republic, ICSID Case No ARB/01/12, Award (14 July 2006)

TABLE OF CASES 253

Azurix Corp v The Argentine Republic, ICSID Case No ARB/01/12, Decision on Jurisdiction (8 December 2003)

Bayindir Insaat Turizm Ticaret Ve Sanayi AS v Islamic Republic of Pakistan, ICSID Case No ARB/03/29, Decision on Jurisdiction (14 November 2005)

Bayview Irrigation District and others v United Mexican States, ICSID Case No ARB(AF)/05/1, Award (19 June 2007)

Bear Creek Mining Corporation v Republic of Perú, ICSID Case No ARB/14/21, Award (30 November 2017)

Beijing Urban Construction Group Co Ltd v Republic of Yemen, ICSID Case No ARB/14/30, Decision on Jurisdiction (31 May 2017)

Biwater Gauff (Tanzania) Ltd v United Republic of Tanzania, ICSID Case No ARB/05/22, Award (24 July 2008)

Blusun SA, Jean-Pierre Lecorcier, and Michael Stein v Italian Republic, ICSID Case No ARB/14/3, Award (27 December 2016)

Bosh International Inc and B&P Ltd Foreign Investments Enterprise v Ukraine, ICSID Case No ARB/08/11, Award (25 October 2012)

Brandes Investment Partners LP v The Bolivarian Republic of Venezuela, ICSID Case No ARB/08/3, Award (2 August 2011)

Bridgestone Licensing Services Inc and Bridgestone Americas Inc v Republic of Panama, ICSID Case No ARB/16/34, Decision on Expedited Objections (13 December 2017)

Burlington Resources Inc v Republic of Ecuador, ICSID Case No ARB/08/5, Decision on Jurisdiction (2 June 2010)

Burlington Resources Inc v Republic of Ecuador, ICSID Case No ARB/08/5, Decision on Liability (14 December 2012)

Burlington Resources Inc v Republic of Ecuador, ICSID Case No ARB/08/5, Decision on Counterclaims (7 February 2017)

Cambodia Power Company v Kingdom of Cambodia and Electricité du Cambodge, ICSID Case No ARB/09/18, Decision on Jurisdiction (22 March 2011)

Capital Financial Holdings Luxembourg SA v Republic of Cameroon, ICSID Case No ARB/15/18, Award (22 June 2017)

Caratube International Oil Company LLP and Mr Devincci Salah Hourani v Republic of Kazakhstan, ICSID Case No ARB/13/13, Award (27 September 2017)

Casinos Austria International GmbH and Casinos Austria Aktiengesellschaft v Argentine Republic, ICSID Case No ARB/14/32, Decision on Jurisdiction (29 June 2018)

Cementownia 'Nowa Huta' SA v Republic of Turkey, ICSID Case No ARB(AF)/06/2, Award (17 September 2009)

CEMEX Caracas Investments BV and CEMEX Caracas II Investments BV v Bolivarian Republic of Venezuela, ICSID Case No ARB/08/15, Decision on Jurisdiction (30 December 2010)

Ceskoslovenska Obchodni Banka AS v The Slovak Republic, ICSID Case No ARB/97/4, Decision of the Tribunal on Objections to Jurisdiction (24 May 1999)

Champion Trading Company and others v Arab Republic of Egypt, ICSID Case No ARB/02/9, Decision on Jurisdiction (21 October 2003)

Churchill Mining Plc v Republic of Indonesia, ICSID Case No ARB/12/14, Decision on Jurisdiction (24 February 2014)

CMC Muratori Cementisti CMC Di Ravenna SOC Coop and others v Republic of Mozambique, ICSID Case No ARB/17/23, Award (24 October 2019)

CMS Gas Transmission Company v Argentine Republic, ICSID Case No ARB/01/8, Decision of the Ad Hoc Committee on the Application for Annulment of the Argentine Republic (25 September 2007)

CMS Gas Transmission Company v The Argentine Republic, ICSID Case No ARB/01/8, Award (12 May 2005)

CMS Gas Transmission Company v The Republic of Argentina, ICSID Case No ARB/01/8, Decision of the Tribunal on Objections to Jurisdiction (17 July 2003)

Compañiá de Aguas del Aconquija SA and Vivendi Universal v Argentine Republic, ICSID Case No ARB/97/3, Decision on Annulment (3 July 2002)

Consorzio Groupement LESI-DIPENTA v People's Democratic Republic of Algeria, ICSID Case No ARB/03/08, Award (10 January 2005)

Continental Casualty Company v The Argentine Republic, ICSID Case No ARB/03/9, Award (5 September 2008)

Corona Materials LLC v Dominican Republic, ICSID Case No ARB(AF)/14/3, Award on the Respondent's Expedited Preliminary Objections in Accordance with Article 10.20.5 of the DR-CAFTA (31 May 2016)

Cortec Mining Kenya Limited, Cortec (Pty) Limited, and Stirling Capital Limited v Republic of Kenya, ICSID Case No ARB/15/29, Award (22 October 2018)

Daimler Financial Services AG v Argentine Republic, ICSID Case No ARB/05/1, Award (22 August 2012)

Desert Line Projects LLC v The Republic of Yemen, ICSID Case No ARB/05/17, Award (6 February 2008)

Duke Energy Electroquil Partners & Electroquil SA v Republic of Ecuador, ICSID Case No ARB/04/19, Award (18 August 2008)

EDF (Services) Limited v Romania, ICSID Case No ARB/05/13, Award (8 October 2009)

EDF International SA, SAUR International SA, and León Participaciones Argentinas SA v Argentine Republic, ICSID Case No ARB/03/23, Award (11 June 2012)

TABLE OF CASES 255

El Paso Energy International Company v The Argentine Republic, ICSID Case No ARB/03/15, Decision on Jurisdiction (27 April 2006)

Emilio Agustín Maffezini v The Kingdom of Spain, ICSID Case No ARB/97/7, Decision of the Tribunal on Objections to Jurisdiction (25 January 2000)

Empresa Eléctrica del Ecuador Inc v Republic of Ecuador, ICSID Case No ARB/05/9, Award (2 June 2009)

Enron Corporation and Ponderosa Assets LP v Argentine Republic, ICSID Case No ARB/01/3, Award (22 May 2007)

Enron Corporation and Ponderosa Assets LP v The Argentine Republic, ICSID Case No ARB/01/3, Decision on Jurisdiction (14 January 2004)

Enron Creditors Recovery Corp and Ponderosa Assets LP v The Argentine Republic, ICSID Case No ARB/01/3, Decision on the Application for Annulment of the Argentine Republic (30 July 2010)

Fedax NV v The Republic of Venezuela, ICSID Case No ARB/96/3, Decision of the Tribunal on Objections to Jurisdiction (11 July 1997)

Flughafen Zürich AG and Gestión e Ingenería IDC SA v Bolivarian Republic of Venezuela, ICSID Case No ARB/10/19, Award (18 November 2014)

Garanti Koza LLP v Turkmenistan, ICSID Case No ARB/11/20, Decision on the Objection to Jurisdiction for Lack of Consent (3 July 2013)

Garanti Koza LLP v Turkmenistan, ICSID Case No ARB/11/20, Dissenting Opinion by Laurence Boisson de Chazournes (3 July 2013)

Gas Natural SDG SA v The Argentine Republic, ICSID Case No ARB/03/10, Decision of the Tribunal on Preliminary Questions on Jurisdiction (17 June 2005)

GEA Group Aktiengesellschaft v Ukraine, ICSID Case No ARB/08/16, Award (31 March 2011)

Generation Ukraine Inc v Ukraine, ICSID Case No ARB/00/9, Award (16 September 2003)

Georg Gavrilović and Gavrilović doo v Republic of Croatia, ICSID Case No ARB/12/39, Award (26 July 2018)

Giovanni Alemanni and others v The Argentine Republic, ICSID Case No ARB/07/8, Decision on Jurisdiction and Admissibility (17 November 2014)

Global Trading Resource Corp and Globex International Inc v Ukraine, ICSID Case No ARB/09/11, Award (1 December 2010)

Gustav F W Hamester GmbH & Co KG v Republic of Ghana, ICSID Case No ARB/07/24, Award (18 June 2010)

H&H Enterprises Investments Inc v The Arab Republic of Egypt, ICSID Case No ARB/09/15, Award (6 May 2014)

Hochtief AG v The Argentine Republic, ICSID Case No ARB/07/31, Decision on Jurisdiction (24 October 2011)

Hussein Nuaman Soufraki v The United Arab Emirates, ICSID Case No ARB/02/7, Decision of the ad hoc Committee on the Application for Annulment of Mr Soufraki (5 June 2007)

İçkale İnşaat Limited Şirketi v Turkmenistan, ICSID Case No ARB/10/24, Award (8 March 2016)

Impregilo SpA v Argentine Republic, ICSID Case No ARB/07/17, Award (21 June 2011)

Impregilo SpA v Argentine Republic, ICSID Case No ARB/07/17, Concurring and Dissenting Opinion of Professor Brigitte Stern (21 June 2011)

Impregilo SpA v Argentine Republic, ICSID Case No ARB/07/17, Decision of the ad hoc Committee on the Application for Annulment (24 January 2014)

Impregilo SpA v Islamic Republic of Pakistan, ICSID Case No ARB/03/3, Decision on Jurisdiction (22 April 2005)

Inceysa Vallisoletana SL v Republic of El Salvador, ICSID Case No ARB/03/26, Award (2 August 2006)

Industria Nacional de Alimentos SA and Indalsa Perú SA v The Republic of Peru, ICSID Case No ARB/03/4, Decision on Annulment (5 September 2007)

Ioan Micula and others v Romania, ICSID Case No ARB/05/20, Decision on Jurisdiction and Admissibility (24 September 2008)

Ioannis Kardassopoulos v Georgia, ICSID Case No ARB/05/18, Decision on Jurisdiction (6 July 2007)

Jan de Nul NV and Dredging International NV v Arab Republic of Egypt, ICSID Case No ARB/04/13, Decision on Jurisdiction (16 June 2006)

Joy Mining Machinery Limited v Arab Republic of Egypt, ICSID Case No ARB/03/11, Award on Jurisdiction (6 August 2004)

Kiliç İnşaat İthalat İhracat Sanayi Ve Ticaret Anonim Şirketi v Turkmenistan, ICSID Case No ARB/10/1, Award (2 July 2013)

Krederi Ltd v Ukraine, ICSID Case No ARB/14/17, Award (2 July 2018)

KT Asia Investment Group BV v Republic of Kazakhstan, ICSID Case No ARB/09/8, Award (17 October 2013)

Lanco International Inc v The Argentine Republic, ICSID Case No ARB/97/6, Preliminary Decision on the Jurisdiction of the Arbitral Tribunal (8 December 1998)

Lao Holdings NV and Sanum Investments Limited v Lao People's Democratic Republic, ICSID Case Nos ARB(AF)/16/2 and ADHOC/17/1, Procedural Order No 2 (23 October 2017)

Le Chèque Déjeuner and CD Holding Internationale v Hungary, ICSID Case No ARB/13/35, Decision on Preliminary Issues of Jurisdiction (3 March 2016)

LESI SpA and ASTALDI SpA v République Algérienne Démocratique et Populaire, ICSID Case No ARB/05/3, Decision (12 July 2006)

LG&E Energy Corp, LG&E Capital Corp, and LG&E International Inc v Argentine Republic, ICSID Case No ARB/02/1, Decision of the Arbitral Tribunal on Objections to Jurisdiction (30 April 2004)

Lighthouse Corporation Pty Ltd and Lighthouse Corporation Ltd IBC v Democratic Republic of Timor-Leste, ICSID Case No ARB/15/2, Award (22 December 2017)

Liman Caspian Oil BV and NCL Dutch Investment BV v Republic of Kazakhstan, ICSID Case No ARB/07/14, Award (22 June 2010)

Malaysian Historical Salvors Sdn Bhd v The Government of Malaysia, ICSID Case No ARB/05/10, Decision on the Application for Annulment (16 April 2009)

Malaysian Historical Salvors Sdn Bhd v The Government of Malaysia, ICSID Case No ARB/05/10, Annulment Proceedings, Dissenting Opinion of Judge Mohamed Shahabuddeen (19 February 2009)

Malaysian Historical Salvors Sdn Bhd v The Government of Malaysia, ICSID Case No ARB/05/10, Award on Jurisdiction (17 May 2007)

Marco Gavazzi and Stefano Gavazzi v Romania, ICSID Case No ARB/12/25, Decision on Jurisdiction, Admissibility, and Liability (21 April 2015)

Marvin Roy Feldman Karpa v United Mexican States, ICSID Case No ARB(AF)/99/1, Interim Decision on Preliminary Jurisdictional Issues (6 December 2000)

Masdar Solar & Wind Cooperatief UA v Kingdom of Spain, ICSID Case No ARB/14/1, Award (16 May 2018)

MCI Power Group LC and New Turbine Inc v Republic of Ecuador, ICSID Case No ARB/03/6, Award (31 July 2007)

MCI Power Group LC and New Turbine Inc v Republic of Ecuador, ICSID Case No ARB/03/6, Decision on Annulment (19 October 2009)

Menzies Middle East and Africa SA et Aviation Handling Services International Ltd v République du Sénégal, ICSID Case No ARB/15/21, Award (5 August 2016)

Mera Investment Fund Limited v Republic of Serbia, ICSID Case No ARB/17/2, Decision on Jurisdiction (30 November 2018)

Middle East Cement Shipping and Handling Co SA v Arab Republic of Egypt, ICSID Case No ARB/99/6, Award (12 April 2002)

Mihaly International Corporation v Democratic Socialist Republic of Sri Lanka, ICSID Case No ARB/00/2, Award (15 March 2002)

Millicom International Operations BV and Sentel GSM SA v The Republic of Senegal, ICSID Case No ARB/08/20, Decision on Jurisdiction of the Arbitral Tribunal (16 July 2010)

Mobil Corporation, Venezuela Holdings BV, and others v Bolivarian Republic of Venezuela, ICSID Case No ARB/07/27, Decision on Jurisdiction (10 June 2010)

Mobil Exploration and Development Argentina Inc Suc Argentina and Mobil Argentina Sociedad Anónima v The Argentine Republic, ICSID Case No ARB/04/16, Decision on Jurisdiction and Liability (10 April 2013)

Mobil Investments Canada Inc v Government of Canada, ICSID Case No ARB/15/6, Decision on Jurisdiction and Admissibility (13 July 2018)

Mondev International Ltd v United States of America, ICSID Case No ARB(AF)/99/2, Award (11 October 2002)

Mr Patrick Mitchell v The Democratic Republic of Congo, ICSID Case No ARB/99/7, Decision on the Application for Annulment of the Award (1 November 2006)

Mr Saba Fakes v Republic of Turkey, ICSID Case No ARB/07/20, Award (14 July 2010)

MTD Equity Sdn Bhd and MTD Chile SA v Republic of Chile, ICSID Case No ARB/01/7, Award (25 May 2004)

MTD Equity Sdn Bhd and MTD Chile SA v Republic of Chile, ICSID Case No ARB/01/7, Decision on Annulment (21 March 2007)

Murphy Exploration and Production Company International v Republic of Ecuador, ICSID Case No ARB/08/4, Award on Jurisdiction (15 December 2010)

Noble Energy Inc and Machalapower Cia Ltda v The Republic of Ecuador and Consejo Nacional de Electricidad, ICSID Case No ARB/05/12, Decision on Jurisdiction (5 March 2008)

Noble Ventures Inc v Romania, ICSID Case No ARB/01/11, Award (12 October 2005)

Nova Scotia Power Incorporated (Canada) v Bolivarian Republic of Venezuela, ICSID Case No ARB(AF)/11/1, Award (30 April 2014)

Occidental Petroleum Corporation and Occidental Exploration and Production Company v The Republic of Ecuador, ICSID Case No ARB/06/11, Decision on Jurisdiction (9 September 2008)

Olguín v Republic of Paraguay, ICSID Case No ARB/98/5, Decision on Jurisdiction (8 August 2000)

Ömer Dede and Serdar Elhüseyni v Romania, ICSID Case No ARB/10/22, Award (5 September 2013)

Pac Rim Cayman LLC v The Republic of El Salvador, ICSID Case No ARB/09/12, Decision on the Respondent's Jurisdictional Objections (1 June 2012)

Pan American Energy LLC and BP Argentina Exploration Company v The Argentine Republic and BP America Production Company and others v The Argentine Republic, ICSID Cases No ARB/03/13 and ARB/04/8, Decision on Preliminary Objections (27 July 2006)

Pantechniki SA Contractors & Engineers (Greece) v The Republic of Albania, ICSID Case No ARB/07/21, Award (30 July 2009)

Parkerings-Compagniet AS v Republic of Lithuania, ICSID Case No ARB/05/8, Award (11 September 2007)

Perenco Ecuador Limited v The Republic of Ecuador, ICSID Case No ARB/08/6, Decision on Perenco's Application for Dismissal of Ecuador's Counterclaims (18 August 2017)

Philip Morris Brands Sàrl, Philip Morris Products SA, and Abal Hermanos SA v Oriental Republic of Uruguay, ICSID Case No ARB/10/7, Decision on Jurisdiction (2 July 2013)

Phoenix Action Ltd v The Czech Republic, ICSID Case No ARB/06/5, Award (15 April 2009)

Plama Consortium Limited v Republic of Bulgaria, ICSID Case No ARB/03/24, Decision on Jurisdiction (8 February 2005)

Plama Consortium Limited v Republic of Bulgaria, ICSID Case No ARB/03/24, Award (27 August 2008)

Planet Mining Pty Ltd v Republic of Indonesia, ICSID Case No ARB/12/40, Decision on Jurisdiction (24 February 2014)

PNG Sustainable Development Program Ltd v Independent State of Papua New Guinea, ICSID Case No ARB/13/33, Award (5 May 2015)

Poštová banka as and Istrokapital SE v The Hellenic Republic, ICSID Case No ARB/13/8, Award (9 April 2015)

Quiborax SA, Non Metallic Minerals SA, and Allan Fosk Kaplún v Plurinational State of Bolivia, ICSID Case No ARB/06/2, Decision on Jurisdiction (27 September 2012)

RREEF Infrastructure (GP) Limited and RREEF Pan-European Infrastructure Two Lux Sàrl v Kingdom of Spain, ICSID Case No ARB/13/30, Decision on Jurisdiction (6 June 2016)

Rumeli Telekom AS and Telsim Mobil Telekomunikasyon Hizmetleri AS v Republic of Kazakhstan, ICSID Case No ARB/05/16, Award (29 July 2008)

Saipem SpA v People's Republic of Bangladesh, ICSID Case No ARB/05/7, Decision on Jurisdiction and Recommendation on Provisional Measures (21 March 2007)

Salini Costruttori SpA and Italstrade SpA v Kingdom of Morocco, ICSID Case No ARB/00/4, Decision on Jurisdiction (31 July 2001)

Salini Costruttori SpA and Italstrade SpA v The Hashemite Kingdom of Jordan, ICSID Case No ARB/02/13, Decision on Jurisdiction (15 November 2004)

Salini Impregilo SpA v Argentine Republic, ICSID Case No ARB/15/39, Decision on Jurisdiction and Admissibility (23 February 2018)

SAUR International SA v Republic of Argentina, ICSID Case No ARB/04/4, Decision on Jurisdiction and Liability (6 June 2012)

Sempra Energy International v Argentine Republic, ICSID Case No ARB/02/16, Award (28 September 2007)

Señor Tza Yap Shum v The Republic of Peru, ICSID Case No ARB/07/6, Decision on Jurisdiction and Competence (19 June 2009)

SGS Société Générale de Surveillance SA v Islamic Republic of Pakistan, ICSID Case No ARB/01/13, Decision of the Tribunal on Objections to Jurisdiction (6 August 2003)

SGS *Société Générale de Surveillance SA v Republic of the Philippines*, ICSID Case No ARB/02/6, Decision of the Tribunal on Objections to Jurisdiction (29 January 2004)

SGS *Société Générale de Surveillance SA v The Republic of Paraguay*, ICSID Case No ARB/07/29, Decision on Jurisdiction (12 February 2010)

Siemens AG v The Argentine Republic, ICSID Case No ARB/02/8, Award (6 February 2007)

Siemens AG v The Argentine Republic, ICSID Case No ARB/02/8, Decision on Jurisdiction (3 August 2004)

Southern Pacific Properties (Middle East) Limited v Arab Republic of Egypt, ICSID Case No ARB/84/3, Decision on Preliminary Objections to Jurisdiction (14 April 1988)

Spence International Investments LLC, Berkowitz, and others v Republic of Costa Rica, ICSID Case No UNCT/13/2, Interim Award (25 October 2016)

Spyridon Roussalis v Romania, ICSID Case No ARB/06/1, Award (7 December 2011)

Standard Chartered Bank (Hong Kong) Limited v Tanzania Electric Supply Company Limited, ICSID Case No ARB/10/20, Decision on the Application for Annulment (22 August 2018)

Suez, Sociedad General de Aguas de Barcelona SA, and Interagua Servicios Integrales de Agua SA v Argentine Republic, ICSID Case No ARB/03/17, Decision on Argentina's Application for Annulment (14 December 2018)

Suez, Sociedad General de Aguas de Barcelona SA, and InterAguas Servicios Integrales del Agua SA v The Argentine Republic, ICSID Case No ARB/03/17, Decision on Jurisdiction (16 May 2006)

Suez, Sociedad General de Aguas de Barcelona SA, and Vivendi Universal SA v The Argentine Republic, ICSID Case No ARB/03/19, and *AWG Group Ltd v The Argentine Republic*, UNCITRAL arbitration, Decision on Jurisdiction (3 August 2006)

Suez, Sociedad General de Aguas de Barcelona SA, and Vivendi Universal SA v The Argentine Republic, ICSID Case No ARB/03/19, and *AWG Group v The Argentine Republic*, UNCITRAL arbitration, Decision on Liability (30 July 2010)

Supervision y Control SA v The Republic of Costa Rica, ICSID Case No ARB/12/4, Award (18 January 2017)

Tecnicas Medioambientales Tecmed SA v The United Mexican States, ICSID Case No ARB(AF)/00/2, Award (29 May 2003)

Teinver SA, Transportes de Cercanías SA, and Autobuses Urbanos del Sur SA v The Argentine Republic, ICSID Case No ARB/09/1, Award (21 July 2017)

Teinver SA, Transportes de Cercanías SA, and Autobuses Urbanos del Sur SA v The Argentine Republic, ICSID Case No ARB/09/1, Decision on Jurisdiction (21 December 2012)

TABLE OF CASES   261

Telefónica SA v The Argentine Republic, ICSID Case No ARB/03/20, Decision of the Tribunal on Objections to Jurisdiction (25 May 2006)

Telenor Mobile Communications AS v The Republic of Hungary, ICSID Case No ARB/04/15, Award (13 September 2006)

The Loewen Group Inc and Raymond L Loewen v United States of America, ICSID Case No ARB(AF)/98/3, Award (26 June 2003)

Tokios Tokelės v Ukraine, ICSID Case No ARB/02/18, Decision on Jurisdiction (29 April 2004)

Toto Costruzioni Generali SpA v The Republic of Lebanon, ICSID Case No ARB/07/12, Decision on Jurisdiction (11 September 2009)

Tradex Hellas SA (Greece) v Republic of Albania, ICSID Case No ARB/94/2, Decision on Jurisdiction (24 December 1996)

Transglobal Green Energy LLC and Transglobal Green Panama SA v Republic of Panama, ICSID Case No ARB/13/28, Award (2 June 2016)

TSA Spectrum de Argentina SA v Argentine Republic, ICSID Case No ARB/05/5, Award (19 December 2008)

Tulip Real Estate Investment and Development Netherlands BV v Republic of Turkey, ICSID Case No ARB/11/28, Decision on Bifurcated Jurisdictional Issue (5 March 2013)

Unión Fenosa Gas SA v Arab Republic of Egypt, ICSID Case No ARB/14/4, Award (31 August 2018)

United Parcel Service of America Inc v Government of Canada, ICSID Case No UNCT/02/1, Award on the Merits (24 May 2007)

Urbaser SA and CABB v The Argentine Republic, ICSID Case No ARB/07/26, Decision on Jurisdiction (19 December 2012)

Urbaser SA and CABB v The Argentine Republic, ICSID Case No ARB/07/26, Award (8 December 2016)

Victor Pey Casado and President Allende Foundation v Republic of Chile, ICSID Case No ARB/98/2, Award (8 May 2008)

Waguih Elie George Siag and Clorinda Vecchi v The Arab Republic of Egypt, ICSID Case No ARB/05/15, Award (1 June 2009)

Waste Management Inc v United Mexican States, ICSID Case No ARB(AF)/98/2, Dissenting Opinion of Keith Highet (8 May 2000)

Waste Management Inc v United Mexican States, ICSID Case No ARB(AF)/00/3, Award (30 April 2004)

Western NIS Enterprise Fund v Ukraine, ICSID Case No ARB/04/2, Order (16 March 2006)

Wintershall Aktiengesellschaft v Argentine Republic, ICSID Case No ARB/04/14, Award (8 December 2008)

World Duty Free Company Limited v The Republic of Kenya, ICSID Case No ARB/00/7, Award (4 October 2006)

PCA-Administered Arbitrations

Chevron Corporation (USA) and Texaco Petroleum Corporation (USA) v The Republic of Ecuador, PCA Case No 34877, Interim Award (1 December 2008)

Chevron Corporation and Texaco Petroleum Company v The Republic of Ecuador, PCA Case No 2009-23, Third Interim Award on Jurisdiction and Admissibility (27 February 2012)

China Heilongjiang International Economic & Technical Cooperative Corp and others v Mongolia, PCA Case No 2010-20, Award (30 June 2017)

European American Investment Bank AG (Austria) v The Slovak Republic, PCA Case No 2010-17, Award on Jurisdiction (22 October 2012)

Guaracachi America Inc and Rurelec PLC v The Plurinational State of Bolivia, PCA Case No 2011-17, Award (31 January 2014)

HICEE BV v The Slovak Republic, PCA Case No 2009-11, Partial Award (23 May 2011)

Hulley Enterprises Limited (Cyprus) v The Russian Federation, PCA Case No AA 226, Final Award (18 July 2014)

Hulley Enterprises Limited (Cyprus) v The Russian Federation, PCA Case No AA 226, Interim Award on Jurisdiction and Admissibility (30 November 2009)

ICS Inspection and Control Services Limited (United Kingdom) v The Argentine Republic, PCA Case No 2010-9, Award on Jurisdiction (10 February 2012)

Iron Rhine Arbitration (Belgium/Netherlands), PCA Case No 2003-02, Award of the Arbitral Tribunal (24 May 2005)

Khan Resources Inc, Khan Resources BV, and CAUC Holding Company Ltd v The Government of Mongolia and MonAtom LLC, PCA Case No 2011-09, Decision on Jurisdiction (25 July 2012)

Larsen v Hawaiian Kingdom, PCA Case No 1999-01, Award (5 February 2001)

Nissan Motor Co Ltd (Japan) v The Republic of India, PCA Case No 2017-37, Decision on Jurisdiction (29 April 2019)

Philip Morris Asia Limited v The Commonwealth of Australia, PCA Case No 2012-12, Award on Jurisdiction and Admissibility (17 December 2015)

Professor Christian Doutremepuich and Antoine Doutremepuich v The Republic of Mauritius, PCA Case No 2018-37, Award on Jurisdiction (23 August 2019)

Resolute Forest Products Inc v Government of Canada, PCA Case No 2016-13, Decision on Jurisdiction and Admissibility (30 January 2018)

TABLE OF CASES 263

Romak SA (Switzerland) v The Republic of Uzbekistan, PCA Case No AA280, Award (26 November 2009)

Sanum Investments Limited v The Government of the Lao People's Democratic Republic, PCA Case No 2013-13, Award on Jurisdiction (13 December 2013)

Serafín García Armas and Karina García Gruber v The Bolivarian Republic of Venezuela, PCA Case No 2013-3, Decision on Jurisdiction (15 December 2014)

South American Silver Limited (Bermuda) v The Plurinational State of Bolivia, PCA Case No 2013-15, Award (22 November 2018)

ST-AD GmbH (Germany) v The Republic of Bulgaria, PCA Case No 2011-06, Award on Jurisdiction (18 July 2013)

The South China Sea Arbitration (The Republic of the Philippines v The People's Republic of China), PCA Case No 2013-19, Award on Jurisdiction and Admissibility (29 October 2015)

Venezuela US SRL v The Bolivarian Republic of Venezuela, PCA Case No 2013-34, Dissenting Opinion of Professor Marcelo G Kohen (26 July 2016)

Venezuela US SRL v The Bolivarian Republic of Venezuela, PCA Case No 2013-34, Interim Award on Jurisdiction (on the Respondent's Objection to Jurisdiction Ratione Voluntatis) (26 July 2016)

William Ralph Clayton and others v Government of Canada, PCA Case No 2009-04, Award on Jurisdiction and Liability (17 March 2015)

WNC Factoring Ltd (United Kingdom) v The Czech Republic, PCA Case No 2014-34, Award (22 February 2017)

Yukos Universal Limited (Isle of Man) v The Russian Federation, PCA Case No AA 227, Final Award (18 July 2014)

SCC-Administered Arbitrations

Anatolie Stati and others v The Republic of Kazakhstan, SCC Case No V 116/2010, Award (19 December 2013)

Charanne BV and Construction Investments SARL v The Kingdom of Spain, SCC Case No V 062/2012, Final Award (21 January 2016)

Isolux Infrastructure Netherlands BV v Kingdom of Spain, SCC Case No V2013/153, Award (12 July 2016)

Ivan Peter Busta and James Peter Busta v The Czech Republic, SCC Case No V 2015/014, Final Award (10 March 2017)

Limited Liability Company Amto v Ukraine, SCC Case No 080/2005, Final Award (26 March 2008)

Mr Franz Sedelmayer v The Russian Federation, SCC arbitration, Arbitration Award (7 July 1998)

Renta 4 SVSA and others v The Russian Federation, SCC Case No 24/2007, Award on Preliminary Objections (20 March 2009)

RosInvestCo UK Ltd v The Russian Federation, SCC Case No V 079/2005, Award on Jurisdiction (October 2007)

Vladimir Berschader & Moïse Berschader v The Russian Federation, SCC Case No 80/2004, Award (21 April 2006)

Vladimir Berschader & Moïse Berschader v The Russian Federation, SCC Case No 80/2004, Separate Opinion of Arbitrator Todd Weiler (7 April 2006)

LCIA-Administered Arbitrations

Occidental Exploration and Production Company v The Republic of Ecuador, LCIA Case No UN3467, Final Award (1 July 2004)

Société Générale v The Dominican Republic, LCIA Case No UN 7927, Award on Preliminary Objections to Jurisdiction (19 September 2008)

Ad Hoc Arbitrations

Alps Finance and Trade AG v The Slovak Republic, UNCITRAL ad hoc arbitration, Award (5 March 2011)

Austrian Airlines v The Slovak Republic, UNCITRAL ad hoc arbitration, Final Award (9 October 2009)

BG Group Plc v The Republic of Argentina, UNCITRAL ad hoc arbitration, Final Award (24 December 2007)

Cargill, Incorporated v Republic of Poland, UNCITRAL ad hoc arbitration, Final Award (29 February 2008)

Ethyl Corporation v The Government of Canada, UNCITRAL ad hoc arbitration, Award on Jurisdiction (24 June 1998)

Eureko BV v Republic of Poland, ad hoc arbitration, Partial Award (19 August 2005)

Glamis Gold Ltd v United States of America, UNCITRAL ad hoc arbitration, Award (8 June 2009)

Grand River Enterprises Six Nations Ltd and others v United States of America, UNCITRAL ad hoc arbitration, Decision on Objections to Jurisdiction (20 July 2006)

TABLE OF CASES 265

Hesham Talaat M Al-Warraq v The Republic of Indonesia, UNCITRAL ad hoc arbitration, Award on Respondent's Preliminary Objections to Jurisdiction and Admissibility of the Claims (21 June 2012)
International Thunderbird Gaming Corporation v The United Mexican States, UNCITRAL ad hoc arbitration, Separate Opinion of Thomas Wälde (1 December 2005)
Methanex Corporation v The United States of America, UNCITRAL ad hoc arbitration, Partial Award (7 August 2002)
National Grid plc v The Argentine Republic, UNCITRAL ad hoc arbitration, Decision on Jurisdiction (20 June 2006)
Ronald S Lauder v The Czech Republic, UNCITRAL ad hoc arbitration, Final Award (3 September 2001)
Saluka Investments BV v The Czech Republic, UNCITRAL ad hoc arbitration, Decision on Jurisdiction over the Czech Republic's Counterclaim (7 May 2004)
Ulysseas Inc v The Republic of Ecuador, UNCITRAL ad hoc arbitration, Interim Award (28 September 2010)
Yaung Chi Oo Trading Pte Ltd v Government of the Union of Myanmar, ASEAN Case No ARB/01/1, Award (31 March 2003)

Other International Cases

Austria v Italy App No 788/60 (Eur Comm'n HR, 11 January 1961)
Chapman v The United Kingdom App No 27238/95 (ECtHR, 18 January 2001)
Essien v The Gambia ECW/CCJ/APP/05/05 (ECOWAS Court of Justice, 14 March 2007)
Islamic Republic of Iran Shipping Lines v Turkey App No 40998/98 (ECtHR, 13 December 2007)
Loizidou v Turkey App No 15318/89 (ECtHR, 23 March 1995)
Prosecutor v Duško Tadić (Decision on the Defence Motion for Interlocutory Appeal on Jurisdiction) ICTY-94-1 (2 October 1995)
Prosecutor v Zlatko Aleksovski (Judgment) ICTY-95-14/1-A (24 March 2000)
Rawle Kennedy v Trinidad and Tobago Comm No 845 (HRC, 31 December 1999)
Soering v The United Kingdom App No 14038/88 (ECtHR, 7 July 1989)
Tyrer v The United Kingdom App No 5856/72 (ECtHR, 25 April 1978)
WTO, *United States: Import Prohibition of Certain Shrimp and Shrimp Products—Report of the Appellate Body* (12 October 1998) WT/DS58/AB/R
Zorica Jovanović v Serbia App No 21794/08 (ECtHR, 26 March 2013)

Domestic Cases

Arrêt du 11 décembre 2018, Tribunal fédéral, 1re Cour de droit civil (Switzerland) 4A_65/2018

Arrêt du 20 septembre 2016, Tribunal fédéral, 1re Cour de droit civil (Switzerland) 4A_616/2015

Arrêt du 25 septembre 2008, Cour d'Appel de Paris, 1ère Chambre - Section C (France) 07/04675

Arrêt du 29 janvier 2019, Cour d'Appel de Paris, Pôle 1 - Chambre 1 (France) 16/20822

Arrêt du 29 novembre 2016, Cour d'Appel de Paris, Pôle 1 - Chambre 1 (France) 14/17964

Arrêt du 7 février 2017, Cour d'Appel de Paris, Pôle 1 - Chambre 1 (France) 14/21103

Ashby v White (1703) 92 ER 126 (KB (England))

BG Group plc v Republic of Argentina (2014) 572 US __

BG Group plc v Republic of Argentina (Roberts CJ dissenting) (2014) 572 US __

Dallal v Bank Mellat [1985] QB 441 (EWCA)

Kingdom of Lesotho v Swissbourgh Diamond Mines (Pty) Limited and others [2017] SGHC 195

Occidental Exploration & Production Company v The Republic of Ecuador [2005] EWCA Civ 1116

The Kyrgyz Republic v Stans Energy Corp and Kutisay Mining LLC [2017] EWHC 2539 (Comm)

The Republic of Ecuador v Occidental Exploration & Production Co [2006] EWHC 345 (Comm)

The Republic of Ecuador v Occidental Exploration & Production Co [2007] EWCA Civ 656

The Republic of Korea v Mohammad Reza Dayyani and others [2019] EWHC 3580 (Comm)

Treaties

Accord entre les Gouvernements du Royaume de Belgique et du Grand-Duché de Luxembourg et le Gouvernement de l'Union des républiques socialistes soviétiques, concernant l'encouragement et la protection réciproques des investissements (signed 9 February 1989, entered into force 18 August 1991)

Agreement Between the Belgium-Luxembourg Economic Union and Barbados for the Reciprocal Promotion and Protection of Investments (signed 29 May 2009, not in force)

Agreement Between the Belgium-Luxembourg Economic Union and the Government of the Republic of Mozambique on the Reciprocal Promotion and Protection of Investments (signed 18 July 2006, entered into force 1 September 2009)

Agreement Between the Belgium-Luxembourg Economic Union and the Government of the People's Republic of China on the Reciprocal Promotion and Protection of Investments (signed 6 June 2005, entered into force 1 December 2009)

Agreement Between the Belgo-Luxembourg Economic Union, on the one hand, and the Serbia and Montenegro, on the other hand, on the Reciprocal Promotion and Protection of Investments (signed 4 March 2004, entered into force 12 August 2007)

Agreement Between the United States of America, the United Mexican States, and Canada (signed 30 November 2018 and 10 December 2019, entered into force 1 July 2020)

Agreement on Free Trade and Economic Partnership Between Japan and the Swiss Confederation (signed 19 February 2009, entered into force 1 September 2009)

Comprehensive Economic and Trade Agreement Between Canada and the European Union (signed 30 October 2016, not in force)

Convention for the Protection of Human Rights and Fundamental Freedoms, as amended by Protocols Nos 11 and 14 (opened for signature 4 November 1950, entered into force 3 September 1953; Protocol No 11 entered into force 1 November 1998; Protocol No 14 entered into force 1 June 2010) 213 UNTS 222

Convention on the Prevention and Punishment of the Crime of Genocide (adopted 9 December 1948, entered into force 12 January 1951) 78 UNTS 277

Convention on the Recognition and Enforcement of Foreign Arbitral Awards (signed 10 June 1958, entered into force 7 June 1959) 330 UNTS 38

Convention on the Settlement of Investment Disputes Between States and Nationals of Other States (signed 18 March 1965, entered into force 14 October 1966) 575 UNTS 159

Energy Charter Treaty (signed 17 December 1994, entered into force 16 April 1998) 2080 UNTS 95

European Convention for the Peaceful Settlement of Disputes (signed 29 April 1957, entered into force 30 April 1958) 320 UNTS 243

EU-Singapore Investment Protection Agreement (signed 19 October 2018, not in force)

EU-Vietnam Investment Protection Agreement (signed 30 June 2019, not in force)

North American Free Trade Agreement (signed 17 December 1992, entered into force 1 January 1994) 32 ILM 289

Protocol No 1 to the European Convention for the Protection of Human Rights and Fundamental Freedoms (signed 20 March 1952, entered into force 18 May 1954) 213 UNTS 262

Reciprocal Investment Promotion and Protection Agreement Between the Government of the Kingdom of Morocco and the Government of the Federal Republic of Nigeria (signed 3 December 2016, not in force)

Rome Statute of the International Criminal Court (signed 17 July 1998, entered into force 1 July 2002) 2187 UNTS 90

Statute of the International Court of Justice (signed 26 June 1945, entered into force 24 October 1945) 3 Bevans 1153

Supplementary Act A/SA.3/12/08 Adopting Community Rules on Investment and the Modalities for Their Implementation with ECOWAS (signed 19 December 2008, entered into force 19 January 2009)

United Nations Convention on Jurisdictional Immunities of States and Their Property (signed 2 December 2004, not in force)

United Nations Convention on Transparency in Treaty-Based Investor-State Arbitration (signed 10 December 2014, entered into force 18 October 2017)

Vienna Convention on the Law of Treaties (signed 23 May 1969, entered into force 27 January 1980) 1155 UNTS 331

Vienna Convention on the Law of Treaties Between States and International Organizations or Between International Organizations (signed 21 March 1986, not in force) 25 ILM 543

Miscellaneous Sources

'ICSID 1984 Annual Report' <https://icsid.worldbank.org/sites/default/files/publications/annual-report/en/1984-ar-final-en.pdf > accessed 28 August 2020

'Report of the Executive Directors on the Convention on the Settlement of Investment Disputes Between States and Nationals of Other States, 1965' (1993) 1 ICSID Reports 23

Arbitration Rules of the Arbitration Institute of the Stockholm Chamber of Commerce (in force 1 January 2017)

Arbitration Rules of the Permanent Court of Arbitration (in force 17 December 2012)

Belgium-Luxembourg Economic Union Model BIT (2019) <https://investmentpolicy.unctad.org/international-investment-agreements/treaty-files/5854/download> accessed 1 September 2020

ECtHR, Rules of Court (in force 14 November 2016)

ICJ, Rules of Court (adopted 14 April 1978, entered into force 1 July 1978)

ICSID Rules of Procedure for Arbitration Proceedings (in force 10 April 2006)

ICSID, 'Proposals for Amendment of the ICSID Rules' (February 2020) Working Paper #4, vol 1 <https://icsid.worldbank.org/sites/default/files/amendments/WP_4_Vol_1_En.pdf> accessed 1 September 2020

ILC, 'Diplomatic Protection', *Yearbook of the International Law Commission 2006*, vol II (Part Two) (UN 2013)

ILC, 'Final Report of the Study Group on the Most-Favoured-Nation Clause' (29 May 2015) UN Doc A/CN.4/L.852

ILC, 'Responsibility of States for Internationally Wrongful Acts', *Yearbook of the International Law Commission 2001*, vol II (Part Two) (UN 2007)

India Model BIT (2015) <https://investmentpolicy.unctad.org/international-investment-agreements/treaty-files/3560/download> accessed 20 August 2020

Rules of Arbitration of the International Chamber of Commerce (in force 1 March 2017)

UK Model BIT (2008) <https://investmentpolicy.unctad.org/international-investment-agreements/treaty-files/2847/download> accessed 20 August 2020

UNCITRAL Arbitration Rules (with new article 1, paragraph 4, as adopted in 2013) (in force 1 April 2014)

UNCITRAL Model Law on International Commercial Arbitration of 1985, with amendments as adopted in 2006 <https://uncitral.un.org/sites/uncitral.un.org/files/media-documents/uncitral/en/19-09955_e_ebook.pdf> accessed 4 April 2021

UNCITRAL Rules on Transparency in Treaty-based Investor-State Arbitration (in force 1 April 2014)

UNCITRAL Working Group III, 'Possible Reform of Investor-State Dispute Settlement (ISDS)' (5 September 2018) UN Doc A/CN.9/WG.III/WP.149

UNCITRAL, 'Report of Working Group III (Investor-State Dispute Settlement Reform) on the Work of Its Thirty-Sixth Session (Vienna, 29 October–2 November 2018)' (6 November 2018) UN Doc A/CN.9/964

UNCITRAL, 'Report of Working Group III (Investor-State Dispute Settlement Reform) on the Work of Its Thirty-Eighth Session (Vienna, 14–18 October 2019)' (23 October 2019) UN Doc A/CN.9/1004

UNCITRAL, 'Report of Working Group III (Investor-State Dispute Settlement Reform) on the Work of Its Thirty-Fourth Session (Vienna, 27 November–1 December 2017)' (26 February 2018) UN Doc A/CN.9/930/Add.1/Rev.1

UNCTAD, 'Most-Favoured-Nation Treatment', *UNCTAD Series on Issues in International Investment Agreements II* (UN 2010)

US Model BIT (2012) <https://investmentpolicy.unctad.org/international-investment-agreements/treaty-files/2870/download> accessed 20 August 2020

Index

Abuse of process   155, 167
Admissibility of claims   81, 173, 183–184
   and denial of benefits   111
   and most-favoured nation clause   102, 104–105, 108
Adventurism   168, 209–210
Agreement
   special   57–58
   to arbitrate   52, 54–55, 55–57, 57, 63, 127, 176, 181, 203–204
Annulment   47, 73, 205–207, see also Control mechanism, see also Review
   duty to state the reasons   75, 206–207
   excess of powers   47, 73–74, 206–207
Arbitration without privity   48, 167–168
Authority to adjudicate   19–20, 52, 56–57, 165, 177, 178, 214–215
   and secondary rules   184, 196–197

Basic norm of international adjudication   36–37
Bias   168
Bilateral investment treaties   39–40, 48–49, 59–60, 176, 177
Burden
   of argumentation   105–107, 182, 184, 195–196
   of proof   34–35, 72

Commercial law
   and arbitration   51–52, 162, 208
   approaches   43–44, 162
   dispute settlement mechanisms   42
Commercial transaction   134–135, 140–141
Communicative process   194–195, 199–200, 219–220
Compétence de la compétence   27–28, 34–35, 75–77
Compulsory jurisdiction   17–18, 33–34
Conditions of access   62, 80
Conditions precedent   183–184
   and admissibility   84
   and most-favoured nation clause   100, 104–105, 108
   bypassing   89

Confidentiality   164–165, 208–209
Consensualism
   and a hybrid regime   44
   and global public goods   38
   and protective regimes   41–42
   and sovereignty   16–17, 171–172
   and the power of arbitral tribunals to raise jurisdictional issues on their own initiative   71–72
   of international adjudication   14, 171–172
   principle of   1, 61–62, 75–76, 173, 174–175, 208–209, 213
Consent   5, 46, 170–171, 181, 184, 214–215
   and global public goods   37
   scope of   129–130, 181
Consistency   10–11, 209–210, 211, 215–216
Contemporaneity, principle of   203–204
Continued act doctrine   115
Contract
   adhesion   33, 49–50, 181
   claims   127, 163–164
   regulating jurisdiction   64–65
Contractual arbitration   143–144
Contractual nature of international adjudication   30
Contractual relationship   162–163
Contribution to the development of the host state   136–138
Control mechanism   73–75, 205, see also Annulment, see also Review
Cooling-off/waiting periods   84–86
Counterclaims   129–130, 181
Counteroffer   54–55, 176, 181
Court of Appeal of England and Wales   55–56, 57, 63–65
Customary international law
   and arbitral practice   187–188
   and rules of interpretation   67
   violations of   129–130

Default rule   182–183, 200–201
Denial of benefits   61, 110
Depoliticization   39–40, 45, 175–176
Diplomatic protection   90–91, 162–163, 172

Dispute 22
    and conditions of access 97
    arbitrable 54–55, 59, 127, 151
    non-justiciable 23–24
Domestic courts 65–66, 73, 205–206, 207
Domestic law 48, 64–65, 67–68, 129–130, 143, 146–147

Energy Charter Treaty 111, 113–114, 143–144
European Convention on Human Rights 27–28, 41
European Court of Human Rights 27–28, 29, 41, 218
    and *Loizidou* case 27–29
Evolutive interpretation, doctrine of 204–205
Ex officio 34–35, 70, see also *Proprio motu*
Excess of powers 34–35, see also Annulment, excess of powers
    and domestic courts 207
Expropriation
    amount of compensation for 59–60, 130
    occurrence of 102–103, 130

Foreign element 148–151, see also Investor, objective definition of
Fork-in-the-road clause 62, 183–184
    bypassing 94
Forum prorogatum 18, 26–27, 46–47, 58
Foundational basis of a claim 96–97
Futility 90, 183–184, 202–203

General international law 36–37
General principle of international law 35
Global governance 212
Global public goods 37, 216–217

High Court of Singapore 149–150
Human rights 37, 39–41
    bodies 32
    courts 122–123, 150

ICSID Convention 5–6, 26–27, 45, 50, 57–58, 112–113, 120, 148, 176, 181
    and admissibility 81, 82–83
    and excess of powers 73–74, see also Annulment, excess of powers
    and mass claims 88–89
    and objective definition of 'investment' 133

    and personal jurisdiction 29–30, 60
    and substantive jurisdiction 59–60
ICSID 5–6, 29–30, 45, 58, 69, 73, 77–78, 154–155, 168–169, 205–207
Identity of claims/disputes 62, 92, 183–184, 202–203
Indirect investments 123, see also Presumption, and indirect investments
International adjudication 12
    and global public goods 38
International Chamber of Commerce 42, 69
International Court of Justice 5–6, 15–16, 29, 31, 50, 81–82, 83–84, 92, 93–94, 112–113, 173, 175, 179–180, 195–196, 198, 218
    and *Certain Norwegian Loans* case 32
    and dispute 22
    and genocide disputes 21
    and *Nicaragua* case 23–24
International Criminal Court 219
International investment law
    and global administrative law 42–43
    and global public goods 38
    as a hybrid regime 42
    as a protective regime 39
International Law Commission 91–92
International public policy 143–144
Inter-state adjudication 173–174, 175–176, 177–178
Inter-state arbitration 48–49, 120
Inter-state law 173–174, 175
Inter-state relations 63–64, 173–174, 177–178
Investment court 10–11, 207–208
Investment laws see Domestic law
Investment restructuring 155–156
Investment
    definition of 60, 119–120, 132, 156
    inherent meaning of 140–141
    objective definition of 133, 144–145, 147, 167, 183–184, 202–203
Investor
    definition of 60, 119–120, 132, 148–149
    objective definition of 148, see also Foreign element

Jura novit curia, principle of 72, 184
Jurisdiction 6, 19–20
    in abstracto and *in concreto* 25–26
    personal 29–30, 60, 110–111
    substantive 59–60

INDEX

substantive, and indirect investments   123–124
substantive, and most-favoured nation clause   102
temporal   61
Jurisdictional bridging   127, 181, see also Presumption, jurisdictional bridging
Jurisdictional regulation
  arbitral   3–4, 161, 170–171, 174, 179–180
  consensual   3–4, 55
  evolutive   192, 196–197
  process of   12, 44–45, 160
  two-layered model of   160–161, 180, 198, 212
Jurisprudence constante   187–188, 195–196
Justiciability   22, see also Dispute, arbitrable, non-justiciable

Legal certainty   202, 224–225
Legal change   198–202, 205–206
Legality requirement   143
  independent   143, 167, 182–183
Legitimacy   214
  normative   214–215
  sociological   215–216
Living instrument doctrine   41
Local litigation, requirement of   62, 86–87, 91–92, 92–94, 100–101, 183–184
Local remedies, exhaustion of   62, 90–91, 93–94, 172

Mass claims   88–89
Mavrommatis principle   92
Most-favoured nation clause   60, 62, 69–70, 98, see also Presumption, and MFN-dispute resolution

Negotiation, requirement of   62, 84–86
New York Convention   65–66
North American Free Trade Agreement   115–116, 148–149
Notification, requirement of   84–86

Offer/acceptance   31, 48–49, 50, 52, 57–58, 181, 204–205

Pacta sunt servanda   33–34
Permanent Court of Arbitration   46, 69
Permanent Court of International Justice

and *Lotus* case   15
and *Mavrommatis* case   22, 92
Power to adjudicate   see Authority to adjudicate
Precedent, doctrine of   179, 187–189, 194–195, 196–197, 208
Presumption   182, 200–201
  and indirect investments   123, 167, 182, 189–190
  and jurisdictional bridging   127, 189–190, see also Jurisdictional bridging
  and MFN-dispute resolution   100, 105, 167, 182, 189–191, 202
Primary rules   181
Private-public adjudication   175–176, 177–178
Privity   49–50, 51
  condition of   151–152, 182–183
Procedural economy   84–86
Proprio motu   34–35, 70, see also *Ex officio*
Protective regime   39, 165–166, 204–205

Reasoning, arbitral   199–200
Reciprocity   51, 56–57
Regulatory deficiency   162–163, 178, 178–179, 214–215
  and contract claims   163–164
  and denial of benefits   114
  and objective definition of 'investor'   148
  and regulatory space   160–161
  and umbrella clauses   151–152
  of party-provided jurisdictional rules   7–8, 68–69
Regulatory space   200–202, 205–206
  and conditions precedent   84
  and denial of benefits   114
  and futility   90–91
  and legality requirement   143–144
  and scope of consent   130
Review   47, 65–66, 73–75, 205–208, see also Annulment, see also Control mechanism
Right to arbitrate   83–84, 102
Rules of procedure   77–78
  and admissibility   88

Scope of protection   119, 132
Screening process   46–47, 58, 69
Secondary rules   182
Self-judging clause   27–29, 32
Shareholder claims   125–126

Southern African Development
    Community   149–151
Sovereignty   14–17, 171–174, 174–175, see also
    Consensualism, and sovereignty
    of arbitral tribunals   194–195
Standard   183–184, 200–201, 202–203
State responsibility, law of   115, 122–123, 153
State-owned companies   120–123, 162–163
Statutory arbitration   63–64
Stockholm Chamber of Commerce   42, 69
Subject matter of dispute   93–94
Substantive protections   98, 178, 209–210, 213
Supreme Court of the United States   87–88

Time of consent   55
Time-bar   115–118

Transparency   164–165, 208
Triple identity test   93–94, 95–96

Umbrella clause   60, 151, 182–183
UNCITRAL arbitration rules   42
UNCITRAL Working Group III   10–11, 211
Unilateral act/obligation   51, 56–57, 67–68
US-Iran Claims Tribunal   63–64

Vienna Convention on the Law of
    Treaties   35–36, 67–68

Withdrawal of an offer   54–55, 56–57, 112–113
World Trade Organization   218–219

Printed in the United States
by Baker & Taylor Publisher Services